Creating iOS Apps

Second Edition

DEVELOP AND DESIGN

Richard Warren

PEACHPIT PRESS
WWW.PEACHPIT.COM

To my wife, Mika; my daughter, Haruko; and my son, Kai.
Thank you for your understanding and patience.
I owe each of you more than I could possibly express.
You've put up with a lot of extremely long hours and
general grumpiness over the last few months.
I really appreciate everything you've done to support me.
I couldn't have made it without you.

ACKNOWLEDGEMENTS

I'd like to start by thanking all the students who have taken my classes and all the people who have visited my web site and posted questions or comments about the first edition of this book. You've given me a lot to think about, and a lot of the changes that I've made have come from your suggestions.

I would also like to thank the developers and Apple engineers on the Apple Developer forums. When working with new technologies, we often don't have an established set of best practices to fall back on. Having such an active group of people to discuss ideas and share notes with makes a huge difference.

Additionally, the book would not have been possible without the editors and production people at Peachpit. You've helped clarify my intentions and made the meaning behind my words come through clear. The layout and design of the new book look stunning, and I'm sure there are a thousand other things you've done that I know nothing about.

Mostly, I'd like to thank everyone who read and enjoyed the first edition. You made the second edition possible.

ABOUT THE AUTHOR

Richard splits his time between software development, teaching, and technical writing. He has a strong background in artificial intelligence research (machine learning and probabilistic decision making) and software engineering. Richard previously worked as a scientist for a small R&D company, developing Java software focused on computer vision and data analysis. Since escaping the Java world, Richard has spent the last three years focusing on hands-on, freelance consulting work for the iOS platform. During that time, he has developed a broad range of iOS apps with an emphasis on casual gaming. Richard is also the author of *Creating iOS 5 Apps: Develop and Design* (December, 2011, Peachpit Press) and *Objective-C Boot Camp: Foundation and Patterns for iOS Development* (July 2011, Peachpit Press). Additionally, he has written articles for *MacTech* magazine over the last seven years. Finally, Richard is one of the senior iOS and Objective-C instructors for About Objects.

CONTENTS

WELCOME TO CREATING iOS 7 APPS

This book serves two goals: introducing new developers to iOS development and educating experienced developers about the changes in iOS 7. We will examine a wide range of subjects—some new and some old—covering everything from building an initial iOS project to submitting your app to the iTunes App Store. For more information, including bonus chapters, sample code, and FAQs, check out www.freelancemadscience.com/books.

IOS 7 TECHNOLOGIES AND TOOLS

Over the course of this book, we will discuss the key technologies and development tools you will need to create high-quality iOS applications. Let's take a look at the most important of these.

STORYBOARDS

Storyboards allow us to rapidly design the relationships and segues between different scenes in our application. This lets us sketch out and edit our entire application's workflow very early in the design process. We can also show the storyboard to our clients, getting approval and feedback before we invest a significant amount of time in writing code.

AUTO LAYOUT

Creating a user interface that can automatically adapt to changes in size has become increasingly important. Whether you're responding to rotation events, trying to design an interface that works on both 3.5- and 4-inch phones or adjusting the user interface because of changes from Dynamic Type, Auto Layout makes creating truly adaptive interfaces possible. Furthermore, iOS 7 and Xcode 5 offer significantly better support for Auto Layout. If you haven't tried Auto Layout lately, you should look at it again.

ANIMATION

While visually stunning animations have always been part of the iOS experience, iOS 7's new user interface places a much greater emphasis on attractive, functional animations. The new, "flatter" look de-emphasizes visual ornamentation but replaces it with custom transitions and interactive animations. Furthermore, new technologies like UIMotionEffects and UIKit Dynamics help give our applications depth.

XCODE

Xcode provides an integrated development environment, giving us a wide range of tools to both create and manage our projects. It handles everything from running and debugging our code to designing our UI and data models. As iOS developers, we will spend most of our time in Xcode. Having a well-grounded understanding of its features is essential to our success.

iOS SIMULATOR

The iOS Simulator application lets us run, debug, test, and profile our code directly on a Mac. While the simulator will never replace testing on an actual device, it has a number of advantages. For example, developers can begin using the simulator before they join the iOS Developer Program. It's also easier and faster to run quick tests in the simulator, letting us perform rapid develop/test/iterate cycles as we add new features to our applications. The simulator also lets us trigger system events, such as memory warnings, that wouldn't be possible when testing on a device.

INSTRUMENTS

Apple's premier profiling tool, Instruments lets us dynamically trace and analyze code running either in the simulator or directly on an iOS device. It lets us track and record everything from object allocations and timer-based samples to file access and energy use. It also provides the tools necessary for sifting through and analyzing the data that it generates. In experienced hands, Instruments can help us to fix bugs and polish our code.

CHAPTER 1

Hello, iOS

Before you can master any skill, you must first become comfortable with the tools. In this chapter, we will gain hands-on experience using some of these tools.

We will start with Xcode, the primary development tool for iOS applications. We will use Xcode to create a new project and then examine the files created by the project template. In particular, we will study how the different pieces of an iOS application fit together.

Once we are familiar with the project template, we will expand upon it, using Xcode's graphical interface editor to add controls and to draw connections between these controls and their actions. Together these exercises will provide a solid foundation for working on more complex projects in later chapters.

AN INTRODUCTION TO iOS

If this is your first exposure to iOS development, welcome to an exciting new world. The iOS lineup provides a number of great devices for you to explore. The iPhone, in particular, brings together a wide range of exciting technologies, including always-on Internet, location awareness, device motion tracking, a responsive multi-touch interface, a high-resolution display, and high-performance graphics acceleration. In the not so distant past, developers had to either build custom hardware or pay tens of thousands of dollars just to experiment with many of these technologies. Now you can fit the entire package in your pocket and carry it with you wherever you go.

The iPhone's hardware opens up previously unimaginable opportunities. Over the last few years, iOS has quietly grown into a surprisingly robust gaming platform. From casual games like Angry Birds to AAA titles like XCOM: Enemy Unknown, we're seeing a growing depth and breadth of games. And, with iOS 7's support for game controllers and other expanded game-based technologies, this trend will undoubtedly accelerate.

Meanwhile, revolutionary new social networking and location-aware apps continue to become a growing part of our digital lifestyle. There's still no sign that this flurry of innovation is slowing. In the first edition of this book, I claimed we had just begun to scratch the surface of what these devices can do. I still feel that way. The best ideas are yet to come.

Apple has also created a rich and vibrant marketplace for our apps. At the 2013 World Wide Developer's Conference, Apple CEO Tim Cook announced that Apple has more than 575 million accounts linked to the App Store, each only one click away. These customers have downloaded more than 50 billion apps, resulting in more than $10 billion paid to developers—$5 billion of that in the last year alone. This makes the App Store one of the biggest marketplaces on the Internet, and its growth continues to accelerate.

This provides exciting opportunities for both large and small development teams. For larger corporations, it opens a specialized, focused channel for interacting with your customers. A well-built, tightly focused application not only enhances your customers' experiences, it becomes a powerful public relations tool. Your app will help build brand loyalty with existing customers, while improving brand awareness among potential customers.

On the other end of the spectrum, the App Store makes it possible for one- or two-person development teams to get their products in front of millions of customers. You don't have to build and maintain your own online store. You don't need to collect money or process credit card transactions. Apple handles those details for you. You can focus on the part you love—building great applications.

Of course, the size of the App Store also brings challenges. With more than 900,000 apps in the store, the competition has become fierce. Just having a good idea isn't enough. You must back it with rock-solid and high-performance code, an intuitive and responsive user interface, and visually appealing layout and design.

So, the App Store is the 800-pound gorilla in the room, but you don't necessarily have to let it distract you. It's not always about producing commercial software. A growing number of developers use iOS devices as platforms for any number of personal or educational projects. You can find iOS-based experiments in everything from middle-school science fairs to robotics labs. And with iPhone's low-power Bluetooth 4.0 and Wi-Fi connections, we can easily interface our apps with other objects out in the real world.

Finally, Apple has given us a set of high-quality development tools. Xcode 5 continues to improve and refine the development environment, providing a wide range of utilities for testing, analyzing, and debugging code.

Apple also provides a top-notch programming language with an excellent set of frameworks. I know, I know...a lot of new iOS programmers balk at learning Objective-C, and I admit that the learning curve can feel quite steep, especially when you're struggling to get started. Still, once you become comfortable with the language, you will quickly begin to appreciate its power and elegance. Besides, learning a new programming language helps stretch your brain in interesting new ways. Objective-C will make you a better developer, even if you never use it for production code.

Objective-C is a dynamic, incredibly flexible programming language. It provides a number of features that will (if used properly) help overcome many difficult programming challenges. Likewise, the iOS software development kit (SDK) provides a wide range of excellent frameworks that let us rapidly build our apps.

Frameworks are one of the most difficult pieces of software to design. Ideally, they should make it simple for developers to perform common tasks, while still giving us enough freedom to strike out into uncharted territory. By those metrics, Cocoa Touch is one of the best frameworks that I have ever used. Indeed, if you find yourself writing a lot of code to do a common task, you are almost certainly doing something wrong.

I hope that this book will provide a gentle introduction to the world of iOS development. While it's not possible to cover every aspect or explore every framework, this book should give you a strong foundation to build on and the tools and skills to continue exploring on your own.

Additionally, while most of the book focuses on developing for the iPhone, the concepts and techniques apply to any iOS device: iPod touch, iPod, iPad Mini, and iWhateverMayCome. There are very few differences between devices. The iPad, for example, has a couple of unique user interface elements—but outside of those, everything else is the same.

While the exact differences between iPhone and iPad development is beyond the scope of this book, detailed information can be found in the bonus chapter "From iPhone to iPad" at www.freelancemadscience.com/creating-ios-7-apps-bonus-chap/.

For now, let's jump right in to our first project. Let's begin by building a simple utility application that displays a one-line message. Don't worry if you don't understand the code the first time through. The "Objective-C" bonus chapter, also at www.freelancemadscience.com/creating-ios-7-apps-bonus-chap/, covers the programming language in more depth. For now, use this as an opportunity to settle into the development environment.

GETTING STARTED WITH iOS

Ask any craftsperson—if you want to succeed, you must have the right tools for the job. For iOS development, this means having a Macintosh running OS X 10.8.4 or newer and a copy of Xcode 5. If you want to run your programs on an actual iOS device, you will also need a compatible device running iOS 7 (iPhone 4, fifth-generation iPod touch, iPad 2, iPad Mini or newer) and the appropriate developer/provisioning profiles.

We'll talk more about provisioning profiles in Chapter 2. For now, begin by downloading the latest version of Xcode from the Mac App Store. This is a free application, and downloading it through the App Store makes keeping all your development tools up-to-date very easy.

If you want to test your code on actual iOS devices or want to submit your application to the iTunes App Store, you will need to join the iOS Developer Program. This costs $99 a year for individuals or organizations. Students at universities can often get free access as part of their coursework, and large organizations may look into getting an enterprise license, letting them develop and distribute proprietary, in-house applications.

However, we can begin using Xcode for free—simply building and testing our apps in the simulator. While we wouldn't want to rely on the simulator for serious testing of production code, it is an easy way to start out.

Xcode is an integrated development environment (IDE) specifically designed for programming both Mac OS X and iOS. As the name suggests, an IDE is more than just a text editor. It is an interconnected suite of tools that helps you organize, edit, debug, manage, and otherwise herd all the resources into your final program. Through Xcode you can manage your assets, visually lay out the user interface, test run your program in an iOS simulator, step through your code one command at a time, analyze your application's performance, and more.

> **NOTE:** All the projects in this book were developed and tested using Xcode 5 and iOS SDK 7.0. If the past is any indication, Apple loves to make small (and sometimes not so small) changes even in minor releases. This means later versions will undoubtedly differ from what you see here. Menu options and the details of project templates will probably change. More rarely, updates to the SDK can affect how projects compile and run. Be aware, if you are using a newer version of either Xcode or the SDK, you may have to do some exploring and possibly even some debugging on your own. As always, if you run into problems and need help, check the errata or forums on the book's website: www.freelancemadscience.com/books/.

Once you have downloaded and installed Xcode (at almost 2GB, this may require a bit of patience), launch it, and let's get started.

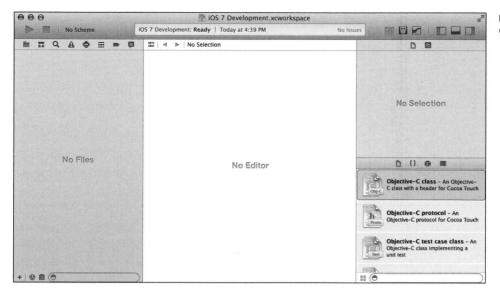

FIGURE 1.1 Our empty workspace

CREATING THE WORKSPACE

We will start by creating a new workspace. In Xcode, a *workspace* is a virtual box for organizing related projects. The workspace contains schemes for building and launching those projects, along with other related data. Xcode will allow you to search through all files in the workspace, and it will support workspace-wide indexing of those files. This allows features such as code completion, Jump to Definition, Open Quickly, and refactoring to operate smoothly across the entire workspace.

Workspaces simply let us organize our projects. They do not define where or how the individual projects are stored. Each workspace can have any number of projects, and each project can exist in any number of workspaces. This gives developers a lot of flexibility in organizing their work. You can even create specialized workspaces that focus on one particular task. For example, you may create one workspace for unit tests, another for debugging, and yet another for performance testing.

You don't need to create a workspace; you could simply start with a freestanding project. Nevertheless, it's a nice way to keep everything tidy. Let's build a workspace that will contain all the projects in this book. In Xcode, select the File > New > New Workspace menu item. Name the workspace iOS 7 Development, choose a location for it, and click Save. Xcode will then open a window that shows your empty workspace: no files, no editor, and no scheme (**Figure 1.1**).

CREATING THE PROJECT

With the workspace open, create a new project. In Xcode, select File > New > Project.... This will open the project template sheet (**Figure 1.2**). Xcode provides a wide range of templates for new projects. In the left column, select iOS > Application. Then, select the icon for Utility Application and click Next.

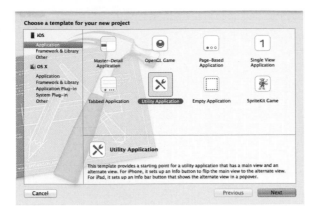

FIGURE 1.2 Selecting the iOS Utility Application template

We're now ready to choose the options for our project. Enter **Hello World** in the Product Name field. The Organization Name field should be either your name or the name of your company.

The Company Identifier field must be a string that uniquely identifies the organization (or you). In most cases, you will use reverse-DNS for the company identifier. This is the domain name of your main website with the levels reversed. Start with the top-level domain and work toward the second- and third-level domains. For example, I would use the reversed domain name from my blog: com.freelancemadscience.

Xcode combines the company identifier and the product name to generate a Bundle Identifier for your app. This is a unique key that Apple will use to refer to your application once you submit it to the App Store.

Next, we have the Class Prefix field. Xcode will automatically add this prefix to all the class names generated by the template. It will also insert the prefix at the beginning of the Class field, whenever we create a new class. This makes it easy to consistently use the same prefix across an entire project.

But, why do we need these prefixes? Well, we can blame them on Objective-C. Unfortunately, unlike many modern languages, Objective-C does not support namespaces. This means each class in our project must have a unique name. That's not a serious restriction when working within a single, isolated project—but once we start to use third-party libraries, we could quickly find ourselves drowning in conflicts.

To prevent naming conflicts, Objective-C developers have adopted the convention of adding prefixes to their class names. Apple, for example, uses a number of prefixes for its classes. Most commonly Apple uses *NS* and *UI*, though other frameworks have their own prefixes. Properly designed third-party libraries will also prefix all their classes.

For our classes, we can use any prefix we like. Just try to pick something unique. We'd definitely want to avoid *NS* or *UI*, since Apple has already claimed them. Actually, Apple is rapidly using up all the good two-letter combinations, so I recommend picking a three-letter prefix.

We can even leave it blank and not add any prefixes to our classes. When developing a self-contained application, as long as everyone else plays by the rules, this works fine. Personally,

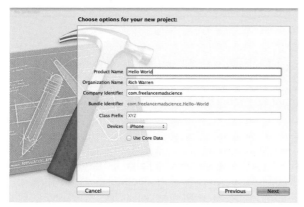

FIGURE 1.3 Selecting the project options

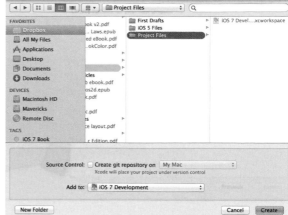

FIGURE 1.4 Selecting the project's location

for application code, I prefer to leave off the prefixes. Having simple, clean class names makes the project easier to read and navigate. So, that's the approach I'll take throughout this book. However, if you're working on a larger project or with a sizeable team, you may find that adding prefixes greatly simplifies the management and coordination of your code.

> **NOTE:** You should always prefix shared code. This is especially true when developing libraries, whether for internal use or to distribute publically. Prefixing your code lets other developers use your code without worrying about possible naming conflicts. It also makes it easier to identify where a class comes from. For example, all classes starting with *RGS* come from my ReallyGreatStuff library. Most importantly, if you don't prefix your classes and I find out, you can expect a sternly worded email! You have been warned.

So, let's leave the Class Prefix field blank. Also, make sure that iPhone is selected in the Devices pop-up menu and that the Use Core Data checkbox is unselected. Our settings should now match those shown in **Figure 1.3**.

This brings up the Save sheet. Select a location for the project. I usually put it in the same folder as the primary workspace. By default, Xcode will create a new folder using the project's name.

You can also create a Git repository for this project. In general, source control is a very good idea and should be included in all your projects. We will begin using source control in Chapter 2, but we won't go into detail about it in this book. If you want more information, I have additional resources at www.freelancemadscience.com/books/.

For now, make sure the Source Control: checkbox is unselected.

Finally, we want to add this project to our workspace. Click the Add to: pop-up and select our iOS 7 Development workspace. The settings should now match **Figure 1.4**.

That's it. Click Create, and Xcode will set up our project.

EXPLORING XCODE

Now that we have a project open, we can explore Xcode. Broadly speaking, we can divide the interface into five main pieces: toolbar, Navigator, Utilities, Debug area, and the Editor (**Figure 1.5**). Of these, we can hide everything except the Editor.

TOOLBAR

The toolbar presents commonly used tools and notifications. From left to right, it contains Run, Stop, Active Scheme, Destination, Status window, Standard Editor, Assistant Editor, Version Editor, Navigator, Debug area, and Utilities area (**Figure 1.6**).

The Run button will build the application using the currently selected scheme and then upload and run it on the currently selected device.

The Stop button will kill the current application.

NOTE: When you click the Stop button, the application is immediately killed. It does not go through the normal shutdown procedure. This distinction will become important when we start saving and loading data. Not surprisingly, we will revisit it in Chapter 5, "Loading and Saving Data."

The next two buttons control the active scheme. In Xcode, *schemes* are used to define both the configuration and device to use when building and running the app. The first button sets the active scheme. You can also use it to create new schemes or edit existing schemes.

The second sets the destination. In our case, this will include the iPhone and iPad simulators, as well as any test devices that are currently attached to the computer. Just pick the location where you want the app to run.

Xcode uses the Status window to display messages as it builds and runs our application. More importantly, it displays errors or warning icons if our code currently has any issues. We can click the error and warning icons in the Status window to navigate directly to the first issue of that type.

NOTE: If you haven't set up your developer's certificate and provisioning profiles yet, you will probably see one or two warnings. It's OK to ignore these for now. The project will still build and run on the simulator.

The Standard Editor, Assistant Editor, and Version Editor buttons let us select the type of editor to we want to use. The Standard editor simply displays a single editor, appropriate to the currently selected file. For code, this will be a text editor. For storyboards, this will be a graphical user interface editor (often referred to as Interface Builder). We will see other editors as we progress through the book.

FIGURE 1.5 Xcode overview

FIGURE 1.6 Toolbar

The Assistant editor displays two editor windows either stacked vertically or side-by-side. Use the View > Assistant Editor menu items to modify how the views are arranged. The main window will show the currently selected file, while the assistant window shows a related file.

The Version editor works with our project's source control management software and lets us view two different versions of the same file, with the differences highlighted. For this project, it won't be very useful, since we did not create a Git repository.

The last three buttons are toggles. They hide or display the Navigator, Debug area, and Utilities, respectively. If the button is blue, the corresponding area will be shown onscreen. If it's grayed out, the area will be hidden.

Finally, we can hide and show the toolbar using the View > Hide Toolbar and View > Show Toolbar menu items.

NAVIGATOR

The Navigator lets us navigate through various aspects of our project. The Navigator has eight tabs, each showing a different view into our project.

The *Project navigator* displays all the files, frameworks, and other resources included in our project. Select a file to open it in the editor. Most of the time, we will use the Project navigator to move around our project.

The *Symbol navigator* shows all the symbols in our project: the classes, methods, protocols, and so on.

The *Find navigator* lets us search through our workspace. Use ⌘F when searching within a single file. Use the File navigator to search across multiple files.

The *Issue navigator* displays our project's warnings and errors. We can click an issue in the Issue navigator, and it will take us to the problem in our code.

The *Test navigator* displays our unit tests. We can see the results of our tests, as well as rerunning individual tests.

The *Debug navigator* displays the stack trace for each thread when debugging. We can use this to move back up the stack trace.

The *Breakpoint navigator* displays all the breakpoints in our project. We can edit and delete breakpoints here. We can also create symbolic or exception breakpoints.

The *Log navigator* shows both the console logs and the build logs. While Xcode is open, it will save these logs each time you build and run the application. When you close and reopen Xcode, it will clear all but the most recent set of logs.

Most of the Navigator tabs have controls on the bottom to let us filter its content. This can be handy as the number of files in your project begins to grow.

NOTE: You don't need to use the Navigator to open files. The File > Open Quickly... menu item (or ⇧⌘O) will open a pop-up window. Type in the name of a symbol or file, and it will display a list of suggestions. Just select the one you want to open it. The Open Quickly window does a great job of intelligently guessing likely matches. If you have a fairly good idea of what you're looking for, Open Quickly will be faster than searching the Navigator.

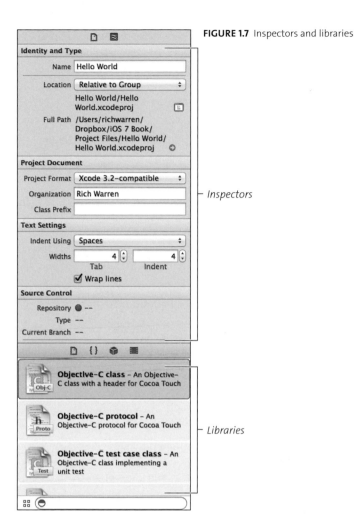

FIGURE 1.7 Inspectors and libraries

— *Inspectors*

— *Libraries*

UTILITIES

The Utilities area consists of two parts: inspectors and libraries (**Figure 1.7**).

Inspectors let us observe and configure the item we are currently editing. Each type of editor has its own set of inspectors. For example, the text editor has only two inspectors: File and Quick Help. Interface Builder has six: File, Quick Help, Identity, Attributes, Size, and Connections. You can find these by clicking on Main.storyboard.

The File inspector provides information about the file itself: where it is saved, which targets it is included in, and so on.

The Quick Help inspector provides a summary of the currently selected object (or, for text, the symbol at the cursor's current location). Quick Help usually includes links to an appropriate header file, to Apple's documentation, and to any appropriate sample projects.

The Identity inspector is primarily used to change the class of an object to a custom subclass when graphically designing user interfaces. The accessibility settings are also located here. We can even set an Xcode-specific label for the object or use Key-Value Coding to set properties not exposed through the Attributes inspector. Don't worry if this doesn't make a lot of sense. We'll see it in action later.

The Attributes inspector is where we will spend most of our time, especially when designing user interfaces. This inspector lets us modify and configure the selected object. Each type of object has a custom set of attributes that we can modify. For example, views have a background color attribute (among many others).

The Size inspector is also commonly used when designing user interfaces. This inspector displays the current position and size of the selected object. We can also view and modify the auto layout constraints for that object.

The Connections inspector displays all the connections for the currently selected object. We will get some hands-on experience drawing connections later in this chapter.

The libraries provide elements that we can drag out and add to our project. Each library works in its own way. There are four tabs, letting us select the four different libraries.

The File Template library, as the name suggests, is a library of file templates. To add a new file to our project, you can simply drag an item from the library and drop it into the Project navigator.

The Code Snippet library lists the commonly used code snippets. This is a great place to look if you cannot remember how to write a proper init method, fast enumeration, or a dispatch once block. Just drag an item out into the text editor and then modify it as needed.

The Object library is honestly the library I use 90 percent of the time. This is strictly used for interface development. This library contains all the controls, controllers, and containers we will use to design our user interface. Simply drag them out into Interface Builder, resize them, and draw the connections. We'll get some hands-on experience using this library later in this chapter.

The Media library displays all the media files added to your project. You can drag and drop these directly onto the user interface; however, in practice I never do this. I typically either programmatically load the media file or I set them using a control's attribute. The Attributes inspector will automatically list all the appropriate media files for a given setting—so there's usually no need to come down here.

DEBUG AREA

The Debug area consists of two parts: Console and Variables. As our application runs, anything printed to the standard output will appear in the Console window. If we stop at a breakpoint, we will get additional information about local variables in the Variables window. Additionally, our Console window becomes an active control. We can type debugger commands directly into the console. For example, we can use the po command to print an Objective-C object, or the p command to print C-data.

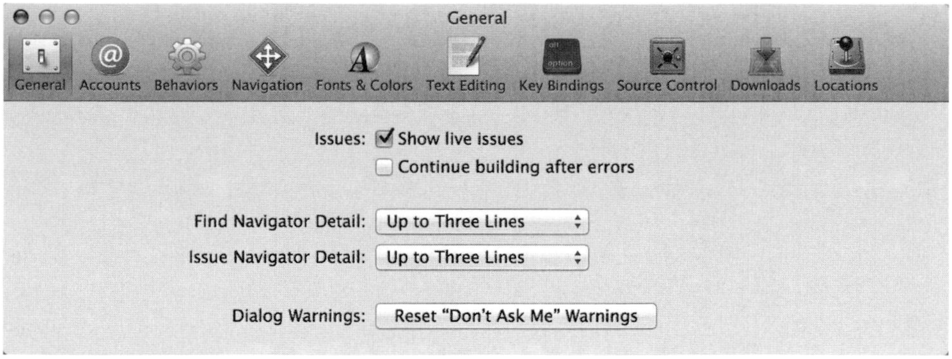

FIGURE 1.8 Xcode preferences window

```
po self.label
<UILabel: 0x8e828e0; frame = (20 225; 280 29); text = 'Hello World';
→ clipsToBounds = YES; opaque = NO; autoresize = RM+BM; userInteractionEnabled
→ = NO; layer = <CALayer: 0x8e829e0>>
```

We will look at this in more depth once we have some code to run.

EDITOR

This is where the rubber hits the road. We will spend most of our time in the Editor, modifying the content of our files. Different file types have their own editors. We'll get a chance to use both the text editor and Interface Builder in this chapter. We will also see other editors in later chapters.

PREFERENCES

One last thing to look at in our whirlwind tour is how to set preferences. Xcode gives us a lot of flexibility when it comes to configuring our work environment, so it's worth spending some time exploring and tweaking the settings to make sure Xcode is working the way you (or your team) want.

We can access the preferences using the Xcode > Preferences... menu. This brings up the preferences window. The window has ten tabs: General, Accounts, Behaviors, Navigation, Fonts & Colors, Text Editing, Key Bindings, Source Control, Downloads, and Locations (**Figure 1.8**).

- **General:** This tab has relatively few settings, most of which (honestly) aren't very interesting. Show live issues is enabled by default. This tells Xcode to analyze your code as you write and to display warnings and errors as they occur. This can be annoying, but in general turning it off is worse. You can also set the number of lines displayed in the Find and Issue Navigator—if you want to see more or less detail.

- **Accounts:** This is where you manage your developer accounts. Notice that you can connect to more than one developer account—and each developer account can belong to more than one team. Highlight a team name and hit the View Details button to see the signing identity and provisioning profiles associated with that account. This tab is also used to manage source control repositories.

- **Behaviors:** This page allows you to set up events (left pane) that trigger actions (right pane). For example, look at the default behaviors for Build > Generates new issues. Whenever the build system generates a new issue, Xcode will show the issue in the Issue navigator. We could modify this to have it also play a sound, display a notification, or even run a script. While behaviors have a lot of potential, I often find that either the events or the actions are too coarse-grained to really do what I want.

- **Navigation:** The Navigation tab lets you set how the navigators respond to clicks, double-clicks, and Option-clicks.

NOTE: I highly recommend setting Double Click Navigation: to Uses Separate Tabs. By default, Xcode opens the file in a separate window with the Toolbar, Navigator, Debug area, and Utilities area all hidden. If you lose track of this window and it happens to be the only window left open when Xcode closes, Xcode will assume you want this format for all future windows. This can be very frustrating, especially if you don't know how to fix it. Hint: Go to the View menu and turn the toolbar back on.

- **Fonts & Colors:** This tab sets the font, font size, and coloring scheme used by the text editor. There are several predefined color settings. You can also manually modify the setting for each category of text (e.g., strings, comments, class names).

- **Text Editing:** This is where you configure how the text editor works and how it indents your code. Developers have been known to argue bitterly over what the "correct" setting should be. Therefore, I will simply present the settings without further comment—OK, only one comment. I typically turn line numbers on.

- **Key Bindings:** This is where you can view and modify all the keyboard shortcuts used by Xcode. While you can use it to set up new shortcuts, it's almost more useful as a reference. Want to know how to run unit tests from the keyboard? Open this tab and do a quick search for "test" (the answer is ⌘U).

- **Source Control:** This has a few, high-level commands for controlling how source control behaves. To add a repository, you need to go back to the Accounts tab.

- **Downloads:** This is where you select which simulators and which document sets are installed. You can also use this tab to check for updates. I typically install all the available simulators, but only install the most recent doc sets.

- **Locations:** Finally, this tab lets you customize where different byproducts will be saved. This includes the snapshots and archives you might make of your project, as well as any derived data generated during compilation.

FIGURE 1.9 Setting the destination

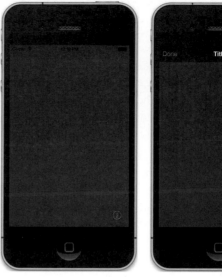

FIGURE 1.10 The main view   **FIGURE 1.11** The flipside view

SURVEYING THE PROJECT

Now that we have a basic understanding of Xcode, let's start exploring our new project. Utility applications should provide easy access to a single screen of information, with a backside view for setting and modifying the preferences. The iPhone's Weather app is a good example. The main screen shows simple weather forecasts for the next week and even lets you page through multiple cities. The flipside view allows you to edit the list of cities, as well as change the temperature display between Fahrenheit and Celsius.

The Utility Application template creates a basic skeleton for this type of application. All of Apple's templates are, by themselves, fully functional apps. They may not do anything particularly interesting, but they will all build and run. In fact, you can often learn a lot about how different technologies can be linked together just by exploring the template code. With that in mind, let's look at all the things Apple gives us for free.

RUNNING THE APPLICATION

Before we can run the app, we need to tell Xcode to use the simulator. Click the destination in the toolbar and select iPhone Retina (3.5-inch) (**Figure 1.9**). Then click the Run button. Xcode will save all of our files, build the project, and launch it in the simulator.

As you can see, the application has a dark gray main view with an info button in the lower-right corner (**Figure 1.10**). If you touch the info button, the screen flips over to show the flipside view with a title bar and a blue Done button (**Figure 1.11**). Tap the Done button, and you flip back to the main view.

EXAMINING THE FILES

Now let's look at the files. The Project navigator should be visible by default. If not, make sure the Navigator button is enabled in the toolbar and then select the Project navigator (the ▮ icon). Alternatively, you can just select the View > Navigators > Show Project Navigator menu item.

The Project navigator will show several groups of resources. The Hello World group contains the header (.h) and implementation (.m) files for all our Objective-C classes. This is where we will do most of our actual coding. It also contains two resource files: Main.storyboard and Images.xassets.

Main.storyboard defines the scenes in our application and the segues between them. Image.xassets manages our image files, keeping track of the different versions needed to support different devices and screen resolutions. We will look at both of these files in more depth in later chapters.

The Supporting Files subgroup contains a variety of secondary files. Initially, this group contains the application's Hello World-Info.plist, InfoPlist.strings, main.m, and Prefix.pch files.

The Hello World-Info.plist file contains a number of key-value pairs used to configure our application. If any of the values are strings that will be displayed to the user, they may need to be localized. This is where the InfoPlist.strings file comes in. When loading a string value, the system will look for a language-specific version first. If this cannot be found, it will use the value from Hello World-Info.plist. We will talk about localization in more detail in Chapter 9, "The Last Mile."

The main.m file contains the main() function. Objective-C, just like C, always begins with main(). This is the first function that is executed when your application launches. It is responsible for setting up and running everything else.

Finally, the Prefix.pch file is the application's precompiled header. To help large projects compile faster, Xcode allows us to create a precompiled prefix header file containing a number of #import, #include, and #define directives common across much of our code. For example, in a typical iOS project, most classes need to access the UIKit and Foundation frameworks. By including the #import statements for these frameworks in our prefix header, Xcode knows to preprocess those files and include the results in all of our source files. This prevents the compiler from processing common files multiple times during each build.

Having said that, Xcode 5 introduces a better technology called *modules*. Modules are an optimized database for system header files. This provides many of the same benefits as Prefix.pch but provides greater performance and removes the need to manually manage the Prefix.pch file.

For the most part, modules are automatic. You simply #import the file, and Xcode looks up the module. In addition, whenever you #import a module, Xcode will automatically link its framework to the project. This is especially good for beginning iOS developers, since link errors can appear somewhat mysterious and confusing when you first encounter them.

Unfortunately, modules support only the system frameworks and libraries provided by Apple. If you want to use a third-party library, you will still need to manually link it to the project, and if it's used across a large portion of your project, you may want to include it in the `Prefix.pch` file.

This may not make a lot of sense right now, and that's OK. Using the `Prefix.pch` is an advanced topic. We won't be touching it in this project. And, honestly, for most iOS projects, the compile time is relatively fast compared to the amount of time it takes to upload the app to the simulator or device. So, unless you're working on a very large, enterprise-scale project, modifying the `Prefix.pch` file is probably a waste of your time.

Finally, the Frameworks group contains all the frameworks explicitly linked to this project (but does not include any modules that are automatically linked in from modules). Meanwhile, the Products group contains the end results—in our case, the compiled application. Again, we won't be touching any of these in this project.

> **NOTE:** Much like Xcode's workspaces, the navigator's groups represent a virtual organization—they exist only within Xcode. These groups do not necessarily have any relationship with how or where the actual resources are stored, or even with what type of files they contain. You are free to place any resource in any group and to add or remove groups or subgroups as needed. Use them to organize the files in your Project navigator as you see fit.

WALKING THROUGH THE PROJECT

When I first started writing Cocoa applications, I did not understand how all the pieces fit together. Sure, I understood each individual part. I had a view and a view controller. They worked together to manage the user interface. However, many of these objects seemed to magically appear at runtime. I had no idea where they came from.

Let me reassure you that there is nothing supernatural going on here. Trust me, I've checked. Still, it's worth taking a few minutes to walk through all the connections, just to understand what is happening. Don't worry about memorizing all the details. Instead, focus on how we trace the connections from one object to the next. That way, you will be able to trace through your own applications later.

Let's start exactly where our application starts. Click `main.m` in the Project navigator (you may need to expand the Hello World and Supporting Files groups if they aren't already visible). This file is actually very short. It imports the UIKit and our application delegate, and then it defines the `main()` function.

```
#import <UIKit/UIKit.h>

#import "AppDelegate.h"

int main(int argc, char * argv[])
{
```

```
@autoreleasepool {
    return UIApplicationMain(argc, argv, nil, NSStringFromClass
    → ([AppDelegate class]));
}
}
```

Basically, `main()` creates an autorelease block. Inside the block, we launch our Objective-C application. You can find a complete discussion on memory management in the "Objective-C" bonus chapter at `www.freelancemadscience.com/creating-ios-7-apps-bonus-chap/`.

The real work happens in the `UIApplicationMain()` function. This function performs four vital tasks:

1. It creates our application object.

2. It creates our application delegate and links it to the application.

3. It starts the application's run loop.

4. Once everything is set up, it calls our delegate's `application:didFinishLaunchingWith Options:` method. This is typically our first opportunity to run our own code.

`UIApplicationMain()` takes four arguments. The first two handle our application's command-line arguments: `argc` gives the number of arguments, while `argv` contains the actual arguments as an array of C-style strings. These arguments are largely a holdover from Unix command-line applications. In iOS, our apps typically have only a single argument, the name of our application's executable file. We almost never use these arguments directly.

The next two arguments define our application and our application delegate, respectively. Each takes a string that corresponds to the desired class name. If the third argument is `nil`, we will use the default `UIApplication` class. If the fourth argument is `nil`, the system will load our `UIApplicationDelegate` from a nib file.

Loading the delegate from a nib file is an older design pattern. You will typically see this if you look at projects designed for iOS 4.0 and earlier. For iOS 7.0, all the application templates use storyboards (except for the empty template, which—as the name suggests—is largely empty). This means we need to manually set our application delegate's name.

We could hard-code in the name as `@"AppDelegate"`. While this saves us a little typing, it has one major limitation. If we refactor our code and change the `AppDelegate` class's name, Xcode won't know to change this string.

In software engineering, the solution to difficult problems often involves adding a layer of indirection. In this case, `NSStringFromClass([AppDelegate class])` indirectly determines the name of our `AppDelegate` class. This gives us a lot of flexibility. In theory, we could override the `+[AppDelegate class]` method to dynamically return our delegate's class, possibly returning a different delegate for the iPad and the iPhones. Most of the time, however, it simply guarantees that when we refactor our delegate's name, `main()` will automatically find and use the new name.

Most applications will follow this pattern. Instead of subclassing the UIApplication, we typically use a standard UIApplication object. Instead, we provide a custom application delegate.

> **NOTE:** You will rarely change anything in main.m. In fact, unless you are doing something very unusual, you should never touch it. Even if you're convinced you really need to make a change or two, please take a step back and think things through one final time. There is almost always a better solution.

EXAMINING THE STORYBOARD

So far so good. The main() function calls UIApplicationMain(). This function instantiates the application and our custom AppDelegate class. Then it sets up the main event loop and begins processing events. It will then call our delegate's application:didFinishLaunchingWithOptions: method. This may kick off some of our own code.

But what about the user interface? In applications that use a storyboard, the application's root view controller is created by the storyboard. But, what is a storyboard?

Storyboards allow us to graphically design our scenes and draw the segues that connect them. This represents the latest step in Xcode's interface development technologies.

Previous versions of Xcode used Interface Builder to graphically design our user interface. Interface Builder saved our designs as binary nib files. Xcode could then include the nibs in our application, loading them at runtime.

In Xcode 4, the Interface Builder application was brought inside Xcode itself. This allows a much tighter integration between the user interface and our code. We can even edit the interface and its related code side by side. With storyboards, Xcode expands this, letting us encapsulate a number of nibs, giving us the power to graphically define multiple scenes and the ability to draw the transitions between them.

As you will soon see, our storyboards contain a lot more than just views, buttons, and text fields. They also contain controller objects, as well as the connections between the various interface objects, views, and controllers. We will get some experience drawing these connections as we expand our Hello World app in the "Modifying the Template" section, later this chapter. Additionally, we will discuss nibs, the underlying technology behind storyboards, in more detail in the Chapter 2 sidebar "The Secret Life of Nibs."

> **NOTE:** Originally, Interface Builder saved nib archives as binary files, with a .nib extension. As of Xcode 3.0, Interface Builder allowed storing the nib files in an intermediate XML format with a .xib extension. This allowed greater compatibility with source control and other development tools. The .xib files are then compiled into binary .nib files when the application is built. For simplicity's sake, both versions are typically referred to as "nib files." In Xcode 4.2, storyboards are also stored as XML files with a .storyboard extension. The system automatically compiles the storyboard into one or more nib files and then loads these nibs as needed at runtime.

FIGURE 1.12 Setting the main storyboard

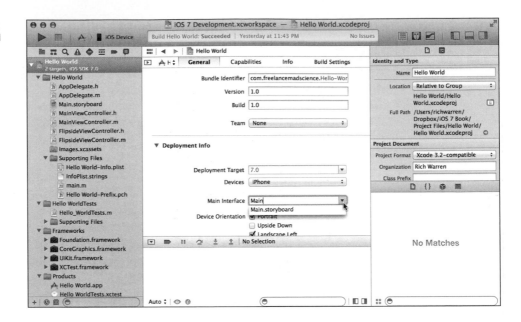

So, how does `UIApplicationMain()` know which storyboard file to open? Simple. It looks in the project's `info.plist`. If you click `Hello World-Info.plist`, you will find a key called "Main storyboard file base name" with the value Main. This tells `UIApplicationMain()` to load the `Main.storyboard` file.

While we can modify the `info.plist` directly, there is a simpler (and safer) way. In the Project navigator, click the blue, Hello World project icon. This will open the project settings editor. Make sure the General tab is selected, and scroll down until you see the Main Interface selection. Clicking this brings up a pop-up menu containing all the storyboard files in our application (right now, we have only one) (**Figure 1.12**). We can simply select the storyboard we want to use.

Let's open the storyboard file. Click `Main.storyboard` in the Project navigator. This will open the storyboard file in Xcode's Editor. You will probably want to close the navigator to give the Editor as much space as possible. You will also want to make sure the Utilities area is open along the right side of the screen. If it's not visible, you can either click the Utilities button or select View > Utilities > Show Utilities.

The Storyboard editor consists of two regions. On the left side is the Document Outline. This sidebar shows all the scenes in our storyboard, as well as every object within each scene.

On the right, we have Interface Builder. This is the graphical editor we use to view and design the actual user interface for our scenes, as well as drawing flow of control among the scenes (**Figure 1.13**).

NOTE: The Document Outline will probably be hidden by default. We can hide and show the Document Outline by clicking the Document Outline button in the bottom-left corner of Interface Builder.

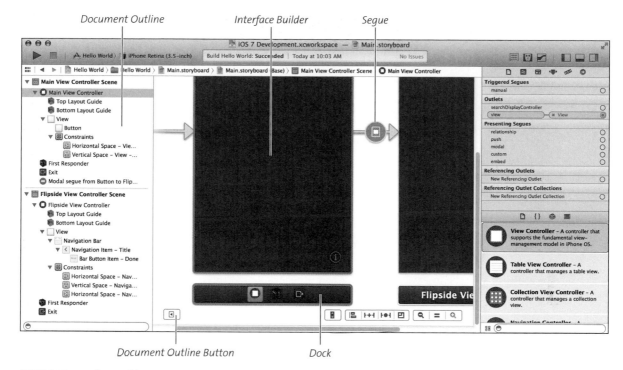

Document Outline   *Interface Builder*   *Segue*

Document Outline Button   *Dock*

FIGURE 1.13 Interface Builder

Our project starts out with two scenes. If you look at the Document Outline, you will see that each scene has at least three top-level objects: the First Responder, the scene's view controller, and an Exit. Let's start with the First Responder. This is, in many ways, a very unusual object. Or rather, it's not an object at all—it's a proxy. The system never creates an instance of the First Responder. Instead, the system will dynamically assign the First Responder at runtime.

Basically, the First Responder represents the first object in our application's responder chain. It can act as a target for any actions that must be sent to the responder chain. For example, a copy action should target the currently selected text, regardless of which control that text may be in. We don't want to hardwire the action to a particular control; instead, we want to route the action to the currently active control. By targeting the first responder, our message is automatically passed to the correct control at runtime. Having said that, we rarely need to interact with the First Responder directly in iOS.

Next, look at the view controller. Each scene has its own view controller—an instance of `UIViewController` or (more likely) one of its subclasses. You can find a complete description of the Model-View-Controller pattern in the "Objective-C" bonus chapter at `www.freelancemadscience.com/creating-ios-7-apps-bonus-chap/`. For now, just think of the controller as the link between the scene and the rest of our code.

FIGURE 1.14 Checking
the class

Expand the view controller. Each view controller contains a top and bottom layout guide-line and a view. The view may, in turn, contain any number of subviews and controls (which may contain their own subviews and controls). We often refer to the entire graph of views and subviews as the view hierarchy. Xcode lets us examine and manipulate both the view hierarchy and the view's actual appearance. The Document Outline shows us the hierarchy, while the Interface Builder shows us the layout.

Finally, we have the Exit. This is even less of an object than the First Responder. At least the First Responder may refer to an object at runtime. Exit is simply a placeholder for segue unwinding actions. We will look at these actions in more depth in Chapter 3, "Developing Views and View Controllers," but won't use them in this project.

Our scenes may also have other top-level objects. For example, the main view control-ler scene has a model segue—the transition between the main view and the flipside view. Scenes may also include gesture recognizers, views, or even data objects as top-level objects.

All of the top-level objects (except the segues) also appear in the scene's dock in Interface Builder. This makes it easier to draw connections between the scene's interface and the top-level objects, especially when the list of scenes begins to grow. Segues, on the other hand, appear between the views they connect. Like the dock, this helps keep them close at hand. Even more importantly, it graphically displays the flow of control through our application, giving us a feel for how everything connects.

Each storyboard designates a single scene as its initial scene. In our case, this is the scene that `UIApplicationMain()` loads when the application first launches.

The initial scene appears in the Interface Builder area with an incoming arrow pointing at it. Unlike segues and other relationships, this arrow doesn't have a scene on the other end. By default, the incoming arrow starts at the left edge of Interface Builder. The initial scene is the first scene, with additional scenes branching out as we move to the right.

We can change the initial scene by selecting a different view controller and selecting its "is Initial View Controller" attribute. Only one view controller can have this attribute enabled at a time. If you enable it in a new view controller, Interface Builder will automatically disable it for the old controller.

In our case, the main view controller scene is our initial scene. This is exactly what we want. Make sure we are zoomed in on the main scene. Double-clicking the background will toggle the zoom between an overview of the entire storyboard and the actual-size view.

Let's start by clicking each object in the main scene and examining their classes. Make sure the Identity inspector is selected (the ▣ tab). Open the Document Outline, and expand all the items in both scenes. Then click the Main View Controller icon. Not surprisingly, our view controller is an instance of the `MainViewController` class (**Figure 1.14**).

> **NOTE:** To select a view controller, you must click its icon, either in the Document Outline or in the scene's dock. When a view controller is selected, the entire scene will be outlined in blue.

Next, look at the top and bottom layout guides. These guides make it easier to define auto layout constraints. We will look at constraints in detail in Chapter 3. For now, you just need to know that the auto layout system uses constraints to resize and reposition our content when the containing view's size changes. Most of the time this happens when the user rotates the device into landscape or portrait orientation.

Basically, we can connect constraints to either the top or bottom layout guidelines instead of connecting directly to the containing view. This is important, since the guides will automatically adjust their position depending on whether or not our view has a navigation, tool bar, status bar or tab bar.

If you select the guides, you will see that they are simple `NSObjects`. However, we will never really interact with these guides, except as reference items in our constraints.

Next, we have the view. It's a simple `UIView` with no additional features or abilities. Inside the view, we have a `UIButton` (the info button at the lower-right corner). Below the button are our view's constraints. While we cannot select the Constraints icon, we can select the individual constraints beneath it. Each one is an instance of `NSLayoutConstraint`.

The First Responder, Exit, and segue don't correspond to actual objects. As a result, none of them has a class. In fact, the Exit and the segue don't have any Identity settings at all.

Moving on to the flipside view controller scene, we have a `FlipsideViewController`. Inside this, we have another `UIView`; however, at the top of this view we have a `UINavigation` bar, with a `UINavigationItem`. Inside that, we have our Done button—a `UIBarButtonItem`.

Now switch to the Connections inspector (the ➡ tab). This lets us view and edit the connections between objects. While it can appear somewhat complex, this inspector shows only five connection types: outlets, actions, events, segues, and relationships.

The first three are used to define connections within a single scene. Outlets are properties that can store a pointer to an object. They define the relationships between objects in our graph, letting the code inside one object refer to another object in the same scene.

Actions, on the other hand, are methods that we can connect to events. When an event occurs, the system automatically calls its corresponding action. Controls define a set of common events that occur when the user interacts with the control. This includes a variety of touch events, value changes, and editing events.

Next, segues and relationships define the connections between scenes. Segues act as transitions. When the application triggers a segue, it transitions to the next scene using the specified animation.

FIGURE 1.15 Displaying the connection

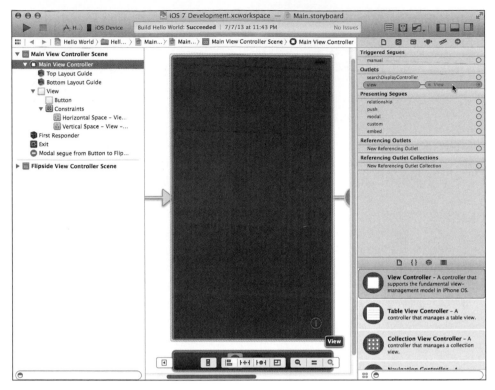

Relationships look a lot like segues, but they are used to show ownership. Container controllers (like tab view controllers) will use relationships to connect to the views they manage.

If we look at the main view controller, we can see that it has a `view` outlet pointing to the contained `view` object. If you hover the mouse over this connection, both the controller and the view will be highlighted (**Figure 1.15**). This connection means that we can refer to our `view` object in our view controller's code.

There's only one other connection in this scene. Select the info button. It has a modal triggered segue to the flipside view controller (**Figure 1.16**). If the user taps the button, they will trigger this segue, moving the application to the flipside view controller scene.

Now let's look at the flipside view controller (**Figure 1.17**). Like the main view controller, it has an outlet connecting it to its view. As you can probably guess, this is a general pattern. All view controllers have an outlet connecting to their view.

The flipside view controller also has two incoming connections. One is the presenting segue from the main view controller's info button. This simply refers back to the triggered segue we have already seen.

The other connection represents an incoming action. Just by looking, we cannot tell which user interface control is triggering the action; however, mouse over the connection and the Done button is highlighted. We'll look at the other side of this connection in a moment.

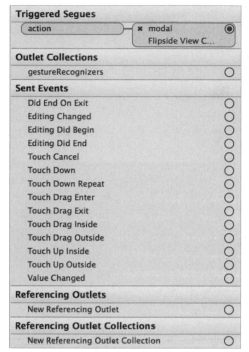

FIGURE 1.16 Info button's connections

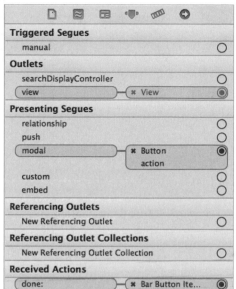

FIGURE 1.17 Flipside view controller's connections

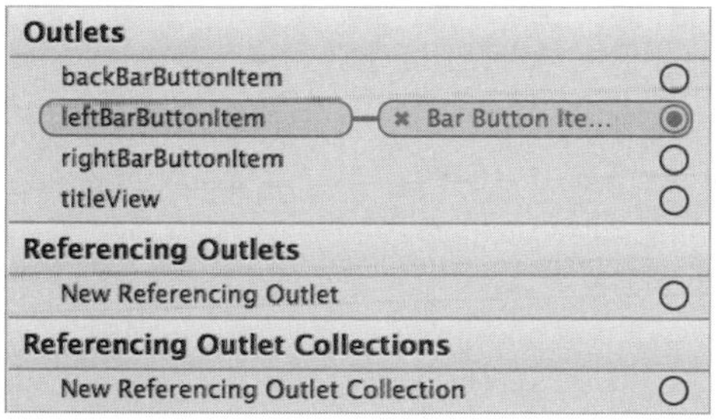

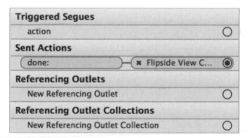

FIGURE 1.18 Navigation item's connections

FIGURE 1.19 Done button's connections

There are only two other connections in this scene. The navigator item's leftBarButton-Item outlet refers to the Done button (**Figure 1.18**). This positions the bar button correctly in the navigation bar. Additionally, we see the action connection from the Done button to the flipside view controller's done: method (**Figure 1.19**). This method will be called whenever the Done button is pressed.

Next, let's look at the constraints. Reading constraints takes a bit of practice, so we'll just touch on the basics here. Don't worry if it doesn't make a lot of sense, we'll get real hands-on experience in Chapter 3.

FIGURE 1.20 Selected constraints are highlighted

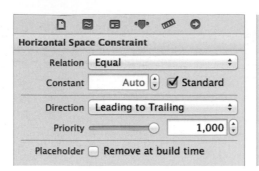

FIGURE 1.21 Constraint attributes

FIGURE 1.22 List of navigation bar constraints

First, switch to the Attributes inspector (the icon). Then, in the Document Outline, select the Main View Controller Scene's Horizontal Space constraint. Notice how the blue I-bar connecting the info button to the right edge of the view is highlighted (**Figure 1.20**). This indicates a constraint between the button and its containing view.

Now look at the attributes (**Figure 1.21**). There are three key pieces of information here. First, the Relationship type is set to Equal. Next, the Standard checkbox is checked. Finally Direction is set to Leading to Trailing. That means we are setting the distance between our button and the view equal to the standard spacing (in this case, 20 points). The Leading to Trailing setting is a bit misleading in this context. Technically we are connecting the button's trailing edge to the view's trailing edge. What it really means is that instead of hard-coding in specific sides (connecting the button's right side to the view's right side), we're going to base the connection on the currently selected language's reading order. In a left-to-right language (like English), the button will appear on the bottom-right corner of the screen. In a right-to-left language (like Arabic), auto layout will automatically reposition it to the bottom-left corner.

If you look at Main View Controller's second constraint, you will see that it is also set equal to the standard spacing; however, there is no direction setting for vertical constraints.

Looking at the flipside scene, it has three constraints, but they are all a bit harder to decipher. Selecting them doesn't reveal the I-bar. Instead, we get a bar across either the entire length or width of the screen. From the attributes, we can see that the spacing is set equal to 0 points—but it doesn't tell us which items are being constrained.

To get the rest of the picture, switch to the Size inspector (the icon) and select the Navigation bar in the Document Outline. All three constraints should show up (**Figure 1.22**). Note, however, that we can hide any section in any of our inspectors. If the Size inspector is empty except for the word "view," then click "view" to display the view settings. We have the leading space to the superview, the top space to the superview, and the trailing space to the superview—all set to zero points.

So, what does this mean? Well, for the main scene, our info button will be held a fixed distance from the bottom-right corner, no matter how tall or wide the containing view is. For the flipside view, the navigation bar will be held flush against the top and stretched from

FIGURE 1.23 Main view landscape orientation

FIGURE 1.24 Flipside view landscape orientation

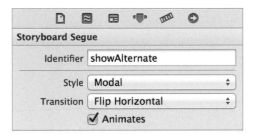

FIGURE 1.25 The segue attributes

edge to edge—again, no matter how wide or tall the view is. We can see this, as we rotate the device from portrait to landscape (⌘⇨ or ⌘⇦ in the simulator). Auto layout repositions our info button and resizes our navigation bar for us automatically (**Figures 1.23** and **1.24**). It even animates the changes for us.

Finally, let's take a closer look at the segue. Select the Attributes inspector (the ⬤ icon), and select the segue between our views. This shows our segue's details (**Figure 1.25**). The Identifier field contains a string we can use to identify this segue in our code. The Style pop-up menu lets us define the segue's type: push, modal, or custom. The Transition pop-up and the Animates checkbox let us control how (and whether) the system animates this transition.

In our case, the segue is named showAlternate. We will present our new scene as a modal view. Animations are enabled, so we will show our main view flipping over horizontally to reveal the flipside view on its back.

In most graphical user interfaces, a modal view is a view that must be dismissed (usually by clicking an OK or Cancel button) before the user can perform any other actions in the application. This forces the user to focus on whatever is inside the modal view—they must finish dealing with it before they can move on. On desktop applications, we generally use modal view to display things like Save or Print dialogs. On the iPhone, modal views cover the entire screen (though the iPad has a few additional options), but their use and meaning are largely the same. We are presenting information and controls that the user must actively dismiss once they are done.

So, what does this all mean? Well, we've gone on a few short tangents, but we're still trying to trace through how all the objects in our application get created.

ADVANCED TOPIC: BOOTSTRAPPING YOUR APP

There are eight tasks that must be completed to properly set up an iOS application. Every application must perform all of these steps.

1. **Create App Object:** Instantiate UIApplication or one of its subclasses.

2. **Create App Delegate:** Instantiate a custom subclass of UIResponder that also adopts the UIApplicationDelegate protocol.

3. **Link the App and Delegate:** Set the App's delegate property to the delegate object.

4. **Create Window:** Instantiate a UIWindow object.

5. **Link the Delegate and Window:** Set the UIApplicationDelegate's window property to the window object.

6. **Create Root View Controller:** Instantiate a custom UIViewController subclass. This view controller is responsible for displaying our app's initial view.

7. **Link Root View Controller and Window:** Set the UIWindow's rootViewController property to our view controller object.

8. **Setup the Window:** Call -[UIWindow makeKeyAndVisible] to make our window the key window, and make it visible.

While our application must either explicitly or implicitly perform all of these steps, the exact procedure can vary considerably from app to app. There are, however, three main approaches: programmatically bootstrapping the app, using a main nib file, or using a storyboard.

Programmatic Bootstrapping

1. When calling UIApplicationMain(), pass nil as the third argument and the name of our UIApplicationDelegate as the fourth.

2. In application:didFinishLaunchingWithOptions: we must instantiate the window and the root view controller. We must link the delegate and the window and then link the window and the root view controller. Finally, we must call makeKeyAndVisible.

Using a Main Nib File

1. When calling UIApplicationMain(), pass nil as both the third and fourth arguments. This tells UIApplicationMain() that we will be instantiating and configuring our delegate object inside the main nib file.

2. Create a nib file. This nib file must instantiate our delegate object and connect it to the File's Owner's delegate outlet. It must create a window and connect it to the delegate's window outlet. Finally, we must create our root view controller and connect it to the window. Note that the root view controller's view hierarchy is often defined in a separate nib file, causing us to chain one nib file to another.

3. Set the nib file as our application's main interface in the info.plist. UIApplicationMain() will automatically call makeKeyAndVisible for us.

Using Storyboards

1. When calling UIApplicationMain(), pass nil as the third argument and the name of our UIApplicationDelegate as the fourth.

2. Create a storyboard file with at least one scene. The storyboard's initial scene will become our root view controller.

3. Set the nib file as our application's main interface in the info.plist. That's it. UIApplicationMain() will automatically handle the rest. Specifically, it will instantiate and link up all the objects for us, and then call makeKeyAndVisible.

In Xcode 5.0, almost all of Apple's project templates use storyboards to bootstrap the iOS apps. This is largely an automated process, automatically handling many details that must be manually performed in the other two approaches.

Throughout this book, we will follow Apple's lead and use storyboards. However, I wanted to at least mention the other approaches, since you may encounter them in older projects, books, and tutorials.

Remember, the `UIApplicationMain()` method creates an instance of the `UIApplication` and of our `AppDelegate` class. If the application uses a storyboard, the `UIApplicationMain()` looks up the main storyboard in our application's `info.plist` file. It creates our application's window and then loads the storyboard's initial scene, setting this as our window's root view controller. Finally, it calls our delegate's `application:didFinishLaunchingWithOptions:` method. Once this method returns, the view is displayed, and our app is ready for user input.

If the user touches the info button, our segue launches. This loads the flipside view controller and displays it as a modal view. When the user presses the **Done** button, it calls flipside view controller's `done:` action. We know this dismisses the flipside view, but we don't yet know how this works. To discover more, we have to look at the code.

EXAMINING THE CODE

While the storyboard gives us a good overview of our application, to really understand it we will need to dig into the code. If you are having trouble following the code, please check out the "Objective-C" bonus chapter at `www.freelancemadscience.com/creating-ios-7-apps-bonus-chap/`. For now, just get a feel for where things are and what they do.

Let's start with `AppDelegate.h`. Select this file in the Project navigator (or use ⇧⌘O to search for it). This is the header file for the `AppDelegate` class. It declares the class's public interface.

You won't find anything terribly surprising here. `AppDelegate` is a subclass of `UIResponder`. This means it can respond to input events: touches, shakes, and remote control events. It also adopts the `UIApplicationDelegate` protocol, which allows it to act as an application delegate.

A delegate is an object that acts on behalf of, or in coordination with, another object. The delegate typically acts as an assistant to the main (or "delegating") object. The main object will call predefined methods on the delegate in response to specified events. The delegate then uses those methods to monitor and control the main object. This lets the delegate alter the main object's behavior without modifying the main object itself.

`AppDelegate` also declares a `window` property. As `UIApplicationMain()` loads our storyboard, it also instantiates a window object and assigns it to this property. Usually, iOS applications have a single window that fills the entire screen. This window acts as the root for our view hierarchy. It both creates a space where other views can be displayed and distributes events to the proper views or subviews.

```
#import <UIKit/UIKit.h>

@interface AppDelegate : UIResponder <UIApplicationDelegate>

@property (strong, nonatomic) UIWindow *window;

@end
```

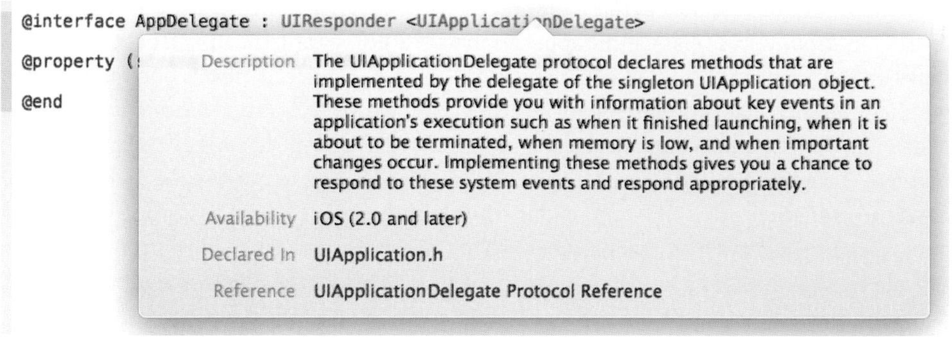

FIGURE 1.26
UIApplicationDelegate
pop-up help

```
@interface AppDelegate : UIResponder <UIApplicationDelegate>
```

Description	The UIApplicationDelegate protocol declares methods that are implemented by the delegate of the singleton UIApplication object. These methods provide you with information about key events in an application's execution such as when it finished launching, when it is about to be terminated, when memory is low, and when important changes occur. Implementing these methods gives you a chance to respond to these system events and respond appropriately.
Availability	iOS (2.0 and later)
Declared In	UIApplication.h
Reference	UIApplicationDelegate Protocol Reference

The UIApplicationDelegate protocol defines a wide range of optional methods that we can implement to observe and modify our application's behavior. These include methods that respond to changes to the application's state, as well as local, remote, and system notifications. You can find a complete list of these methods in the developer documentation.

In the editor, hold down the option key (⌥) and move the mouse so that it's hovering over the word *UIApplicationDelegate*. When the mouse pointer turns into a question mark, click the highlighted word.

This brings up the help pop-up (**Figure 1.26**). The pop-up provides a brief description of the selected symbol. It's not complete, but it does let us get a quick overview of most classes, methods, or functions. Additionally, the pop-up contains hyperlinks to additional resources. We can open the system header file or bring up Apple's full documentation from here.

Click the "UIApplicationDelegate Protocol Reference" link to bring up the full documentation. This opens the Documentation viewer in a separate window. Scroll down until you see the Tasks section. This lists all the methods we can implement. If we want to receive one of these notifications from the application, we simply need to implement the corresponding method.

Now, open the AppDelegate.m file (select it in the Project Manager or search for it using ⇧⌘O). You can see that the template has already implemented several of these methods—but none of them do anything. Right now, they are simply method stubs—placeholders, waiting for us to fill in the details.

```
#import "AppDelegate.h"

@implementation AppDelegate

- (BOOL)application:(UIApplication *)application didFinishLaunchingWithOptions:
→ (NSDictionary *)launchOptions
{
    // Override point for customization after application launch.
    return YES;
}
```

```objectivec
- (void)applicationWillResignActive:(UIApplication *)application
{
    // Sent when the application is about to move from active to inactive
    // state. This can occur for certain types of temporary interruptions
    // (such as an incoming phone call or SMS message) or when the user quits
    // the application and it begins the transition to the background state.
    // Use this method to pause ongoing tasks, disable timers, and throttle
    // down OpenGL ES frame rates. Games should use this method to pause
    // the game.
}


- (void)applicationDidEnterBackground:(UIApplication *)application
{
    // Use this method to release shared resources, save user data, invalidate
    // timers, and store enough application state information to restore your
    // application to its current state in case it is terminated later.
    // If your application supports background execution, this method is called
    // instead of applicationWillTerminate: when the user quits.
}


- (void)applicationWillEnterForeground:(UIApplication *)application
{
    // Called as part of the transition from the background to the inactive
    // state; here you can undo many of the changes made on entering the
    // background.
}


- (void)applicationDidBecomeActive:(UIApplication *)application
{
    // Restart any tasks that were paused (or not yet started) while the
    // application was inactive. If the application was previously in the
    // background, optionally refresh the user interface.
}


- (void)applicationWillTerminate:(UIApplication *)application
{
    // Called when the application is about to terminate. Save data if
    // appropriate. See also applicationDidEnterBackground:.
}

@end
```

These methods respond to changes in our application's state. They are called when our application first loads, when it becomes active or inactive, when it goes into or out of the background, or when it prepares to terminate. We will discuss these (and other) methods in more detail in the Chapter 2 sidebar "Common Tasks Every Application Should Perform." For now, read the comments in these method stubs. They should give you a good overview of their intended use.

Next, look at `MainViewController.h`. This is even simpler than the app delegate's interface declaration. We define our class as a subclass of `UIViewController`. It also adopts a custom protocol, `FlipsideViewControllerDelegate`. That's it.

```
#import "FlipsideViewController.h"

@interface MainViewController : UIViewController <FlipsideViewControllerDelegate>

@end
```

> **NOTE:** FlipsideViewControllerDelegate is not a protocol provided by Apple. Therefore, Option-clicking FlipsideViewControllerDelegate only brings up a pop-up with a single link to `FlipsideViewController.h`. This is where the protocol is defined in our project. We can use this link to quickly move about inside our code. Alternatively, we could Control-click FlipsideViewControllerDelegate and select Jump to Definition from the pop-up menu.

Now let's look at the implementation. Select `MainViewController.m`. Much like the app delegate, the `UIViewController` class has a number of methods that we can override to monitor our view. In particular, this includes any methods with `will` or `did` in their name. The `will` methods are called just before the event takes place. The `did` methods are called just after. Look up `UIViewController` in the developer documentation to see the complete list. Option-click the symbol and then click the link to the full documentation.

> **NOTE:** Option- and Control-clicking symbols can be frustratingly difficult. When Option-clicking, it's easiest if you hold down the Option button, then maneuver the mouse over the symbol. When the cursor changes to a question mark and the symbol turns blue, click on it. When Control-clicking, it's easiest to double-click the symbol first, selecting it. Once the correct symbol is selected, Control-click it.

If you scan through our file, you will see that it includes a few of these as method stubs. Again, the implementation doesn't do anything; it just calls the superclass's implementation.

There are only two methods containing functional code: `flipsideViewControllerDidFinish:` and `prepareForSegue:sender:`.

```
#pragma mark - Flipside View

- (void)flipsideViewControllerDidFinish:
(FlipsideViewController *)controller
{
    [self dismissViewControllerAnimated:YES completion:nil];
}


- (void)prepareForSegue:(UIStoryboardSegue *)segue sender:(id)sender
{
    if ([[segue identifier] isEqualToString:@"showAlternate"]) {
        [[segue destinationViewController] setDelegate:self];
    }
}
```

Let's take these in order. The flipsideViewControllerDidFinish: method is a delegate method for our flipside view controller. As you might guess from the name, the flipside view controller will call this method when it is finished. Our current implementation simply dismisses the current modal view. You probably remember, when we examined the segue, we saw that it displayed our flipside view controller as a modal view. Therefore, this method simply removes our flipside view, using the same transition (horizontal flipping) to return to the main view.

Next, prepareForSegue:sender: is called whenever a segue is triggered from the current scene. Although the implementation looks a little complex, it simply checks to make sure our segue's id matches the expected value, showAlternate. If it does, we assign our main view controller as the destination's delegate.

It's always a good idea to check the segue's identifier before doing anything in the prepareForSegue:sender: method. Right now it's not strictly necessary. We have only one segue, so we know the identifier will always match. However, checking the identifier helps future-proof our code. We won't suddenly have odd bugs or crashes just because we added a new segue.

The destinationViewController is simply the controller that the segue is creating and presenting for us. Unfortunately, there is no way to know what this controller will be, just by looking at the code. We need to examine the storyboard to understand the full picture. If you remember, in the storyboard the showAlternate segue connects our main view controller scene with our flipside view controller scene. This means the destinationViewController will be our FlipsideViewController.

So, the user presses the info button, triggering our segue. The system instantiates a copy of our `FlipsideViewController` and then calls the `MainViewController`'s `prepareForSegue:sender:`. Here, `MainViewController` assigns itself as `FlipsideView Controller`'s delegate. The transition occurs, and our view flips over horizontally, revealing the flipside view. When the flipside view is finished (which we will see in a minute), the flipside view controller calls `flipsideViewControllerDidFinish:` on its delegate, `MainView Controller`. `MainViewController` then dismisses the flipside view controller and our views flip back over, revealing the main view again.

It's important to realize that this pattern demonstrates the preferred technique for passing data from one scene to another across a segue. When passing data from the originating view controller to the destination view controller, we override the originating view controller's `prepareForSegue:sender:` method and pass the data along.

Passing data back gets more complicated. In this project, we make the originating view a delegate of the destination view and then call the appropriate delegate methods. In Chapter 3, we will see a simpler approach using segue unwinding. But, for now, let's look at what's going on inside `FlipsideViewController`.

Open `FlipsideViewController.h`. Here, we start by declaring our `FlipsideView ControllerDelegate` protocol. This has only a single method, which we have already seen, `flipsideViewControllerDidFinish:`. Next, we declare the `FlipsideViewController` class. This is also simple, containing only two items: the delegate outlet property and the done: action.

We've seen both of these before. We just discussed the `delegate` property in relationship to our `MainViewController`, and we saw the done: action back when we were exploring our storyboard. It is connected to the Done button in the navigation bar. Pressing that button will trigger this method.

```objc
#import <UIKit/UIKit.h>

@class FlipsideViewController;

@protocol FlipsideViewControllerDelegate
- (void)flipsideViewControllerDidFinish:
→ (FlipsideViewController *)controller;
@end

@interface FlipsideViewController : UIViewController

@property (weak, nonatomic) id <FlipsideViewControllerDelegate> delegate;

- (IBAction)done:(id)sender;

@end
```

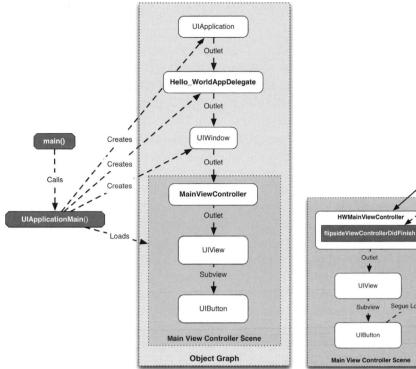

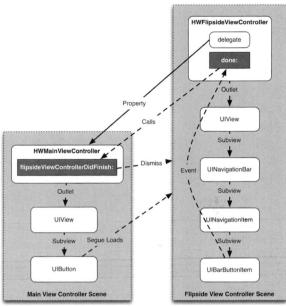

Now open `FlipsideViewController.m`. Much like `MainViewController.m`, this largely contains method stubs. However, at the bottom we have the implementation for our `done:` action.

```
- (IBAction)done:(id)sender
{
    [self.delegate flipsideViewControllerDidFinish:self];
}
```

This simply calls the delegate's `flipsideViewControllerDidFinish:` method. And that brings everything around full circle. When the user presses the Done button, the event triggers the `done:` action. This then calls `MainViewController`'s `flipside ViewControllerDidFinish:`, which dismisses the flipside view controller scene.

Everything in our application is now connected (**Figures 1.27** and **1.28**).

Again, there is nothing magical going on here. If you ever feel lost in a new project, start with the main storyboard file (as defined in the project's `info.plist` file) and walk your way through. You should be able to trace a series of connections from `UIApplication` object to any object in your project. Some may be defined in code and some in the storyboard, but with a little patience, you will be able to track everything down.

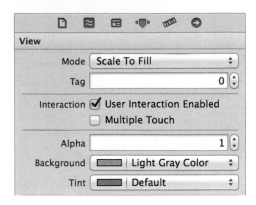

FIGURE 1.29 Setting the background color

MODIFYING THE TEMPLATE

OK, enough chatter. Let's build something new. We're going to add a label to the main view that will display a short message. We will also add a text box to the flipside view, letting the user change this message. So, let's get started.

MODIFYING THE MAIN VIEW

Open `Main.storyboard` and zoom in on the main view controller scene. The background is a little too dark for my taste. Select the View object, and then switch to the Attributes inspector. Change the Background attribute to Light Gray Color (**Figure 1.29**).

Now we need to add a label. Xcode makes it easy to add common user interface objects. In the bottom half of the Utilities, select the Object library (the 📦 icon). Scroll down until you find the label (if you are having trouble, use the filter bar at the bottom of the library). Click the label and drag it from the library pane onto Main View Controller Scene's view. The mouse pointer should have a green plus symbol. This indicates that we can add the object to this location.

Xcode will help you correctly place the control. As you drag the label across the Editor area, it highlights and labels the current view. It also adds blue guidelines to help properly position your objects. Drag the label until it is centered vertically and aligned with the view's left margin, as shown in **Figure 1.30**.

When you release the label, it will appear surrounded by eight white squares. You can click and drag these anchor points to resize the label. Grab the right side and stretch it until you hit the right-margin guide.

This gives us a label that is centered vertically and that is stretched to fill the screen from margin to margin. The problem is, it won't stay that way. Build and run the app. Depending on your settings, you may immediately notice a problem. If you designed the storyboard for the 4-inch iPhone but run it on the 3.5-inch simulator, it will appear too low on the screen.

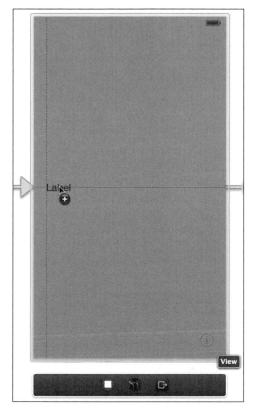

FIGURE 1.30 Properly aligning the label

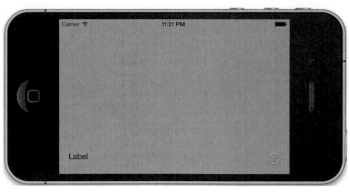

FIGURE 1.31 The label is no longer centered vertically.

FIGURE 1.32 Adding a center vertically constraint

FIGURE 1.33 The label and its constraints

Even worse, rotate the simulator into the landscape orientation. No matter what your settings, now things definitely look wrong (**Figure 1.31**).

The problem is, by default all user interface elements are kept a fixed distance from the upper-left corner of their containing view. If we want our layout to adapt to different screen sizes and different orientations, we need to add a few Auto Layout constraints.

I'll cover the details of Auto Layout in Chapter 3. For now, let's just use enough to make things work. Make sure the label is selected, and then Control-click the label and drag to the left. A blue line should stretch from the point where you Control-clicked to the mouse. Let go of the mouse when you are between the edge of the label and the edge of its view. In the pop-up window, select Center Vertically in Container (**Figure 1.32**).

Repeat the gesture. This time select Leading Space to Container. Next, Control-click and drag off the right edge and select Trailing Space to Container. We should now have a blue I-bar on each side of the label, a blue line running through the middle of the label (**Figure 1.33**). Build and run the app again. The label will be vertically centered, no matter which simulator or which orientation you choose.

FIGURE 1.34 Setting the font

Make sure the label is still selected, and open the Attributes inspector. In the Alignment attribute, click the button for centered text (the ≡ button). Next, we want to change the font. Click the T icon inside the Font attribute's text field. This brings up the font pop-up window. Here, change the font to System Bold and the size to 24 points (**Figure 1.34**).

Next, let's change the text. Double-click the label. It should be highlighted in blue. Type in **Hello World** and hit Return. Notice that Interface Builder automatically resizes the label after we edit its text.

If you modify the label's text by double-clicking on the label and editing it directly, it will automatically resize. If you select the label and modify its text attribute in the Attributes inspector, it won't. As a result you will have a "Misplaced Views" warning. The label will appear with an orange and a dashed-red box around it. You can always force Auto Layout to update a frame to match its current constraints by selecting the interface element. Next, click the "Resolve Auto Layout Issues" tool (the ⊢•⊣ button on the bottom-right edge of Interface Builder), and select Update Frames from the pop-up menu. We will go over this technique and other methods for managing Auto Layout in Chapter 3.

Run the application. Our new label should appear centered in the screen both vertically and horizontally. Rotate the app, and it remains centered.

ADDING AN OUTLET

If we want to change the label's text during runtime, we need a way to access it in our code. The easiest way is to add an outlet to the view's controller. In the pre–Xcode 4.0 days, this meant jumping back and forth between Xcode and Interface Builder as we modified our code by hand. Now there's a much simpler way.

First, we should probably collapse the Document Outline. Click the Document Outline button (the ◁ button in the lower-left corner of the Editor area). Next, switch to the Assistant editor (the icon on the toolbar).

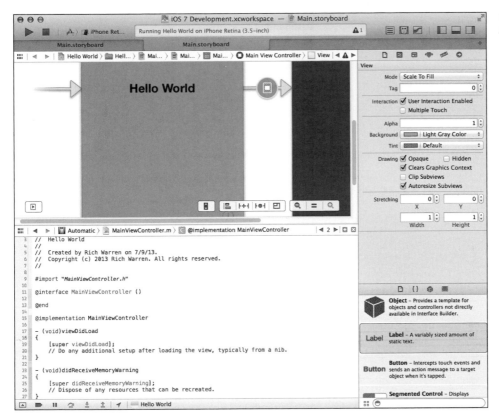

FIGURE 1.35 Stacked Assistant editor

This will display two Editor areas side by side. The leftmost area contains the selected file, while the rightmost contains a closely related file. For example, if you select the MainViewController.h header file, the right editor should display the MainViewController.m implementation file. In our case, the left editor shows the storyboard, while the right editor shows the selected controller's implementation file.

There is actually one small change that I want to make. I prefer to have my editors stacked vertically. Select the View > Assistant Editor > Assistant Editors on Bottom menu item. Then click inside the main view. Your interface should look like **Figure 1.35**.

NOTE: Although Xcode generally does a great job auto-selecting the correct companion file, there may be times when it does not work properly or when you want to select a different file instead. You can do this in the jump bar. Selecting the leaf item will let you choose an alternate file based on the same general selection rules. Selecting the root item will allow you to choose different selection rules. Xcode provides a number of different, context-specific selection rules. You can also choose to manually select the companion file, if necessary.

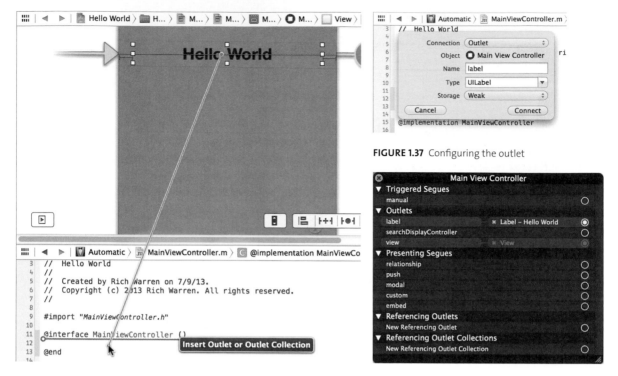

FIGURE 1.37 Configuring the outlet

FIGURE 1.36 Adding an outlet

FIGURE 1.38 Main view controller Connections HUD

Control-click the label and drag it down into the `MainViewController.m` file. Again, a blue line will stretch from the point where you clicked to your mouse. When you move it between the `@interface` and the `@end` directives, you should see a blue line marking the insertion point, with a pop-up menu offering to Insert Outlet or Outlet Connection (**Figure 1.36**). Once you see this, release the mouse.

A pop-up dialog will now allow you to configure the outlet. Make sure the Connection setting is set to Outlet. In the Name field, enter **label**. The type should be `UILabel`, and the storage should be Weak (**Figure 1.37**). Click Connect to continue.

Xcode will make the following change to `MainViewController.m` (in pink):

```
@interface MainViewController ()
@property (weak, nonatomic) IBOutlet UILabel *label;

@end
```

This defines an outlet that we can connect to in Interface Builder.

In the storyboard file, Xcode has already connected the label to our newly created outlet. You can view this using the Connections inspector. Alternatively, Control-click the Main View Controller icon in either the Document Outline or the scene's dock to bring up a Connections HUD (**Figure 1.38**).

FIXING THE NAVIGATION BAR

If you run the application and tap on the info button, you can see that our navigation bar and our status bar overlap. In previous versions of iOS, the status bar was typically an opaque strip across the top of the screen. The top of our user interface would start just below the status bar. In iOS 7, the status bar is transparent, and we must stretch our interface to the very top of the screen.

Apparently, the Utility Application template still uses an old-style navigation bar. We could make the navigation bar 20 points taller so that it fit nicely under the status bar, but the easiest fix is to just hide the status bar in this scene.

Unfortunately, this requires a tiny bit of code. Open FlipsideViewController.m and find the didReceiveMemoryWarning method. Add the following code right after didReceiveMemoryWarning:

```
- (BOOL)prefersStatusBarHidden
{
    return YES;
}
```

That's it. Now when you run the app, and navigate to the flipside view, the status bar is gone, and the navigation bar is properly aligned across the top.

ADDING THE TEXT FIELD

The first few steps are very similar to what we did for the main view. We will be adding a Text Field control instead of a Label, and we will place it just below the navigation bar (so it is out of the way when the keyboard appears, even in landscape orientation). But, otherwise the steps are the same.

Switch back to the Standard Editor, and make sure Main.storyboard is open. Zoom in on the Flipside View Controller Scene. Now, drag a Text Field control from the Object library. Position it a bit below the navigation bar, and resize it so that it fills the view from margin to margin.

Control-click and drag to the left of the text field. Again, release the mouse between the edge of the text field and the edge of the view. This time select Leading Space to Container. Next, Control-drag to the right and select Trailing Space to Container. Remember, Xcode tries to be helpful and uses the direction you drag to determine which constraints you may be looking for. If you drag in the wrong direction, you won't find the constraints you're looking for.

Next, we want to create a constraint between the text field and the navigation bar. Unfortunately, if we Control-drag from the text field to the navigation bar, we will either get the navigation item or the top layout guide. Instead, make sure the Document Outline is expanded, and Control-drag from the Round Style Text Field to the Navigation Bar, and select Vertical Spacing in the pop-up.

We can always use the Document Outline to draw our constraints, outlets, or actions. This can be handy whenever we cannot draw the connection in the interface builder.

Again, we want to be able to access the value of the text field in our code. That means we need an outlet. Open the Assistant editor again. Make sure the bottom editor is showing `FlipsideViewController.m`. Control-drag from the text field to between the `@interface` and `@end` directives. Connection should be Outlet. Name the outlet `textField`. Type should be `UITextField`, and Storage should be Weak. When you click Connect, it should make the following change to `FlipsideViewController.m`:

```
@interface FlipsideViewController ()
@property (weak, nonatomic) IBOutlet UITextField *textField;

@end
```

Whenever we want to change the label's text, we just need to get the value from our `textField` outlet and copy it into our `label` outlet. However, there's a slight problem. We created our outlets inside their respective `.m` files. This means they are private, implementation details of their respective classes. We cannot access the `label` outlet from outside our `MainViewController` class. Likewise, we cannot access the `textField` outlet from outside the `FlipsideViewController` class.

While this may seem like a problem, it is actually a very good thing. Each class has a clearly defined, separate set of responsibilities. `MainViewController` is responsible for managing everything in its view hierarchy. `FlipsideViewController` is responsible for managing everything in its view hierarchy. Neither class should be reaching inside the other's view hierarchy. This is covered in more depth in the "Objective-C" bonus chapter at www.freelancemadscience.com/creating-ios-7-apps-bonus-chap/.

This means we need to create a public property to act as the bridge between these two classes. Switch back to the Standard editor, and open `FlipsideViewController.h`. We just need to add a single line of code, as shown here:

```
@interface FlipsideViewController : UIViewController

@property (weak, nonatomic) id <FlipsideViewControllerDelegate> delegate;
@property (strong, nonatomic) NSString *text;

- (IBAction)done:(id)sender;

@end
```

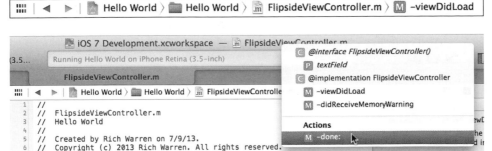

FIGURE 1.39
The jump bar

FIGURE 1.40
Navigating to the done:
method.

This creates a public property to hold our text. Now, when the user dismisses the flipside view, we need to copy the value from our textField outlet to our text property. Switch to FlipsideViewController.m (you can use ⌃⌘⇧ or ⌃⌘⇩ to switch between corresponding .h and .m files). We need to find the done: method. Currently our files are not very long, so you can probably spot it right away. Still, it is often easiest to use the editor's jump bar to move to a specific method (**Figure 1.39**).

The bar across the top of the Editor area shows you the item you are editing. Click the rightmost item and select the done: method (**Figure 1.40**). The editor will select the method and (if necessary) scroll so that it is visible.

Modify the done: method as shown here:

```
- (IBAction)done:(id)sender
{
    self.text = self.textField.text;
    [self.delegate flipsideViewControllerDidFinish:self];
}
```

This line simply copies the current value from the private textField outlet to the public text property, before calling our delegate's flipsideViewControllerDidFinish: method.

Now we need to use this text property. Open MainViewController.m and navigate to the flipsideViewControllerDidFinish: method. Modify the method as shown here:

```
- (void)flipsideViewControllerDidFinish:
(FlipsideViewController *)controller
{
    self.label.text = controller.text;
    [self dismissViewControllerAnimated:YES completion:nil];
}
```

The new line simply copies the text from our flipside controller and assigns it to our label.

That's it. Run the application again. It should display the default "Hello World" message when it launches. Click the info button, and type new text into the text field. Click the Done button. The label should now show your new text.

REFINING THE INTERFACE

Functionally, everything is OK, but it's not the most polished (or, for that matter, useful) app in the world. Let's make it a little bit better. When the flipside view appears, let's fill the text field with the label's current value. Additionally, let's go ahead and dismiss the flipside view when the user taps the Return key.

Let's start by passing the text from our main view's label to our flipside controller. Just like the flipside controller's delegate property, we will assign this value in our prepareForSegue:sender: method.

Navigate to MainViewController's prepareForSegue:sender: method and add the highlighted line:

```
- (void)prepareForSegue:(UIStoryboardSegue *)segue sender:(id)sender
{
    if ([[segue identifier] isEqualToString:@"showAlternate"]) {
        [[segue destinationViewController] setDelegate:self];
        [[segue destinationViewController] setText:self.label.text];
    }
}
```

And, again, we need to use this value. Switch back to FlipsideViewController.m. This time we're going to add an entirely new method. Insert the following code after the viewDidLoad:

```
- (void)viewDidAppear:(BOOL)animated
{
    [super viewDidAppear:animated];
    self.textField.text = self.text;
}
```

This method is called every time the flipside view appears. Here, we're just assigning the value stored in our text property to the text field.

Now let's dismiss the flipside view when the user hits the Return key. Open Main.storyboard, and zoom in on the Flipside View Controller Scene. Control-click the text field to bring up the Connections HUD. At the top of the Sent Events section, there should be an event named "Did End on Exit." Click and drag from the event's circle to the view controller icon in the dock (the HUD will automatically fade to get out of the way, if necessary) (**Figure 1.41**).

When you release the mouse, a second, smaller HUD will appear. This has only one option showing, the done: method. Fortunately, that's exactly what we want. Click it.

There are several other equally valid ways to draw this connection. We could Control-click the FlipsideViewController icon in the scene's dock and then drag from the done: action to the text field. Xcode will then prompt us for the correct event. We could also use the Connections inspector in the Utilities area, instead of using the pop-up dialogs. Most of these approaches are equivalent. Feel free to experiment with the different approaches and see which one works best for you.

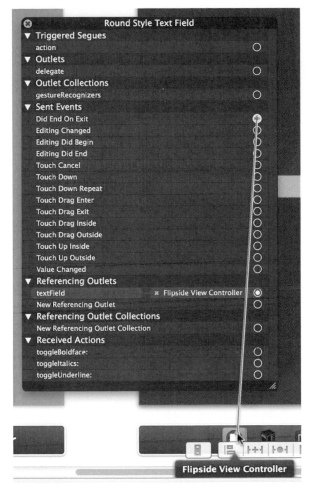

FIGURE 1.41 Connecting the Return key to the done: method

Be aware, however, that for text field events, the system will often try to automatically select the "Editing did End" event. This is not what we want. This limits our options somewhat. We need to use an approach that explicitly lets us select the "Did End on Exit" event.

> **NOTE:** Each event can be connected to more than one action, and a single action can connect to multiple events. In this case, we have both the text field and the Done button connected to the done: action.

While we're at it, let's change the appearance of the keyboard's Return key. Select the text field and open the Attributes inspector. Set the Return Key attribute to **Done**. While this doesn't change the keyboard's functionality, it helps communicate our intent.

You may also want to set the Clear Button attribute to "Appears while editing." After all, using the Backspace key to delete large amounts of text gets tedious very quickly.

FIGURE 1.42 Final app main view

FIGURE 1.43 Final app flipside view

That's it. Run the application. It should appear as shown in **Figure 1.42**. Touch the info icon to switch to the flipside view. The text field should display the current message. Touch the text field, and the keyboard and clear buttons should appear (**Figure 1.43**).

If you tap and hold on the text, the magnifying glass will appear. Let go and a pop-up menu appears. If you tap Select, the menu changes. We have the option to cut, copy, replace, or define the current word. Tap Define and the system's dictionary opens to the selected word (note: on the simulator, no definition will be found). Tap Done to dismiss the dictionary. Modify the text, and then shake the device (^ ⌘Z in the simulator). An alert message will ask if we want to undo our typing.

That's quite a bit of functionality, and we get it all for free—just because we are using one of the system's text fields. Dismiss the alert, change the text, and press either Return or Done. The main screen's text should change to match.

WRAPPING UP

And that's it for our Hello World app. In this chapter, we've examined how iOS applications are pieced together. We've built and modified our own (albeit incredibly simple) application, and we've gotten some hands-on experience using the development tools. This should give you a good jumping-off point for the rest of the book.

In Chapter 2, we will take everything we've learned so far and start building a more complex, real-world application. We will continue to work with this application throughout the rest of the book, expanding it and enhancing it as we go along.

OTHER RESOURCES

For more information, check out the following resources:

- **Xcode User Guide**

  iOS Developer's Library

  An excellent and thorough guide to using Xcode. This goes into considerable detail, covering every aspect of the IDE.

- **iOS App Programming Guide**

  iOS Developer's Library

  This is a somewhat eclectic collection of topics relating to app development. It would be worth looking at some of the more general topics—but much of the information probably won't be useful quite yet.

- **View Controller Programming Guide for iOS**

  iOS Developer's Library

  An exhaustive look at view controllers and their role in iOS. This includes some details about storyboards and segues that would be relevant to this chapter. Again, much of this guide will be more useful once we get a few more chapters under our belts.

CHAPTER 2

Our Application's Architecture

Much of the rest of this book will focus on developing a single application. Chapter by chapter, we will cover the major steps required to build and test this application, from creating the initial project to prepping it for sale.

In this chapter, we will focus on our application's overall architecture. We will define the user's flow through the application, connecting our basic views and the transitions between them. We will also build our application's model and link it to our view controllers. Finally, we will touch on a number of smaller topics: enabling compiler warnings to produce cleaner code, implementing several key methods that every app must have, running our application on iOS devices, and even exploring the inner workings of nib files.

STARTING WITH THE BASIC BUILDING BLOCKS

We can divide our application into three major modules: the model, our view hierarchies, and our view controllers.

The model handles our application's data. It is also responsible for persisting the data—saving it to and reading it from disk. We have a lot of flexibility when it comes to building our model layer. It may consist entirely of custom classes that we create, it could be built entirely using Apple's Core Data framework, or it could use some hybrid approach.

The view interacts directly with the users. It displays information and responds to touches, taps, and swipes. Typically, we don't do a lot of coding for our views. Until we start making custom views (see Chapter 4, "Custom Views and Custom Transitions"), we will largely lay out our view layer in Interface Builder using standard UIKit controls.

Finally, the view controllers are the peanut butter that holds this sandwich together. It's important to note that there are two main categories of view controllers: content controllers and container controllers. These play very different roles in our application.

Content controllers are views that manage roughly a screen's worth of information. As we saw in Chapter 1, "Hello, iOS," there is a separate view controller for each scene in our storyboard. These controllers act as the content controllers for their scenes. They are responsible for coordinating between the scene's views and the application's model. They request data from the model, passing that data to the views to be displayed. Similarly, they respond to any user interaction: button presses, slider changes, text edits, and so on. Finally, the controller passes these changes back to the model, when appropriate.

Container controllers act somewhat differently. Typically, they have a very limited user interface, perhaps just a bar across the top or the bottom. They are primarily responsible for managing and displaying other view controllers. This includes managing the transition between view controllers. In this way, the container controllers largely define our application's workflow.

Originally, as developers we could only create our own content controllers. Apple provided a limited set of container view controllers (e.g., the navigation controller or tab controller), and we had to use those to manage our application's flow.

However, with iOS 5, Apple formalized the relationship between content and container view controllers, opening up the API and letting us create our own content controllers as well.

As we start designing an application, we need to think about how the user will move through the application. Often this is driven by the data our application uses. Look at the Music app, for example. It manages our music library—however, this isn't simply a flat list of songs. Our music library has a hierarchical structure to it. Songs are organized into albums, which are further organized into artists and genres. The users need a way to move through these layers of complexity. We manage this using a combination of container and content view controllers.

The iOS SDK provides five tools for organizing the application: `UITabBarController`, `UINavigationController`, `UITableViewController`, `UICollectionViewController`, and presented controllers. You may not need all of these, but they are the basic building blocks of most applications.

The `UITabBarController` lets the user switch between different tasks or different groups of data. For example, the Clock application lets the user choose between the different time-related tasks: World Clock, Alarm, Stopwatch, and Timer. The Music app, on the other hand, allows the user to select different views of their data: Albums, Artists, Genres, Songs, and Playlists, among others The App Store mixes both approaches, displaying three data groups (Features, Top Charts, and Near Me) and two tasks (Search and Updates).

The tab bar can support any number of tab items. However, it can show only five tabs at a time. `UITabBarController` automatically manages any extra tab items by providing a More button and letting the user customize the items that appear on the tab bar. Note that if you have more than five tabs, the tab bar will display only four of them, since the More button takes up the fifth space.

Next, the `UINavigationController` lets users move from scene to scene. This controller maintains a stack of views. When a new view is added to the top of the stack, that view slides in from the right while the old view slides off to the left. When the top view is popped from the top of the stack, the animation is reversed. This provides an intuitive interface for moving through a hierarchy of views.

With iOS 7, Apple has introduced a new transition when moving back down the stack. As before, we can still just tap the back button, and the system will animate our return to the previous scene. However, we can also drag our finger across the screen from the left edge. This is an example of an interactive transition. The transition's pace matches that of our finger, and we can cancel the transition at any point. If we stop dragging too early, it will simply slide back to the top view. After a certain point, it will continue to animate the transition, even without our control. We will look at interactive transitions, including creating our own interactive transitions, in more detail in Chapter 4.

Both `UITabBarController` and `UINavigationController` are examples of container controllers. They define how we move from scene to scene in our application. `UITableView Controller` and `UICollectionViewController`, on the other hand, are content controllers. While they appear quite differently, their role and operations are largely identical. These controllers present a number of items onscreen, letting the user select one or more of these items.

The table view controller simply displays its data as a single column with any number of rows. Individually, each row could be quite complex, combining images, icons, and formatted text. In general, a single row type is used throughout the table. Each row represents a different entry from a list of similar items.

The user can scroll up and down through the rows, selecting any item they want. Tables are often used to present lists, such as the list of email accounts, the list of mailboxes within a single account, or even the list of messages within a single mailbox.

NESTING CONTAINERS

While each of the basic view controllers is a powerful tool by itself, we can combine them to create even more sophisticated view hierarchies. However, we need to take some care when nesting containers inside other containers, especially since many container controllers expect to manage a fixed-size view. Trying to place one fixed size view inside another will undoubtedly result in odd layout issues.

Apple recommends always maintaining the following order (from parent to child):

1. Split View Controller (iPad only)

2. Tab Bar Controller

3. Navigation Controller

4. Content view controllers and container view controllers that have flexible bounds (e.g., the Page View Controller).

Modal views act as a release valve of sorts. Since they take up the whole screen, we can usually place any container controller inside a modal view. The same basic logic applies to pop-up view controllers on the iPad.

This means we can place a `UINavigationController` inside a `UITabBarController`, but we cannot place a `UITabBarController` inside a `UINavigationController`. For iPhone apps, typically either `UITabBarControllers` are the window's root view controller or they are displayed modally.

Apple's documentation strongly recommends having a single tab bar, making it your application's root view, and having it visible and accessible in every scene. If this does not fit your application's needs, then perhaps you should rethink your user interface. For example, a table view controller, collection view controller, or even a custom view controller might better fit your needs.

`UITableView` has a common secondary use as well. We can create a static table to organize a fixed set of heterogeneous pieces of data. In this case, the entire table is typically used to represent a single entry. Each row has its own unique formatting, displaying some aspect of this entry. As we change entries, the number and type of rows remain the same; only the data changes. We often use static tables to create forms that the user will fill in or to display detailed information about a selected leaf object in our data hierarchy.

The collection view controller has considerably more flexibility. We can customize both how the individual items are displayed and how the collection is organized. However, at their most basic, we can use collection view controllers to display a grid of items. Again, the user can scroll through the grid, selecting any item they want. This lets us easily display a set of images or icons. More generally, we will use collection views whenever we need something a little more complex than what a table view can handle.

Finally, any view controller can present another view controller. By default, these are presented as modal view controllers. The incoming scene will fill the full screen, covering the current view controller, and it will remain until dismissed. While we should avoid layering multiple presented view controllers on top of each other—they are useful for quickly popping up forms or controls that the user must interact with or cancel before proceeding.

Most applications combine some or all of these tools into a user interface that naturally matches the application's data. In general, `UITabBarController` provides the coarsest organization, defining our broadest groups. Within each group, `UINavigationController` lets the user move through the data's hierarchy from general to specific, while `UITableViewControllers` or `UICollectionViewControllers` displays the information available at each level of detail.

KICKING OFF THE HEALTH BEAT PROJECT

If you're like me, you spend most of your day sitting in front of a computer. This has led to an ongoing battle to lose weight. To help in this fight, let's build an application that will let us track our weight over time.

Health Beat will have three main tasks: Users can enter new weights, they can view a graph showing how their weight changes over time, and they can view the complete history showing all their weight entries. We will use a tab view to navigate between the weight history data and the graph. In addition, we will use a table view/navigation controller combination to manage our history view. The table view will show all the weights in our history. If you tap a weight, the navigation controller will bring up a detail view for that entry. Finally, we will present a modal view to enter new weights.

This chapter will focus on the overall architecture of this application; on building a storyboard that connects our tab bar, table view, and navigation controllers; and on building and attaching our application's model. We will flesh out this design and cover additional topics, such as saving and loading the data and drawing custom views, in later chapters.

CREATING THE PROJECT

Open the workspace we created in Chapter 1. Look for "iOS 7 Development" in Xcode's list of recent projects, or just find and double-click the iOS 7 Development.xcworkspace file. The workspace should contain our Hello World project. Add a new project by selecting File > New > Project... from the menu. Then select iOS > Application > Tabbed Application and click the Next button (**Figure 2.1**).

In the "Choose options for your new project" panel, name the project Health Beat. Fill in the Organization Name and Company Identifier fields. Leave Class Prefix blank, and set Devices to iPhone. Then click Next (**Figure 2.2**).

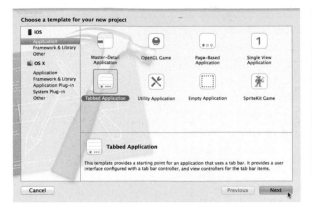

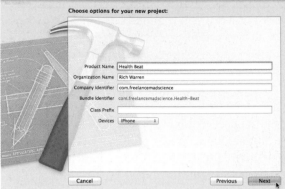

FIGURE 2.1 Creating a tabbed application

FIGURE 2.2 Setting the project options

FIGURE 2.3 Saving the project

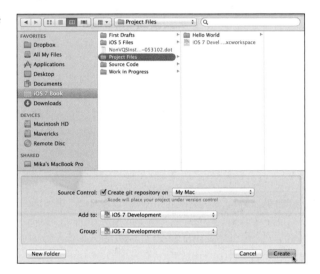

In the final panel, select the location for the project. Make sure the "Create git repository on" checkbox is selected. Unless you have a build server set up, it should create the repository locally on My Mac.

Make sure the "Add to" drop-down is set to iOS 7 Development. The group should also be set to iOS 7 Development, creating a new top-level project in our workspace (**Figure 2.3**).

This creates a basic tabbed application. In Xcode's toolbar, change the scheme to Health Beat > iPhone Retina (3.5 inch) (**Figure 2.4**) and run the application.

As you can see, the application template gives us a simple two-tab application (**Figure 2.5**). You can press the tab buttons to switch between the first and second views.

FIGURE 2.4 Setting the scheme

FIGURE 2.5 Running the template

Looking at the files in the Project navigator, our template created an app delegate (App-Delegate), two view controllers (FirstViewController and SecondViewController), and the storyboard (MainStoryboard.storyboard). Our assets catalog (Images.xcassets) contains the icons for our first and second tab bar. We also have support files and a new group for our unit tests.

CLEANING HOUSE

Before we start building our application, let's tidy things up. First, while we could modify the existing controllers and storyboard elements, it will be easier to just create our own from scratch. So, let's delete them. Delete FirstViewController.h, FirstViewController.m, SecondViewController.h, and SecondViewController.m.

Open Images.xcassets and delete the first and second icons. You can simply select "first" from the list of assets and hit the Delete key. Then repeat for the second icons.

Next, open the storyboard and delete the first and second view controllers. There are a couple of ways to do this—but let's look at the simplest approach. The trick to removing scenes from a storyboard is to select and delete the view controller itself.

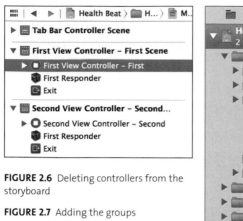

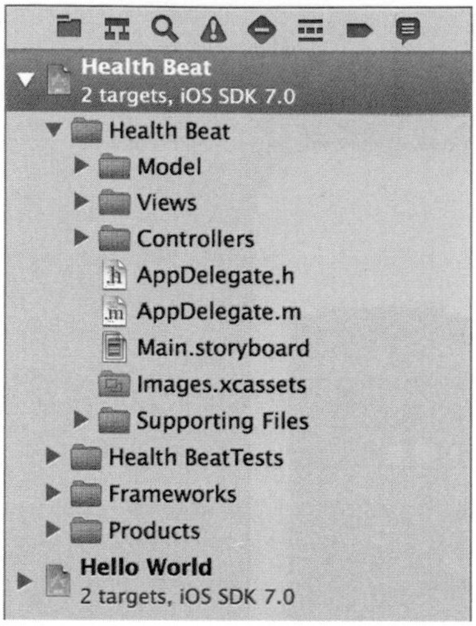

FIGURE 2.6 Deleting controllers from the storyboard

FIGURE 2.7 Adding the groups

Make sure the Document Outline is visible, and then expand the First View Controller – First Scene. Inside that scene, select the First View Controller – First line (**Figure 2.6**). This is the view controller object.

In the editor area, the view should appear with a blue line around it. Just hit the Delete key, and the entire scene will disappear from the storyboard. Repeat for the second view controller. This should just leave the Tab Bar Controller Scene.

Now, let's add some organization. We want to add four groups to our Project navigator: Model, Views, and Controllers. In the Project navigator, right-click the Health Beat group, select New Group, and then give it an appropriate name. When you're done, move the groups around so they match **Figure 2.7**.

SETTING ADDITIONAL WARNINGS

Xcode can perform sophisticated analysis and provide quite a bit of feedback on your code, helping to avoid a great number of common programming errors. Unfortunately, many of these settings are turned off by default. Let's fix that.

Click the Health Beat project icon (blue icon at the top). This allows us to edit numerous project and target settings. Make sure the Health Beat target is selected and click the Build Settings tab. Verify that the All and Combined buttons are pressed, and then type **analyzer** in the search bar. This will bring up the Static Analyzer setting. Change "Analyze During 'Build'" to **Yes**. Also change "Mode of Analysis for 'Build'" to **Deep**. This will force the compiler to run the static analyzer every time you build your application.

While we're at it, scroll down to the Static Analyzer—Issues—Security settings. Some of these checks are turned off by default. They won't really have any effect on the current application, but we may as well turn them on. Change "Floating Point Value used as Loop Counter," "Use of 'rand' Functions," and "Use of 'strcpy' and 'strcat'" to **Yes**.

Running the static analyzer on every build provides a great sanity check; however, it can significantly slow down compile time. You may find that you need to turn it off when working on very large projects or when developing on slower computers. In my experience, however, it takes such a long time to upload a new copy of the application onto the device (or even onto the simulator) that a little extra compile time is hardly noticeable. Still, your mileage may vary.

Next, clear the search bar, and scroll until you find the section labeled Apple LLVM 5.0 - Warning Policies. This section, along with the other Warning sections that follow, contains settings that let us configure the warnings and errors that the compiler will generate.

Let's start by changing "Treat Warnings as Errors" to Yes. If you don't change anything else, at least change this. Treating warnings as errors forces you to clean up your code and get rid of all your warnings. This is a very important habit. As frustrating as it may be, you really want to clear out all warnings on every single build. Otherwise, sooner or later, you will overlook something truly important.

Trust me, nothing is worse than compiling someone else's code and watching a steady stream of warnings scroll by. You get that sinking feeling in the pit of your stomach. Are these serious issues that need to be resolved, or are they trivial matters that you can simply ignore? Do everyone a favor and get rid of all your warnings.

However, it shouldn't end there. Here is the complete list of warnings that I recommend turning on. Some will be turned on by default, but I am listing them for completeness (and in case Apple changes the defaults in future Xcode releases).

- Treat Warnings as Errors
- Check Switch Statements (on by default)
- Deprecated Functions (on by default)
- Direct usage of 'isa' (on by default)
- Documentation Comments
- Hidden Local Variables
- Implicit Boolean Conversions (on by default)
- Implicit Constant Conversions (on by default)
- Implicit Conversion to 32 Bit Type (on by default)
- Implicit Enum Conversions (on by default)
- Implicit Integer to Pointer Conversions (on by default)
- Implicit Signedness Conversion
- Initializer Not Fully Bracketed
- Mismatched Return Type (on by default)
- Missing Braces and Parentheses (on by default)
- Missing Fields in Structure Initializers
- Missing Function Prototypes
- Missing Newline At End Of File

- Pointer Sign Comparison (on by default)
- Sign Comparison
- Suspicious Implicit Conversions
- Typecheck Calls to printf/scanf (on by default)
- Uninitialized Variables (on by default)
- Unknown Pragma
- Unused Functions (on by default)
- Unused Labels
- Unused Values (on by default)
- Unused Variables (on by default)
- Implicit Atomic Objective-C Properties
- Incomplete Objective-C Protocols (on by default)
- Overriding Deprecated Objective-C Methods
- Strict Selector Matching
- Undeclared Selector (on by default)
- Unintentional Root Class (on by default)
- Implicit ownership types on out parameters
- Implicit retain of 'self' within blocks
- Using __bridge Casts Outside of ARC (on by default)

Now, I'm not going to lie to you. In the short run, turning these warnings on may force you to do some extra typing—sometimes a lot of extra typing. You will occasionally have to add unnecessary steps to your methods just to keep the compiler happy. Some developers prefer to turn these warnings off when focusing on rapid build-test-modify cycles and then turn them back on when polishing the code. Of course, there's a risk you might never have time to come back and fix things. I recommend leaving them on as much as possible. One of these days they will save you from an embarrassing bug and you will thank me.

Of course, not all developers will follow this advice. You will find that some third-party libraries may trigger hundreds or thousands of warnings. As always, it's better to be pragmatic and finish a project than to be dogmatic and proud of yourself. If you have to turn off some of the warnings to move forward, then just turn off the warning.

ADDING IMAGES

We will need icons for our tab buttons, and I'll admit, these images are a little odd. They need to be 30 by 30 PNG files (60 by 60 @2x.png files for phones with the Retina display). The actual color of the image does not matter; the tab-bar icons just use their alpha level. In iOS 7, these are called *template images*. Their color is based on the tintColor of the containing UI element.

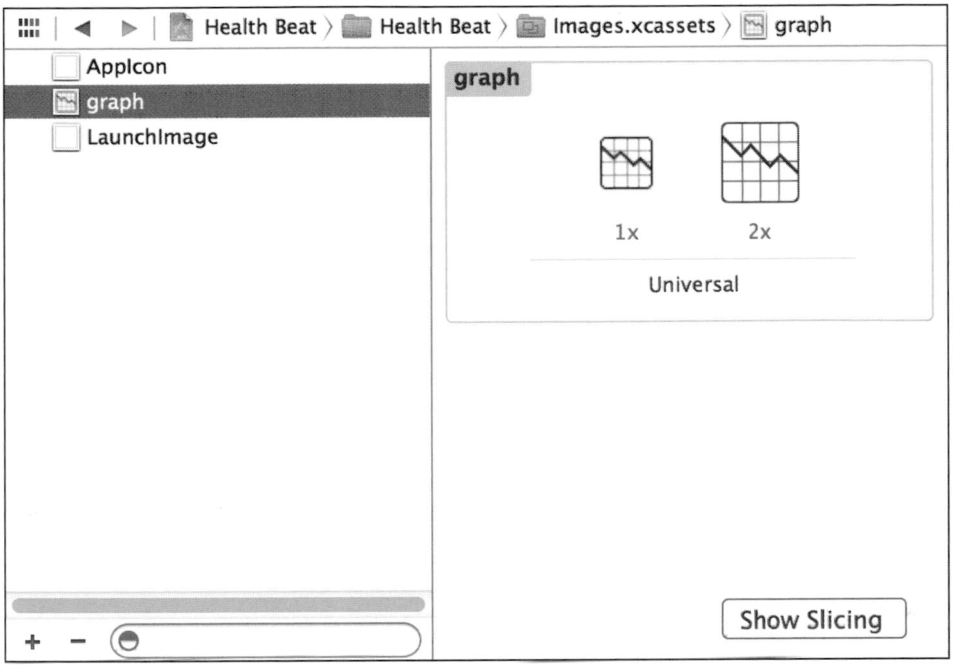

FIGURE 2.8 Adding the graph tab icon

Since the color doesn't matter, I find it easiest to draw the icons in black on a transparent background. If I want shading, I change the opacity of the black ink. That way, the image I see is at least close to what I get when my app displays the template image.

Feel free to create your own icons. Alternatively, you can just download the source code from www.freelancemadscience.com/ios7_source/ and copy over the artwork. Select Images.xcassets in the Project navigator. The editor should show a list of assets on the left and the image editor on the right. There should be only two assets currently, AppIcon and LaunchImage.

Drag graph.png into the list. This should create a new asset named graph. Select that asset, and you should see the placeholders for the 1x and 2x images. Currently, only the 1x is filled.

Drag graph@2x.png into the 2x placeholder. This should set both image resolutions (**Figure 2.8**). We can now simply load the graph image at runtime, and the system will automatically select the correct resolution for our device.

Repeat this procedure for graph_selected.png and graph_selected@2x.png. We should now have four assets in our Images.xcassets folder.

As the name suggests, the graph icon will be used for our graph view tab. We will use a built-in icon for the history view tab and our add button, so they don't need any additional artwork.

RUNNING AND TESTING ON iOS DEVICES

If you are running Mountain Lion or Mavericks, you can download Xcode 5.0 from the App Store for free. This gives you full access to the iOS SDK and the simulator. However, if you want to build and run your applications on actual iOS devices, then you need to join the iOS Developer Program. You can register as either an individual or a company team for $99 a year.

There are also a few less-common options. The iOS Developer University Program is free for qualifying academic institutes, allowing universities to offer iOS development classes as part of their curriculum. At the higher end, the iOS Developer Enterprise Program allows larger companies to produce and deploy proprietary, in-house applications. Still, most of us will probably either purchase an individual membership or find ourselves added to an existing company team.

Once you have an iOS Developer membership, you must set up the proper developer certificates and provisioning profiles before you can build and test on your devices. Originally, this was a tedious and somewhat error-prone process. The Certificates, Identifiers & Profiles page has detailed information covering all the necessary steps (https://developer.apple.com/ios/manage/overview/index.action).

However, I have some good news. Apple has worked hard to automate and simplify these procedures over the years. Most of the time, Xcode can set everything up for you automatically.

If you are getting error messages about your signing entities or provisioning profiles, make sure everything is set up properly. First, in the Project navigator, select the project icon. Make sure the correct build target is selected and click the General tab. Scroll through this page and look for any warnings. If there are any warnings, you should also see a button you can click to fix the issue. If you don't find anything there, try checking the Capabilities tab.

If you still cannot run your app on a physical device, check your preferences. Select the Xcode > Preferences... menu. In the preference sheet, select the Accounts tab. On the right side, select your account and click the View Details button.... From here, make sure you have a valid signing identity. You should also refresh your provisioning profiles.

If all else fails, go to Apple's Certificates, Identifiers & Profiles page (https://developer. apple.com/ios/manage/overview/index.action). This gives you a complete set of tools for managing your certificates, App IDs, and profiles. This is definitely the last resort. You don't get all the nice, automated tools—but you should be able to go in, find the problem, and fix it.

BUILDING THE MODEL

We are now ready to start building. Let's begin with the model, since we will need a minimally functional model before our view controllers will do any real work.

One of our goals in designing the model is to make it as modular as possible. This means creating a well-defined interface through which we will communicate with the rest of our application. For Health Beat, this will be our WeightHistoryDocument class. We will also create a WeightEntry class. This will hold the data for an individual entry. Finally, we will create WeightUnits.h and WeightUnits.m files. WeightUnits won't be a class, but it will be an enum and related functions that we want to use in various places throughout our application. Giving them their own header and implementation file makes it easy to import them wherever we need them.

CREATING OUR FILES

Let's start by adding the WeightHistoryDocument class to the project, Control-click the Model group, and select New File... from the pop-up menu. This will bring up the "Choose a template..." page. Make sure to select an iOS > Cocoa Touch > Objective-C Class and click Next.

On the "Choose options..." page, make sure the "Subclass of" setting is set to **NSObject**, and then name the class **WeightHistoryDocument**. I always set the superclass before the name, since some superclasses will automatically modify the name. For example, UIView Controller adds ViewController to the end of the current class name. After accidentally creating a number of MyViewControllerViewControllers, I decided it was best to just set the superclass first. Once the name and superclass are set, click Next.

The final page lets us choose where to save our class. We can use the default location, but make sure you look at the options at the bottom. The Group should be set to Model, and the Health Beat target should be selected. If everything looks OK, click Create.

Xcode will add the class to our project and will open the .m file in the editor. I typically start by modifying the .h file. Fortunately, we can switch between the .h and .m files by pressing ⌃⌘⇧ or ⌃⌘⇩.

Repeat the procedure for WeightEntry. Control-click the Model group and select New File.... Set the superclass to NSObject and the name to WeightEntry, and make sure the files are added to the correct group and target.

For the enum and utility functions, we could create a header file and a C file from the iOS > C and C++ templates. However, this won't actually work for us. C implementation files end with a .c. Objective-C implementation files end with an .m. The compiler will compile our code as Objective-C only if it has an .m extension.

Now, we're not creating a class—but we still want to be able to use Objective-C classes in our functions, so we need our code to be compiled as Objective-C. The easiest way to get an .h and .m pair is actually to create an Objective-C object and then delete the object declaration. Let's do that.

Again, Control-click the Model group and select New File.... Name the class `WeightUnits`. This will determine the .h and .m names. The superclass doesn't matter; leave it set to the current default. Then make the following two changes:

- In `WeightUnits.m`, delete everything after `#import "WeightUnits.h"`.
- Switch to `WeightUnits.h` and delete everything after `#import <Foundation/Foundation.h>`.

  This gives us an empty `.h` and `.m` pair.

If you did everything correctly, you should have added six files to the Model group: `WeightHistoryDocument.h`, `WeightHistoryDocument.m`, `WeightEntry.h`, `WeightEntry.m`, `WeightUnits.h`, and `WeightUnits.m`. Make sure you have all six files before proceeding to the next step.

IMPLEMENTING WEIGHTUNIT

Let's start with `WeightUnit`, since it's the simplest. Open `WeightUnits.h`, and add the following code:

```
#import <Foundation/Foundation.h>

typedef enum {
    LBS,
    KG
} WeightUnit;


WeightUnit getDefaultUnits(void);
```

Here, we're simply declaring our `WeightUnit` enum. Notice that we are combining the declaration and the typedef into a single expression. Feel free to separate it into two steps, if you prefer.

Initially, we will use only two different weight units, LBS and KG. However, since we are defining our units as an enum, it will be relatively easy to add additional units later—for example if we wanted to add STONE, OZ, or even TON.

We are also declaring a single function, `getDefaultUnits()`. Initially, this will simply return LBS. However, we will add the ability to change the default units in Chapter 5, "Loading and Saving Data."

Now, switch to `WeightUnits.m`. We simply need to define our `getDefaultUnits()` method.

```
#import "WeightUnits.h"


WeightUnit getDefaultUnits(void)
{
    return LBS;
}
```

That's it. `WeightUnit` is done (for now).

IMPLEMENTING WEIGHTENTRY

The WeightEntry class is only slightly more complicated than WeightUnit. Let's start by opening WeightEntry.h and replacing all the existing code with the code shown here:

```objc
#import <Foundation/Foundation.h>
#import "WeightUnits.h"

/**
 * The WeightEntry class holds the weight and date data for a single entry.
 */
@interface WeightEntry : NSObject

/// Stores the weight for this entry in US pounds
@property (assign, nonatomic, readonly) float weightInLbs;

/// Stores the date for this entry
@property (strong, nonatomic, readonly) NSDate* date;

/**
 * Convenience method for instantiating new WeightEntry objects
 *
 * @param weight Weight for this entry
 * @param unit Unit type for the weight parameter
 * @param date Date for this entry
 * @return A newly instantiated WeightEntry object
 */
+ (instancetype)entryWithWeight:(float)weight
                     usingUnits:(WeightUnit)unit
                        forDate:(NSDate *)date;

/**
 * Class method for converting from US pounds to kilograms
 *
 * @param lbs The weight in pounds
 * @return The weight in kilograms
 */
+ (float)convertLbsToKg:(float)lbs;

/**
 * Class method for converting from kilograms to US pounds
```

```
 *
 * @param kg The weight in kilograms
 * @return The weight in pounds
 */
+ (float)convertKgToLbs:(float)kg;
```

```
@end
```

We start by importing our `WeightUnits` declarations. Then we add two properties to our `WeightEntry` class: `weightInLbs` and `date`. Each `WeightEntry` will store a single entry. For Health Beat, this means storing the weight and the date on which the weight was taken.

Notice that these properties are read-only. This means our `WeightEntry` objects will be immutable. Once we create one, we cannot change its values. If we want to modify a `Weight-Entry`, we must create a new object with the correct values and delete the old ones.

While this may seem a little inconvenient, immutable data objects can greatly simplify our code. For example, we don't need to worry about some other part of our application changing their values while we are using them.

Also, for simplicity's sake, we will always store the weight in pounds. We can then convert it into whatever format the user wants when we display the weights.

Additionally, we are specifically using `float` instead of `double` for our weight. We want to use the same data type in both 32- and 64-bit applications, to make saving and loading our data easier. Using 64-bit data would both require more memory and slow down our 32-bit versions. And, since our weight values will never need the additional range or accuracy of a double, it would just be wasted effort.

Next, we declare a convenience method to let us easily instantiate new `WeightEntry` objects. This is a class method that takes three arguments: the weight, the units for the weight, and the date.

Then, since we will be converting our weights, we add methods to manage the conversion from pounds to kilograms and back. These methods do not use any of the `WeightEntry` object's internal data, so we will make them class methods.

Finally, notice that I've added Doxygen-formatted documentation comments to this header file. Documentation comments are primarily used to create docsets for your classes. You can then add these docsets to your `~/Library/Developer/Shared/Documentation/DocSets` folder, allowing Xcode to access them through its Documentation viewer. However, creating docsets is most useful when you are creating shared libraries—particularly when publicly distributing those libraries or when sharing them with other members of your team. For most small to medium applications, docsets are probably overkill.

However, the documentation comments are still useful, even within a small project. Xcode is smart enough to pick up on these documentation comments and use them when presenting the quick help pop-up for these symbols. With these comments in place, I can Option-click either the class, property, or method names to bring up this information (**Figure 2.9**). All of this happens automatically once I create the comments; I don't need to do any additional work.

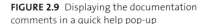

FIGURE 2.9 Displaying the documentation comments in a quick help pop-up

Unfortunately, because of the space they require, I won't be including documentation comments in the rest of the book. However, I strongly recommend adding them to all of your .h files. It is especially useful when maintaining code that may be months or years old.

OK, we still have more work to do. Let's switch to WeightEntry.m. First, we need to implement our creating methods. We will need three creation methods. We want to create a private, custom init method. We want to override the superclass's init method, and we want to implement our convenience method.

Add the following code inside WeightEntry's @implementation block (between the @implementation line and the @end directive):

```
#pragma mark - Init Methods

// Designated initializer.
- (id) initWithWeight:(float)weight
        usingUnits:(WeightUnit)unit
          forDate:(NSDate*)date
{
    self = [super init];
    if (self)
    {
        if (unit == LBS) {
            _weightInLbs = weight;
        }
        else {
            _weightInLbs = [WeightEntry convertKgToLbs:weight];
        }
        _date = date;
    }
    return self;
}
```

```
// Must override the superclass's designated initializer.
- (id)init
{
    NSDate* referenceDate = [NSDate dateWithTimeIntervalSince1970:0.0f];

    return [self initWithWeight:0.0f
                     usingUnits:LBS
                        forDate:referenceDate];
}


+(instancetype)entryWithWeight:(float)weight
                    usingUnits:(WeightUnit)unit
                       forDate:(NSDate *)date
{
    return [[self alloc] initWithWeight:weight usingUnits:unit forDate:date];
}
```

The initWithWeight:usingUnits:forDate: method is our designated initializer. It sets our weightInLbs property—converting the weight from kilograms to pounds, if necessary. It is also a private method, which means it should not be called from outside the class. Here, we are trying to force people to instantiate our WeightEntry class through our public convenience method—which we will define in a minute.

For completeness, we need to override the superclass's designated initializer. Our class's superclass is NSObject, which means we simply need to override init. In this case, our init method simply calls initWithWeight:usingUnits:forDate: creating a weight entry of 0.0 lbs., dated on January 1, 1970, GMT.

Finally, the convenience method simply allocs and inits a WeightEntry object using our new designated initializer. It passes along all of its arguments to the designated initializer and returns the result.

This is a pretty standard set of initialization methods. If you are having trouble understanding them, please review the "Writing Initialization Methods" and "Convenience Methods" sections of the "Objective-C" bonus chapter (www.freelancemadscience.com/creating-ios-7-apps-bonus-chap/).

We still need to implement our conversion methods. However, before we can do that, we need to declare a constant to represent the conversion rate between pounds and kilograms.

At the top of WeightEntry.m, add the following line:

```
#import "WeightEntry.h"

static const float LBS_PER_KG = 2.20462262f;

@implementation WeightEntry
```

This simply declares a constant floating-point value that we can use for our calculations. Now, at the bottom of the @implementation block, right before the @end directive, add the following two methods:

```
#pragma mark - Conversion Methods
+ (float)convertLbsToKg:(float)lbs
{
    return lbs / LBS_PER_KG;
}


+ (float)convertKgToLbs:(float)kg
{
    return kg * LBS_PER_KG;
}
```

These simply convert from pounds to kilograms, using the constant we just defined.

Finally, let's modify the class's description. Every object has a description method that it inherits from NSObject. This method creates a string representation for our class. By default, it simply creates a pair of angled brackets with the class name and the pointer value inside. Unfortunately, this isn't useful when you are trying to debug your code.

We won't be using the description directly in our production code—but it will be quite helpful during our initial testing and development. Add the following code to the bottom of the file, before the @end directive:

```
#pragma mark - NSObject Methods


-(NSString *)description
{
    NSString *date = [NSDateFormatter
                      localizedStringFromDate:self.date
                      dateStyle:NSDateFormatterMediumStyle
                      timeStyle:NSDateFormatterShortStyle];


    return [NSString stringWithFormat:
    @"%0.2f lbs entry from %@", self.weightInLbs, date];
}
```

Here, we are using the NSDateFormatter to create a properly localized string for our date. This will take into account both the device's language and its region.

We really should do something similar for the weight—and later, we will build helper functions to help us better display our weight. For now, we're just going to display it as a number out to two decimal places.

This isn't ideal, but it's good enough for our current testing needs.

IMPLEMENTING WEIGHTHISTORYDOCUMENT

By far, the WeightHistoryDocument will be the most complex piece of our model. And this isn't even the full WeightHistoryDocument implementation. We won't be worrying about saving and loading our data. Nor will we be syncing our data using iCloud. Those features will be added in future chapters. Instead, this is the simplest, most basic implementation that will still let us test our user interface.

Still, there are a lot of tasks that it must perform. It must store all of our weight entries and give us a way to access that data. It must also notify other parts of our application when the underlying data has changed. Specifically, it needs to post notifications when changes begin, when an entry has been added to our history, when an entry has been deleted from our history, and when the changes end.

Let's start by declaring string constants for the notification names. There are also a few other things we need to set up before we get started. Open WeightHistoryDocument.h. Between the line importing the foundation framework and the beginning of the @interface block, add the following code:

```
#import "WeightUnits.h"

@class WeightEntry;
typedef void (^EntryEnumeratorBlock) (WeightEntry *entry);


// Use to register for update notifications
extern NSString * const
WeightHistoryDocumentBeginChangesNotification;

extern NSString * const
WeightHistoryDocumentInsertWeightEntryNotification;

extern NSString * const
WeightHistoryDocumentDeleteWeightEntryNotification;

extern NSString * const
WeightHistoryDocumentChangesCompleteNotification;

// Use to access data in the notifications
extern NSString * const WeightHistoryDocumentNotificationIndexPathKey;
```

The first line imports our weight unit enum and functions. Next we have a forward declaration for the WeightEntry class. Typically we want to keep all #import directives out of the .h files. #import is a lot smarter than it's C cousin, #include. #import will include each file only once. So, we don't have to worry too much about creating infinite loops. Still, having header files that import other header files, which import still other header files, can bog down the build system.

We couldn't do anything about `WeightUnits.h`'s enum or function—but we can use forward declarations to handle both protocols and classes. Basically, the `@class` line tells the compiler that the `WeightEntry` class exists, and that the compiler doesn't need to worry about the details right now. We promise to provide all the necessary information before it becomes important.

This works because all classes are pointers—which mean they are all the same size. As long as the code in our file only passes the pointer around or saves it (e.g., passing the object as arguments or return values or saving it in instance variables or properties), the compiler doesn't need to know anything else. We only need to import the header file when we want to access the object's public properties or methods. Most of the time this means we use a forward declaration in the `.h` file and import the header file in the `.m` file.

After the forward declaration, we're creating a typedef for a block type. The syntax is...well, let's be generous and say it's a little bit hard to follow, in the same way that Swedish death metal is a little bit loud. Basically, we're creating a data type named `EntryEnumeratorBlock`, which is an alias for a block that takes a single `WeightEntry` argument and has no return value. We'll use this block type to create a block-based interface for our collection of `WeightEntrys`.

If you're using blocks as arguments, return types, or properties, typedefs like this help keep your code manageable. As ugly as the previous line is, it's a lot nicer than just shoving this whole mess into your method prototype.

Finally we declare five string constants. The first four are the names for our notifications. The fifth one is a key that we can use to get and set the index path in the notification's user info dictionary.

That's a lot of work, and we still haven't modified the `WeightHistoryDocument` class itself yet. Let's declare our properties and methods. Add the following code inside the `@interface` block:

```
@property (nonatomic, readonly) NSUInteger count;

- (WeightEntry *)entryAtIndexPath:(NSIndexPath *)indexPath;
- (NSIndexPath *)indexPathForEntry:(WeightEntry *)weightEntry;
- (void)addEntry:(WeightEntry *)weightEntry;
- (void)deleteEntryAtIndexPath:(NSIndexPath *)indexPath;

- (void)enumerateEntriesAscending:(BOOL)ascending
                         withBlock:(EntryEnumeratorBlock)block;
```

This class has only one public property, count. Actually, count will be a virtual property. We won't use an instance variable to store the number of items in our history. Instead, we will calculate this value whenever the accessor is called.

Admittedly, we could have just declared count as a method—however, by declaring it as a virtual property, we can use dot notation to access it. This streamlines our code, but it comes at a slight cost. If we declare it as a property, we should really make sure it's KVC and KVO compliant. As you will soon see, we will spend a little extra time and effort setting up the property in order to simplify its use later on.

After the property, we declare a number of methods. The entryAtIndexPath: method lets us access the entry for a given index path. Table views (among others) use index paths to refer to items by their section and their row numbers. Since we will primarily be displaying the entries in a table, we will match that indexing here.

The indexPathForEntry: method searches through the weight history for a matching entry. If it finds one, it returns the entry's index path. The addEntry: method simply adds another entry to our history, while deleteEntryAtIndexPath: deletes the corresponding entry.

Finally, the enumerateEntriesAscending:withBlock: method will let us iterate over all the entries in our history. We can choose to iterate in ascending order (going forward in time from the earliest date to the most recent date) or in descending order (going backward in time). For each entry in our history, this method will call the provided EntryEnumeratorBlock, passing in the current entry.

These methods let us manipulate our entry history without exposing the history itself. While this is generally a cleaner way to code, since other parts of our application cannot modify our history without going through these methods. The real benefit comes from hiding the underlying implementation. As you will see in Chapter 7, "Core Data," when we move from custom objects to Core Data, WeightHistoryDocument's interface will remain unchanged. We may gut and rewrite the underlying implementation, but the rest of our application won't even notice the difference.

And, speaking of the implementation, let's open WeightHistoryDocument.m and begin defining our methods. Much like the .h file, we will start by importing files and declaring our constants. Add the following code under the WeightHistoryDocument.h import, before the beginning of the @interface block:

```
#import "WeightEntry.h"

// Use to register for update notifications
NSString * const WeightHistoryDocumentBeginChangesNotification =
@"WeightHistoryDocumentBeginChangesNotification";

NSString * const WeightHistoryDocumentInsertWeightEntryNotification =
@"WeightHistoryDocumentInsertWeightEntryNotification";

NSString * const WeightHistoryDocumentDeleteWeightEntryNotification =
@"WeightHistoryDocumentDeleteWeightEntryNotification";
```

```
NSString * const WeightHistoryDocumentChangesCompleteNotification =
@"WeightHistoryDocumentChangesCompleteNotification";

// Use to access data in the notifications
NSString * const WeightHistoryDocumentNotificationIndexPathKey =
@"WeightHistoryDocumentNotificationIndexPathKey";
```

Here we import the WeightEntry class—following up on the promise we made with our forward declaration. We are also defining our string constants. It doesn't really matter what value these strings have, as long as they're unique within our application. When I'm using string constants as keys or notification names, I typically use the constant's name for the string's content.

Next, we're going to add an extension to the class. Place the following code after our constant definitions but before the @implementation block:

```
@interface WeightHistoryDocument()
@property (strong, nonatomic)NSMutableArray *weightHistory;
@end
```

Extensions are typically used to add private properties to a class. In this case, we will store our history in a mutable array—however, this is purely an internal implementation detail and should not be exposed outside our class.

Next, we need a custom init method. Since we are simply overriding the superclass's designated initializer, we need only one init method in this class. Put the following code inside WeightHistoryDocument's @implementation block:

```
#pragma mark - Initialization Methods


- (id)init
{
    self = [super init];
    if (self) {
        _weightHistory = [NSMutableArray array];
    }
    return self;
}
```

This is a standard designated initializer. Most of the method is boilerplate. The only real work is the line in the middle, where we create a new, empty array for our weightHistory property.

Next, we need to implement the getter for count. This has two effects. First, it lets us dynamically calculate the count, rather than storing and retrieving the value. More importantly, since the complier isn't creating any accessors for this property, it won't create the _count instance variable either. Add the following code beneath our init method but before @end:

```
#pragma mark - Accessor Methods

-(NSUInteger)count
{
    return [self.weightHistory count];
}


+ (NSSet *)keyPathsForValuesAffectingCount
{
    return [NSSet setWithObjects:@"weightHistory", nil];
}
```

Here, our count method simply calls our mutable array's count method and returns the result. The keyPathsForValuesAffectingCount method is used by the system to determine when our count property has change. If you are using Key-Value Observing to monitor the count property, you will receive an update notification every time our weightHistory changes.

This, however, isn't quite enough to make count KVO compliant. It turns out that making collections Key-Value Coding compliant (which is a prerequisite for KVO compliance) is more difficult than it seems. Basically, we must implement and use KVC-compliant getters and setters for the elements in our array. There are a couple of different ways to do this, but for this project, we will add the following methods to WeightHistoryDocument:

```
#pragma mark - KVO Accessors

- (void)insertObject:(WeightEntry *)object
inWeightHistoryAtIndex:(NSUInteger)index
{
    [self.weightHistory insertObject:object atIndex:index];
}


- (void)removeObjectFromWeightHistoryAtIndex:(NSUInteger)index
{
    [self.weightHistory removeObjectAtIndex:index];
}
```

This is where Objective-C's dynamic underpinnings really begin to shine. The system will dynamically look for these methods based on our property's name. If it finds both of these methods, it will enable Key-Value Observing using these methods. Any calls to these methods will generate change notifications.

However, we must implement both of these methods. Just implementing one will not make the class KVC compliant—and Key-Value Observing won't register any changes. Optionally, we could add a third method `replaceObjectInWeightHistoryAtIndex:withObject:`; however, that won't be necessary for this project.

With these methods in place, our count property will be properly KVO compliant—provided, of course, we modify the underlying data only using `insertObject:inWeightHistoryAtIndex:` and `removeObjectFromWeightHistoryAtIndex:`. That's a bit annoying, but it's not too hard to guarantee. Fortunately, `weightHistory` is a private property, so it cannot be modified from outside our class. As long as our `WeightHistoryDocument` class is correct, everything will work as expected. It's yet another win for encapsulation!

Now, let's look at the accessor methods. The first two are easy.

```
#pragma mark - Public Methods

- (WeightEntry *)entryAtIndexPath:(NSIndexPath *)indexPath
{
    return self.weightHistory[(NSUInteger)indexPath.row];
}


- (NSIndexPath *)indexPathForEntry:(WeightEntry *)weightEntry
{
    NSUInteger row = [self.weightHistory indexOfObject:weightEntry];
    return [NSIndexPath indexPathForRow:(NSInteger)row inSection:0];
}
```

Here, we're simply converting between the array index and an `NSIndexPath`. When working with tables, `NSIndexPath` has two components, a row and a section. In our application, we will have only a single section. So, all the items will be placed in section 0. The entry's row is just equal to its index in the array.

So, for `entryAtIndexPath`, we extract the row number from the `indexPath` argument. Then we use Objective-C's new subscript notation to look up the object at that index.

There is, unfortunately, one smallish hitch in the process. `NSIndexPath` uses signed integers, while the subscript notation uses unsigned integers. Assuming you enabled all the warnings I recommended earlier in this chapter, you will need to cast from the signed to the unsigned variant to get rid of the warning. As I said, the extra typing can be annoying—but it will help you prevent a potentially embarrassing mistake one day.

indexPathForEntry: is the reverse. We get the index number for the desired weight entry. Then we use that number to create a new NSIndexPath (casting to a signed integer, when necessary).

Next, let's add the addEntry: method.

```
- (void)addEntry:(WeightEntry *)weightEntry
{
    NSUInteger index = [self insertionPointForDate:weightEntry.date];
    NSIndexPath *indexPath =
    [NSIndexPath indexPathForRow:(NSInteger)index inSection:0];

    NSNotificationCenter *center = [NSNotificationCenter defaultCenter];

    [center
     postNotificationName:WeightHistoryDocumentBeginChangesNotification
     object:self];

    [self insertObject:weightEntry inWeightHistoryAtIndex:index];

    [center
     postNotificationName:
     WeightHistoryDocumentInsertWeightEntryNotification
     object:self
     userInfo:@{WeightHistoryDocumentNotificationIndexPathKey:indexPath}];

    [center
     postNotificationName:WeightHistoryDocumentChangesCompleteNotification
     object:self];
}
```

This method is starting to get a bit more complex. Here we start by determining the insertion point for our entry. We want our WeightEntry elements to remain in chronological order, and it's faster to just insert each new element into its proper position—rather than sorting the entire array after each change.

If you're not familiar with WeightHistoryDocument's insertionPointForDate: method, that's because we haven't written it yet. We will add this as a private method soon. For now, let's just assume it works as advertised.

Next, we convert the index to an index path. Then we get a reference to the default notification center. We then send a notification, stating that our document is about to change. We add the entry using our KVO-compliant accessor method. Then we send a second notification stating that we've inserted an object into our history and a third notification stating that the changes are done.

Of these notifications, the `WeightHistoryDocumentInsertWeightEntryNotification` is the most complex. Here, we don't just send it; we also pass in an `NSDictionary` containing information about the change. Specifically, we include the index path of the newly inserted object. Notice that we are using Objective-C's new literal dictionary syntax to create our dictionary inline.

Destruction is often easier than creation, and Health Beat is no exception, as you will see. Add the `deleteEntryAtIndexPath:` method as shown here:

```objc
- (void)deleteEntryAtIndexPath:(NSIndexPath *)indexPath
{
    NSNotificationCenter *center = [NSNotificationCenter defaultCenter];

    [center
     postNotificationName:WeightHistoryDocumentBeginChangesNotification
     object:self];

    [self removeObjectFromWeightHistoryAtIndex:(NSUInteger)indexPath.row];

    [center
     postNotificationName:
     WeightHistoryDocumentDeleteWeightEntryNotification
     object:self
     userInfo:@{WeightHistoryDocumentNotificationIndexPathKey:indexPath}];

    [center
     postNotificationName:WeightHistoryDocumentChangesCompleteNotification
     object:self];
}
```

In many ways, this is very similar to `addEntry:`. We grab a reference to the default notification center. We then use that reference to send the begin changes notification. We remove the `WeightEntry` object using our KVO-compliant accessor. Then we send two additional notifications. First the weight entry deleted notification, and then the changes completed notification.

Now let's look at the block enumeration method. Despite the scary technology involved, this is actually one of the easier methods.

```objc
- (void)enumerateEntriesAscending:(BOOL)ascending
                        withBlock:(EntryEnumeratorBlock)block
{
    NSUInteger options = 0;
    if (ascending)
    {
```

```
        options = NSEnumerationReverse;
    }

    [self.weightHistory
     enumerateObjectsWithOptions:options
     usingBlock:^(id obj, NSUInteger idx, BOOL *stop) {
        block(obj);
    }];
}
```

Here, we start by creating an `options` local variable and setting this to 0 (no options). Next we check to see whether we are enumerating our entries in ascending order. If we are, we set our options to `NSEnumerationReverse`. This will cause our enumeration code to start at the tail end of the array and work toward the first object. Of course, this assumes our `weightHistory` array is kept in descending order. We will take care of that in a minute.

Then we just call `enumerateObjectsWithOptions:usingBlock:`. We pass in our `options` variable for the first argument. For the second argument we create a block that simply calls our block, passing in the current entry as an argument.

Yes, we have a block inside a block. Yes, that may seem odd, and we could have simply changed our `EntryEnumeratorBlock` definition so that it matched the blocks required by `enumerateObjectsWithOptions...`. That way, we could just pass our block directly to `enumerateObjectsWithOptions...`. However, we are interested only in the current entry—we don't need the index or the stop output argument. In fact, we really shouldn't expose those details to the outside. Calling our block inside their block lets us simplify, focus, and clean up the interface.

Finally, we need to implement our private `insertionPointForDate:` method. I typically place private methods at the bottom of the file, just before the @end directive.

```
#pragma mark - Private Methods

- (NSUInteger)insertionPointForDate:(NSDate *)date
{
    NSUInteger index = 0;
    for (WeightEntry *entry in self.weightHistory)
    {
        if ([date compare:entry.date] == NSOrderedDescending)
        {
            return index;
        }
        index++;
    }
    return index;
}
```

We want our `weightHistory` array to be kept in descending order. To do this, we start with an index of 0. Then we iterate over our current array. For each entry in the array, we check to see whether its date is after the date of our new entry. If it is, we've found the correct position. We simply return the current index. If it's not, we increment the index and check the next item. If we reach the end of the array, we simply return the length of the array, effectively inserting our object at the end.

This algorithm works as long as the array is already in descending order. Fortunately, if we start with an empty array and we always use this algorithm to add new items, it can never get out of order. This is also the reason we don't allow replacing or modifying entries. If we did, we would have to check any time a change was made and reorder our array, if necessary. That gets messy fast.

As written, if you want to replace an entry, you must delete the old entry and insert a new entry. Of course, when you add the new entry, our code will automatically insert it in the proper position, based on its new date. So, everything stays properly ordered.

There's one last step. We should probably override the description method to provide more useful information during testing. Add the following method. I usually add overridden methods near the bottom of the class, just before the private methods.

```
#pragma mark - NSObject Methods


-(NSString *)description
{
    return [NSString stringWithFormat:
            @"WeightHistoryDocument: count = %@, history = %@",
            @(self.count), self.weightHistory];
}
```

Here, we need to make sure our formatting string works for both 32-bit and 64-bit. The problem is, `self.count` returns an NSUInteger, and NSUInteger's size changes between 32- and 64-bit. This means its placeholder must also change. In 32-bit, it requires a %d, in 64-bit it requires a %ld. We solve this problem by using an object placeholder, %@, and converting our integer to an NSNumber using the literal syntax.

That's it for now. We'll add a few bells and whistles in later chapters, but this is enough to let us build and test our user interface. And speaking of user interfaces....

LAYING OUT THE STORYBOARD

FIGURE 2.10
Our mostly empty
storyboard

It's time to start building our application's workflow. We already have a tab bar controller—but it doesn't currently have any tabs. If you run the application now, you'll see. It doesn't do a whole lot.

We want to add two tabs: one for our history view and one for our graph view. We do this by adding two view controllers to our storyboard and connecting them as relationships to the tab bar controller.

Open Main.storyboard. Working with storyboards requires a lot of screen space (or you need to get very good at zooming in and zooming out). So, you probably want to hide the Navigator and the Debug area to give yourself as much room as possible. We will often use the Document Outline and Utilities area, so I leave them on the screen. At this point, our storyboard should just have a single tab bar controller (**Figure 2.10**).

Let's start by adding our history view controller. This will be a table view controller, so in the Object library, find the Table View Controller icon (it should be near the top of the list), and drop it to the right of the tab view controller. Double-clicking the background will zoom in and out. You may want to zoom out to more easily adjust the table view controller's position.

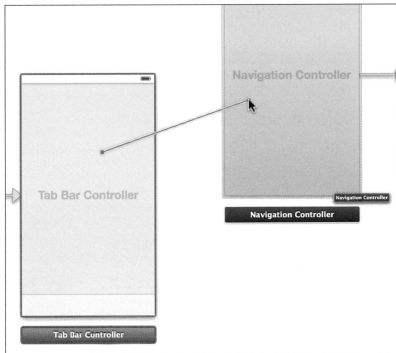

FIGURE 2.11 Selecting the view controller   **FIGURE 2.12** Connecting the controllers

Now, our history view should be inside a navigation controller, letting us easily bring up a detailed view for each entry. We could find a navigation controller in the Object library, and drag it out and link everything by hand, but there's a quicker way.

Select the table view controller. Again, selecting the controller can be a bit tricky. If you're zoomed out, you can just click anywhere inside the scene. If you're zoomed in, you need to actually select the view controller icon either in the scene's dock or in the document outline. Clicking the scene will usually select the view, not the view controller. You can tell that the view controller is selected, because the entire scene will be surrounded by a blue line (**Figure 2.11**).

With the table view controller highlighted, select the Editor > Embed In > Navigation Controller menu item. This will automatically add a navigation controller to our storyboard, setting our table view controller as the navigation controller's root view controller.

Now, we need to connect the navigation controller to our tab bar controller. Control-click the tab bar controller and drag to navigation controller (**Figure 2.12**). When you let go of the mouse, a pop-up menu will appear. It lists four options. Three manual segues (push, modal, and custom) and a single relationship segue (view controllers). Select "view controllers." This will add our history view as our tab bar controller's first tab.

Next, we need our graph view. This will be somewhat simpler. Drag a View Controller out from the Object library, and place it in the storyboard below the navigation controller. Then Control-drag from the tab bar controller to our new view controller. Again, select "view controllers" from the pop-up menu.

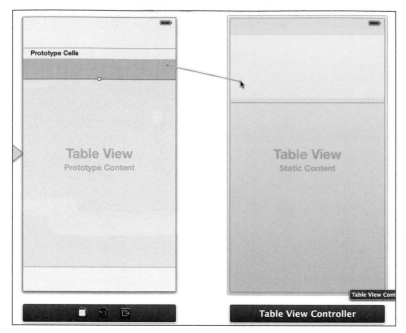

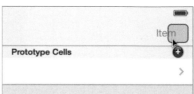

FIGURE 2.13 Connecting our history view's cell to the detail scene

FIGURE 2.14 Adding a navigation bar button

Two more scenes to go. We want a scene to display the detailed information about each weight entry. One of the easiest ways to do this is to use a static table. So, let's drag out another Table View Controller from the Object library. Place it to the right of our current table view.

Now let's configure it as a static table. Zoom in on our new table view controller, and select the table view. You should be able to just click the middle of the scene. In the Attributes inspector, change the Contents from Dynamic Prototypes to Static Cells. We also want to change the Style from Plain to Grouped. That's it for now; we will lay out the content in the next chapter.

We still need to connect this scene to our history view scene. Basically, whenever the user taps a row in the history view, we want to push our detail view on to the navigation stack. This is easy to set up. Control-click the table view cell in our original table view and drag over to our second table view (**Figure 2.13**). When you release the mouse, select the push segue. This will connect the view controllers, add the navigation bar to our detail table, and add the gray disclosure indicator to our original table view cell.

We still need a scene to let us add new weight entries. For this, we need to add a button to the history table's navigation bar. Then we will connect a modal view to this button.

Zoom in on our original table view controller (the one attached to the navigation controller). In the Object library, scroll down until you find a Bar Button Item. Drag this out and place it on the right side of the table view's navigation bar (**Figure 2.14**).

Now select the button, and in the Attributes inspector, change the Identifier to Add. The button should now appear as a plus sign.

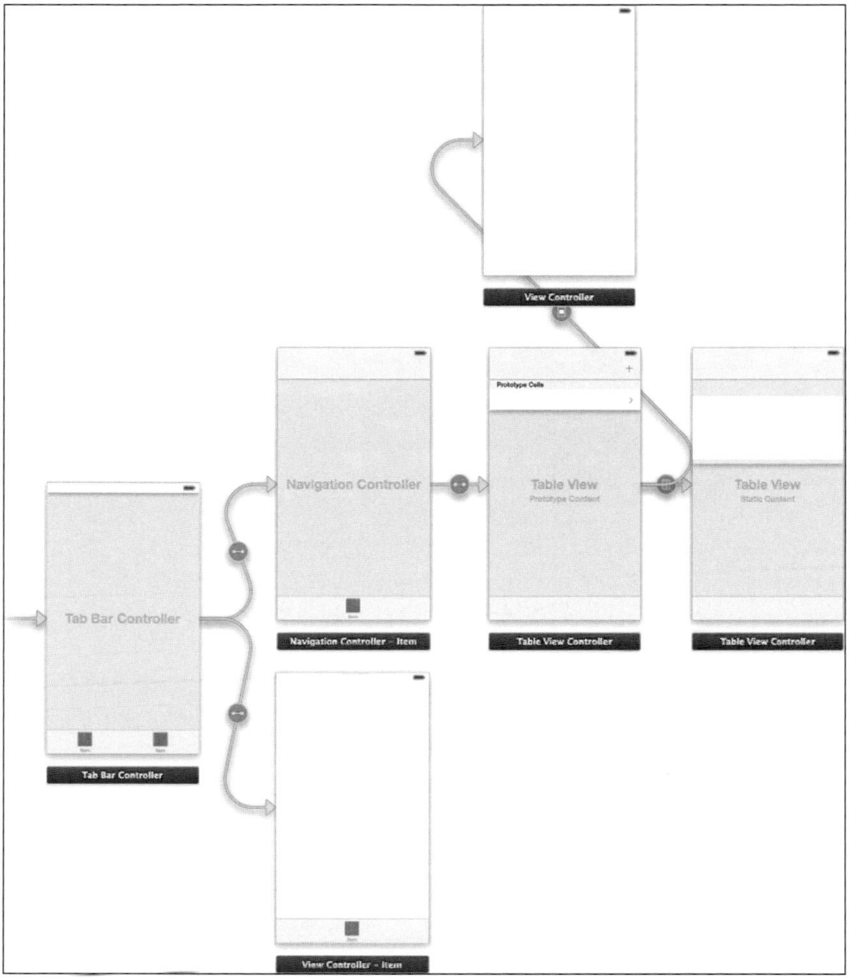

FIGURE 2.15 The complete scene layout

Drag out another View Controller and place it above our table view controller. Now, Control-click the add button and drag up to our new view controller. This time, select the modal segue.

> **NOTE:** We are using three different navigation techniques in our application. The tab bar controller lets us switch between the history view and our graph view. The navigation controller lets us slide easily between the history view and the detailed views for any particular entry. The history view also displays our add entry scene as a modal view, temporarily covering the entire user interface until the add entry scene is explicitly dismissed (until the new entry is saved or canceled).

So far, the storyboard gives us the basic framework for our application. Zoom out and reposition the scenes so they match **Figure 2.15**.

ADDING CUSTOM VIEW CONTROLLERS

Currently, our storyboard will use default UIKit view controllers for all of our scenes: UIViewController, UITabBarController, UINavigationController, or UITableViewController. However, we want to provide a custom subclass for each of these, letting us customize their behavior.

This is a two-step process. First, we need to create the custom classes. Second, we need to tell the storyboard to use our new classes.

Let's start by adding a custom tab bar controller. If you previously hid the Navigator, you will have to show it again. Then, in the Project navigator, right-click the Controllers group, and select New File.... We want to create a new Objective-C Class. The class name should be **RootTabBarController**. It should be a subclass of **UITabBarController**. Make sure the Targeted for iPad and "With XIB for user interface" boxes are not checked. Finally, make sure it's added to the Controllers group and the Health Beat target.

Repeat this procedure for the other controllers. Their names and subclasses are listed in **Table 2.1**.

TABLE 2.1 Storyboard's UIViewController Subclasses

CLASS NAME	SUBCLASS OF
RootTabBarController	UITabBarController
HistoryNavigationController	UINavigationController
HistoryTableViewController	UITableViewController
EntryDetailViewController	UITableViewController
AddEntryViewController	UIViewController
GraphViewController	UIViewController

Once we're done, we should have added six classes (12 different files) to our Controllers group. Except for the table view controller subclasses, these are primarily empty. They just have stubs for initWithNibName:bundle:, viewDidLoad, and didReceiveMemoryWarning:. We could delete these to clean up our classes, but they won't hurt anything. Besides, we will use many of the viewDidLoad methods later, so let's leave them alone for now.

The table view controller subclasses have a number of additional stubs to support loading and displaying the table data. These stubs can be useful when setting up a table view—they serve as reminders for all the tasks we need to perform to get the table up and running. However, we won't end up using most of them for our detail scene, since it is a static table. Its content won't be dynamically loaded at runtime. Instead, we will design its interface in Interface Builder.

So, let's clear it out. Open the EntryDetailViewController.m file. Delete everything between @implementation and @end. That is it, our custom controllers are ready to use.

Open `Main.storyboard` again. With the storyboard zoomed out, click the tab bar scene. Switch to the Identity inspector. It should show that our view controller's class is currently a `UITabBarController`. Change the class setting to `RootTabBarController`. This should be one of the options listed in the drop-down menu. Notice that the controller's name changes both in the scene and in the Document Outline.

We will repeat this for all of our controllers. Change the Navigation Controller's class to `HistoryNavigationController`. The view controller attached to the `RootTabBarController` should be our `GraphViewController`. The first table view controller is our `HistoryTableViewController`. The second is our `EntryDetailViewController`. Finally, the view controller attached to `HistoryTableViewController`'s add button is our `AddEntryViewController`.

With this step complete, when the scenes load, they will use our custom classes.

NAVIGATION ITEMS, TAB BAR ITEMS, AND SEGUES

There are a few, minor settings we should set. First, we want to set the titles on our navigation bars. With the storyboard open, zoom in on our history table view controller. Double-click the center of the navigation bar, and type **History** in the text box. This sets the navigation title for that scene.

Do the same thing for the Entry Detail View Controller, but type **Weight Entry** instead.

> **NOTE:** If you're having trouble editing the navigation bar titles, you can always select the scene's Navigation Item in the Document Outline, and modify its title in the Attributes inspector.

Similarly, we will want to set the titles and images of our tabs. The tab bar item is part of the scene that is being displayed—this means both our History Navigation Controller and our Graph View Controller scenes have tab bar items that we can modify.

Zoom in on the History Navigation Controller first. Click the tab bar icon to select it. It should be a square with the word item underneath. In the Attributes inspector, change the Identifier to History. This will automatically change both the image and the title.

As you can see, iOS provides a number of built-in tab identifiers. These will handle many of the common tasks, and we should use them wherever appropriate. Users will already recognize these icons and should have a rough understanding of what they will do.

Unfortunately, there isn't an appropriate identifier for our graph view. So, we'll have to provide both a custom image and a title. Zoom in on the Graph View Controller scene. Again, select the tab icon. In the Attributes inspector, change the Title to Graph. Then change the Image to Graph. If you click the drop-down arrow, it should be the only option listed.

This sets up the unselected image. We would like to be able to use a slightly bolder, selected image as well. Unfortunately, we need to set this up in code. Open `GraphViewController.m` and add the following line to its `viewDidLoad:` method:

```
self.tabBarItem.selectedImage = [UIImage imageNamed:@"graph_selected"];
```

Nibs are the underlying technology behind story-boards. The compiler will break the storyboard into a number of nib files, loading them as necessary. Therefore, to understand what happens when a storyboard loads a scene, we really need to understand the life cycle of the underlying nibs. I give a brief summary here, but for the full blow-by-blow details, check out Apple's Resource Programming Guide.

Nibs can be thought of as freeze-dried view hierarchies. When we create a nib, we are simply saving everything inside the nib to disk. This uses the same basic technology we will use in Chapter 5.

When a nib loads, memory is set aside for all the objects and resources stored inside that nib. Then the entire object graph is instantiated. Objects that conform to the NSCoding protocol will be instantiated by calling initWithCoder:. All other objects are instantiated by calling init.

The system then connects all the outlets by calling the setValue:forKey: method. It connects all the actions using addTarget:action:forControlEvents:. Once the entire object graph is linked together, UIKit calls awakeFromNib on each of the objects created by the nib. You can implement an object's awakeFromNib method to perform any additional configuration steps after all the outlets and actions have been properly configured.

Note: UIViewController subclasses should do their additional configuration in viewDidLoad instead. We often create the view controllers in one nib and create their contents in another. As a result, the awakenFromNib method may be called before the view has loaded, and any outlets connecting the controller to user interface elements in the view's nib will not be set up yet.

After the nib has finished loading, any objects that are not stored in a strong reference will be deallocated. Most of the time, we won't need to worry about this. Unless we're programmatically loading the scene ourselves, the system will automatically store a reference to the view controller in our view controller hierarchy. The main view is stored in the view controller, and any other user interface elements and gesture recognizers are automatically stored in their containing view.

However, if we add any new top-level objects (data objects or views not yet placed into the view hierarchy), we will need to store a reference to them somewhere. Typically, this means creating an outlet in our view controller and connecting the object to that outlet.

This will automatically load the correct resolution image from Images.xcassets and assign it as our selected image. Now, whenever the graph tab is selected, the area under the line will also be filled in with a solid color—similar to the way the clock face is filled in when the history tab is selected.

The navigation titles and tab icons are now set properly. We just need to set up our segues. Switch back to Main.storyboard. If you look at the storyboard, you will see a number of connections between our scenes. Three of these are relationships. These show the connection between the tab bar controller and the view controllers it manages or between the navigation controller and its root view controller. The container controllers need these relationships to operate properly, but they aren't really something we can modify.

There are, however, two segues: a push segue between History Table View Controller and Entry Detail View Controller and a modal segue between History Table View Controller and the Add Entry View Controller.

There are a few key points worth emphasizing:

1. Many of the details of how nibs are loaded are different on Mac OS X and iOS. If you are moving back and forth between desktop and mobile development, be sure to double-check the documentation.

2. Any object that conforms to NSCoding will be loaded using initWithCoder:. Unlike other init methods, this does not end up calling your designated initializer. If you are loading custom objects (including UIViewController subclasses) in your nibs, be sure to perform all additional initialization steps in the awakeFromNib method (or viewDidLoad for UIViewController subclasses). If you do custom setup in your designated initializer, you will need to duplicate this in initWithCoder: (or, better yet, have both methods call a private method that handles the configuration and setup).

3. If you add a top-level object, be sure to add an outlet for it in your view controller. We need a strong reference to the top-level object; otherwise, it will disappear after the nib loads.

4. A new destination UIViewController is created every time your app performs a segue. This means some of our nibs may be loaded multiple times during the application's lifetime. You cannot assume that a nib will be loaded only once.

5. Xib files are a newer, XML-formatted nib file. Xib files were added to better support source control software. In theory, they are human readable. That means we can look at the difference between two xibs and perhaps make changes by hand to merge conflicts. However, in practice the XML gets rather opaque, and merging nibs (or storyboards) is difficult if not impossible. When we build our project, the compiler will compile xib files into binary nib files. The nib files are then added to the application bundle. So, we are still loading binary nib files at runtime. The documentation often refers to xibs and nibs interchangeably. For hIstorical reasons (and reasons of consistency) I will use "nib" throughout this book, unless I'm explicitly talking about the word *xib*.

Select the push segue, either by selecting it in the Document Outline or by clicking on the segue icon in the storyboard. In the Attributes inspector, set its Identifier to Entry Detail Segue. Next, select the modal segue, and set its identifier to Add Entry Segue. We will use these to identify our segues in code.

FIGURE 2.16 Final
application workflow

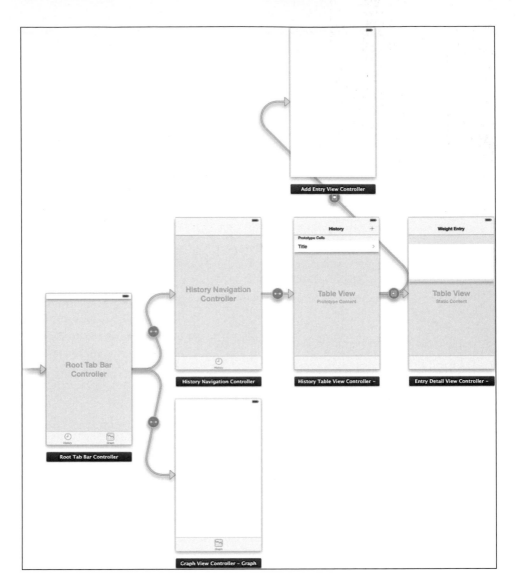

That's it. The basic workflow is done (**Figure 2.16**). We still need to build the actual
interfaces for each scene, of course. But, we'll handle that in the next chapter. For now, let's
connect our model to our view controllers and verify that our data gets passed along as we
navigate from one scene to the next.

CONNECTING THE MODEL

Now we need to connect our model objects to our controllers. This often causes some confusion—after all, the controllers are created by our storyboard. How do we get our data objects to them?

In theory, we could add our model objects to the storyboard and let it create them as well. This isn't a bad approach; however, we lose some control over when and how our objects are loaded. Any objects in the storyboard will be created when the scene is loaded. If our data object is loaded as part of our initial scene, it could cause a delay when launching our application—especially when loading a particularly large file or loading resources from the network. If it's part of a different scene, it would get loaded each time we segue to that scene. This means it might be loaded multiple times during the application's lifetime.

More importantly, we cannot connect the outlets in one scene to objects in another. If we could add our model to our initial scene and then connect it to outlets in all our other scenes, I would be strongly tempted to add objects to storyboards. As it is, there are better solutions.

A second, common approach involves creating a singleton class for our model or storing our model in the app delegate (which effectively does the same thing). Personally, I find the app delegate approach a little sloppy, and I try to avoid the dark temptation of singleton classes whenever possible.

Instead, let's use lazy initialization to create our model in our initial scene's controller and then pass the data to our new scenes when they are loaded. This is often referred to as the *baton passing* approach. It also means that we need to add a property to our RootTabBarController to hold a reference to our model.

Open RootTabBarController.h. Modify it as shown here:

```
@class WeightHistoryDocument;

@interface RootTabBarController ()

@property (strong, nonatomic) WeightHistoryDocument
*weightHistoryDocument;

@end
```

There should be no surprises here. First, we have to create a forward declaration for our WeightHistoryDocument class. Then we declare a property to hold our weight history inside our @interface block.

Switch to RootTabBarController.m. We need to import our WeightHistoryDocument class. At the top of the file, just under the line to import RootTabBarController.h, add the following line:

```
#import "WeightHistoryDocument.h"
```

Now, scroll down to `viewDidLoad`. Modify the code as shown here:

```
- (void)viewDidLoad
{
    [super viewDidLoad];
    self.weightHistoryDocument = [[WeightHistoryDocument alloc] init];
    [self documentReady];
}
```

Here, we're just instantiating a new `WeightHistoryDocument` object and assigning it to our property. Then we call the `documentReady` method. Again, you may not recognize this method. That's because we haven't written it yet.

The `documentReady` method will pass the document to all of the tabs. We will do this dynamically. If, in the future, we decide to add additional tabs, they can automatically take advantage of this code.

Add the following code to the bottom of the file, before the @end directive:

```
#pragma mark - Private Methods


- (void)documentReady
{
    // automatically passes the weight history document
    // on to any of the controlled view controllers.
    for (id controller in self.viewControllers) {
        if ([controller respondsToSelector:
            @selector(setWeightHistoryDocument:)])
        {
            [controller setWeightHistoryDocument:
             self.weightHistoryDocument];
        }
    }
}
```

We start by iterating over all the controllers in the tab view controller's `viewControllers` property. Notice that we are using the `id` dynamic type, instead of statically typing each controller as a `UIViewController`.

Next, we check to see whether the `controller` responds to the `setWeightHistoryDocument:` method. If it does, we call that method, passing in our document. We have to use `id` for controller, since `UIViewController` doesn't declare a `setWeightHistoryDocument:` method. The compiler has, however, seen a `setWeightHistoryDocument:` before (it was implicitly declared as part of our `weightHistoryDocument` property), so it freely lets us call that method on any `id` types. It just assumes we know what we're doing. Fortunately, since we check this method before calling it, this is perfectly safe.

The upshot is, if either our `HistoryNavigationController` or `GraphViewController` want access to the document, all they need to do is declare their own `weightHistoryDocument` property, and the model will automatically get passed along to them. If we add another tab, it can also gain access to our document by simply implementing `weightHistoryDocument`.

So, let's do that. Open `GraphViewController.h`. Add the forward declaration and property, just like we did in `RootTabBarController.h`.

```
#import <UIKit/UIKit.h>
@class WeightHistoryDocument;


@interface GraphViewController : UIViewController
@property (strong, nonatomic) WeightHistoryDocument
*weightHistoryDocument;
@end
```

Repeat this process in the `HistoryNavigationController.h` and `HistoryTableViewController.h`.

We need a little more work to pass the document from the navigation controller to the history table controller. Remember, our `HistoryTableViewController` is the root view of our navigation controller. It was never directly added to the tab bar. As a result, it won't automatically get our document.

The easiest way to chain the document along is to override `HistoryNavigationController`'s `setWeightHistoryDocument:` method. This method would normally be automatically generated by the property—but, if we provide our own implementation, the system will use our version instead.

Open `HistoryNavigationController.m` and add the following code before the @end directive:

```
#pragma mark - Accessor Methods


-(void)setWeightHistoryDocument:
(WeightHistoryDocument *)weightHistoryDocument
{
    _weightHistoryDocument = weightHistoryDocument;

    id rootViewController = self.viewControllers[0];
    if ([rootViewController respondsToSelector:
        @selector(setWeightHistoryDocument:)])
    {
        [rootViewController setWeightHistoryDocument:
         weightHistoryDocument];
    }
}
```

Here, we start by assigning our incoming value to the property's instance variable. Then we get a dynamic reference to the navigation controller's root view controller. Just like in the tab bar controller, we check to see whether the root view controller responds to the `setWeight-HistoryDocument:` method. If it does, we call that method, passing our document along.

There are only two scenes left. We actually don't want to pass the document to either of them. Our `AddEntryViewController` will simply let the user select a weight and date. If the user then clicks Save, the displaying controller will grab those values and create a new entry, adding it to our document.

Similarly, the `EntryDetailViewController` doesn't need access to the entire document. It just needs the currently selected entry. We'll actually add some additional information to provide richer, statistical data in the next chapter. But, for now, let's just add a `WeightEntry` property.

Open `EntryDetailViewController.h`. Add a forward declaration for the `WeightEntry` class. Then add a property to hold our weight entry, as shown here:

```
#import <UIKit/UIKit.h>
@class WeightEntry;
@interface EntryDetailViewController : UITableViewController
@property (strong, nonatomic) WeightEntry *entry;
@end
```

SETTING UP HISTORYTABLEVIEWCONTROLLER

We still need to pass the entry from our history table view to the entry detail view. However, before we can do that, we need to set up our table view.

Table view controllers use both a delegate and a data source to configure their contents. Both of these protocols declare a number of methods that we can use to modify the content and their appearance of our table view at runtime. They also let us respond to row selections and other user interactions. You can see the complete list of methods in the `UITableViewDelegate` and `UITableViewDatasource` protocol references.

It's a little inconvenient. You have to look at both protocols to see the full range of methods we can implement. In general, the data source methods are used to gather information about the data that will fill our table, while the delegate handles the table's appearance, user interactions, and other miscellaneous things. However, I could pick some nits over the exact division of labor.

Fortunately, when we create a table view controller, the controller is automatically set as both the delegate and the data source. It also automatically adopts both protocols. This means we just need to implement a few methods, and our table is ready to go.

There are really only two required data source methods: `tableView:numberOfRows InSection:` and `tableView:cellForRowAtIndexPath:`. We will also go ahead and implement the `numberOfSectionsInTableView:` method, since the template has already provided a stub for us.

Whenever the table needs to reload its data, it will first call `numberOfSectionsInTableView:` to determine the number of sections. Then, for each section, it will call `tableView:numberOfRows`

InSection: to determine the number of rows. Finally, for each row currently on screen, it will call tableView:cellForRowAtIndexPath:. This last call is where we configure our cell, displaying the correct information for that row.

Open HistoryTableViewController.m. At the top of the file, import our EntryDetail-ViewController, WeightHistoryDocument, and WeightEntry classes.

```
#import "EntryDetailViewController.h"
#import "WeightHistoryDocument.h"
#import "WeightEntry.h"
```

Next, all view controller subclass templates automatically include a class extension. Often, we will use this as a place to hold private properties that refer to user interface elements. However, currently, we need a different sort of private property. We want to observe all of the document's change notifications. Whenever we register for a notification, we need to make sure we unregister as well. Otherwise, we may leave dangling pointers behind in the notification center.

Since we will be using the block-based notification API, we will need to store opaque observer objects so that we can unregister them when we are done. We don't actually know the observer object's type—and it really doesn't matter. We can just save them as ids.

Inside the class extension, declare the following properties:

```
@interface HistoryTableViewController ()
@property (strong, nonatomic) id documentBeganObserver;
@property (strong, nonatomic) id documentInsertedObserver;
@property (strong, nonatomic) id documentDeletedObserver;
@property (strong, nonatomic) id documentChangeCompleteObserver;
@end
```

Next, navigate down to the numberOfSectionsInTableView: method. Our table view will always have just a single section. We could delete this method, since it defaults to 1; however, I usually like to leave it, just in case I want to add sections later.

Modify the method as shown here:

```
- (NSInteger)numberOfSectionsInTableView:(UITableView *)tableView
{
    return 1;
}
```

After that, scroll down to the tableView:numberOfRowsInSection: method. Here, we need to return the number of entries in our history. Fortunately, we created our count property, making this easy to do. Modify the method as shown here:

```
- (NSInteger)tableView:(UITableView *)tableView
 numberOfRowsInSection:(NSInteger)section
{
    return (NSInteger)self.weightHistoryDocument.count;
}
```

Again, our count property is an unsigned integer, and this method returns a signed integer. Since we turned on the more extreme warnings, we need to cast our count value into a signed value before we can return it.

Next, we need to modify tableView:cellForRowAtIndexPath:, but, before we do this, we need to discuss how table view cells are used.

Whenever we create a table view (or really, any scrolling view), we need to make sure it is as high-performance as possible. We want to avoid any hesitation or stuttering in the animation. The system should respond as if the user were actually moving the images behind the glass.

Obviously, if we created new cells for each row, we would be wasting a lot of time and effort. We only need enough cells to cover the whole screen. As they scroll off the top, they can be reused on the bottom.

To help support the recycling of cells, the system doesn't dispose of cells when they are removed from the table. Instead, it puts them in a pool to be reused. We can request these cells with one of two methods: dequeueReusableCellWithIdentifier: or dequeueReusable CellWithIdentifier:forIndexPath:.

The first is an older method. It will look for a cell in the pool with a matching identifier. If it cannot find one, it will return nil. To use this method, we must check the return value and create a new cell whenever it returns nil.

The second version is more advanced. It will always return a cell—automatically creating a new cell if there aren't any in the pool. Unfortunately, this means we also need to tell the system what type of cell to create for each identifier. We can do this automatically in our storyboard, or we could programmatically register our cells using registerNib:forCell ReuseIdentifier: or registerClass:forCellReuseIdentifier:.

Each unique cell layout needs its own identifier. Typically a table has only one type of cell, so we need only a single, unique identifier per table. However, we could use multiple cell styles inside a single table. In that case, each one must have its own, unique identifier.

Let's open Main.storyboard and set the cell type and identifier. Zoom in on the History Table View Controller, and select the Table View Cell.

Next chapter, we will learn how to create a custom cell for our table. For now, let's just use one of the standard cells. In the Attributes inspector, change the cell's Style to Basic. Then, in the Identifier text field, type **History Cell**.

Now, let's go back to HistoryTableViewController.m. Replace the existing tableView: cellForRowAtIndexPath: method with the implementation listed here:

```
- (UITableViewCell *)tableView:(UITableView *)tableView
        cellForRowAtIndexPath:(NSIndexPath *)indexPath
{
    static NSString *CellIdentifier = @"History Cell";

    UITableViewCell *cell =
    [tableView dequeueReusableCellWithIdentifier:CellIdentifier
                                   forIndexPath:indexPath];
```

```
WeightEntry *entry = [self.weightHistoryDocument
                         entryAtIndexPath:indexPath];

    cell.textLabel.text = [entry description];

    return cell;
}
```

We start by creating a cell identifier that matches the identifier we set in the storyboard. Next, we call dequeueReusableCellWithIdentifier:forIndexPath:. Since we're using the newer API, we do not need to check the return value. It will always return a valid cell—even if it has to create one for us. Finally, we use the entryAtIndexPath: method we created earlier to get the entry for this index path. We then set the cell's text to our entry's description.

As you can see, the work we did in WeightHistoryDocument is already starting to pay off. There's a very natural interface between our model and our history table view.

PASSING DATA ACROSS SEGUES

We have already set up the storyboard to create and display a new EntryDetailViewController whenever the user selects a row. However, we still need some way of passing our WeightEntry to the incoming view controller.

We do this using the prepareForSegue:sender: method. This method will be called after the incoming view controller is instantiated but before it is added to the view hierarchy. This means the controller has not yet loaded its view, so none of its outlets or actions are set yet.

Typically we use prepareForSegue:sender: to pass data over to the incoming view controller. The incoming view controller will then use this data to fill in its own views during its viewWillAppear: method.

In HistoryTableViewController.m, scroll down to the bottom and uncomment the prepareForSegue:sender: stub. Then modify the stub as shown here:

```
#pragma mark - Navigation


- (void)prepareForSegue:(UIStoryboardSegue *)segue sender:(id)sender
{
    if ([segue.identifier isEqualToString:@"Entry Detail Segue"])
    {
        EntryDetailViewController *controller =
        segue.destinationViewController;

        NSIndexPath *indexPath = [self.tableView indexPathForSelectedRow];
        controller.entry =
        [self.weightHistoryDocument entryAtIndexPath:indexPath];
    }
}
```

We start by checking to see which segue we are traversing. Our `HistoryTableViewController` has two separate segues—so we need to make sure it's the Entry Detail Segue, not the Add Entry Segue. It's probably obvious, but the segue's identifier property will match the identifiers we set in the storyboard.

Then we grab a reference to the destination view controller. Here we're using a common Objective-C trick. Since the destination view controller is an id type, we can freely assign it to any static object variable. The compiler will simply assume we know what we're doing. This is conceptually identical to casting the destination to a specific type; however, it looks a lot cleaner.

Next, we get the index path for the selected row and then use the index path to get the correct entry. We then pass this entry to the destination view controller.

NOTE: We should always perform some sort of check before working with the destination view controller—even if we have only a single segue from our view controller. This is a nice sanity check, and it prevents us from accidentally introducing errors later, when we add additional segues without modifying our code.

NOTE: Often, we will pass the same data to multiple segues. Sometimes it's easier to check and see whether the destination view controller has a given setter and then call the setter whenever it's available. This is conceptually similar to the way the tab bar controller passes the document to all its children. When used properly, this technique can keep our `prepareForSegue:sender:` method from getting too repetitive.

LISTENING FOR NOTIFICATIONS

One last task is left to set up. We need to update our table whenever our data changes. To do this, we will listen for the notifications sent by our `WeightHistoryDocument` object.

Using notifications is a little bit complicated. In many cases, we could achieve the same effect with less work using delegates, callback blocks, or other techniques. However, notifications have one huge advantage over all other technologies. Any number of observers can register for a single notification. This means we could have any number of views or controllers listening and updating whenever there is a change to the underlying document. This is important, since we're going to have at least two views that need to be updated: the History Table View and the Graph View.

Let's start by creating two methods: one to register for notifications and one to unregister. Let's start with the remove method, since it is easier. Place this method in `HistoryTableViewController.m`, after `prepareForSegue:sender:` and before `@end`.

```
- (void)removeNotifications
{
    NSNotificationCenter *center = [NSNotificationCenter defaultCenter];
```

```
if (self.documentBeganObserver)
{
    [center removeObserver:self.documentBeganObserver];
    self.documentBeganObserver = nil;
}

if (self.documentInsertedObserver)
{
    [center removeObserver:self.documentInsertedObserver];
    self.documentInsertedObserver = nil;
}

if (self.documentDeletedObserver)
{
    [center removeObserver:self.documentDeletedObserver];
    self.documentDeletedObserver = nil;
}

if (self.documentChangeCompleteObserver)
{
    [center removeObserver:self.documentChangeCompleteObserver];
    self.documentChangeCompleteObserver = nil;
}
}
```

While this looks big, it's really just the same step repeated over and over again. First, we grab a reference to the default notification center. Then, we check each of our observer properties. If the property has a valid value, we remove it from the notification center and set it to `nil`. This last step is a safety check, since removing the same observer twice will create errors.

Now, let's set up the notifications.

```
- (void)setupNotifications
{
    NSNotificationCenter *center = [NSNotificationCenter defaultCenter];
    NSOperationQueue *mainQueue = [NSOperationQueue mainQueue];
    WeightHistoryDocument *doc = self.weightHistoryDocument;
    __weak HistoryTableViewController *_self = self;

    self.documentBeganObserver =
```

```objc
    [center
     addObserverForName:WeightHistoryDocumentBeginChangesNotification
     object:doc
     queue:mainQueue
     usingBlock:^(NSNotification *note) {
         if ([_self isViewLoaded])
         {
             [_self.tableView beginUpdates];
         }
     }];

    self.documentInsertedObserver =
    [center
     addObserverForName:WeightHistoryDocumentInsertWeightEntryNotification
     object:doc
     queue:mainQueue
     usingBlock:^(NSNotification *note) {
         NSIndexPath *indexPath =
         note.userInfo[WeightHistoryDocumentNotificationIndexPathKey];
         NSAssert(indexPath != nil,
                  @"We should have an index path in the "
                  @"notification's user info dictionary");

         if ([_self isViewLoaded])
         {
             [_self.tableView
              insertRowsAtIndexPaths:@[indexPath]
              withRowAnimation:UITableViewRowAnimationAutomatic];
         }
     }];

    self.documentDeletedObserver =
    [center
     addObserverForName:WeightHistoryDocumentDeleteWeightEntryNotification
     object:doc
     queue:mainQueue
     usingBlock:^(NSNotification *note) {
         NSIndexPath *indexPath =
         note.userInfo[WeightHistoryDocumentNotificationIndexPathKey];
```

```
        NSAssert(indexPath != nil,
                @"We should have an index path in the "
                @"notification's user info dictionary");

        if ([_self isViewLoaded])
        {
            [_self.tableView
             deleteRowsAtIndexPaths:@[indexPath]
             withRowAnimation:UITableViewRowAnimationAutomatic];
        }
    }];

    self.documentChangeCompleteObserver =
    [center
     addObserverForName:WeightHistoryDocumentChangesCompleteNotification
     object:doc
     queue:mainQueue
     usingBlock:^(NSNotification *note) {
         [_self.tableView endUpdates];
     }];
}
```

Again, this looks like a wall of code, but it's basically just minor variations on a theme. We start by grabbing references to all the data we will need: the notification center, the main queue, our document, and a weak reference to self. We shouldn't let our blocks capture self, since this can introduce retain cycles. In fact, it actually does create retain cycles in this case. Worse yet, the compiler and the static analyzer aren't smart enough to catch them.

With our data prepared, we register for the four notifications, passing a block that will get called whenever we receive that notification. The WeightHistoryDocumentBeginChanges Notification and WeightHistoryDocumentChangesCompleteNotification are the simplest. They just check to see whether the view has been loaded. If it has, they call beginUpdates and endUpdates, respectively. The table view will group all the changes that occur between the beginUpdates and endUpdates call into a single animation.

For WeightHistoryDocumentInsertWeightEntryNotification, we extract the index path from the notification's userInfo dictionary. The NSAssert() function ensures that we actually received a valid index path. If we don't, it throws an exception. Finally, we check to see whether the view is loaded. If it is, we insert a row at the given index path. By specifying UITableViewRowAnimationAutomatic, we tell the table view to pick the best animation given the current state. It will then select an animation based on the row's position on the screen and the number of rows in the table.

`WeightHistoryDocumentDeleteWeightEntryNotification` is virtually identical to `WeightHistoryDocumentInsertWeightEntryNotification`, except we are deleting the row at the index path. Everything else is the same.

With these notifications in place, our table view will automatically adjust its contents to any changes in the underlying document.

Now, we just need to call `setupNotification` and `removeNotification`. We will start by setting up the notifications whenever our `weightHistoryDocument` property is set. This means we need to implement a custom setter.

Add the following method to `HistoryTableViewController.m`:

```
#pragma mark - Accessor Methods
- (void)setWeightHistoryDocument:(WeightHistoryDocument *)weightHistoryDocument
{
    if (_weightHistoryDocument)
    {
        [self removeNotifications];
    }

    _weightHistoryDocument = weightHistoryDocument;
    [self setupNotifications];
}
```

First, we check to see whether we already have a weight history document. If we do, we need to clear all our current notifications. Then we assign the incoming document to our property's instance variable. Finally we set up the notifications for the new document.

We also need to make sure we clear all the notifications when our class is deallocated. This means we must add a `dealloc` method, as shown here. I typically place the `dealloc` method at the top of the file, right after the `init` methods.

```
- (void)dealloc
{
    [self removeNotifications];
}
```

That's it. The basic features are in place. We'll expand on it more next chapter, as we add the ability to insert and delete `WeightEntries`. However, this is enough to do some rudimentary testing and make sure our document data is getting passed from scene to scene correctly.

TESTING OUR ARCHITECTURE

Right now we can run our application. It doesn't do much. We have our history with no entries. We can switch to the graph, which is completely blank. Going back to the history, we can tap the plus button to bring up the add entry scene—however, since we haven't added any way to dismiss this scene, we're now stuck.

Let's make sure the data is at least getting passed to our leaf views. As a quick check, add the following code to HistoryTableViewController.m, EntryDetailViewController.m, AddEntryViewController.m, and GraphViewController.m:

```
// TODO: Delete This After Testing!
- (void)viewDidAppear:(BOOL)animated
{
    [super viewDidAppear:animated];
    NSLog(@"%@ appeared", [self class]);
}
```

Now when we run the application and cycle through the views, we should get the following data printed to the console:

```
2013-08-21 22:04:40.852 Health Beat[11784:70b] HistoryTableViewController
→ appeared
2013-08-21 22:04:42.512 Health Beat[11784:70b] GraphViewController appeared
2013-08-21 22:04:43.645 Health Beat[11784:70b] HistoryTableViewController
→ appeared
2013-08-21 22:04:45.554 Health Beat[11784:70b] AddEntryViewController appeared
```

So far, so good. But, let's expand this to make sure our data is actually getting across. Modify the NSLog statement in HistoryTableViewController.m and GraphViewController.m to print out our document as well.

```
NSLog(@"%@ appeared, document = %@",
    [self class], self.weightHistoryDocument);
```

In EntryDetailViewController, we don't have a document, but we do have a weight entry. Modify the log message to print out the entry instead.

```
NSLog(@"%@ appeared, entry = %@",
    [self class], self.entry);
```

Now, run the application and cycle through the views. We should get the following printout:

```
2013-08-21 22:18:25.372 Health Beat[11994:70b] HistoryTableViewController
→ appeared, document = WeightHistoryDocument: count = 0, history = (
)
2013-08-21 22:18:40.172 Health Beat[11994:70b] GraphViewController appeared,
→ document = WeightHistoryDocument: count = 0, history = (
)
2013-08-21 22:18:41.298 Health Beat[11994:70b] HistoryTableViewController
→ appeared, document = WeightHistoryDocument: count = 0, history = (
)
2013-08-21 22:18:42.867 Health Beat[11994:70b] AddEntryViewController appeared
```

The iOS SDK has a handful of methods that are commonly used to perform vital tasks. We don't necessarily need to implement each of these in every application; however, we should at least give each one some thought. In addition, most of these methods have a corresponding notification that we could use to monitor these events in other parts of our code.

App Opening

These methods are called when the application first launches or when it returns from the background state. We will often use these methods to load the application's state and to perform other one-time configuration activities.

`application:didFinishLaunchingWithOptions:`

UIKit calls this `UIApplicationDelegate` method when the application first launches. We typically use it to perform one-time configuration tasks. Note, however, that the application will not appear onscreen until after this method returns. Therefore, we should avoid doing any potentially time-consuming activities during this method.

In particular, try to avoid tasks such as accessing remote servers. These may work fine in testing but fail when deployed to actual users (especially when people start using their phone in areas with poor reception). This could cause the application to freeze until the network connection times out, creating an unacceptably long delay when launching.

Basically, if we're going to read any data from disk or perform any network operations, we should launch it as an asynchronous task on a background thread. That way, our application will launch quickly and will remain responsive.

`applicationWillEnterForeground:`

UIKit calls this `UIApplicationDelegate` method when the application returns from the background state. This may be called multiple times as the user closes and opens the app.

`applicationDidBecomeActive:`

This `UIApplicationDelegate` method is called whenever the application becomes active. This includes both when the application first launches and after it returns from the background—however, it will also be called in a number of other situations, such as if the user ignores an incoming phone call or SMS message.

`viewDidLoad`

UIKit calls this `UIViewController` method once the controller's view has fully loaded. This method is called regardless of how the view was created—it could be loaded from a nib or programmatically built using the `loadView` method.

Note that views are lazily loaded. A view controller will wait to load its view until someone accesses its view property. Before this point, if the controller has any properties that refer to items in the view hierarchy, they will still be set to `nil`. However, by the time `viewDidLoad` is called, those properties will contain their correct values. This often makes `viewDidLoad` a convenient and safe place to perform additional setup or configuration.

In previous versions of iOS, views could be loaded and unloaded multiple times because of memory pressure. Unfortunately, the multiple loading/unloading tended to cause bugs when not handled properly. With iOS 6 and newer, the view will be loaded only once. If the system memory starts to run low, it may simply dispose of the graphics bitmap that stores the view's appearance—provided the view is not currently being displayed. This may cause the view to be redrawn, but it will not load or unload the view itself. This still gives us most of the memory savings we used to get by unloading the whole view, while avoiding most of the bugs.

Of course, you may still see references to `viewDidUnload` in older tutorials or code, but that method is now deprecated and will never get called.

App Closing

These methods are called when the application is closing or when it is moving to the background. You will often use these methods to save the application's state or to perform any cleanup activities before the application closes. In general, `applicationWillTerminate:` will be called only on applications that continue performing background tasks when the user switches to another application. Most applications will simply receive an `applicationDidEnterBackground:` as they go to the background. Once in the background, the system may silently kill them to free up more memory. As a result, we often need to perform identical cleanup operations in both methods.

`applicationWillTerminate:`

UIKit calls this `UIApplicationDelegate` method just before an application terminates. Somewhat surprisingly, modern iOS applications rarely receive this notification. The application must be executing in the background when it needs to terminate suddenly—usually in response to a low memory warning. More typically, when the user taps the home button, your application will move first to the background and will then become suspended. The application's current state is frozen in memory, but it's not actually running. If the system needs more memory, it will begin killing suspended applications, reusing their memory. In this case, the app dies silently without any additional notifications.

The `applicationWillTerminate:` method has approximately five seconds to perform any cleanup activities and return. If it takes longer than five seconds, the system watchdog will kill the application.

`applicationDidEnterBackground:`

This `UIApplicationDelegate` method is called before the application is sent to the background. We should perform any cleanup activities here, since our application may be terminated while in the background. As mentioned earlier, `applicationWillTerminate:` is

not called when our application is suspended, so this method is often our last chance to clean up the application before it dies.

Like `applicationWillTerminate:`, we have approximately five seconds to complete any actions. However, we can request additional time by calling `beginBackgroundTaskWithExpirationHandler:`.

Low Memory Warnings

These methods are called whenever our application receives a low memory warning. We should implement these methods to free up any unneeded resources. If the low memory condition persists, our app may crash. Remember, memory shortages are the most common source of iOS application crashes.

`applicationDidReceiveMemoryWarning:`

This `UIApplicationDelegate` method is called when the application receives a low memory warning. We can use it to free up any unneeded memory (for example, any cache memory our app may be holding onto) at the application level.

`didReceiveMemoryWarning`

This `UIViewController` method is called when the application receives a low memory warning. By default, if the controller's view is not currently in the view hierarchy (so it is not currently being displayed onscreen), the system will mark the graphical bitmap used by its view as available for reuse. If the system ends up using some of this memory, it will need to redraw the view the next time it is used. If the system does not end up using this memory, it will simply reclaim the memory and continue as if nothing had happened.

Most of the time, the default implementation is sufficient. We can override this method and perform any additional actions to free up memory here, but we must call the super method before we are done.

That's pretty good, but we don't actually have any entries, so we cannot test our EntryDetailViewController. Let's add some mock data whenever our application first launches. This will also be helpful when designing our user interfaces in Chapter 3, "Developing Views and View Controllers."

Open RootTabBarController.m. At the top of the file, import our WeightEntry class.

```
#import "WeightEntry.h"
```

Now, in the private method section, add the addMockData method.

```
- (void)addMockData
{
    NSTimeInterval twentyFourHours = 60.0 * 60.0 * 24.0;
    NSDate *now = [NSDate date];

    NSDate *yesterday =
    [now dateByAddingTimeInterval:-twentyFourHours];

    NSDate *twoDaysAgo =
    [yesterday dateByAddingTimeInterval:-twentyFourHours];

    WeightEntry *entry1 =
    [WeightEntry entryWithWeight:150.0 usingUnits:LBS forDate:twoDaysAgo];

    WeightEntry *entry2 =
    [WeightEntry entryWithWeight:152.0 usingUnits:LBS forDate:yesterday];

    WeightEntry *entry3 =
    [WeightEntry entryWithWeight:148.5 usingUnits:LBS forDate:now];

    [self.weightHistoryDocument addEntry:entry1];

    [self.weightHistoryDocument performSelector:@selector(addEntry:)
                             withObject:entry2
                             afterDelay:2.0];

    [self.weightHistoryDocument performSelector:@selector(addEntry:)
                             withObject:entry3
                             afterDelay:4.0];
}
```

FIGURE 2.17 Displaying the mock data

There's some complicated stuff going on here, so let's take it slowly. At the top, we're simply creating four dates. One is the current date and time. One is 24 hours ago. The last is 48 hours ago.

We then use these dates to generate three different WeightEntry objects. We add the first one immediately. Then we use performSelector:withObject:afterDelay: to add the second weight entry in two seconds, and the third in four seconds. If you just want to run code after a slight delay, performSelector:withObject:afterDelay: is a very easy way to set it up. There are other options (NSTimer or Grand Central Dispatch's dispatch_after()), but these are all more complicated than we need.

Then, modify viewDidLoad: to call this method as shown:

```
- (void)viewDidLoad
{
    [super viewDidLoad];
    self.weightHistoryDocument = [[WeightHistoryDocument alloc] init];
    [self addMockData];
    [self documentReady];
}
```

The end result is that our document will start with a single entry. A second entry will be added two seconds later. The third entry two seconds after that. If you run the app now and let it sit on the history scene, you can watch the animation as each entry is added (**Figure 2.17**). Good news! Not only is our communication working, but our notifications and updates are working as well.

Now, select one of the rows. The app should transition to the Weight Entry scene. It won't display anything interesting on the screen, but you should see something similar appear in the console:

```
2013-08-21 22:48:19.453 Health Beat[12400:70b] EntryDetailViewController
appeared, entry = 148.50 lbs entry from Aug 21, 2013, 10:46 PM
```

That's it. If the data is getting all the way out to our detail view, then we're done. If not, try to identify where the system breaks down, and go back and double-check those instructions. If it still doesn't work, download the source code for this chapter (http://www.freelancemadscience.com/ios7_source/) and make sure my code still works properly—sometimes updates to the OS can cause things to break. If the sample code works, compare it to your code and see whether you can find the problems.

WRAPPING UP

Our app builds and launches. We can switch between our tabs and our detail view and even bring up the modal view. Yes, it's just a skeleton—but the next few chapters will put some meat on these bones. In Chapter 3, we will flesh out the AddEntryViewController and continue to add features to HistoryTableViewController. In Chapter 4, we will look at drawing custom views with the GraphViewController, and in Chapter 5, we will save both the application data and set up the user defaults. In Chapter 6, we will add iCloud syncing. Finally, in Chapter 7, we will replace Health Beat's current model with Core Data.

There's one last step before we go. Let's commit our changes to the git repository. It's best to get into the habit of committing changes early and often. That way we can compare our current files with any of the previously committed versions, and if we have to roll back our changes, we can minimize the amount of work we're undoing. It's always better to have a large number of small, incremental steps than to have a few giant strides.

To commit all our changes, select Source Control > Commit. Enter **Chapter 2** as the commit message, and click Commit. That's it. Xcode should take care of the rest.

As we go through the book, try to commit your changes after we finish adding each feature to the application. That should give you several commits per chapter. Unfortunately, I don't have space to talk about Git further in this book; I will cover it in more detail in the "Other Tools of the Trade" bonus chapter, which can be found at www.freelancemadscience.com/creating-ios-7-apps-bonus-chap/.

OTHER RESOURCES

For more information, check out the following resources:

- **Peter Hosey's Warnings I turn on, and why**

  http://boredzo.org/blog/archives/2009-11-07/warnings

  This is the original source on enabling high-octane warnings in Xcode.

- **Freelance Mad Science: Advanced Storyboard Techniques**

  www.freelancemadscience.com/fmslabs_blog/2012/9/24/advanced-storyboard-techniques.html

  This is a blog post I wrote that contains quite a bit of useful, advanced information about storyboards, including detailed information about timing and advice on chaining storyboards, nibs, and programmatically loaded views together.

- **Key-Value Coding Programming Guide and Key-Value Observing Programming Guide**

  iOS Developer's Library

  These are the go-to resources for all information about KVC and KVO. KVC can be a surprisingly complex, especially when it comes to collections. So, this is well worth a read.

- **View Controllers Programming Guide for iOS**

  iOS Developer's Library

  This is an extensive discussion on view controllers. In many ways, view controllers are the backbones of our applications. The more you know about them, the better off you will be.

- **Resource Programming Guide**

  iOS Developer's Library

  This has all the squirrely details about nibs, storyboards, and much, much more.

CHAPTER 3

Developing Views and View Controllers

In this chapter, we will flesh out Health Beat's History, Entry Detail, and Add Entry scenes. As we proceed, we will gain more experience graphically laying out views and linking user interface elements to their view controllers. We will also build adaptive user interfaces using Auto Layout, add the ability to insert and delete weight entries, and adjust our font sizes using Dynamic Type. Through it all, you should get a better understanding of the role that views and view controllers play in a typical iOS app.

INITIAL HOUSEKEEPING

FIGURE 3.1 Searching our workspace

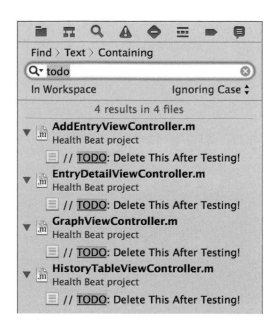

If you haven't done so already, we should delete the log messages we added in the previous chapter. If you followed my example and added the `//  TODO:` comments in the previous chapters, these will be easy to find.

Comments that start with `//  TODO:` show up in the jump bar when editing the file. This can act a great reminder, constantly nagging us to come back and fix unresolved issues—but it helps you find code only when you already know where to look. Fortunately, we can also search for *todo* and find all of these references.

Switch to the Find navigator and type **todo** in the search field. Make sure In Workspace and Ignore Case are selected. This should find all four locations (**Figure 3.1**). If you didn't add the comment, you can also search for *NSLog*. The project is currently small enough that this won't return too many references. You can then sort through them by hand.

Using the search as our guide, remove the `viewDidAppear:` method from `AddEntryViewController.m`, `EntryDetailViewController.m`, `GraphViewController.m`, and `HistoryTableViewController.m`.

NOTE: You can click the search result to open the code.

We're going to leave the mock data in place for now. It will be useful when developing and testing our user interfaces.

ROTATIONS, RESIZING, AND REDRAWING

Before we modify the user interface, let's launch the application and look at what we've built so far. Right now, the only interesting view is the History view, so we'll focus our attention there. Try rotating the device (⌘⇨ and ⌘⇦ in the simulator). Notice that we can rotate into the normal portrait orientation, to either the landscape-left or landscape-right orientation, but we cannot rotate it upside down.

This is the default behavior for an iPhone app. In general, we want to let the user decide how they want to hold their device. For iPad apps, this means letting them rotate it into all four orientations. On the iPhone, we generally prohibit turning the phone upside down. Why? Because it's a phone. If a call comes in, we don't want the user accidentally talking into the speaker and listening at the microphone (yes, not only do Apple engineers think about these things, but they write them into their HIG guidelines).

The default rotations are managed (in part) by the target settings. Click the blue Health Beat icon in the Project navigator. Make sure the Health Beat target and the General tab are selected. In the Deployment Info settings, you should see Device Orientation settings. Portrait, Landscape Left, and Landscape Right are selected.

Deselect everything but Portrait, and run the app again. Now, when you rotate the device, the screen does not change. It remains locked in the portrait orientation.

Try checking all four orientations. Run the app again. You'll notice that despite checking Upside Down, we can still rotate only into the default three orientations. That's because these settings are only half of the story.

The system will also call the supportedInterfaceOrientations method to calculate which rotation orientations are allowed. This is a UIViewController method—but the system doesn't call this on every view controller. It simply calls it on our application's root view controller—or on the topmost presented view controller that fills the entire screen. This means only our RootTabBarController and our AddEntryViewController (when displayed) have any say in the matter.

> **NOTE:** supportedInterfaceOrientations was introduced with iOS 6. Before then, many of the container view controllers would first ask their child controllers before allowing rotation. This often meant every view controller contributed to rotation decisions. If you didn't correctly implement the rotation methods in one controller, you could disable rotations throughout the entire app. By putting control in the hands of a single controller at a time, supportedInterfaceOrientations significantly simplifies our rotation logic.

Open RootTabBarController.m and add the following method:

```
- (NSUInteger)supportedInterfaceOrientations
{
    return UIInterfaceOrientationMaskAll;
}
```

Now run the app. The screen should freely rotate into all four orientations.

`supportedInterfaceOrientations` simply returns a bitmask of the orientations. The `UIInterfaceOrientationMask` enum defines the four basic orientations, plus a few useful combinations. Here, we're using `UIInterfaceOrientationMaskAll` to enable all four orientations. There's also `UIInterfaceOrientationMaskLandscape` for just the left and right landscape orientations, and there's `UIInterfaceOrientationMaskAllButUpsideDown` for the default iPhone behavior.

The system takes the intersection of the orientations specified in `supportedInterface Orientations` and the target settings when determining whether an orientation is allowed. An orientation must be enabled in both places before the rotation will occur. By default, `supportedInterfaceOrientations` returns `UIInterfaceOrientationMaskAllButUpsideDown` on the iPhone and `UIInterfaceOrientationMaskAll` on the iPad. With very few exceptions—such as games that must be played in a landscape orientation—we probably shouldn't change these settings.

We actually want the default behavior for our app, so delete the `supportedInterface Orientations` method and uncheck Health Beat's Upside Down setting.

However, we're not quite done with rotations. Launch the app again and rotate into the three supported orientations. Notice how the table automatically resizes to take advantage of the wider screen. Now try launching the app using a different sized simulator—for example, iPhone Retina (4-inch). Again, the History table view automatically adapts to the longer screen.

The size of our application's user interface can change for a number of reasons. Rotations and screen sizes are the two most obvious examples—but they are not the only ones. We will also lose 20 points off the top of our screen if the user is currently on a phone call or recording audio.

Regardless, our interface needs to adapt to these changes in size. There are three main approaches: programmatically laying out the UI, autoresizing masks, and Auto Layout.

NOTE: Spoiler alert: Auto Layout is the newest, most powerful, and most complicated solution to this problem. It is also essentially required if we want to take advantage of Dynamic Type. We'll discuss this in greater depth in the "Auto Layout" section.

PROGRAMMATICALLY LAYING OUT THE UI

The first option is to programmatically define the location of all our user interface elements. We can then update their position and size on demand. As you can probably guess, this is a tedious and error-prone process. So, we probably want to use one of the automated APIs whenever possible. There are, however, two good reasons for learning to lay things out programmatically.

- We need to understand how the system lays out views if we want to be able to use autoresizing masks or Auto Layout effectively.

- Sometimes we just can't get the automated systems to do what we want. In those cases, we have no choice but to modify part of the layout in code. Note: this mostly occurs when using autoresizing masks. Unless you are radically changing the view's layout between orientations, there are few situations that Auto Layout cannot handle.

Before we look at methods for laying out our views, we need to know a bit about the view hierarchy and view geometry.

THE VIEW HIERARCHY

The view hierarchy defines our application's user interface. This is a collection of nested UIView and UIView subclasses. The hierarchy starts with our application's window. The window typically contains a single view, our application's root view. The root view then contains any number of subviews, controls, and other user interface elements. If we want something to appear on the screen, we must add it to the view hierarchy.

The inverse is also true. Everything that appears on the screen is a UIView or a subclass of UIView. The UIView class manages a rectangular region onscreen. As we will see, each view is defined in terms of its upper-left corner, its width, and its height.

UIView defines a number of properties that let us specify its position, size, and appearance. These include frame, backgroundColor, tintColor, alpha, and clipsToBounds. Many of these can also be set in the Attributes inspector in Interface Builder. As we will see in Chapter 4, "Custom Views and Custom Transitions," some of these properties are also animatable. See the UIView Class Reference for a complete description of the UIView class and all its properties.

Each view also has its own coordinate system. By default, the origin is in the upper-left corner—though this can be modified by adding affine transforms to rotate, translate, or scale the coordinate system.

VIEW GEOMETRY

Positions in the coordinate system are given using a wide range of Core Graphics data types. Their definitions are shown in **Table 3.1**.

TABLE 3.1 Core Graphics Data Types

TYPE	DEFINITION
CGFloat	`typedef float CGFloat; // on 32-bit devices`

CGPoint	`struct CGPoint {`
	`    CGFloat x;`
	`    CGFloat y; };`
	`typedef struct CGPoint CGPoint;`

CGSize	`struct CGSize {`
	`    CGFloat width;`
	`    CGFloat height; };`
	`typedef struct CGSize CGSize;`

CGRect	`struct CGRect {`
	`    CGPoint origin;`
	`    CGSize size; };`
	`typedef struct CGRect CGRect;`

These are all defined in the CGGeometry reference. CGGeometry also defines a number of functions to help create, compare, and manipulate these values. We will get some experience using these functions in both this and the next chapter.

Each view's size and location are defined by three interrelated properties: frame, bounds, and center.

- **Frame:** The frame is a CGRect that defines our view's size and position in its superview's coordinate system.
- **Bounds:** The bounds is a CGRect that defines our view's size and position in its own coordinate system. Most of the time, the bounds' size will be equal to the frame's size, and the bounds' origin will be set to {0, 0}. This may change; however, if you're deliberately offsetting the view's content or if you apply a rotation, scale, or translation transformation to the view.
- **Center:** The center is a CGPoint that defines the position of our view's center in the superview's coordinate system. We often use the center to move or align views.

Changing any of these will affect the others. Specifically, when you modify the frame, the system will automatically recalculate the bounds and center. When you modify the bounds, the center remains fixed, but the system recalculates the frame. Finally, when you modify the center, the bounds remain unchanged, but the frame is modified.

NOTE: Our application's main screen and window will always have their origins in the upper-left corner in the device's portrait orientation. This does not change as you rotate the device. Our root view, however, may rotate, giving it a different coordinate system. The difference between the screen/window coordinate system and the rest of the view hierarchy can easily cause layout bugs if not handled properly.

Pragmatically this means if we want to resize a view around its center, we can change its bounds. If we want to resize it relative to the upper-left corner, we can change its frame. If we just want to move it around, we can modify the center.

We also need to think about the coordinate system when using these values. If possible, we want to grab the coordinates in the correct coordinate system. This is probably easier to show than to describe. Consider the following code:

```
CGSize size = superview.bounds.size;
CGFloat width = size.width / (CGFloat)2.0;
leftView.frame = CGRectMake(0.0, 0.0, width, size.height);
rightView.frame = CGRectMake(width, 0.0, width, size.height);
```

We are going to lay out our left and right views inside our superview, so we start by grabbing our superview's bounds. Specifically, we grab the size from our superview's bounds.

As I said earlier, the size will often be the same in both the frame and the bounds. So, why do we specifically grab the bounds' size? Well, if we add a scale or rotation transformation to this view, the frame and bounds sizes will no longer match. So, while using the frame may work (at least initially), it's always safest to grab the correct value.

OS X and iOS use different coordinate systems. OS X places the origin in the bottom-left corner, while iOS uses the top left. Most of the time, we can ignore these differences, unless we're porting code between the desktop and our mobile devices.

However, some of the low-level frameworks will default to the OS X coordinate system. If you're doing low-level graphics or text manipulation, you may find that your results are upside down and backward. If this happens, the solution is easy. We just need to modify the coordinate system before drawing.

For example, we could transform the graphic context, translating the y-axis by the view's height and then setting the y-scale to -1.0. Sample code is shown here:

```
CGContextTranslateCTM(context, 0, self.bounds.size.height);

CGContextScaleCTM(context, 1.0, -1.0);
```

We then use the `size` to calculate the sizes and positions of our `leftView` and `rightView`. Note that we specify their position and size by setting each view's `frame`. The subview's `frame` and the superview's `bounds` use the same coordinate system. So, everything here works as expected.

Unfortunately, we cannot always get the values in the coordinate system we want. Fortunately, `UIView` defines a number of methods to help us convert from one coordinate system to another. These methods include `convertPoint:fromView:`, `convertPoint:toView:`, `convertRect:fromView:`, and `convertRect:toView:`.

For example, we often want to center a view in its superview. It may, therefore, be tempting to set our subview's center equal to our superview's.

```
subview.center = view.center;
```

This, however, may not work as expected. The problem is, we want the view's center in its own coordinate system, but `view.center` returns the value in its superview's coordinate system. These values could be considerably different—especially if the view is our application's root view and our device is rotated. Remember, the application's window does not rotate; it is always in portrait orientation.

We can solve the problem by converting the center to our view's coordinate system before using it.

```
CGPoint center = [view convertPoint:view.center fromView:view.superview];
subview.center = center;
```

There's one last point that's worth mentioning. If you use a transform to rotate a view to an arbitrary angle, its `frame` becomes its bounding box in the superview's coordinate system. This means there is no longer a direct relationship between the `frame` property and our view's upper-left corner or size. If you're rotating views, you typically need to use `center` and `bounds` to perform your calculations, not `frame`.

ADDING, REMOVING, AND REORDERING VIEWS

Each view maintains an array of its subviews. When the screen is drawn, the view is drawn first; then its subviews are drawn in order. This proceeds, depth-first, down the entire view hierarchy. UIView defines a number of methods to let us add, remove, and reorder our subviews. The most common methods, and a brief description, are listed here:

- addSubview: Adds the provided view as a subview.
- bringSubviewToFront: Moves the specified subview to the end of the subview array. This means it will appear on top of its siblings.
- sendSubviewToBack: Moves the specified subview to the beginning of the subview array. This means it will appear below its siblings.
- removeFromSuperview   Removes the target from its superview. Notice that adding and removing are asymmetrical. We call addSubview: on the superview, but we call removeFromSuperview on the subview.
- insertSubview:atIndex: Adds the provided subview at the specified index in the subviews array.
- insertSubview:aboveSubview: This method takes two view arguments. It adds the first view as a subview but positions it immediately after the second view in the subview array. This means it will appear just above the second view, when drawn.
- insertSubview:belowSubview: This method takes two view arguments. It adds the first view as a subview but positions it immediately before the second view in the subview array. This means it will appear just below the second view, when drawn.
- exchangeSubviewAtIndex:withSubviewAtIndex: This method swaps the two views in the subview array, changing the drawing order.

As we will see in Chapter 4, there are also transition animations to let us animate adding, removing, and exchanging our views.

RESPONDING TO CHANGE IN SIZE

A view's size and position are determined by its frame property. This means all views have a fixed height and width. Their location is also defined as a fixed distance from the top and a fixed distance from the left edge of their superview.

While this lets us easily specify an unambiguous layout for our controls, it doesn't give us any flexibility. If the view's size changes, we must re-layout everything, cycling through all our interface elements and repositioning and resizing each one.

Fortunately, this is fairly easy (albeit tedious to the extreme). We can reposition a view by modifying either its center or frame property. We can also resize it by modifying either the frame or bounds properties. Of course, the calculations required to properly resize and reposition our view may be arbitrarily complex, but the act of resizing and repositioning it is easy enough.

If we want to programmatically lay out our views, we typically modify these properties in our view controller's viewWillLayoutSubview or viewDidLayoutSubview methods. These methods are called when our view is first created and whenever our view's bounds change. We can also implement the UIView layoutSubviews method to similarly fine-tune the layout of a custom view's subviews.

UIViewController also defines a few methods for specifically dealing with rotations. willRotateToInterfaceOrientation:duration: is called just before the rotation occurs. We might override it to stop expensive drawing or updating operations during rotation. Additionally, if we want to use completely different user interfaces in the landscape and portrait orientations, we can use this method to swap our views.

didRotateFromInterfaceOrientation: is called just after the rotation completes. We usually use this to reenable anything we disabled in willRotateToInterfaceOrientation: duration:. Finally, willAnimateRotationToInterfaceOrientation:duration: is called from within the rotation's animation block. We can override this to add animations that should occur as part of the rotation.

Notice that we don't typically use these methods to lay out our subviews as a result of the rotation. The viewWillLayoutSubview or viewDidLayoutSubview methods should automatically handle that for us. Remember, the rotation will change our bounds—and changing the bounds will trigger the layout methods.

AUTORESIZING MASKS

While programmatically repositioning one or two subviews isn't hard, the task quickly becomes unwieldy for even moderately complex user interfaces. Ideally, we would like to automate some, if not all, of this work. In many cases, we can do this by simply setting each view's Autoresizing mask.

Autoresizing lets us define six parameters that describe how a view will respond to changes in its superview size. These are the left margin, right margin, top margin, bottom margin, height, and width. Each of these can be set to be either fixed or flexible.

Here are the rules: Fixed parameters have a set size. They will not change as the superview shrinks and grows. Flexible parameters, on the other hand, can shrink and grow. Left margin + width + right margin will always equal the superview's width. Similarly, top margin + height + bottom margin will equal the superview's height.

If you have more than one flexible parameter for a given dimension, the changes will be split between them. On the other hand, the margins have a higher priority than the height and width—so if you set all three to fixed, the size parameter will be ignored, and the height (or width) will change with the superview.

By default, views have fixed top and left margins, fixed height and width, and flexible bottom and right margins.

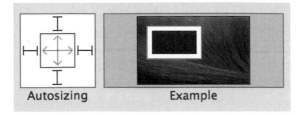

FIGURE 3.2 Interface Builder's Autosizing tool

The masks can be set programmatically by passing a bitmask to the view's `autoresizeMask` property. Or it can be configured in Interface Builder using the Autosizing tool in the Size inspector (**Figure 3.2**).

When using Interface Builder's Autosizing tool, the red I-bars indicate a fixed margin, while the red arrows indicate a flexible height or width. Tap the control to turn them on or off. The Example shows a mini-animation demonstrating how your view's size will change as its superview shrinks and grows. This makes it easy to visually verify your settings.

NOTE: The Autosizing tool will only appear if Auto Layout is turned off. By default, Auto Layout is turned on for all nib files or storyboards. You can turn it off on a file-by-file basis. Open the storyboard or nib, and select the File inspector. In the Interface Builder Document settings uncheck the "use Autolayout" checkbox.

This system has several advantages. It is relatively simple. Use it once or twice and you understand how it handles most common layout situations. Its biggest problem, however, comes from this simplicity. It can handle only relatively simple layouts. Specifically, it works best when only one element in a row (or column) is flexible. Trying to manage multiple flexible elements tends to produce an interface that feels somewhat sloppy, as the space between elements grows and shrinks with the view's size.

If we want more precise, complex changes, we need to either manage the layout programmatically or switch to Auto Layout.

AUTO LAYOUT

Auto Layout is a declarative, constraints-based layout engine. Apple created Auto Layout to fill in the gaps left by Autoresizing. In theory, it should eliminate the need to programmatically lay out our view hierarchies. Instead of specifying a view's size or location, Auto Layout lets us define complex relationships between views, giving us an incredible amount of power—but this power comes at a cost. Auto Layout is much harder to understand and set up than Autoresizing.

There are two main challenges to using Auto Layout. The first is the technical challenge. We must learn the Auto Layout API and Interface Builder's controls before we can use it effectively.

The second challenge is mental. Auto Layout requires a fundamental shift in the way we think about views. When using Auto Layout, we no longer specify a view's size and position using its `frame`, `bounds`, and `center`. Instead, we specify a number of constraints. Picking the correct set of constraints is like solving logic problems. And, like any new puzzle, it can be baffling and frustrating at first. Rest assured, it gets easier.

Auto Layout's constraints can be represented as linear equations, as shown here:

```
Attribute_1 = Multiplier * Attribute_2 + Constant
```

The attributes can be any of the following:

```
Left Edge
Right Edge
Top Edge
Bottom Edge
Leading Edge
Trailing Edge
Width
Height
CenterX
CenterY
Baseline
Not An Attribute
```

Of these, three merit special mention. Leading Edge is the first edge you run across based on the current local's reading direction. For left-to-right languages like English, this would be the left edge. Trailing Edge is the opposite, the right edge for English. By using the Leading Edge and Trailing Edge (instead of Left Edge and Right Edge), our UI elements will automatically reorder themselves when we switch from a left-to-right language to a right-to-left language.

"Not An Attribute" indicates that the attribute (and multiplier) will not be used in this calculation. We can use this to define constant values.

Here are some examples in pseudo-code:

```
// Example 1: Setting a constant height
View's Height = 0.0 * Not An Attribute + 40.0;


// Example 2: Setting a fixed distance between two buttons
Button_2's Leading Edge = 1.0 * Button_1's Trailing Edge + 8.0;


// Example 3: Make two buttons have the same width
Button_2's Width = 1.0 * Button_1's Width + 0.0;
```

```
// Example 4: Centering a view in its superview
View's CenterX = 1.0 * Superview's CenterX + 0.0;
View's CenterY = 1.0 * Superview's CenterY + 0.0;

// Example 5: Giving a view a constant aspect ratio
View's Height = 2.0 * View's Width + 0.0;
```

To use Auto Layout, we define a set of rules, and the system tries to fulfill them. Unfortunately, like most rules-based systems, each individual constraint may seem simple enough—but as they are combined, they may create unintended consequences. As the number of constraints grows, it gets harder and harder to accurately guess what the system will do at runtime. My advice is to build your interfaces iteratively and test them often.

SUFFICIENT, NONAMBIGUOUS LAYOUTS

To generate predictable results, we must declare constraints that are both sufficient and nonambiguous. Typically this means we need at least four constraints per view: one to define its height, one to define its width, one to define its x-coordinate, and one to define its y-coordinate. Of course, there are many ways to skin this cat, but as long as we declare two of the possible attributes for each dimension, we should be fine. For example, to specify a view's y-axis, we could specify the Top and Bottom, Top and Height, Bottom and Height, Center Y and Height, or Baseline and Height. Other combinations are possible (Top and Center Y, for example), but these will be somewhat rare.

We also need to avoid assigning too many constraints—creating conflicts that cannot be simultaneously satisfied. For example, I cannot define a view's Top, Height, and Bottom. One of these will need to change as the superview's height changes.

So far this seems fairly straightforward. Just create two and only two x-dimension constraints and two and only two y-dimension constraints for each view in your view hierarchy. You should be good to go. Of course, nothing about Auto Layout will ever be that straightforward. The problem is that I lied.

Actually constraints don't have to be linear equations. They can also be inequalities. For example, we could define a minimum width for a view as shown here:

```
View's Width >= 0.0 * Not An Attribute + 20.0;
```

When you use inequalities, you will need more than four constraints to specify an unambiguous layout. To make matters worse, each constraint also has a priority. Priorities range from 1 to 1,000. If it's set to 1,000, the constraint is required. Anything less than 1,000 is optional. The system will try to satisfy all the optional constraints in order from highest priority to lowest.

Finally, some controls have a natural size. Buttons, for example, are typically 30 points tall and wide enough to hold their title text. Text fields, on the other hand, are also 30 points tall but don't have a preferred width. We say that these views have an intrinsic size—and this automatically generates a whole new set of optional constraints for us.

INTRINSIC SIZES

We can set the intrinsic size of a `UIView` subclass by overriding its `intrinsicContentSize` method. This method should return a `CGSize`. This could be a fixed size, or a size calculated from the view's contents. If the view does not have an intrinsic size for a given dimension, it should use `UIViewNoIntrinsicMetric` for that dimension. By default, `UIView` returns {`UIViewNoIntrinsicMetric` , `UIViewNoIntrinsicMetric`}.

If we need to recalculate the intrinsic size (for example, after changing the view's content), we should call `invalidateIntrinsicContentSize`. The system will then use the new intrinsic size on the next layout pass.

Auto Layout creates four constraints based on a view's intrinsic size: two pairs of inequalities per axis. The compression resistance maintains the view's minimum height and width, while the content hugging defines its maximum. The linear equations are shown here:

```
// Compression Resistance
View's Height >= 0.0 * Not An Attribute + View's Intrinsic Height;
View's Width >= 0.0 * Not An Attribute + View's Intrinsic Width;


// Content Hugging
View's Height <= 0.0 * Not An Attribute + View's Intrinsic Height;
View's Width <= 0.0 * Not An Attribute + View's Intrinsic Width;
```

By default, the content hugging priority is set to 250, and the compression resistance priority is set to 750. Some elements may have different defaults. For example, the content hugging priority for `UILabel` is 251. This means most other user interface elements will be stretched before the label. We can modify the priorities for these constraints by calling `setContentCompressionResistancePriority:forAxis:` and `setContentHuggingPriority:forAxis:`. Note that Apple has provided a few constants to make setting the priorities easier (see **Table 3.2**).

TABLE 3.2 Priority Constants

CONSTANT NAME	VALUE
`UILayoutPriorityRequired`	1,000
`UILayoutPriorityDefaultHigh`	750
`UILayoutPriorityDefaultLow`	250

This gives us considerable flexibility when it comes to our views. For one button, we might set both the compression resistance and the content hugging to `UILayoutPriorityRequired`. This would force the button to a fixed size. For another, we might set the x-axis content hugging to `UILayoutPriorityDefaultLow` and set all others to `UILayoutPriorityRequired`. This would give it a fixed height and a minimum width but would allow it to grow to fill the available space.

SPECIFYING CONSTRAINTS

There are four ways to set up a view's constraints. We can simply use the default constraints. We can programmatically define each constraint. We can programmatically set multiple constraints using the Visual Format language. Finally, we can set up the constraints in Interface Builder.

While we will primarily use Interface Builder throughout this book, understanding how to build constraints in code really helps clarify exactly what Interface Builder is doing for us.

DEFAULT CONSTRAINTS

Whenever we add a view to the view hierarchy, the system automatically generates a set of constraints to match the view's Autoresizing mask. As we saw earlier, all views have an Autoresizing mask with a fixed left margin, fixed top margin, fixed height, and fixed width.

Sometimes these default constraints can prove useful. In many cases, it might be easier to define the Autoresizing mask and use the auto-generated constraints, rather than creating our own constraints by hand. Additionally, the default constraints act as an escape valve. As long as we are using the default constraints, we can continue to modify the view's size and position by simply modifying its frame, bounds, and center properties. As we will see, this can be particularly helpful when animating views or using UIDynamics.

However, we will often want to use our own constraints—and that means we need to disable the default constraints first. To disable the default constraints, simply call setTranslatesAutoresizingMaskIntoConstraints: and pass NO.

CONSTRAINT API

Our constraints are instances of the NSLayoutConstraint class. We can create new constraints by calling NSLayoutConstraint's constraintWithItem:attribute:relatedBy: toItem:attribute:multiplier:constant: method. This method is a direct translation of the linear equation we saw earlier.

The first two arguments define the view and the attribute we are constraining. The attribute must be of type NSLayoutAttribute, as shown here:

```
enum {
    NSLayoutAttributeLeft = 1,
    NSLayoutAttributeRight,
    NSLayoutAttributeTop,
    NSLayoutAttributeBottom,
    NSLayoutAttributeLeading,
    NSLayoutAttributeTrailing,
    NSLayoutAttributeWidth,
    NSLayoutAttributeHeight,
    NSLayoutAttributeCenterX,
    NSLayoutAttributeCenterY,
    NSLayoutAttributeBaseline,
```

```
    NSLayoutAttributeNotAnAttribute = 0
};
typedef NSInteger NSLayoutAttribute;
```

Next we pass an NSLayoutRelation to define the type of equation, as shown here:

```
enum {
    NSLayoutRelationLessThanOrEqual = -1,
    NSLayoutRelationEqual = 0,
    NSLayoutRelationGreaterThanOrEqual = 1,
};
typedef NSInteger NSLayoutRelation;
```

The next two arguments define the view and the attribute for the right side of the equation. Again, the attribute must be an NSLayoutAttribute. These are followed by the multiplier and the constant (both CGFloats).

So, the following call:

```
NSLayoutConstraint *constraint =
[NSLayoutConstraint constraintWithItem:view1
                            attribute:attribute1
                            relatedBy:relationship
                               toItem:view2
                            attribute:attribute2
                           multiplier:mx
                             constant:c];
```

defines the following linear equation:

```
view1.attribute1 view2.attribute2 * mx + c;
```

Now, I described the items as views. That's not 100 percent correct. Technically, they are ids. Most of the time we will be creating constraints between views (or other UIView subclasses). However, there are two notable exceptions. UIViewController defines two properties that we can also use in our constraints: topLayoutGuide and bottomLayoutGuide.

The exact location of the top layout guide will change depending on which bars are visible. If the scene has a navigation bar, it will be the bottom of the navigation bar. If the scene has only a status bar, it will be the bottom of the status bar. If the scene doesn't have any bars, it will use the top of the view. By creating a constraint to the top layout guide, we can guarantee that our controls are positioned correctly below the scene's bars and that the location will automatically adapt if we change the bars.

The bottom Layout Guide works similarly. If the scene has a toolbar or tab bar, it will be at the top of the bar. If not, it will be the bottom of the view in the current orientation.

These guides are particularly important in iOS 7. Our views should extend under the bars, which are semi-transparent, allowing a highly blurred and somewhat desaturated hint of our view to show through. This adds a touch of context to our layout and can be particularly effective when displaying scrolling content. However, obviously, when designing nonscrolling views, we don't want our controls to accidentally slide up under the bars.

When laying out nonscrolling scenes, we should always create our constraints to the layout guides instead of the top and bottom of the scene's main view. This will guarantee that our layouts adapt, even if we change the workflow. For example, we can embed the scene in a navigation controller or change the incoming segue from push to modal, and our layout will automatically adjust.

Once we have created a constraint, we still need to add it to the system. Constraints should be added to the closest ancestor of both views in the constraint. By ancestor, I mean either the view itself, its superview, its superview's superview, or any other superview moving up the view hierarchy.

For example, if we create a constraint between a view and its superview, we should add the constraint to the superview. If we add a constraint between two sibling buttons, we should add the constraint to their shared superview.

We add constraints by calling UIView's addConstraint: method and passing our constraint.

The following code unambiguously defines a set of constraints for a button and a text view. In a left-to-right language (like English), the button should be a constant distance from the superview's upper-left corner. It also has a fixed width. The text field should be a fixed distance from the button's right edge. It is also vertically centered on the button. Finally, the right edge of the text field should be a fixed distance from the superview's right edge. Therefore, as our superview resizes, the text field's width will grow and shrink to fill the space.

```
// Setup Button's Constraints
NSLayoutConstraint *buttonX =
[NSLayoutConstraint
 constraintWithItem:myButton
 attribute:NSLayoutAttributeLeading
 relatedBy:NSLayoutRelationEqual
 toItem:view
 attribute:NSLayoutAttributeLeft multiplier:1.0
 constant:20.0];

[view addConstraint:buttonX];

NSLayoutConstraint *buttonY =
[NSLayoutConstraint
 constraintWithItem:myButton
 attribute:NSLayoutAttributeTop
 relatedBy:NSLayoutRelationEqual
```

```objc
  toItem:view
  attribute:NSLayoutAttributeTop
  multiplier:1.0
  constant:20.0];

[view addConstraint:buttonY];

// Setup Button's Intrinsic Size Priorities
[myButton
  setContentHuggingPriority:UILayoutPriorityRequired
  forAxis:UILayoutConstraintAxisHorizontal];

[myButton
  setContentCompressionResistancePriority:UILayoutPriorityRequired
  forAxis:UILayoutConstraintAxisHorizontal];

// Setup Textfield Constraints.
NSLayoutConstraint *textX =
[NSLayoutConstraint
  constraintWithItem:myTextField
  attribute:NSLayoutAttributeLeading
  relatedBy:NSLayoutRelationEqual
  toItem:myButton
  attribute:NSLayoutAttributeTrailing
  multiplier:1.0
  constant:5.0];

[view addConstraint:textX];

NSLayoutConstraint *textY =
[NSLayoutConstraint
  constraintWithItem:myTextField
  attribute:NSLayoutAttributeCenterY
  relatedBy:NSLayoutRelationEqual
  toItem:myButton
  attribute:NSLayoutAttributeCenterY
  multiplier:1.0
  constant:0.0];
```

```
[view addConstraint:textY];

NSLayoutConstraint *textWidth =
[NSLayoutConstraint
 constraintWithItem:myTextField
 attribute: NSLayoutAttributeTrailing
 relatedBy:NSLayoutRelationEqual
 toItem:view
 attribute: NSLayoutAttributeTrailing
 multiplier:1.0
 constant:-20.0];

[view addConstraint:textWidth];
```

In many ways, these are the easiest constraints to understand. However, as you can see, they require a lot of typing. Fortunately, the Visual Formatting language greatly reduces this—but it can also obscure some of the details, making it somewhat harder to understand.

VISUAL FORMATTING SYNTAX

Hands up if you ever spent an afternoon drawing ASCII art. This feature is for you.

NSLayoutConstraint supports a visual formatting syntax for constraints. This allows us to "draw" our constraints using an ASCII-art like syntax. The full details can be found in the iOS Document and API Reference, Cocoa Auto Layout Guide, but I'll go through the basics here.

We start by creating an NSString that defines a group of constraints. These strings will use the symbols shown in **Table 3.3**.

NOTE: Do not use any spaces in your visual format string.

Here are a few examples:

- |-[view1]: Sets the standard spacing between the superview's leading edge and view1's leading edge.
- [view1]-[view2]: Sets the standard spacing between the leading edge of view2 and the trailing edge of view1.
- [view1][view2]: Aligns the leading edge of view2 to the trailing edge of view1. There will be no space between the views.
- V:|-[view1]: Sets the standard vertical spacing between the superview's top and view1's top.

TABLE 3.3 Auto Layout Visual Format

SYMBOL	MEANING
|	The edge of the containing superview.
[<view_string>] [<view_string>(<width>)] [<view_string>(<width>@priority>)]	Specifies a view in our UI. Optional arguments can be used to declare the view's width and the width's priority. The width and priority values can be literal numbers or constants. The width value can also be an inequality. You can also set a view's width equal to another view. Simply use the other view's view string for the width. Finally, we can create complex arguments by providing multiple width@priority pairs separated by commas.
- -<width>- -<width@priority>-	These represent the space between views. If no width is specified, the system will use standard spacing. The width and priority can be a literal number or constant. The width value can also be an inequality. And we can create complex arguments by providing multiple width@priority pairs separated by commas.
<view_string>	Used to refer to a view in the views dictionary.
<metric_string>	Used to refer to constant values in the metrics dictionary. These can be used for width and priority values.
<= == >=	Used to specify the relationship when setting inequalities. By default, relationships are assumed to be equal (==).
V:	Vertical layout. All descriptions that refer to width refer to height instead.

- [view(200)]: Sets view's width to 200 points.
- [view(<=200)]: Sets view's width to 200 points or less.
- [view(>= 50,<=200)]: Sets view's width to greater than 50 but less than 200 points.
- [view1(==view2)]: Sets view1's width equal to view2's width. Note that the equal relationship is optional; however, it can make the formatting string easier to read.
- [view(200@500)]: Sets view's width to 200 points and its priority to 500.
- [view(standard@high)]: Sets view's width to the standard constant. Also sets its priority to the high constant.

We can also combine these strings into complex statements. The following example lays out three equal-sized buttons using standard system spacing between all the elements:

```
|-[view1]-[view2(==view1)]-[view3(==view2)]-|
```

We create these constraints using `NSLayoutConstraint`'s `constraintsWithVisual Format:options:metrics:views:` method. The first argument is our visual formatting string. The second argument specifies how the elements should be aligned and whether we should use LTR, RTL, or Leading-To-Trailing relationships. Finally, we pass in two dictionaries. The first defines our constants, and the second contains our list of views.

The keys in these dictionaries must match the metric_strings and view_strings used in our visual formatting. The values must be an `NSNumber` (for metrics) or `UIView` (for views). We can also place the top and bottom layout guides in the views dictionary, letting us draw constraints to them as well.

While we can create the view dictionary by hand, we can also use the `NSDictionary OfVariableBindings()` function to automatically build one for us. To call this method, pass in our views as arguments. It returns a dictionary that uses our view's name as the key.

This means the following two definitions for views are identical:

```
// Create a local variable for the guide
id topGuide = self.topLayoutGuide;


// Version 1
NSDictionary *views =
NSDictionaryOfVariableBindings(view1, view2, view3, view4, topGuide);


// Version 2
NSDictionary *views =
@{@"view1":view1, @"view2":view2, @"view3":view3,
  @"view4":view4, @"topGuide":topGuide};
```

`constraintsWithVisualFormat:options:metrics:views:` returns an array of constraints. We can add these to a view by calling `addConstraints:`.

So, we can redefine our button and text field's constraints using visual formatting, as shown here:

```
NSDictionary *views =
NSDictionaryOfVariableBindings(myTextField, myButton);


// Defines both the horizontal constraints and the vertical alignment
NSArray *constraints =
[NSLayoutConstraint
```

```
constraintsWithVisualFormat:@"|-[myButton]-[myTextField]-|"
options:NSLayoutFormatAlignAllCenterY |
NSLayoutFormatDirectionLeadingToTrailing
metrics:nil
views:views];

// Define's the button's vertical position
NSArray *verticalConstraints =
[NSLayoutConstraint
 constraintsWithVisualFormat:@"V:|-[myButton]"
 options:0
 metrics:nil
 views:views];

[view addConstraints:constraints];
[view addConstraints:verticalConstraints];



// Still need to set the button's intrinsic size priorities
[myButton
 setContentHuggingPriority:UILayoutPriorityRequired
 forAxis:UILayoutConstraintAxisHorizontal];

[myButton
 setContentCompressionResistancePriority:UILayoutPriorityRequired
 forAxis:UILayoutConstraintAxisHorizontal];
```

It's still a large chunk of code, but we've managed to compress five separate constraints into two visual syntax calls. Obviously, the more UI elements you have in each row or column, the greater the savings.

However, there are some limitations. For example, we cannot set a view's width relative to its height. If we want that sort of relationship, we will need to explicitly define the constraint in code.

EDITING CONSTRAINTS IN INTERFACE BUILDER

Auto Layout took a fair bit of criticism in iOS 6. Most people agreed that it was potentially useful and powerful—what they objected to was the way Interface Builder handled Auto Layout.

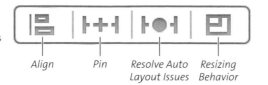

FIGURE 3.3 Interface Builder's onscreen tools

Align   Pin   Resolve Auto Layout Issues   Resizing Behavior

Interface Builder tried to be too helpful. Whenever we added a view to a storyboard or nib file, it automatically added constraints for that view based on its position in the scene. It would also actively prevent us from making ambiguous or invalid constraints.

This worked great for simple layouts—but once things got a bit complex, you would inevitably want to change Interface Builder's default constraints. The problem was, you couldn't necessarily just add or delete constraints—that would create an invalid set of constraints. If you were clever, careful, and a little bit obsessive, you could manage to work around these restrictions and massage the constraints until they were exactly the way you wanted them. However, if you then made any changes to the user interface, Interface Builder would re-generate all your constraints, undoing all your hard work.

Fortunately, all of that is behind us. With Xcode 5, Interface Builder no longer tries to be helpful. Ironically, by doing less, it has become a lot more useful. Yes, there's a downside. We have to specify each and every constraint ourselves. It won't make any assumptions for us. However, we have complete freedom to add, modify, and remove as many constraints as we want. Even more importantly, since it no longer tries to help us, it won't accidentally undo our work.

When you add a user interface element in Interface Builder, the system will begin by using its default constraints. The element will have a fixed position relative to the top-left corner of its containing view. It will also have a fixed width and a fixed height. As soon as we add our first constraint, Interface Builder removes the default constraints. We must then add a full set of constraints for that item.

Interface Builder has many constraint editing features. We won't be able to cover them all here. Instead, we will do a quick overview of the most important editing features and then get some real-world experience using these tools in Health Beat.

Interface Builder provides four onscreen constraints: Align, Pin, Resolve Auto Layout Issues, and Resizing Behavior (**Figure 3.3**).

The Align tool lets us select two or more elements and then set constraints to align their edges, centers, or baselines. We can also align elements with the containing view (**Figure 3.4**). We can also specify which frames get updated when we add these constraints.

For the Pin tool, we can select a single item and then set constraints to its nearest neighbor (which may be the containing superview a nearby view, or the closest layout guide). We can also specify a fixed height or width for the item. Finally, we can select multiple items and give them equal heights or widths or even align them (**Figure 3.5**). I'd be a bit careful using the "nearest neighbor" controls, especially in complex scenes. Its definition of nearest neighbor may be different than yours. However, notice that you can click the drop-down arrow on the nearest neighbor settings to specify the correct neighbor.

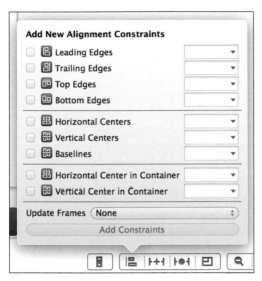

Add New Alignment Constraints

☐ ⊞ Leading Edges ▾
☐ ⊟ Trailing Edges ▾
☐ ⊡ Top Edges ▾
☐ ⊞ Bottom Edges ▾

☐ ⊞ Horizontal Centers ▾
☐ ⊞ Vertical Centers ▾
☐ ⊞ Baselines ▾

☐ ⊞ Horizontal Center in Container ▾
☐ ⊞ Vertical Center in Container ▾

Update Frames (None ⬍)

Add Constraints

FIGURE 3.4 Auto Layout's Align tool

Add New Constraints

▾

▾ ⊡ ▾

▾

Spacing to nearest neighbor

☐ ⊟ Width ▾
☐ ⊟ Height ▾

☐ ⊟ Equal Widths
☐ ⊟ Equal Heights

☐ ⊞ Align (Leading Edges ⬍)

Update Frames (None ⬍)

Add Constraints

FIGURE 3.5 Auto Layout's Pin tool

Update Frames   ⌥⌘=
Update Constraints   ⇧⌘=
Add Missing Constraints
Reset to Suggested Constraints ⌥⇧⌘=
Clear Constraints

Update All Frames in View Controller
Update All Constraints in View Controller
Add Missing Constraints in View Controller
Reset to Suggested Constraints in View Controller
Clear All Constraints in View Controller

FIGURE 3.6 Auto Layout's Resolve Auto Layout Issues tool

When Resizing Views Apply Constraints to...
  Siblings and Ancestors
✓ Descendants

FIGURE 3.7 Auto Layout's Resizing Behavior tool

We will primarily use the Resolve Auto Layout Issues tool to update our view's frame based on its current constraints, or to clear away all the constraints, giving us a fresh start. There are some controls to autogenerate missing constraints or revert to recommended constraints—but I don't recommend using them. In my experience, they rarely do what I expect and typically cause more problems than they solve. Notice that the menu is divided into two parts. The top half acts on the currently selected item. The bottom half acts on all the user interface elements in the view controller (**Figure 3.6**).

Finally, we have the Resizing Behavior tool (**Figure 3.7**). This provides toggles that let us define which constraints are updated live while we resize views within the scene. I typically leave this set to the defaults.

The Editor > Canvas menu can also be useful when working with constraints. We can control exactly what we want Interface Builder to show. We can even set the canvas to automatically update our frames as we add constraints. While this may sound like a good idea, it usually isn't. Typically we need to set a number of constraints before updating the frame makes sense. Otherwise, it may be swept off the screen or shrunk until it is teeny-tiny. Usually I leave the canvas settings alone, unless I'm debugging a specific problem, and I think the additional visualizations will help.

The Size inspector also has a number of useful settings. It lets us set the content hugging and compression resistance priorities for our selected view. It also lists all the constraints for a given view, letting us delete, select, or edit those constraints.

Onscreen constraints appear as little I-bars or lines. Orange constraints are warnings. These can occur either because the layout is still ambiguous or because our view is in the wrong location or is the wrong size. In the latter case, it will also show the correct frame as a dashed orange box. Red constraints indicate errors. These occur when we have conflicting constraints. Blue constraints mean everything is fine. The element's position and size are uniquely defined by our constraints.

We can select the constraints, either by clicking them directly in the editor or by selecting them in the Document Outline or Size inspector. Once selected, we can modify the constraint's relationship type, constant value, and priority from the Attributes inspector. We can also specify that a constraint is a placeholder, which will be removed at build time. Presumably, we would programmatically replace it at runtime.

Finally, we can draw connections between our constraints and outlets in our Interface Builder. This lets us programmatically modify or replace the constraints.

OTHER CONSTRAINT METHODS

We can override a few other methods to help control Auto Layout. These may not be particularly useful in our day-to-day coding, but it's nice to know that they exist.

The first is `requiresConstraintBasedLayout`. This `UIView` class method returns `NO` by default. Our custom `UIView` subclasses should override this to return `YES` if they require Auto Layout.

NOTE: In my testing, I haven't found any cases where the system's behavior changes based on the `requiresConstraintBasedLayout` method's return value. If you add a view that uses Auto Layout to a view hierarchy using Autoresizing, the system simply converts the entire view hierarchy to Auto Layout. However, future code—including our own code or third-party libraries—may check this value, so we should make sure our `UIView` subclasses behave correctly.

Next, when Auto Layout aligns two views, it actually aligns them based on their alignment rectangle—not on their frames. This might not be immediately apparent, since the alignment rectangle is set to the view's `frame` by default. Still, if our view has some content that shouldn't be considered when aligning, a badge icon that sticks out past the view's regular content, for example, we may want to set the alignment rectangle to a subsection of its frame.

The easiest way to set the alignment rect is to override the view's `alignmentRectInsets` method. This returns the `UIEdgeInsets` that define the offset between the alignment rectangle and the view's `frame`. Alternatively, we can override `alignmentRectForFrame:` and `frameForAlignmentRect:` methods to convert between the alignment rect and its `frame`. By default, these methods call `alignmentRectInsets` and perform the conversion based on those insets.

Finally, a view can save some or all of its constraints when it is archived. Each constraint has a `shouldBeArchived` property. By default, this is set to `NO`, and the constraint is not saved with the view. However, if we want the constraint to be saved, we can simply set its `should-BeArchived` property to `YES`.

TROUBLESHOOTING AUTO LAYOUT

With Xcode 5's Auto Layout support, troubleshooting is a lot easier than it used to be. We can visually see whether we have ambiguous or conflicting layouts. Warnings and errors will also appear in the Document Outline. Still, sometimes we need to dig a bit deeper to figure out what, exactly, is going wrong.

There are really three types of problems we can run into when creating constraints. Our constraints could be ambiguous, they could have conflicts, or they could be logically incorrect.

DETECTING AMBIGUOUS LAYOUTS

A view has an ambiguous layout if there is more than one possible layout that satisfies all its constraints. Typically ambiguous layouts cause our view to appear in the wrong location or to have the wrong size. Sometimes the layout may change between one run and the next, or the view may otherwise jump or shift unexpectedly.

Usually this means we need to add constraints. As stated earlier, each view needs at least four constraints to specify both its position and its size. If you are using inequalities, more constraints are needed.

However, we can also have ambiguous layouts when we have conflicting nonrequired constraints with exactly the same priority. The system won't be able to determine which constraint should be fulfilled. In these cases, we have to modify one of the priorities to break the tie.

If we're programmatically creating constraints, we won't be able to rely on Interface Builder to detect ambiguous layouts for us. In these cases, detecting and debugging ambiguous layouts is largely a matter of trial and error; however, the system does provide a few tools to help. First, we have a variety of debugging methods. These methods should be used only during debugging, such as while writing code to explore the layout and determine why our application is not behaving properly.

`UIView`'s `hasAmbiguousLayout` is our front-line tool. Quite simply, it will return `YES` if the view has an ambiguous layout. It will return `NO` otherwise. This provides a quick test. If the layout is ambiguous, we can explore further. If not, then either our constraints are either just buggy or there's something else wrong with our code.

Next, `UIView`'s `exerciseAmbiguityInLayout` will randomly change the view's frame to another value that also satisfies its constraints. By cycling through several alternates, you should soon get a feel for the missing constraint.

Finally, `constraintsAffectingLayoutForAxis:` returns an array containing all the constraints affecting the view's layout along the specified axis. We can then examine these constraints to get a better feel for the problem.

Remember, if you can find a good place to set a breakpoint, you can call these methods from the debugger's console:

```
p (BOOL)[self hasAmbiguousLayout]
```

Instruments also provides some assistance. There is a Cocoa Layout instrument that will track any changes to our constraints. Again, this is primarily used when programmatically modifying or replacing constraints—we can use Instruments to verify that the constraints are changing when and where we expect.

DETECTING CONFLICTS

Conflicts are both more serious and easier to detect. Conflicts occur when two (or more) required constraints cannot both be satisfied. Fortunately, the system throws an exception when it detects conflicting constraints.

By default, the system also catches this exception. It logs a warning to the console and then chooses one of the constraints to ignore. It will then continue to lay out our views.

A sample warning is shown here:

```
2012-12-28 01:07:09.880 AutoLayoutTest[43733:c07] Unable to simultaneously
→ satisfy constraints.
Probably at least one of the constraints in the following list
→ is one you don't want. Try this: (1) look at each constraint and
→ try to figure out which you don't expect; (2) find the code that
→ added the unwanted constraint or constraints and fix it. (Note:
→ If you're seeing NSAutoresizingMaskLayoutConstraints that you don't
→ understand, refer to the documentation for the UIView property
→ translatesAutoresizingMaskIntoConstraints)
(
    "<NSLayoutConstraint:0x7581490 H:[MyView:0x7580c30(60)]>",
    "<NSLayoutConstraint:0x7581320 H:[MyView:0x7580c30(80)]>"
)

Will attempt to recover by breaking constraint
<NSLayoutConstraint:0x7581320 H:[MyView:0x7580c30(80)]>
```

> **NOTE:** When possible, `NSLayoutConstraint`'s description method uses visual formatting. Where this is not possible, it will use pseudocode to write out the linear equation directly.

In this example, you can see that we've set two different constraints specifying the height of MyView. In one case, we set the height to 60 points. In the other, we set it to 80 points. The system chose to ignore the 80-point constraint and continue to lay out the view.

We can set a breakpoint to detect this exception. Either set an exception breakpoint or set a symbolic breakpoint for objc_exception_throw. However, this will provide useful information only for constraints set in a view's updateConstraints method. Constraints added anywhere else will throw an exception during the next update phase—not at the point when the constraint was added.

LAYOUT TIMING

Whether we use Auto Layout, Autoresizing, or old-school programmatic layouts, our views are processed in three phases: Update Constraint, Layout, and Display.

The system performs these phases once each time we cycle through the run loop. These phases affect only dirty views—views that have been explicitly marked as needing an update. The system will check to see whether our view needs to have its constraints updated, needs to have its layout updated, or needs to be redrawn before calling the relevant method. Therefore, if nothing has changed, nothing much happens.

UPDATE CONSTRAINTS PHASE

This constraint is useful only if you are using Auto Layout. Here, the system starts with the leaf views and works up the view hierarchy toward the application's window. If a view's constraints need to be updated, the system will call the view's updateConstraints method. We typically override this method in our view subclasses to dynamically provide constraints at runtime.

We should never call updateConstraints directly. Instead, call setNeedsUpdateConstraints. This will mark the view for updating, and the system will call updateConstraints for us on the next pass through the Update Constraints phase.

UIViewController has a similar method named updateViewConstraints. We can alternatively override this method to programmatically provide constraints at the controller layer. updateViewConstraints is also triggered by setNeedsUpdateConstraints, and it is called after its view's updateConstraints method.

If we ever need to change a view's constraints at runtime, we should remove the old constraints and then call setNeedsUpdateConstraints. Our custom updateConstraints or updateViewConstraints methods can then provide the new constraints.

LAYOUT PHASE

The Layout phase proceeds in a similar manner; however, it starts with the window and works down toward the leaf views. Again, if a view's layout needs to be updated, the system will call the view's layoutSubviews method. We indicate that a view's layout needs to be updated by calling the setNeedsLayout method.

Additionally, if a view's content has changed, we can invalidate its intrinsic content size by calling invalidateIntrinsicContentSize. The next time through the layout phase, the system will call the view's intrinsicContentSize method to get its new content size.

If you're not using Auto Layout, the default implementation of layoutSubviews does not do anything. However, we can override this method to provide our own custom layouts. With Auto Layout enabled, the view will take its list of constraints and calculate the proper bound, center, and frame properties for its contained views.

While I do not recommend mixing code that directly modifies the bounds, center, and frame with Auto Layout, if you need to do this, be sure to set your custom values after the call to [super layoutSubviews]. Otherwise, the system will clobber your values with its newly calculated values.

DISPLAY PHASE

Finally, we have the Display phase. This works the same with or without Auto Layout. The system will call drawRect: as necessary for our views. We can trigger drawing by calling set-NeedsDisplay or setNeedsDisplayInRect:.

Note that iOS heavily caches its views. Often, we draw the view once, and then we never draw it again. The system will continue to reuse the cached version, even if we move the view, cover and uncover it, change its size, rotate it, or even fade it in and out.

This can cause rendering problems when enlarging a view's frame. By default the system will simply stretch the cached version to fit. We can force our views to redraw whenever their frame changes by setting their content mode, as shown here:

```
self.view.contentMode = UIViewContentModeRedraw;
```

There is one time when the system will redraw our views. If a view is not currently part of the view hierarchy and a memory warning comes in, then the system may clear the view's graphics cache. If this happens, the next time you place the view onscreen, the system will call drawRect: to redraw it.

UPDATING HEALTH BEAT

We have a lot to accomplish, so let's get back to our project. We want to let users add and remove weight entries. We need to design both our Add Entry and Entry Detail views. And, we want to spruce up our history view. Let's start with the history view.

CUSTOM TABLE VIEW CELLS

Currently we are displaying our weight entries using one of the prebuilt cell layouts. The basic cell gives us a single black, left-aligned label and an optional image view. iOS actually defines four prebuilt cell layouts. However, we often want to create our own. And, with storyboards, custom cells are very easy to use.

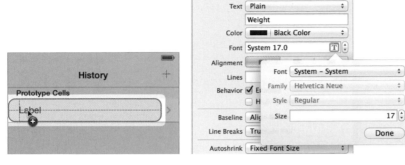

FIGURE 3.8 Editing the table view cell's content

FIGURE 3.9 Changing the font

FIGURE 3.10 Our custom table view cell

NOTE: Interface Builder's support for custom table view cells and static tables are built into storyboards. You cannot use them on nib files. In fact, I find the storyboard's expanded table view support so useful, I feel that it is one of the most compelling reasons to use storyboards.

Open Main.storyboard and navigate to the History Table View Controller. Select our table view cell, and in the Attributes inspector, change the Style to Custom. We now have an almost blank slate to work with. Our cell is empty except for the disclosure indicator on the right side.

Drag a label from the library into the cell. Use the guidelines to make sure the label is against the left margin and centered in the cell. Also note how the cell's content area is highlighted in blue—this is the only space we have to work with (**Figure 3.8**).

Double-click the label and change its text to Weight. Then drag a second label, and line it up on the content area's right margin. Double-click this label and change its text to Date. These are just placeholders—we'll dynamically replace them with real data at runtime.

Select the Weight label. We want to change its font. In the Attributes inspector, click the icon inside the Font text field. This will bring up the fonts control (**Figure 3.9**).

Click the Font pop-up button. This will bring up a list of fonts. In particular, look at the fonts listed under Text Styles. These are our Dynamic Types. We will talk about Dynamic Types more in the "Dynamic Type" section. For now just understand that the user will be able to set the font size for their device, and we will update our user interface to match their settings.

For the Weight label, set the font to Headline. For the Date, set it to Subhead. We should also set the Date's Alignment to right-aligned (⊟). Our custom cell should look like **Figure 3.10**.

FIGURE 3.11 Drawing
the constraint

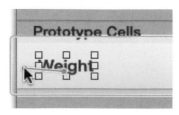

ADDING AUTO LAYOUT CONSTRAINTS

Now we need to add our Auto Layout constraints. Our goal is to have the weight fixed on the left side. The date label will stretch to fill the remaining space, with the standard spacing between them. Everything should be centered vertically in the cell.

Let's start with the Weight. Control-click the Weight label and drag to the left. Let go of the mouse anywhere inside the cell but left of the label (**Figure 3.11**). From the pop-up menu, select Leading Space to Container. This places an orange I-bar to the left of our label, and a dashed orange box now surrounds our label. Congratulations, we've successfully created an ambiguous layout.

Let's take a quick look at the problem. In the top-right corner of the History Table View Controller scene's section in the Document Outline, you should see a little reddish-orange arrow icon. If you click this, it will show you all the warnings and errors for our constraints. We can get similar information in the Issue navigator—but I like the feedback that the Document Outline provides.

In our case, it shows us that we're missing a constraint for our Weight label. We need to specify its Y position. It also says that we have a misplaced view. The Weight label's frame isn't quite in the correct position given its current constraints.

We always want to completely constrain our layout before we update our frames. In this case, adding the Y constraint is easy. Repeat the procedure we performed before. Control-drag from the Weight label to someplace in the cell left of the label. This time, select Center Vertically in Container. Interface Builder will add a blue line across the middle of our cell. Also notice that our I-bar has turned blue.

Our label has an intrinsic height and width, so this should be enough to unambiguously constrain it. Remember, we need only two vertical constraints and two horizontal constraints, and the intrinsic sizes act as one constraint in each dimension.

Unfortunately, the dashed box around our label indicates that something's still not quite right. If you look at our warnings again, you'll see that the view is still misplaced.

Select the Weight label, and then click the Resolve Auto Layout Issues button. In the pop-up menu, select Update Frames. Note: you could alternatively select the Editor > Resolve Auto Layout Issues > Update Frames menu item.

Once that's done, the orange box should vanish. Our Document Outline will also show that there are no Auto Layout issues.

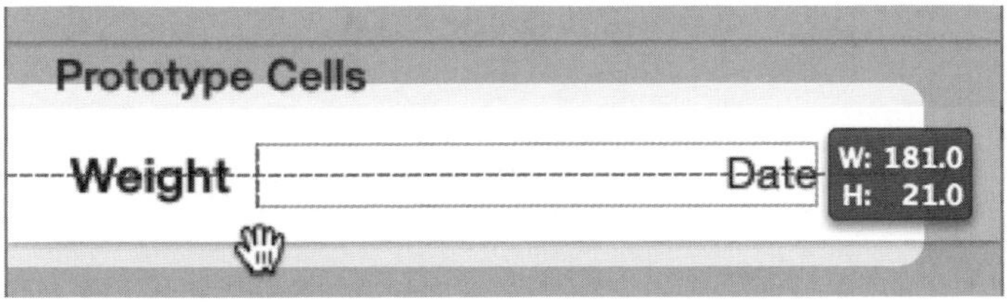

FIGURE 3.12 Stretching the Date label to fit

Date is going to be similar. However, before we begin, stretch the Date label so that its right edge is next to the Weight label. You should see a short blue guideline when you get close. Use that to line up the edges (**Figure 3.12**).

Now Control-drag from the Date label to someplace inside the cell but to the right of the label. Select Trailing Space to Container. Now, Control-drag from Date to Weight. Select Center Y. Control-drag from Date to Weight again, this time selecting Horizontal Spacing.

Once we do that, we get all kinds of orange. What happened here? If we look at the Auto Layout warnings and errors in our Document Outline, it says that we have content priority ambiguity. The layout engine cannot fulfill all our constraints. Specifically, it cannot fulfill the content hugging constraints for both our Weight and Date labels. Fortunately, both of these constraints are optional. Unfortunately, they have the same priority. The system doesn't know which one to choose.

We want our Weight to remain static and have our Date stretch to fill the space. So, let's make Weight's intrinsic size mandatory. Select the Weight label and switch to the Size inspector. Set its Content Hugging and its Content Compression Resistance Priorities to 1000. This means our weight label will always be the correct size for its content. Of course, this size will vary depending on the font size and the amount of text—but the layout engine won't stretch or shrink it in response to rotations or other resizing events.

While this looks good, it might not be pixel perfect. The problem with drawing the constraints this way is that the system will use the current spacing to determine its constraints. So, if you're 21 points from the side, it will set a 21-point constraint, not the standard 20-point constraint.

So, let's double-check everything. In the Document Outline, expand the list of constraints. For the Center Y and Baseline alignments, the Constant should be 0. For the Horizontal spaces, the Constant should be 20 for the margins and 8 between the labels. However, I typically just click the Standard checkbox and let the system sort out the exact sizes.

With that done, everything is blue except Date's frame. Update its frame, and we're good to go.

CONNECTING OUR OUTLETS

Now we need some way to programmatically change our Weight and Date's text when we configure the cell. There are two ways of doing this. We could just add a unique tag to each of the labels. Then, in our view controller, we could simply search for the labels by their tag number. This is simple, in that it doesn't require any extra classes. However, I don't think it really communicates the developer's intent. Four months down the line, we might not remember what tag 23 meant.

Instead, I like to make custom `UITableViewCell` subclasses. These subclasses will have properties for all the UI elements we need access to. It's a little more work to set up, but I think it's a lot cleaner, easier to understand, and, in the long run, more maintainable.

Let's start by creating our new class. In the Project navigator, Control-click the Views group and select New File… > iOS > Cocoa Touch > Objective-C class. Make it a subclass of `UITableViewCell`, and name it **HistoryCell**.

We need to declare two outlets for our labels. Unfortunately, we cannot Control-drag from Interface Builder to our code this time. We have to create them the old fashioned way—by typing.

Open `HistoryCell.h` and add the following two lines to the `@interface` block:

```
@property (weak, nonatomic) IBOutlet UILabel *weightLabel;
@property (weak, nonatomic) IBOutlet UILabel *dateLabel;
```

These are simply property declarations; however, we've added the `IBOutlet` keyword. `IBOutlet` is simply defined as white space. The compiler doesn't see it at all. However, Xcode is smart enough to search for it and knows that it defines a drag target for Interface Builder.

Also, we're deliberately putting the outlets in the public interface this time. When it comes to view controllers, I see a real benefit to hiding away our interface outlets. We don't want anything outside our view controller manipulating them directly. However, for simple views like this, it seems like an exercise in busywork with no real concrete benefits. These labels will be part of `HistoryTableViewController`'s view hierarchy, and it's OK for the view controller to modify any part of its hierarchy. Furthermore, `HistoryCells` will still be hidden away inside `HistoryTableViewController`. So, that's good enough for me.

OK, let's wire up our cells. Open `Main.storyboard` again. Make sure you're zoomed in on the History Table View Controller scene, and select our custom cell. In the Identity inspector, set its class to **HistoryCell**. Then, Control-click the cell to bring up its connections HUD. Connect our `dateLabel` outlet to our Date label and our `weightLabel` outlet to our Weight Label (drag from the circle beside the outlet to the control and let go).

Now we just need to use these outlets. But, before we can do that, let's add some helper methods to let us more easily create properly formatted weight strings.

FORMATTING WEIGHT STRINGS

Numbers are surprisingly complex. Different parts of the world have different ways of representing them. In particular, the decimal mark—the symbol that separates the integer part and the fractional parts of a number—can change from region to region. Some places use a period. Others use a comma. The choice of a decimal mark also affects the thousands separator. When you start representing percentages or currency, it just gets more complex.

And dates are even worse. There are a number of ways to represent a date, even in a single region. Some formats spell out the month names or use abbreviations; others use just numbers and punctuation. Furthermore, the order of the elements and the exact means of separating them can vary.

Ideally, we would like to internationalize the presentation of numbers and dates. We've already seen this done for dates in Chapter 2, "Our Application's Architecture." We used an NSDateFormatter to produce localized dates in our WeightEntry's description method.

Now, we should do the same thing for the weight value. But it's more than just using a correctly localized number. We should also create methods to properly append the correct weight unit as well. Wrapping all this in a few helper methods will make displaying our weight data and switching units much easier.

> **NOTE:** Localization is a big topic. A full description is outside the scope of this book. However, we will look at the basics in Chapter 9, "The Last Mile."

Open WeightEntry.h, and add the following method declarations just before the @end directive:

```
+ (NSString*)stringForUnit:(WeightUnit)unit;

+ (NSString*)stringForWeight:(float)weight ofUnit:(WeightUnit)unit;

+ (NSString*)stringForWeightInLbs:(float)weight inUnit:(WeightUnit)unit;


- (float)weightInUnit:(WeightUnit)unit;

- (NSString*)stringForWeightInUnit:(WeightUnit)unit;
```

Now, switch to WeightEntry.m, and let's implement the methods. But, before we do, we need to create a static NSNumberFormatter. Add the following, just after our LBS_PER_KG constant declaration:

```
static NSNumberFormatter* formatter;
```

There are two ways to use number formatters. We could use the localizedString FromNumber:numberStyle: class method, but that offers only six predefined styles. We need to customize the default decimal style a bit, which means we need to create our own NSNumberFormatter instance.

However, we don't want to create a new number formatter every time we display a weight string. Instead, let's create a static formatter, which we can then freely access anywhere in the WeightEntry.m file. Unfortunately, we cannot create a number formatter constant— since there is no way to instantiate the number formatter at compile time. Instead, we'll do the next best thing. We will use a regular static variable and set its value during our class's initalize method.

There are actually two class methods that we can use to initialize class-level resources. One is load, and the other is initialize. They both have their little quirks and gotchas.

The load method runs early. Very early. In fact, it runs before main(). As a result, the system may not be properly set up yet. For example, we won't have an autorelease pool—if we're using any Objective-C code, we need to provide our own. Also, other classes may not be properly loaded. In general, all the frameworks we link to should be loaded. Other classes in our project may or may not be loaded, and any frameworks that link to our code will not be loaded.

Another oddity, when we looked at Categories in the bonus chapter, "Objective-C," I emphasized how important it was to never, never, ever override methods in a category. Turns out, there is one exception: load. Load is not called like other methods.

The system calls load only if it is implemented in the class or one of the class's categories. It will call the class's load method first and will then call any of the categories' load methods. This lets us provide custom initialization in both our classes and our categories and often makes load an ideal place to do dangerous things such as dynamically implementing methods or even replacing existing methods.

initialize runs much later. It is run the first time a class is used. This means it won't run if the class is never used. At this point, we have a full Objective-C runtime available, and all our classes are loaded, so it is a generally a safer place do our custom initialization. There is one small catch, however. initialize might get called multiple times.

If you override initialize in a class and then create subclasses of that class, your initialize method will get called once for the class and then once for each subclass that doesn't also override initialize. As a result, we always want to check our classes before running any code. This is true, even if we don't currently plan on making any subclasses. You never know what the future might hold.

So, let's add the initialize method as shown here:

```objc
+ (void)initialize
{
    if (self == [WeightEntry class])
    {
        formatter = [[NSNumberFormatter alloc] init];
        [formatter setNumberStyle:NSNumberFormatterDecimalStyle];
        [formatter setMinimum:[NSNumber numberWithFloat:0.0f]];
        [formatter setMaximumFractionDigits:2];
    }
}
```

We start by making sure that the WeightEntry class, and not one of its subclasses, is indeed calling this. Then we instantiate our number formatter. We set it to the decimal style and then modify it so that it has a minimum value of 0.0 and so that it will show our weights to only two decimal places.

With our formatter in place, let's look at our string methods, one at a time.

```objc
#pragma mark - String Methods

+ (NSString*)stringForUnit:(WeightUnit)unit
{
    switch (unit)
    {
        case LBS:
            return @"lbs";

        case KG:
            return @"kg";

        default:
            [NSException
             raise:NSInvalidArgumentException
             format:@"The value %d is not a valid WeightUnit", unit];
    }

    // This will never be executed.
    return @"";
}
```

The stringForUnit: method simply takes a WeightUnit value and returns the corresponding string. If we pass in a value that does not correspond to one of our defined units, it throws an exception. Note that the final return is simply added to make the compiler happy. That code cannot be reached.

```objc
+ (NSString*)stringForWeight:(float)weight ofUnit:(WeightUnit)unit
{
    NSString* weightString =
    [formatter stringFromNumber:@(weight)];

    NSString* unitString = [WeightEntry stringForUnit:unit];

    return [NSString stringWithFormat:@"%@ %@",
            weightString,
            unitString];
}
```

This method creates a complete weight string. The @(weight) call converts our floating-point value to an NSNumber object. We then pass the number object to our number formatter's stringFromNumber: method. This will create a properly localized number string, using the format that we set in our initialize method.

Next, we call stringForUnit: to get our unit string. We then combine the two strings with a space between. This will produce results like "125.32 lbs" or "45.53 kg."

```
+ (NSString*)stringForWeightInLbs:(float)weight inUnit:(WeightUnit)unit
{
    float convertedWeight;
    switch (unit)
    {
        case LBS:
            convertedWeight = weight;
            break;
        case KG:
            convertedWeight = [WeightEntry convertLbsToKg:weight];
            break;
        default:
            [NSException raise:NSInvalidArgumentException
                        format:@"%d is not a valid WeightUnit", unit];
    }


    return [WeightEntry stringForWeight:convertedWeight ofUnit:unit];
}
```

This method makes it easier to print out strings directly from our WeightEntry objects. Since our objects store the weight in pounds, this method will take the weight in pounds and automatically convert it if necessary.

The code is actually very similar to stringForUnit: We check the unit type. If it's LBS, we use the weight value directly. If it's KG, we convert it. If it's anything else, we throw an exception. Once that's done, we simply call stringForWeight:ofUnit: to produce the weight string.

So far, we've just added class methods. However, we'd like to add instance methods that let us directly request a weight string from our WeightEntry objects. We'll start by adding a method to request the weight value in a given unit.

```
- (float)weightInUnit:(WeightUnit)unit
{
    switch (unit)
    {
```

```
        case LBS:
            return self.weightInLbs;

        case KG:
            return [WeightEntry convertLbsToKg:self.weightInLbs];

        default:
            [NSException raise:NSInvalidArgumentException
                        format:@"The value %d is not a valid WeightUnit", unit];
    }

    // This will never be executed.
    return 0.0f;
}
```

This is the same basic construction. If the unit is LBS, we return our weightInLbs directly. If the unit is KG, we convert it and return the result. Otherwise, we throw an exception.

> **NOTE:** We've seen the same basic switch statement three times, with only subtitle variations in the code. When you see this type of repetition, it's often a sign that the class needs to be refactored, in this case, rewriting the class to get rid of the duplicate switch statements. One solution would be to provide separate subclasses for the different units (e.g., WeightEntryInLBS and WeightEntryInKG). However, given the size of the class and the relatively small amount of repetition, I think the cure would be worse than the disease in this case. I'd rather leave the repetition as is.

With the rest of the code in place, our stringForWeightInUnit: method ends up being very simple. All the heavy lifting is done by the methods we defined earlier.

```
- (NSString*)stringForWeightInUnit:(WeightUnit)unit
{
    return [WeightEntry stringForWeight:[self weightInUnit:unit]
                                ofUnit:unit];
}
```

DISPLAYING OUR WEIGHTS

Now we just need to combine our weight string methods with our new custom cell. Open HistoryTableViewController.m and at the top and add an import directive for HistoryCell.h.

```
#import "HistoryCell.h"
```

Next, let's add a private method to configure our cells.

```
- (void)configureCell:(HistoryCell *)cell forIndexPath:(NSIndexPath *)indexPath
{
    WeightEntry *entry =
    [self.weightHistoryDocument entryAtIndexPath:indexPath];

    cell.weightLabel.text =
    [entry stringForWeightInUnit:getDefaultUnits()];

    cell.dateLabel.text = [NSDateFormatter
                            localizedStringFromDate:entry.date
                            dateStyle:NSDateFormatterShortStyle
                            timeStyle:NSDateFormatterShortStyle];
}
```

Here, we grab the entry for the given index path. Then we use our new `stringFor` `WeightInUnit:` method to get the weight string, using our `getDefaultUnits()` function to retrieve the default units. Then we use a date formatter to create a localized string for our date. It will use the short style for both the date and the time.

Since the cell configuration is so short, it's often tempting to put it directly inside the `tableView:cellForRowAtIndexPath:` method. However, this is usually a mistake. In most projects, we will end up needing to reconfigure cells outside the `tableView:cellForRowAt` `IndexPath:` method. For example, if we let users modify entries, then we would need to update the cell content if that entry was currently being displayed.

Now we just need to call this method. Modify `tableView:cellForRowAtIndexPath:` as shown here:

```
- (UITableViewCell *)tableView:(UITableView *)tableView
cellForRowAtIndexPath:(NSIndexPath *)indexPath
{
    static NSString *CellIdentifier = @"History Cell";
    HistoryCell *cell =
    [tableView dequeueReusableCellWithIdentifier:CellIdentifier
                                    forIndexPath:indexPath];

    [self configureCell:cell forIndexPath:indexPath];

    return cell;
}
```

Build and run the application. Our history view should now use our custom cells, as shown in **Figure 3.13**.

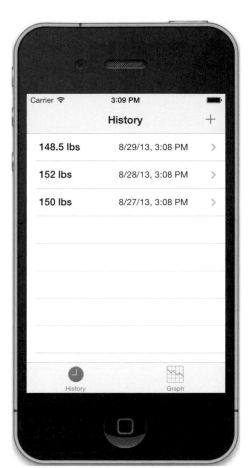

FIGURE 3.13 Our new history cells

ENTRY DETAIL VIEW

Next we need to set up our Entry Detail View. Currently we have a static table—but we haven't yet filled in its contents. We want to use this view to display a table of data. We'll have headers on the left with the values on the right. This is very similar to the layout for our rows in the history view.

Open `Main.storyboard` and zoom in on the Entry Detail View Controller scene. You should see the static table from the previous chapter. Currently it has one section and three rows. Delete two of these rows. You can select them, either in the editor or in the Document Outline, and then press the Delete key. We now have a single row to edit. We'll use this as a template for all our rows.

To begin with, we don't want to let users select the row. The easiest way to disable this is to select the Table View Cell and change its Selection attribute in the Attributes inspector to None.

FIGURE 3.14 Laying out our detail view cell

Now, drag out a label. Vertically center it in the row's content area and align it with the left margin guideline. In the Attributes inspector, set its Font to Headline and its Text to Max Loss. We're going to make labels for weight, date, average, max loss, and max gain. Max loss happens to be the longest. Using it now will make laying out the later rows easier.

Next, drag out a text field. Line it up so that it is also vertically centered and aligned with the guideline just to the right of our label. Then stretch it to the right margin guideline. Set its Font to Subhead and its text to 100. Right-align the text. Then scroll down to the Control section of the Attributes inspector, and uncheck the Enabled setting. This will let us display text but will prevent the users from editing it.

The layout should look like **Figure 3.14**.

Why are we using a text field this time? Two reasons. First, I wanted to show you something new. Second, if we ever decide to expand the app to make these values editable, we will already have the text fields in place. All we need to do is enable the relevant text fields and add the code to handle the edits.

Also, we will eventually want to get rid of the text field's border—but, having the border visible will make it easier to work with. So, let's leave that alone for now.

Let's add our constraints. Select the label and click the Pin tool at the bottom of the editor. In the Add New Constraints section, click the disclosure view for the left constraint. Make sure the Content View is selected (it should be the only option), and select Use Standard Value. For the right constraint, we want the Round Style Test Field (should be the default) and Use Standard Value. Click the "Add 2 Constraints" button to add these constraints.

With the label still selected, click the Align tool. Check the Vertical Center in Container and make sure the value is set to 0. Click the Add 1 Constraint button.

Now select our text field. Use the Pin tool to pin its right side to the content view using the standard value. Now select both the label and the text field. In the Alignment tool, check Baselines and make sure the value is set to 0. Click the Add 1 Constraint button to add this constraint.

Now we want to set the text field's Border Style to no border (⬚) and update its frame. That should clear out all of our warnings and errors. We have a valid, unambiguous layout.

Notice that this time we did not have to change our label's content hugging. By default, the text field has a content hugging of 250. This is lower than the label's 251, so the system will automatically choose to expand and contract our text field—which is what we want.

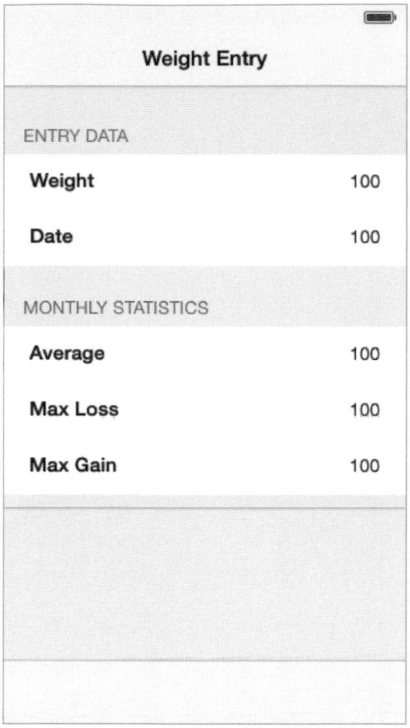

FIGURE 3.15 Our completed Entry Detail View

We also don't have to worry about checking the constraint values this time around. Using the Pin and Align tools guarantee that we will have exactly the values we want. However, we have to be careful when using them in complex layouts and make sure they are adding constraints to the correct views.

Now, let's add our other rows. In the Document Outline, select the Entry Detail View Controller scene's Table View Section. In the Attributes inspector, change Rows to 3. Interface Builder makes two copies of our row. It copies everything across—even our constraints.

Now select the Table View and change its Sections attribute to 2. We should now have two sections with three rows in each. Delete one row from the top section.

Select the first section and set its Header attribute to Entry Data. Select the second section and set its header to Monthly Statistics. Now we want to edit our labels. From top to bottom they should be Weight, Date, Average, Max Loss, and Max Gain. Update the frames, if necessary. Our completed table should look like **Figure 3.15**.

CREATING OUR OUTLETS

If we want to set our text field's values, we need to have outlets that connect to them. Let's create those now. With the Entry Detail View Controller scene still open in Interface Builder, switch to the Assistant Editor. Make sure EntryDetailViewController.m is open in the second edit window.

Control-drag from the text fields to the class extension. Create all the properties as shown here:

```
@property (weak, nonatomic) IBOutlet UITextField *weightTextField;

@property (weak, nonatomic) IBOutlet UITextField *dateTextField;

@property (weak, nonatomic) IBOutlet UITextField *averageTextField;

@property (weak, nonatomic) IBOutlet UITextField *lossTextField;

@property (weak, nonatomic) IBOutlet UITextField *gainTextField;
```

UPDATING OUR VIEW

As we discussed in the previous chapter, we typically pass the data to our new view controller during the prepareForSegue:sender: method. We then use the data to update our view during viewWillAppear:. We already took care of the first step. Let's do the second.

Let's start by adding an updateUI method. Switch back to the Standard Editor and open EntryDetailViewController.m. At the top of the file, import WeightEntry.h, and then add the following method:

```
#pragma mark - Private Methods

- (void)updateUI
{
    WeightUnit unit = getDefaultUnits();
    self.weightTextField.text =
    [self.entry stringForWeightInUnit:unit];

    self.dateTextField.text =
    [NSDateFormatter localizedStringFromDate:self.entry.date
                              dateStyle:NSDateFormatterMediumStyle
                              timeStyle:NSDateFormatterShortStyle];

}
```

So far, this looks a lot like our configureCell:forIndexPath: method. The biggest difference is that we are using the medium date style instead of the short date style. Also, we're setting only the weight and date fields so far. We'll come back and handle the rest soon.

Now, we need to override viewWillAppear: and call our update method.

```
- (void)viewWillAppear:(BOOL)animated
{
    [super viewWillAppear:animated];
    [self updateUI];
}
```

If you run the application and select one of the entries, it will display our new view. The weight and detail text should be filled in, as expected.

To calculate our monthly statistics, we need more information. That means we need an additional property. Switch to `EntryDetailViewController.h` and add the following property:

```
@property (strong, nonatomic) NSArray *lastMonthsEntries;
```

Now, switch back to the implementation file. Let's add the following code to the end of the `updateUI` method (after we set the `dateTextField`'s text but before the final curly bracket).

```
float average =
[[self.lastMonthsEntries valueForKeyPath:@"@avg.weightInLbs"] floatValue];

float min =
[[self.lastMonthsEntries valueForKeyPath:@"@min.weightInLbs"] floatValue];

float max =
[[self.lastMonthsEntries valueForKeyPath:@"@max.weightInLbs"] floatValue];

float lossFromMax = max - self.entry.weightInLbs;
NSAssert(lossFromMax >= 0.0f, @"This should always be a non-negative number");

float gainFromMin = self.entry.weightInLbs - min;
NSAssert(gainFromMin >= 0.0f, @"This should always be a non-negative number");

self.averageTextField.text =
[WeightEntry stringForWeightInLbs:average inUnit:unit];

self.gainTextField.text =
[WeightEntry stringForWeightInLbs:gainFromMin inUnit:unit];

self.lossTextField.text =
[WeightEntry stringForWeightInLbs:lossFromMax inUnit:unit];
```

This code assumes that `lastMonthsEntries` is an array of `WeightEntries`. Here, we are using Key-Value Coding's collection operators. These operators rely on a specially formatted key path. Normal key paths act similarly to dot notation. Here, however, our leftmost segment is a KVC operator—a keyword that begins with an @.

Apple defines a number of collection operators: @count, @average, @min, @max, and @sum. It also defines a number of union operators: @distinctUnionOfObjects, @unionOfObjects, @distinctUnionOfArrays, @unionOfArrays, and @distinctUnionOfSets.

All KVC operators, except @count, require a right key path. That is, they require a dot after the keyword, with the property name of the value the operator will be using. This could be self, to use the object itself.

In our case, we will use @avg.weightInLbs. This will calculate the average of the weightInLbs property for every item in our array. @min.weightInLbs returns the minimum weight, while @max.weightInLbs returns the maximum. These values are returned as NSNumber objects, so we have to call floatValue to get the underlying floating-point value.

We do a little more math to calculate how much we've gained from the minimum or lost from the maximum. There are a few assertions, which just act as sanity checks. Then we use these values to set our text fields. Note that since we don't have an entry object to represent our average, max loss, or max gain, we're using the stringForWeightInLbs:InUnit: class method to create the weight string.

If you run the code, it will actually crash. Our first assertion is triggered. We haven't set our array yet, so its value is nil. This means any calls we make will return nil or 0. Our average, min, and max values are therefore all equal to 0, and max - self.entry.weightInLBS is a negative number.

The problem is, we need to pass along an array of entries when we segue to this scene. Let's fix that.

FILTERING OUR ARRAY

Let's add a method to WeightHistoryDocument that can return a subset of our entries. Open WeightHistoryDocument.h and declare the following method just after enumerateEntries Ascending:withBlock::

```
- (NSArray*)weightEntriesAfter:(NSDate *)startDate
                        before:(NSDate *)endDate;
```

Next, switch to the .m file and add the following implementation (also after enumerate EntriesAscending:withBlock:):

```
- (NSArray *)weightEntriesAfter:(NSDate *)startDate
                         before:(NSDate *)endDate
{

    NSPredicate *betweenDates =
    [NSPredicate predicateWithBlock:^BOOL(WeightEntry *entry,
                                          NSDictionary *bindings) {
        return ([entry.date compare:startDate] != NSOrderedAscending) &&
        ([entry.date compare:endDate] != NSOrderedDescending);
    }];

    return [self.weightHistory filteredArrayUsingPredicate:betweenDates];
}
```

The viewWillAppear: and viewDidAppear: methods can be somewhat confusing. Generally speaking, the system calls these methods whenever a view controller is used to display another view controller. This includes displaying modal views, adding new views to a navigation controller, or switching between views on a tab bar. The system will even call these notification methods when a view reappears, such as when returning from a modal view or when a covering view is popped off the navigation stack.

Technically, viewWillAppear: and viewDidAppear: are called whenever our controller's view is added to the view hierarchy. viewWillDisappear: and viewDidDisappear: are called when the view is removed from the view hierarchy. It has nothing to do with the visual appearance. The view could be covered. It could be hidden. It could have an alpha of 0.0. None of that matters.

However, manually adding a view using the addSubview: method does not trigger these notifications. While this may seem confusing, it points to a common design problem. If your view appears onscreen but your view controller's viewWillAppear: and viewDidAppear: methods are not called, you probably have an inconsistent view hierarchy. This occurs when you add a view to the view hierarchy without properly adding its view controller to the view controller hierarchy.

The view and view controller hierarchies are related but separate. The controller hierarchy is typically smaller, since each controller will manage a large number of views. On the other hand, controllers may have views that are not currently in the view hierarchy. For example, when a navigation or tab controller moves from one child view controller to the next, it removes the old controller's views from the view hierarchy; however, those controllers are still part of the view controller hierarchy.

To have a consistent view controller hierarchy, look at each view controller's view property. That view's superview must be part of the view hierarchy managed by the controller's parentViewController. It doesn't need to be the parent's view property, but it must be a view directly created by and managed by the parent controller.

Most of the time inconsistent hierarchies come from adding a view to the view hierarchy without adding the controller to the controller hierarchy. There are a few ways to fix this. Most simply, you could get rid of the view's controller and add the view directly to its superview's controller. After all, view controllers already manage a number of views. Adding a property to a view that may be added and removed dynamically is no different than adding properties and outlets to other interface elements.

Alternatively, we could create a custom container view controller and use it to present our subview's controller. As the name suggests, a container view controller manages one or more child view controllers. We talked about container view controllers in Chapter 2. UIKit provides a few common container view controllers, including UINavigationController, UITabBarController, and UIPageViewController.

However, we're not limited to those. We can create our own container view controllers. The UIViewController class reference has a detailed explanation about creating custom container view controllers. However, there are four essential methods (addChildViewController:, removeFromParentViewController, willMoveToParent ViewController:, didMoveToParentViewController:) as well as the childViewControllers property. Outside code should never call these methods directly. Rather, we should create a public interface for adding and removing our child view controllers and then use these methods in our implementation.

Here, we're creating an NSPredicate object using a block. Predicates have a number of uses. One is to filter arrays. When we use the predicate, it will iterate over the array, calling our block once for each item. If our block returns YES, then it will include the item in the returned array. If it returns NO, it will skip the item. Our block code simply checks to make sure each entry is between the two dates, inclusively.

Now we just need to call this method and pass the results to our detail view. We could put this code directly in HistoryTableViewController's prepareForSegue:sender: method. But that method can get cluttered fast. Let's create a private method to handle all our configuration needs.

Open HistoryTableViewController.m, and add the following method to the end of our private methods:

```
- (void)configureWeightEntryViewController:
(EntryDetailViewController *)controller
{
    NSIndexPath *selectedPath = [self.tableView indexPathForSelectedRow];
    WeightEntry *entry =
    [self.weightHistoryDocument entryAtIndexPath:selectedPath];

    NSCalendar *calendar =
    [[NSCalendar alloc] initWithCalendarIdentifier:NSGregorianCalendar];

    NSDateComponents *dateComponents =
    [calendar components:NSYearCalendarUnit | NSMonthCalendarUnit |
     NSDayCalendarUnit fromDate:entry.date];

    [dateComponents setMonth:[dateComponents month] - 1];
    NSDate *lastMonth = [calendar dateFromComponents:dateComponents];

    controller.entry =entry;
    controller.lastMonthsEntries =
    [self.weightHistoryDocument weightEntriesAfter:lastMonth
                                    before:entry.date];
}
```

The beginning should be familiar. We get the index path of the currently selected row, and then we grab the weight entry for that index path. What comes next requires a bit of explaining. Basically we want to calculate the date exactly one month before our entry's date. We will then pass along both the current entry and all the entries in the month leading up to it—including the current entry.

However, date arithmetic gets hard fast. Different months have a different number of days, not to mention issues like leap years and leap seconds. And that's just the Gregorian calendar. Different calendars may also track things differently.

Therefore, instead of trying to do the date calculation ourselves, we will use an NSCalendar object to handle all these messy details. We start by instantiating a Gregorian calendar object. The Gregorian calendar is simply the 12-month, January to December calendar most of us use every day.

We then use the calendar to get the date components for our entry date. Specifically, we ask for the year, month, and day. We can then modify these date components. In our code, we decrease the month component by one month. The calendar object is smart enough to adjust the year component as well, if necessary. Finally, we use the new components to calculate a new date. Note, since we don't use the time components, the new date object will be set to midnight of the specified day.

We use the calculated date and our entry's date to get our filtered array of dates. We then pass both the entry and the filtered list to our incoming detail view.

Now, we just need to call this method. Modify prepareForSegue:sender: as shown here:

```
- (void)prepareForSegue:(UIStoryboardSegue *)segue sender:(id)sender
{
    if ([segue.identifier isEqualToString:@"Entry Detail Segue"])
    {
        [self configureWeightEntryViewController:
         segue.destinationViewController];
    }
}
```

If you run the app and select our sample entries, you will see that the statistics data is now filled in. Notice that we always get all the entries in the month leading up to our selected date. So, if you pick the top date, you will get the stats for all three entries (**Figure 3.16**). If you pick the bottom date, there are no earlier dates, so the average will be equal to the weight, and the loss values will both be 0.

ADDING AND DELETING ENTRIES

We also need a way to add and delete our entries. Let's look at deleting first, since it's the easiest.

Open HistoryTableViewController.m and navigate to the viewDidLoad method. Notice the commented code that says, "Uncomment the following line to display an Edit button in the navigation bar?" That code will add an edit button to our navigation bar. The only problem is, it will add it to the right side. We already have a button on the right side, so we want our edit button on the left.

Instead, add the following code to viewDidLoad:

```
self.navigationItem.leftBarButtonItem = self.editButtonItem;
```

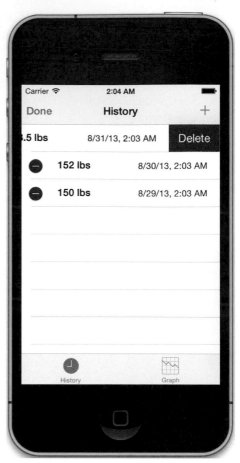

FIGURE 3.16 The completed detail view   **FIGURE 3.17** Editing mode

The edit button is provided by the system. When the button is tapped, it puts our table into the editing mode. Run the application, and tap the edit button. Delete icons will appear before each of our rows. If you tap one, a red delete button will slide in from the right (**Figure 3.17**). However, tapping the delete button does not do anything.

Scroll down until you find the commented-out `tableView:commitEditingStyle:forRow AtIndexPath:` method. Uncomment that method.

The current method checks the editing style and then has a stub for each style. As you can see, there are two editing styles that can be triggered from editing mode: inserts and deletes. In our app, we will never get an insert method. To trigger that, we'd have to create a row with a `UITableViewCellEditingStyleInsert` editing style. I find that, unless your table will only ever display a limited number of items, adding an "add entry" row is just more trouble than it's worth. Our plus button in the navigation bar will work better, since we won't need to worry about it scrolling off the screen.

So, we need to worry only about the `UITableViewCellEditingStyleDelete` branch. Currently, it contains a comment telling us to delete the item from our data source. Then it removes the row from the table. Actually, we only need to delete the item from our data source. We've already written the code to update our table whenever the data source changes.

So, modify the method as shown here:

```
- (void)tableView:(UITableView *)tableView
commitEditingStyle:(UITableViewCellEditingStyle)editingStyle
forRowAtIndexPath:(NSIndexPath *)indexPath
{
    if (editingStyle == UITableViewCellEditingStyleDelete) {
        [self.weightHistoryDocument deleteEntryAtIndexPath:indexPath];
    }
    else if (editingStyle == UITableViewCellEditingStyleInsert) {
        // Create a new instance of the appropriate class, insert
        // it into the array, and add a new row to the table view
    }
}
```

Run the application again. Now, when you delete rows, they are actually deleted from the screen. Also note, there is a slight bug. If you happen to put the table into edit mode while a new row is being inserted, you can end up with blank rows in your table. This is hard to trigger, and it shouldn't occur during normal use. In later chapters we will disable the user interface when loading and syncing our data, which will prevent the problem.

Now we just need to add our entries.

LAYING OUT THE ADD ENTRY VIEW

Open `Main.storyboard` and zoom in on the Add Entry View Controller scene. We want to start by adding a title to the top. This is our most complex layout yet, so let's take it in steps. Drag out a label, and set the following:

1. Pin the left and right sides to the View and the top to the Top Layout Guide using the standard value.

2. Set its Text attribute to Add a New Weight Entry.

3. Center align the text.

4. Set its font to Headline.

5. Update the frame, if necessary.

Now drag out another label. Use the guidelines to position it against the right margin and below our title. Give it the following settings:

1. Pin the left side to the View using the standard value.

2. Select the Vertical Space constraint between the two labels. Set its Relationship attribute to Greater Than or Equal.

3. Set the label's Text attribute to Weight.

4. Set the Font to Subhead.

Since our vertical constraint is now an inequality, we need more constraints to unambiguously define our position. Control-drag between the Weight label and our title label. Create a second Vertical Space constraint. Select the new constraint and, in the Attributes inspector, set the following:

1. Set its Constant by checking the Standard box.

2. Set the Relationship to Less Than or Equal.

3. Set the Priority to 250.

The first vertical constraint means our Weight label will never be closer to our Headline than the standard distance. The second constraint says that it will try to stay as close to the standard distance as possible—but it's a relatively low priority, letting it move further down the screen if necessary.

Next, drag out a text field and position it next to our Weight label. Set it up as shown here:

1. Pin the left side to our Weight label and the right side to the View using the standard value.

2. Create a vertical constraint between the text field and our title label, using the standard spacing, greater than or equal relationship, and a priority of 1000.

3. Create a second vertical constraint between the text field and our title label, using the standard spacing, less than or equal relationship, and a priority of 250.

4. Select both the Weight label and the text field. Align their baselines.

5. Set the text field's Font to Body.

6. Set the Clear Button attribute to Appears while editing.

7. Set its Keyboard attribute to Decimal Pad.

8. Update the frames, as necessary.

This should create a label and text field pair. The text field will be nicely positioned next to the label and will shrink and stretch horizontally to fill the screen. The pair's position beneath the title is determined by the taller of the two. Initially this is the text field—but that could change (e.g., if we later changed the text field to a borderless text field or greatly increased the label's font).

We've also set the text field to use a number pad for entering data. This lets us type any numbers, plus the period and a Delete key. We've also enabled the clear button when the text field is being edited. This lets the user quickly clear the content of the text field and start over.

Run the app, and press the plus button to bring up this view. Make sure everything adjusts properly as you rotate between landscape and portrait. Tap the text field, and the number pad should come up. We can enter numbers and delete or clear the numbers, but we don't have any way to dismiss the number pad. We'll fix that shortly.

MAKING ROOM FOR THE KEYBOARD

Tapping the text field will automatically display the specified keyboard. The system slides the keyboard up from the bottom, covering the lower portion of your content. This will not trigger any Auto Layout or Autoresizing behaviors (the view's size remains unchanged, and the bottom portion is simply covered).

We need to make sure our users can see the selected text field and reach the controls. This can create problems, especially in landscape orientation, since the keyboard will cover most of the screen. One option is to deliberately position all the controls so that they are still visible even in landscape orientation. However, this has two limitations: It makes the view appear somewhat top-heavy, and it's possible only for the simplest views.

Most of the time, you will need to manually reposition or resize the controls (typically using a scroll view) so that the selected control is visible. The keyboard sends out a number of notifications that you can use to make these modifications: `UIKeyboardWillShowNotification`, `UIKeyboardDidShowNotification`, `UIKeyboardWillHideNotification`, and `UIKeyboardDidHideNotification`.

Note: if you use a static table view to lay out your forms, the view will automatically scroll as necessary to avoid the keyboard. If we use a custom view inside a scroll view, we will have to code this behavior ourselves.

For the Health Beat application, our `AddEntryViewController` works well in portrait orientation. In landscape, the date text field may be partially covered, depending on the font size. We will fix this next chapter when we introduce custom transitions and animation.

Repeat this procedure to create a second label and text field pair. This time, the label's text should be Date. The Date label's two vertical constraints should be drawn between it and the Weight label, while the Date text field's two vertical constraints should be drawn between it and the Weight text field. Also, leave the Date's Keyboard as Default, and change its Return Key to Done. This will give us the standard keyboard but will change the appearance of the Return key to make it more appropriate for our app. Otherwise, all the settings are the same.

To make the Return key dismiss our keyboard, Control-click the second text field. Then drag from the "Did End on Exit" Sent event to the Add Entry View Controller, and select doneEditing: from the pop-up HUD.

At this point, we should have no warnings or errors with our layout. The views should adjust nicely as we rotate from landscape to portrait. We can select either of the text fields, and we get a different keyboard for each. The only problem is, the layout looks a bit odd. It would be nice if we could align the two text fields.

Now, we could easily hard code in a value—but since we're using Auto Layout, let's do something a bit more dynamic. We will modify our horizontal constraints between the labels and the text fields, similar to how we set the paired vertical constraints earlier. This will let our layout adapt, even if we change our labels' text. That could be handy, for example, when translating the app to other languages.

Let's start by making the text fields an equal width. Select both text fields. In the Pin tool, check the Equal Widths, and create the constraint.

Now, let's start working on the Weight label and text field.

1. Select the Horizontal Spacing constraint between the label and the text field.

2. Set its Relationship to Greater Than or Equal. Make sure its Constant is set to the standard value.

3. Create a second horizontal constraint.

4. Select the new constraint and set its Relationship to Less Than or Equal.

5. Set its Constant to the standard value.

6. Set its Priority to 250.

7. Select the text field. In the Size inspector, set its Content Hugging priority to 100.

This gives us the following. The vertical space between the text field and the label has a fixed minimum size, but can grow larger, if necessary. However, the text field's hugging constraint has a lower priority, so it will be resized first, if possible. Repeat these steps for the Date label and text field, and resize all the frames in the view controller. This should give us an unambiguous layout with no warnings or errors. The text fields should be perfectly aligned and should be 8 points away from our Weight label—with a slightly longer distance between the Date label and its text field. When you run the app, it should rotate nicely.

Let's add Save and Cancel buttons to the bottom of the screen. Generally you want the safer option closer to the bottom-right corner. This is just playing the odds. Most people hold their phones in their right hand. The button in the bottom-right corner is the one most likely to be pressed by accident. In our case, canceling is safer than saving, so it goes on the right.

Drag out two buttons. Align one with the guidelines in the bottom-left corner. Align the other with the guidelines in the bottom right. Set the left button's title to Save and the right button's to Cancel.

Then set the following:

1. Pin the Save button's left side to the View, its right side to the Button, and its bottom to the Bottom Layout Guide using the standard spacing.

2. Pin the Cancel button's right side to the View and its bottom to the Bottom Layout Guide using the standard spacing.

3. Select both buttons, and pin their widths equal.

4. Update both frames.

The buttons will now resize automatically to fill the bottom of the screen with a nice space between them. Run the app again and make sure everything looks right.

NOTE: We deliberately created a highly dynamic layout using a large number of constraints. This has the advantage of automatically adjusting should the relative size of any of our user elements change. However, we could simplify the constraints by making a few assumptions. For example, it's probably safe to assume that our text field will always be taller than our label. Also, if you're having trouble getting the layout to work, try downloading the sample code from the book's site (www.freelancemadscience.com/ios7_source/), and go through the user interface, comparing your constraints to the sample code.

UPDATING THE TEXT FIELDS

Now, let's set up the view's contents. We're not passing any data to this view when it loads. However, we still want to set the date to the current date and time. We also want to select the weight text field so that the user can start entering data immediately.

With Main.storyboard still open to the Add Entry View Controller scene, switch to the Assistant Editor. Control-drag from the text fields to the class extension to create the following three outlets:

```
@property (weak, nonatomic) IBOutlet UITextField *weightTextField;
@property (weak, nonatomic) IBOutlet UITextField *dateTextField;
@property (weak, nonatomic) IBOutlet UIButton *saveButton;
```

Switch to the Standard Editor. This time open AddEntryViewController.h. Import WeightUnits.h, and then add three properties to the public interface.

```
@property (assign, nonatomic, readonly) WeightUnit units;
@property (assign, nonatomic, readonly) float weight;
@property (strong, nonatomic, readonly) NSDate *date;
```

This will allow outside code to access, but not modify, these values. However, we also want to declare them as readwrite in the private class extension, so we can modify them internally. Switch to AddEntryViewController.m, and insert the following properties into the class extension:

```
@property (assign, nonatomic, readwrite) WeightUnit units;
@property (assign, nonatomic, readwrite) float weight;
@property (strong, nonatomic, readwrite) NSDate *date;
```

We aren't passing any data to this view controller. Instead, we should set up our default values when the controller first loads. Modify viewDidLoad as shown here:

```
- (void)viewDidLoad
{
    [super viewDidLoad];
    self.date = [NSDate date];
    self.weight = 0.0;
    self.units = getDefaultUnits();
}
```

Next, we want to update the user interface when the view appears. Just like the `EntryDetailViewController`, let's create an `updateUI` method to do the real work. Add this code to the bottom of `AddEntryViewController.m`.

```
#pragma mark - Private Methods

- (void)updateUI
{
    [self updateWeightText];
    [self updateDateText];
    [self enableSaveButton];
}
```

The update logic gets a little complex, so we're going to split it into three separate functions. Let's add them as private methods.

```
- (void)updateWeightText
{
    if (self.weight == 0.0)
    {
        self.weightTextField.text = @"";
    }
    else
    {
        self.weightTextField.text =
        [NSNumberFormatter
         localizedStringFromNumber:@(self.weight)
         numberStyle:NSNumberFormatterDecimalStyle];
    }
}
```

The `updateWeightText` method just checks to see whether our weight is set to 0.0. If it is, it clears out the text field. If not, it fills in the text field using a decimal style number formatter.

```
- (void)updateDateText
{
    if (self.date == nil)
    {
        self.dateTextField.text = @"";
    }
    else
    {
```

```
    self.dateTextField.text =
    [NSDateFormatter
     localizedStringFromDate:self.date
     dateStyle:NSDateFormatterMediumStyle
     timeStyle:NSDateFormatterShortStyle];

    self.dateTextField.textColor =
    [UIColor blackColor];
  }
}
```

updateDateText is very similar. Here, we check to see whether our date property is nil. If it is, we clear the date text field. If not, we fill the date text field using the medium date style and the short time style. We also set the date field's text color to black. We will be changing the text color later—this line guarantees that the text color gets reset to the default color if we have a valid date.

```
- (void)enableSaveButton
{
    BOOL enabled = YES;
    enabled &= (![self.weightTextField.text isEqualToString:@""]);
    enabled &= (![self.dateTextField.text isEqualToString:@""]);
    self.saveButton.enabled = enabled;
}
```

This method calculates whether both the weight and date text fields have a valid entry. If they both have valid data, it enables the save button. If they don't, it disables the button. This prevents the user from saving data unless we have a valid weight and date.

Now we just need to call these methods. After viewDidLoad, add the following viewWillAppear: method:

```
- (void)viewWillAppear:(BOOL)animated
{
    [super viewWillAppear:animated];
    [self updateUI];
    [self.weightTextField becomeFirstResponder];
}
```

Here, we simply call our new updateUI method. Then we call the weight text field's becomeFirstResponder method. This will assign our text field first responder status, letting it receive keyboard events. It will also display the keyboard.

Run the app and bring up the scene. The date text field should be filled in with the current date and time. The weight text field should be empty but selected and waiting for text. The keyboard should be visible. We cannot see the Save button, but it will be disabled, at least until we enter weight data.

However, clearly we need some way to dismiss the keyboard. Often, I like to have the keyboard dismissed when the user taps the Return key—however, our number pad doesn't have a Return key. We will have to add our own Done button in an inputAccessoryView.

ADDING AN INPUT ACCESSORY VIEW

UIViewResponder defines two input properties: the inputView and the inputAccessoryView. The inputView is the view that the responder will display as a custom keyboard. If it is set to nil, the responder simply displays the default keyboard. The inputAccessoryView is displayed above the keyboard. Typically this is a toolbar with one or more buttons on it. If it is set to `nil`, the system does not display any accessory views. Both of these properties are set to nil by default, and both are defined as `readonly` for `UIResponder`.

Fortunately, for both the `UITextView` and `UITextField`, these properties are re-declared as `readwrite`. This lets us easily set our own custom keyboards or keyboard accessories.

For this project, we're going to add a simple keyboard accessory. I want to lay out the accessory in Interface Builder. Unfortunately, it's not part of the storyboard—and we cannot have free-floating views in our storyboards. We can, however, have them in nib files. So, let's start by adding a new nib file to our project.

Control-click the Controllers group in the Project navigator, select New File… > iOS > User Interface > Empty, and click Next. Set the Device Family to iPhone. Click Next again. Name it AddEntryAccessory and click Create.

This will create an empty nib file. Notice that the user interface is somewhat different than when editing storyboards. The Document Outline is gone. Instead we have a dock. It's similar, but instead of showing all the scenes in our storyboard, it just shows the items in this particular nib. Right now it only has our placeholder objects. The First Responder, which we discussed in Chapter 1, and the File's Owner.

The File's Owner is our link to the outside world. It is not created by the nib. It already exists in our code, and acts as the bridge between our code and the objects in the nib.

Select the File's Owner icon. You can expand the dock to see the icon's names, if necessary. Then switch to the Identity inspector. It is currently set as an `NSObject`. Let's change its custom class to **AddEntryViewController**. Unfortunately, sometimes Xcode doesn't properly update the list of custom classes in the drop-down menu. If `AddEntryViewController` isn't listed, you can either type it in (which can be a bit difficult due to autocomplete's "help-fulness"), or you can close the project and reopen it. That should force Interface Builder to properly update its list of custom classes.

This setting does not change anything. As I said earlier, our File's Owner will already exist before the nib loads. However, by telling Interface Builder the File's Owner type, we're able to set actions and outlets.

This may also seem a bit odd. Our `AddEntryViewController` will now be associated with at least two separate nib files. The storyboard will create at least one nib file, which will lay out most of the view's contents. Now, our new nib file will load supplementary views— things that are not normally part of the storyboard layout, but still need to be associated with the controller.

As long as there is no overlap between the two sets of outlets, there's no problem. We can load the storyboard and our nib separately. Each one will set up and configure their own views and outlets.

Next, drag out a toolbar from the Object library and place it in the editor window. You can see the toolbar is added as a top-level object in our nib. As we saw last chapter, after our nib loads, all the top-level objects are autoreleased. They will be deleted from memory unless something in our code refers to them. Typically that means assigning them to one of our File's Owner's outlets.

FIGURE 3.18
Our accessory view

Open the Assistant editor. It should automatically bring up AddEntryViewController.m. Control-drag from the toolbar to our class extension to create the following outlet.

```
@property (strong, nonatomic) IBOutlet UIToolbar *accessoryToolbar;
```

Now let's lay out our toolbar. It already has a single button named Item. However, we really want the button on the right side. Drag a Flexible Space Bar Button Item from the Object library and place it to the left of our Item button. The Item button should automatically slide to the right. Double-click the item button and type **Done**. Our toolbar should now look like **Figure 3.18**.

Next, Control-click the Done button and drag down into our code. Position the cursor below our didReceiveMemoryWarning method, and let go. Name the action **doneEditing**. Now modify the doneEditing: method as shown.

```objectivec
#pragma mark - Action Methods

- (IBAction)doneEditing:(id)sender {
    if ([self.weightTextField isFirstResponder])
    {
        [self weightEditingDone];
    }

    if ([self.dateTextField isFirstResponder])
    {
        [self dateEditingDone];
    }
}
```

We start by checking to see which text field is currently the first responder. Then we close a corresponding …Done method for that text field. Now we just need to add these methods to the bottom of our private methods.

```objectivec
- (void)weightEditingDone
{
    self.weight = [self.weightTextField.text floatValue];
    [self updateUI];
    [self.weightTextField resignFirstResponder];
}
```

Here, we start by converting our weight text field's text into a floating-point value, and assigning that to our weight. Then we update our user interface and resign first responder status—dismissing the keyboard.

Now, since we are using a highly restricted keyboard, the user input will almost always be a valid floating-point number. The only thing the user can mess up is the decimal point. They could, in theory, enter **.....04..20.32.** or something similar. floatValue will do its best to interpret anything the user throws at it. If it cannot make sense of the gibberish, it will simply return 0.0. Since we are immediately updating our user interface, this will cause the text field to clear, making it obvious that the user needs to try again.

```
- (void)dateEditingDone
{
    [self updateUI];
    [self.dateTextField resignFirstResponder];
}
```

The date editing method is even simpler. Here, we just update the UI and dismiss our keyboard. We're done. Well, not really. Entering dates is a rather complex and difficult topic. We'll be handling it in a bit.

Now, let's just add our input accessory view to our text fields. Add another private method, as shown below:

```
- (void)setupInputAccessories
{
    UINib *nib =
    [UINib nibWithNibName:@"AddEntryAccessory" bundle:nil];

    [nib instantiateWithOwner:self options:nil];

    NSAssert(self.accessoryToolbar != nil,
            @"We should have a valid input accessory toolbar");
    NSAssert(self.weightTextField != nil,
            @"we should have a valid weight text field");
    NSAssert(self.dateTextField != nil,
            @"we should have a valid date text field");

    self.weightTextField.inputAccessoryView = self.accessoryToolbar;
    self.dateTextField.inputAccessoryView = self.accessoryToolbar;
}
```

FIGURE 3.19
Our accessory view

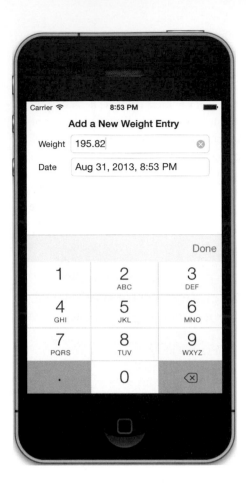

We start by creating a `UINib` object for our nib file. Then we load the nib, passing in `self` as the File's Owner. There are several different ways to load nib files. This one has the advantage of caching the nib's contents. It's probably not going to make a big difference to our application's speed or memory usage—but we might end up loading the nib multiple times during our application's lifetime. We may as well cache it.

Next, we have a series of asserts—we just want to verify that our accessory bar and text field all exist. If any of these fail, they will throw an exception and the app will crash.

Finally, we assign our new toolbar to our text fields' `inputAccessoryView` properties.

We just need to call this method from `viewDidLoad`. Add the following line to the bottom of `viewDidLoad`, after we assign our units but before the closing curly bracket.

```
[self setupInputAccessories];
```

Now run the app. When you bring up the Add Entry view, our new accessory bar should appear above the keyboard (**Figure 3.19**). Try entering a valid weight and tap the Done button. The keyboard should disappear and the Save button will be enabled. Try entering an invalid weight or clearing the date. The Save button will be disabled.

ENTERING DATES

How are we going to let the user enter dates? We could force them to enter a specifically formatted date string—but that doesn't lead to a very friendly user interface. Alternatively, we could replace the default keyboard with a date picker, and grab the results directly from the picker. That works well—but there's actually an approach that I like even better.

The Foundation framework provides a very powerful data detection tool. The NSDataDetector class is a subclass of NSRegularExpression. It is designed to detect a wide range of data elements in text. For example, we can use it to detect phone numbers, addresses, hyperlinks, flight numbers, or even dates.

We will use a data detector to find dates in our user's string. If the string is a date string, we will use it to calculate the date. If it isn't, we will display the text in red and change the Done button's title to Cancel. If the user presses Cancel, we will reset the date to the last selected date and time.

Since we're going to change the Done button's text, we need an outlet to our button. Open AddEntryAccessory.xib and switch to the Assistant editor. Control-drag from the Done button to create the following outlet in AddEntryViewController.m's class extension.

```
@property (weak, nonatomic) IBOutlet UIBarButtonItem *accessoryDoneButton;
```

Switch back to the Standard editor, and open AddEntryViewController.m again. Let's add a couple additional private methods. The first one will determine if a string is a properly formatted date string.

```
- (NSDate *)dateFromString:(NSString *)dateString
{
    NSError *dateDetectionError;
    NSDataDetector *dateDetector =
    [NSDataDetector dataDetectorWithTypes:NSTextCheckingTypeDate
                                    error:&dateDetectionError];

    // Trim off any white space at the beginning or end of our string
    dateString =
    [dateString stringByTrimmingCharactersInSet:
     [NSCharacterSet whitespaceAndNewlineCharacterSet]];

    NSRange allText = NSMakeRange(0, [dateString length]);

    NSTextCheckingResult *result =
    [dateDetector firstMatchInString:dateString
                             options:0
                               range:allText];

    // If our string is a date string, return the date
```

```
    if (NSEqualRanges(result.range, allText))
    {
        return result.date;
    }


    // If not, return nil
    return nil;
}
```

We start by creating our data detector, and we set it to detect dates. Note that the type argument is a bitmask. We could combine multiple NSTextCheckingType values, but we are only interested in dates here.

Then we trim the white space off the beginning and end of our string. We calculate the NSRange for our entire, newly trimmed string, and we check to see if we find any dates.

If the range of the first date we find is the same as the range for our string, we have a match. This means, there could be a valid date buried somewhere in our string, but we'd consider it a failure. In order to get unambiguous results, we only count the user's input as a match if the entire string is a single date value.

If we've found a date, we return it. Otherwise we return nil.

```
- (void)setDateStatusForString:(NSString *)dateString
{
    // if it's an empty string, we will simply use the current date
    if ([dateString isEqualToString:@""])
    {
        self.dateTextField.textColor = [UIColor redColor];
        self.accessoryDoneButton.title = @"Cancel";
        return;
    }


    if ([self dateFromString:dateString])
    {
        self.dateTextField.textColor = [UIColor darkTextColor];
        self.accessoryDoneButton.title = @"Done";
    }
    else
    {
        self.dateTextField.textColor = [UIColor redColor];
        self.accessoryDoneButton.title = @"Cancel";
    }
}
```

This method sets the text color and Done button text based on the dateString argument. First it checks to see if we have a valid date string. If we do, it sets the text color to the default darkTextColor and the button's title to Done. If we don't it sets the text color to red and the button's title to Cancel.

Now, to use these methods, we need to set our view controller as the text field's delegate. Let's start by adopting the delegate protocol. Still in AddEntryViewController.m, scroll up to the class extension, and modify the @interface line as shown below:

```
@interface AddEntryViewController () <UITextFieldDelegate>
```

Now, we need to set ourselves as the text field's delegate. Open Main.storyboard. Zoom in on our Add Entry View Controller scene. Control-click the date text field to bring up the connections HUD. Then drag from the delegate's circle to our view controller icon (either in the dock or in the Document Outline). This sets our controller as that view's delegate.

Now we just need to implement a couple of delegate methods. I recommend adding them after the Action Methods section.

```
#pragma mark - UITextFieldDelegate Methods

- (BOOL)textField:(UITextField *)textField
shouldChangeCharactersInRange:(NSRange)range
replacementString:(NSString *)string
{
    NSString *potentialDateString =
    [textField.text stringByReplacingCharactersInRange:range
                                            withString:string];

    [self setDateStatusForString:potentialDateString];
    return YES;
}
```

This method will be called whenever the user makes any changes to our text field. This is a "should" method, so we can return YES or NO. If we return YES, the change occurs. If we return NO, then the change is canceled. This is one of the easiest ways to filter user input into a text field.

Here, however, we aren't interested in filtering. We simply want to be alerted to any changes. Whenever a change occurs, we take the change and apply it to the current string value. This gives us the value that the text field will have once the change is accepted. We then call setDateStatusForString: to set our button name and text color based on that string. Then we return YES to accept the change.

```
- (BOOL)textFieldShouldClear:(UITextField *)textField
{
    self.accessoryDoneButton.title = @"Cancel";
    return YES;
}
```

The second `UITextFieldDelegate` method simply sets the Done button's title to "Cancel" whenever the user presses the clear button.

Finally, make the following changes to our `dateEditingDone` method.

```
- (void)dateEditingDone
{
    NSDate *date = [self dateFromString:self.dateTextField.text];

    if (date) {
        self.date = date;
    }

    [self updateUI];
    [self.dateTextField resignFirstResponder];
}
```

Here, we start by grabbing the date from our text field's text. If we have a valid date, we assign it to `self.date`. Then we update our UI as before.

Run the application and try to enter date values. Notice that you can enter dates in a number of different formats. You can use the mm/dd/yy format. You could type it out in words or abbreviations. You can even use phrases like "today in the morning" or "yesterday afternoon."

It's very powerful and moderately amazing. Not perfect, however. I'd probably add a few pre-processing steps. For example, I wish it would detect the phrase "now." But, I'll leave that as an exercise for the reader.

ADDING THE UNITS BUTTON

Now, let's add a button to change the units. However, instead of just adding a button anywhere on the screen, let's place it inside the weight text field. And let's have the button toggle between pounds and kilograms.

Let's start by creating the button. We need a button that isn't already part of any view hierarchy. We could programmatically create it—but, again, I like to use Interface Builder whenever possible. Just like the input accessory, we cannot have free-floating buttons in our storyboard—but we can put it in a nib file.

And, conveniently, we already have a nib file associated with the correct view controller. Open `AddEntryAccessory.xib`. Drag a button from the library and place it somewhere beneath our tab bar. Change its title to **lbs**. Switch to the Size inspector and change its height to **17** points and its width to **25** points.

Now, open the Assistant Editor and Control-drag our new button down to `AddEntryViewController.m`'s class extension. Add a new outlet, as shown:

```
@property (strong, nonatomic) IBOutlet UIButton *unitButton;
```

Now our button will automatically get assigned to this outlet when our nib is loaded. However, we also want the button to trigger an action. Control-drag again, but this time drag down to the bottom of the Action methods. Create the following action:

```
- (IBAction)unitButtonTapped:(id)sender {
}
```

Switch back to the Standard editor and open AddEntryViewController.m again. At the top of the file, import WeightEntry.h. Then add the following code to the end of setupInputAccessories, just before its closing curly bracket.

```
NSString *unitString = [WeightEntry stringForUnit:self.units];
[self.unitButton setTitle:unitString forState:UIControlStateNormal];
self.weightTextField.rightViewMode = UITextFieldViewModeAlways;
self.weightTextField.rightView = self.unitButton;
```

We start by getting the unit string for our current units. Then we set that string as the button's title. Finally we set the text field to always display our button, and add our button to the right side of the text field.

Now, implement unitButtonTapped: as shown:

```
- (IBAction)unitButtonTapped:(id)sender {

    if (self.units == LBS)
    {
        self.units = KG;
    }
    else
    {
        self.units = LBS;
    }

    NSString *unitString = [WeightEntry stringForUnit:self.units];
    [self.unitButton setTitle:unitString forState:UIControlStateNormal];
}
```

We're just checking the current value of self.unit, and switching it from LBS to KG or from KG to LBS as necessary. Then we update our button's title to match.

Run the application. You should now be able to tap on the unit button to toggle between lbs and kg (**Figure 3.20**).

FIGURE 3.20 Adding the unit button

TABLE 3.4 Control States

STATE	TRIGGER
UIControlStateNormal	Default control state.
UIControlStateHighlighted	The highlighted state is often used to alter the control's appearance when it is touched. This state is automatically set and cleared as touches enter and leave the control. Our application can also access this state through the `highlighted` property.
UIControlStateSelected	Often, this state has no effect on the control's appearance; however, controls like the `UISwitchControl` will use it when toggling between the ON and OFF states. This state can also be accessed through the control's `selected` property.
UIControlStateDisabled	This state is typically set using the control's `enabled` property. When disabled, the control does not respond to touch events. Many controls also change their appearance when disabled.

Both setTitle:forState: and setTitleColor:forState: refer to the button's state. Every control has a state: normal, highlighted, selected, or disabled. Different actions can change the control's state (see **Table 3.4**). Our button uses only two. It is highlighted when touched; otherwise, it is normal.

When setting per-state attributes, if you don't explicitly assign a value to a given state, that state will default back to the UIControlStateNormal setting. For example, in our code we only had to set the title once. Unless we say otherwise, every other state will use this value as well.

This brings up a point that is often confused. If you look up UIControlState in the developer documentation, the enum is defined as a bitmask. This means we should be able to combine multiple states using the bitwise OR operator (|). As a result, you might be tempted to explicitly set the title for all the states using code like this:

```
UIControlState all =  UIControlStateNormal |

                      UIControlStateSelected |

                      UIControlStateHighlighted |

                      UIControlStateDisabled;

[self.button setText:@"default text" forState:all]
```

Unfortunately, this does not work. Instead of setting the title for all states, you are actually setting the title for a single state: specifically, the state in which the control is selected, highlighted, and disabled—all at the same time (in this case, UIControlState-Normal is ignored).

This can be handy when creating things like custom two-state buttons. These buttons have an ON and an OFF state, and each of these states can be displayed either normally or highlighted. This means we need to define four different appearances for these four different states.

We can use the button's selected property to indicate its ON/OFF state. Our appearances are then defined as follows: UIControlStateNormal means the button is OFF; UIControl-StateHighlighted means the button is OFF and touched; UIControlStateSelected means the button is ON; and UIControlStateHighlighted | UIControlStateSelected means the button is both ON and touched. Note that UIControlStateDisabled is not used here.

Again, if you're simply trying to set a default appearance across all the states, just use UIControlStateNormal and let the others default back to it.

SEGUE UNWINDING

We want to have our Save and Cancel buttons take us back to our history view. However, we cannot simply draw a segue from these buttons back to that scene. Remember, when we perform a segue, we create a new instance of the destination, so drawing a segue back to the history view wouldn't return us to the old view, it would create an entirely new view. As we added new entries to our history, we would continue layering view upon view upon view.

Instead, we want to unwind the segue, or return to a previous point in our workflow. Segue unwinding lets us move back down the chain of segues towards our initial scene. We can move as far as we wish back along this chain. To do this, we must create unwind action methods in the view controller of the scene we wish to return to.

Since we want to go back to the history view, open `HistoryTableViewController.m`. Start by importing `AddEntryViewController.h`. Then add the following methods, after the Navigation methods.

```
#pragma mark - Storyboard Unwinding Methods

- (IBAction)addNewEntrySaved:(UIStoryboardSegue *)segue
{
    AddEntryViewController *controller = segue.sourceViewController;

    WeightEntry *entry = [WeightEntry entryWithWeight:controller.weight
                                           usingUnits:controller.units
                                              forDate:controller.date];

    [self.weightHistoryDocument addEntry:entry];
}

- (IBAction)addNewEntryCanceled:(UIStoryboardSegue *)segue
{
    // We don't need to do anything here.
}
```

These methods look exactly like our other action methods, except they take a `UIStoryboardSegue` argument. The Save method creates a new `WeightEntry` instance, grabbing the weight, unit, and date values from our Add Entry view. Then it adds this entry to our weight history document. Of course, modifying the document triggers a notification, which will then update our table view.

The canceled method doesn't need to do anything. Once we unwind back to this scene, we're done.

Let's connect these methods to our buttons. Open `Main.storyboard` again. We still want to work with the Add Entry View Controller scene. Control-drag from the Save button to the Exit icon in the scene's dock. When you let go, you will see that our new segue unwinding actions show up as options in the pop-up HUD. Select `addNewEntrySaved:`. Do the same thing for the Cancel button, but select `addNewEntryCanceled:`.

Now, run the application. Try adding a new weight entry and click Save. The new weight entry should show up at the top of the History view. Try again, this time click Cancel. You return to the history view, but nothing changes.

With this code in place, we no longer need our mock data. The user can now enter his own data. Of course the data is deleted as soon as the app exits—but we'll look at saving this data in Chapter 5, "Loading and Saving Data" and Chapter 7, "Core Data."

Open `RootTabViewController.m`. Navigate to the `addMocData` method, and comment it out. You can select the entire method and type ⌘ / to comment out all the highlighted code. This, however, creates an error. To fix it, we also need to scroll up to the `viewDidLoad` method and comment out the following line:

```
//    [self addMocData];
```

DYNAMIC TYPE

Dynamic Type really addresses three issues:

1. It gives the user a way to set the font size for all of their apps. Any application that supports Dynamic Type will automatically adjust its font size per the user's request.

2. Fonts that look good in a larger font size are often hard to read when reduced to a smaller font sizes. Similarly, fonts that are clear and legible when small tend to look too heavy when enlarged. To solve this problem, Dynamic Type uses a collection of similar fonts, each one finely tuned for a particular size. The exact font it returns will vary depending on both the user's font settings as well as the particular style requested.

3. Dynamic Type declares a number of different font styles: headline, subhead, body, footnote, caption1, and caption2. By declaring fonts based on their intended use in the user interface, we should be able to create a more consistent look and feel across applications.

Unfortunately, the "dynamic" in Dynamic Type refers to the fact that the fonts are dynamically selected based on the user's size selection and the style. They do not dynamically update when the user changes his font selection. In fact, supporting Dynamic Type requires a fair bit of work to update all the fonts properly.

We need to update the fonts when the application first launches to grab the current font sizes specified by the user. We also need to listen for the `UIContentSizeCategoryDid ChangeNotification`, and update all of our fonts whenever the user changes the font setting.

This is potentially a lot of work spread across a large number of files. However, we can use a few Objective-C tricks to streamline it somewhat. To start with, we don't want to force each and every view controller to observe `UIContentSizeCategoryDidChangeNotification`. Instead, let's have the app delegate listen for changes. When that change occurs, we send a message down the view controller hierarchy. Unfortunately, to really get this to work, we need to add new methods to the `UIViewController` class—which all of our view controllers would then inherit. Fortunately, in Objective-C this is relatively easy. We just need to use a category.

Let's start by creating a category on `UIViewController`. Control-click the Controller's group in the Project navigator and select New File... > iOS > Cocoa Touch > Objective-C Category. Set the Category to **HBTUpdateFonts** and the "Category on" to **UIViewController**. Click Next, and when the next sheet appears, click Create.

Open `UIViewController+HBTUpdateFonts.h`. Declare our new method as shown:

```
@interface UIViewController (HBTUpdateFonts)
- (void)HBT_updateFonts;
@end
```

Remember, when using categories we should always add a prefix to our methods. Since Apple is rapidly using up all the good two-letter prefixes for their own frameworks, I prefer to use three letter prefixes. Unfortunately, HBT was the best three-letter prefix I could come up with for Health Beat. Sorry about that.

Now, lets switch to `UIViewController+HBTUpdateFonts.m` and implement this method.

```
-(void)HBT_updateFonts
{
    for (UIViewController *controller in self.childViewControllers)
    {
        [controller HBT_updateFonts];
    }

    if (self.presentedViewController.presentingViewController == self)
    {
        [self.presentedViewController HBT_updateFonts];
    }
}
```

This will become the default implementation for all our view controllers. It simply iterates over all the view controller's children and calls `HBT_updateFonts` on them. It also checks to see if there is a presented view controller, and calls `HBT_updateFonts` on it as well. The code here gets a bit odd, but it's important because of the way views are presented.

When you call `presentViewController:animated:completion:`, or use a modal segue, the system will start with the current view controller and begin searching for the correct presentation context. Basically, it calls `definesPresentationContext` on the presenting view controller. If this returns NO, it moves up the view controller hierarchy, calling `definesPresentationContext` on each controller. If it doesn't find a match, it will use the application's window as the presentation context.

By default, `definesPresentationContext` returns NO. This means, when you press the plus button in the History scene, our `HistoryTableViewController` is not actually presenting our Add Entry scene. It's actually passed all the way back to our tab view controller.

Similarly, `presentedViewController` returns the view controller presented by the current view controller or any of its ancestors. In our case, if the Add Entry scene is shown, `RootTabBarController`, `HistoryNavigationController`, and `HistoryTableViewController` will all return our `AddEntryViewController` object as their `presentedViewController`.

This means we cannot just use the value of `presentedViewController`. Instead, we use a slight trick. We ask the presented view controller for the controller that is presenting it. If this value matches the current view controller, we know that we've found the presentation context. This is the controller that is actually presenting our scene. We will also let it update the presented view controller's fonts.

Additionally, we are modeling this method on other methods that get passed along the view controller hierarchy. The default implementation doesn't do anything. We can override this method to take specific actions in our classes; however, when we override it, we must call super at some point in our implementation. This is exactly how methods like `viewWillAppear:` operate.

So, let's add the notification that will trigger all this. Open AppDelegate.m. At the top, we need to import our new class category.

```
#import "UIViewController+HBTUpdateFonts.h"
```

Next, let's add a class extension on the AppDelegate. Add the following code before the @implementation block:

```
@interface AppDelegate()
@property (strong, nonatomic) id fontChangeObserver;
@end
```

Now, modify the application:didFinishLaunchingWithOptions: method to register for notifications.

```
- (BOOL)application:(UIApplication *)application didFinishLaunchingWithOptions:
→ (NSDictionary *)launchOptions
{

    __weak AppDelegate *_self = self;
    self.fontChangeObserver =
    [[NSNotificationCenter defaultCenter]
     addObserverForName:UIContentSizeCategoryDidChangeNotification
     object:[UIApplication sharedApplication]
     queue:[NSOperationQueue mainQueue]
     usingBlock:^(NSNotification *note) {
         [_self.window.rootViewController HBT_updateFonts];
     }];

    return YES;
}
```

The content size category is the setting that determines which font size we should use for our dynamic fonts. Whenever this changes, we will update our fonts.

As always, whenever we register for notifications, we also need to make sure we unregister. Add the following dealloc method:

```
- (void)dealloc
{
    if (self.fontChangeObserver)
    {
        [[NSNotificationCenter defaultCenter] removeObserver:
            self.fontChangeObserver];
    }
}
```

This isn't, strictly speaking, required. Our app delegate should exist throughout the entire lifetime of our application. Still, this is a good habit to get into. If you start cutting corners, you may forget it when it really is important.

So, which classes need to have their fonts updated? We've used the Dynamic Type settings in our History Table, Entry Detail, and Add Entry scenes.

UPDATING THE HISTORY TABLE'S FONTS

Let's start with the History Table. Open HistoryTableViewController.m and modify the configureCell:forIndexPath: method as shown:

```
- (void)configureCell:(HistoryCell *)cell forIndexPath:(NSIndexPath *)indexPath
{
    WeightEntry *entry =
    [self.weightHistoryDocument entryAtIndexPath:indexPath];
    cell.weightLabel.text =
    [entry stringForWeightInUnit:getDefaultUnits()];
    cell.dateLabel.text = [NSDateFormatter
                            localizedStringFromDate:entry.date
                            dateStyle:NSDateFormatterShortStyle
                            timeStyle:NSDateFormatterShortStyle];

    cell.weightLabel.font =
    [UIFont preferredFontForTextStyle:UIFontTextStyleHeadline];

    cell.dateLabel.font =
    [UIFont preferredFontForTextStyle:UIFontTextStyleSubheadline];
}
```

The preferredFontForTextStyle: method simply returns the correct, dynamic font for the requested style, given the user's current settings.

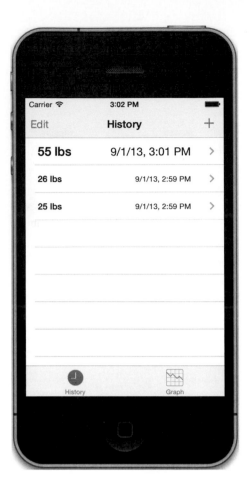

FIGURE 3.21 One cell using the new font size

Run the application again. Create a few entries. So far, everything looks the same. Press the home button (⇧⌘**H** in the simulator) and open the Settings app. In General > Text Size, change the size of the text. If you go back to our app, you will see that nothing has happened. However, create a new entry, and it will appear in the newly selected font size (**Figure 3.21**).

We're using the user specified font—but we're not updating our interface when the setting changes. At the top of `HealthTableViewController.m`, import our `HBTUpdateFonts` category. Then add the following method just below `didReceiveMemoryWarning`:

```
- (void)HBT_updateFonts
{
    [super HBT_updateFonts];
    [self.tableView reloadData];
}
```

This simply reloads our table. Now, if you run the app, you can switch the fonts, and our table automatically updates in response.

UPDATING THE ADD ENTRY SCENE'S FONTS

In the Add Entry scene, we need to update the fonts on both text fields, and on all three labels. We already have outlets for the text fields, but we need to add outlets for our labels. Open Main.storyboard. Switch to the Assistant editor and Control-drag the following outlets to AddEntryViewController.m

```objc
@property (weak, nonatomic) IBOutlet UILabel *titleLabel;
@property (weak, nonatomic) IBOutlet UILabel *weightLabel;
@property (weak, nonatomic) IBOutlet UILabel *dateLabel;
```

Switch back to the Standard editor and open AddEntryViewController.m. Import our HBTUpdateFonts category at the top. Next, we need to update our fonts both when the view first appears and when we receive our update notifications. Since we will be using the same code in two places, let's create a private method to handle the actual updates.

Add the following method just below updateDateText:

```objc
- (void)updateFonts
{
    self.titleLabel.font =
    [UIFont preferredFontForTextStyle:UIFontTextStyleHeadline];

    self.weightLabel.font =
    [UIFont preferredFontForTextStyle:UIFontTextStyleSubheadline];

    self.dateLabel.font =
    [UIFont preferredFontForTextStyle:UIFontTextStyleSubheadline];

    self.weightTextField.font =
    [UIFont preferredFontForTextStyle:UIFontTextStyleBody];

    self.dateTextField.font =
    [UIFont preferredFontForTextStyle:UIFontTextStyleBody];
}
```

This just goes through and sets all of our fonts to use Dynamic Type. Notice that we're using the same styles here that we used when creating the interface in Interface Builder.

Now, we just need to call this method. Override HBT_updateFonts just below didReceiveMemoryWarning:

```objc
- (void)HBT_updateFonts
{
    [super HBT_updateFonts];
    [self updateFonts];
}
```

And add the following line to `viewWillAppear:`.

```
- (void)viewWillAppear:(BOOL)animated
{
    [super viewWillAppear:animated];
    [self updateFonts];
    [self updateUI];
    [self.weightTextField becomeFirstResponder];
}
```

That's it. Run the application and make sure this scene updates its fonts and layout as expected.

UPDATING THE ENTRY DETAIL SCENE'S FONTS

Our entry detail scene has five labels and five text fields. All of them need to be updated. Fortunately, the general procedure is the same as our Add Entry scene.

We already have outlets for all the text fields, so let's start by adding outlets for the labels. Create the following outlets:

```
@property (weak, nonatomic) IBOutlet UILabel *weightLabel;
@property (weak, nonatomic) IBOutlet UILabel *dateLabel;
@property (weak, nonatomic) IBOutlet UILabel *averageLabel;
@property (weak, nonatomic) IBOutlet UILabel *lossLabel;
@property (weak, nonatomic) IBOutlet UILabel *gainLabel;
```

Now open `EntryDetailViewController.m` and import our category's header. Then add the following private method:

```
- (void)updateFonts
{
    self.weightLabel.font =
    [UIFont preferredFontForTextStyle:UIFontTextStyleHeadline];

    self.dateLabel.font =
    [UIFont preferredFontForTextStyle:UIFontTextStyleHeadline];

    self.averageLabel.font =
    [UIFont preferredFontForTextStyle:UIFontTextStyleHeadline];

    self.lossLabel.font =
    [UIFont preferredFontForTextStyle:UIFontTextStyleHeadline];
```

```
    self.gainLabel.font =
    [UIFont preferredFontForTextStyle:UIFontTextStyleHeadline];

    self.weightTextField.font =
    [UIFont preferredFontForTextStyle:UIFontTextStyleSubheadline];

    self.dateTextField.font =
    [UIFont preferredFontForTextStyle:UIFontTextStyleSubheadline];

    self.averageTextField.font =
    [UIFont preferredFontForTextStyle:UIFontTextStyleSubheadline];

    self.lossTextField.font =
    [UIFont preferredFontForTextStyle:UIFontTextStyleSubheadline];

    self.gainTextField.font =
    [UIFont preferredFontForTextStyle:UIFontTextStyleSubheadline];
}
```

Now add our `HBT_updateFonts` method:

```
- (void)HBT_updateFonts
{
    [super HBT_updateFonts];
    [self updateFonts];
}
```

And call `updateFonts` from within `viewWillAppear`:

```
- (void)viewWillAppear:(BOOL)animated
{
    [super viewWillAppear:animated];
    [self updateFonts];
    [self updateUI];
}
```

Again, run the application and make sure the fonts change as expected.

CUSTOMIZING OUR APPEARANCE

Finally, let's make a few, minor changes to our application's appearance.

Originally, with iOS applications, we were relatively limited in our ability to change the appearance of the built-in controls. Yes, we could set a view's backgroundColor. We could modify a label's textColor. But, if we wanted to go beyond this, we would have to custom draw our own controls.

With iOS 5, Apple introduced UIAppearance. This was an easy way to customize the appearance of the views and controls in UIKit. It came in two parts. First, it added a number of methods to let us modify the appearance of our controls directly. For example, the UISwitch gained methods like onImage:, offImage:, onTintColor:, and offTintColor:. Second, the UIAppearance proxy let us make these changes on every instances of a class in our application, or even on all the instances of a class placed within a given view.

Now, not surprisingly, with the radical UI changes in iOS 7, there have also been a number of changes to UIAppearance. Many of the customization methods no longer do anything in iOS 7—so be sure to read the documentation carefully before you call them.

Mostly, however, the tintColor: method has gained new prominence. Previously, tintColor: was used by a few controls to set some sort of coloration—now, however, it has been added as a property of UIView. That means everything displayed on our screen has a tint color.

Many classes, like UIView, UILabel, or UITextField, don't really use it to do anything. Other controls, however, will take the tint color and use it to somehow modify their appearance. For example, it is used to set a button's text color. Furthermore, if you don't set a view's tint color, it will inherit the tint color of its superview. This means we can set our window's tint color, and (more or less) customize our entire application's appearance (more or less).

Let's try that. Add the following code to AppDelegate.m's application:didFinishLaunchingWithOptions: method.

```
self.window.tintColor =

[UIColor colorWithRed:0.5f green:0.0f blue:0.0f alpha:1.0f];
```

Now run the application. Notice how our navigation bar, toolbar, and buttons have all changed to a darker red color? In fact, the only thing that hasn't changed is the button on our accessory view. The keyboard and keyboard accessory aren't part of our view hierarchy. We'll need to set that tint color manually.

Open AddEntryViewController.m and navigate to the setupInputAccessories method. Add the following line to the bottom of the method:

```
self.accessoryDoneButton.tintColor =

[[[[UIApplication sharedApplication] delegate] window] tintColor];
```

Here, we are grabbing the tint color from our application's window and applying it to our Done button. Now, if you run the application, it picks up our custom color as well.

Also notice that the tint color does not change the color of our labels or text views. Those we must specifically change using their textColor property. We've already seen this. We modified the text color in our date text field to turn red whenever the user entered an invalid date string.

Let's also add a tiny splash of color to our Entry Detail scene. When the weight is below the monthly average, show the weight in green. When it's above, show it in red.

To do this, let's add the following code to the bottom of EntryDetailViewController's updateUI method:

```
if (self.entry.weightInLbs > average)
{
    self.weightTextField.textColor = [UIColor redColor];
}
else if (self.entry.weightInLbs < average)
{
    self.weightTextField.textColor =
    [UIColor colorWithRed:0.0f green:0.5f blue:0.0f alpha:1.0f];
}
else
{
    self.weightTextField.textColor = [UIColor darkTextColor];
}
```

Here, we're using the standard red color for weights above average. For weights below average, I've selected a custom green color. [UIColor greenColor] was simply too bright for my taste.

That's it. Setting the tint color and a couple of text colors really only scratches the surface when it comes to customizing our application's appearance. For even greater customization, we could still use the old UIAppearance methods and proxies. We can also do custom drawing, when necessary. Though, honestly, in iOS 7, the application's appearance has become somewhat secondary. In many cases, we want our application to fade into the background. It simply exists to highlight the user's content. Instead, we're encouraged to customize the animations used to present and dismiss our views.

WRAPPING UP

Throughout this chapter, we dug into the details behind views and view controllers as we fleshed out our History, Add Entry, and Entry Detail scenes. In Chapter 4, "Custom Views and Custom Transitions," we will begin working on our graph view. We will look at both drawing custom views and providing custom animations. Looking further down the road, we will add even more advanced UI features in Chapter 8, "Advanced User Interfaces."

OTHER RESOURCES

- **Cocoa Auto Layout Guide**

  iOS Developer's Library

  This is the ultimate authority on all things Auto Layout. It's not necessarily the first place I would go, if I had a quick question. But, it is great when you really want to dig into the details.

- **WWDC Videos**

  https://developer.apple.com/videos/

  These are videos of Apple engineers talking about the tools and technologies that they have created. You can pick up a ton of great tips and tricks by watching these videos. In particular, however, I wanted to point out the Auto Layout videos. There are three Auto Layout videos in the WWDC 2012 set: Introduction to Auto Layout for iOS and OS X, Auto Layout by Example, and Best Practices for Mastering Auto Layout. Just ignore everything they say about Interface Builder—the rest is golden. For Xcode 5 Interface Builder instructions, check out the WWDC 2013 video, Taking Control of Auto Layout in Xcode 5.

- **View Controller Programming Guide for iOS**

  iOS Developer's Library

  If you have any questions on how to best use view controllers, I recommend reading through this guide. This includes information on using Interface Builder and storyboards.

- **Key Value Coding Programming Guide: Collection Operators**

  iOS Developer's Library

  This has additional information on the collection operators with examples.

- **NSHipster**

  http://nshipster.com

  As always, a great source for information. Particularly relevant to this chapter are the articles on KVC Collection Operators and NSDataDetector.

CHAPTER 4

Custom Views and Custom Transitions

This chapter will focus on customizing the user interface. First, we will look at drawing. By drawing our own views, we can create a wide range of visual effects—and by extension, a wide range of custom controls. Then we will look at setting the transitions between scenes and providing animations for those transitions.

In previous versions of iOS, custom drawing grew to become a large part of many applications. As developers tried to give their applications a unique look and feel or tried to push beyond the boundaries of the UIKit controls, they began to increasingly rely on custom drawing to make their applications stand out.

However, iOS 7 is different. In iOS 7, Apple recommends pushing the application's user interface into the background. It should, for the most part, disappear, focusing attention on the user's data rather than drawing attention to itself. As a result, the developers are encouraged to create their own unique look and feel through less visually obvious techniques. In this new paradigm, custom animations may replace custom interfaces as the new distinguishing feature.

CUSTOM DRAWING

In previous chapters, we set up the `GraphViewController` and made sure that it received a copy of our `weightHistoryDocument`. However, it is still just displaying an empty, white view. Let's change that. We're going to create a custom view with custom drawing—actually, to more easily handle the tab bar and status bar, we will be creating two custom views and split our drawing between them.

Let's start with the background view. This will be the backdrop to our graph. So, let's make it look like a sheet of graph paper.

DRAWING THE BACKGROUND VIEW

Create a new Objective-C class in the Views group. Name it **BackgroundView**, and make it a subclass of **UIView**. You should be an expert at creating classes by now, so I won't walk through all the steps. However, if you need help, just follow the examples from previous chapters.

There are a number of values we will need when drawing our graph grid. For example, how thick are the lines? How much space do we have between lines, and what color are the lines?

We could hard-code all this information into our application; however, I prefer to create properties for these values and then set up default values when the view is instantiated. This gives us a functional view that we can use right out of the box—but also lets us programmatically modify the view, if we want.

Open `BackgroundView.h`. Add the following properties to the header file:

```
@property (assign, nonatomic) CGFloat gridSpacing;
@property (assign, nonatomic) CGFloat gridLineWidth;
@property (assign, nonatomic) CGFloat gridXOffset;
@property (assign, nonatomic) CGFloat gridYOffset;
@property (strong, nonatomic) UIColor *gridLineColor;
```

Now, open `BackgroundView.m`. The template automatically creates an `initWithFrame:` method for us, as well as a commented-out `drawRect:`. We will use both of these.

Let's start by setting up our default values. Views can be created in one of two ways. We could programmatically create the view by calling `alloc` and one of its `init` methods. Eventually, this will call our `initWithFrame:` method, since that is our designated initializer. More likely, however, we will load the view from a nib file or storyboard. In this case, `initWithFrame:` is not called. The system calls `initWithCoder:` instead.

To be thorough, we should have both an `initWithFrame:` method and an `initWithCoder:` method. Furthermore, both of these methods should perform the same basic setup steps. We will do this by moving the real work to a private method that both init methods can then call.

Add the following line to the existing initWithFrame: method:

```
- (id)initWithFrame:(CGRect)frame
{
    self = [super initWithFrame:frame];
    if (self) {
        [self setDefaults];
    }
    return self;
}
```

This calls our (as yet undefined) setDefaults method. Now, just below initWithFrame:, create the initWithCoder: method as shown here:

```
- (id)initWithCoder:(NSCoder *)aDecoder
{
    self = [super initWithCoder:aDecoder];
    if (self) {
        [self setDefaults];
    }
    return self;
}
```

We discussed initWithCoder: in the "Secret Life of Nibs" section of Chapter 2, "Our Application's Architecture." It is similar to, but separate from, our regular initialization chain. Generally speaking, initWithCoder: is called whenever we load an object from disk, and nibs and storyboards get compiled into binary files, which the system loads at runtime. Not surprising, we will see initWithCoder: again in Chapter 5, "Loading and Saving Data."

Now, we just need to create our `setDefaults` method. Create the following code at the bottom of our implementation block:

```
#pragma mark - Private Methods

- (void)setDefaults
{
    self.backgroundColor = [UIColor whiteColor];
    self.opaque = YES;

    self.gridSpacing = 20.0;

    if (self.contentScaleFactor == 2.0)
    {
        self.gridLineWidth = 0.5;
        self.gridXOffset = 0.25;
        self.gridYOffset = 0.25;
    }
    else
    {
        self.gridLineWidth = 1.0;
        self.gridXOffset = 0.5;
        self.gridYOffset = 0.5;
    }

    self.gridLineColor = [UIColor lightGrayColor];
}
```

We start by setting our view's background color to clear. This will override any background color we set in Interface Builder. I often use this trick when working with custom views, since they will not get drawn in Interface Builder. By default, all views appear as a rectangular area on the screen. Often we need to set a temporary background color, since the views otherwise match the parent's background color or are clear (letting the parent view show through). This, effectively, makes them invisible in Interface Builder.

By setting this property when the view is first loaded, we can freely give it any background color we want in Interface Builder. This make our custom views easier to see while we work on them. Plus, by setting the value when the view is created, we can still override it programmatically in the controller's `viewDidLoad` if we want.

Next, we set the view to opaque. This means we promise to fill the entire view from corner to corner with opaque data. In our case, we're providing a completely opaque background color. If we programmatically change the background color to a translucent color, we should also change the opaque property.

Next, we check the view's scale factor. The default value we use for our line width, the x-offset and the y-offset, all vary depending on whether we are drawing to a regular or a Retina display.

All the iPhones and iPod touches that support iOS 7 have Retina displays. However, the iPad 2 and the iPad mini still use regular displays—so it's a good idea to support both resolutions. After all, even if we are creating an iPhone-only app, it may end up running on an iPad.

Additionally, Apple may release new devices that also have non-Retina displays. The iPad mini is a perfect example. It has the same resolution as a regular size iPad 2; it just shrinks the pixel size down by about 80 percent. Also, like the iPad 2, it uses a non-Retina display, presumably to reduce cost and improve performance and energy use.

We want to draw the smallest line possible. This means the line must be 1-pixel wide, not 1-point wide. We, therefore, have to check the scale and calculate our line width appropriately. Furthermore, we also need to make sure our lines are properly aligned with the underlying pixels. That means we have to offset them by half the line's width (or, in this case, half a pixel).

Now we need to draw our grid. Uncomment the drawRect: method. The system calls this method during each display phase, as discussed in Chapter 3, "Developing Views and View Controllers." Basically, each time through the run loop, the system will check all the views in the view hierarchy and see whether they need to be redrawn. If they do, it will call their drawRect: method.

Also as mentioned in the previous chapter, our views aggressively cache their content. Therefore, most normal operations (changing their frame, rotating them, covering them up, uncovering them, moving them, hiding them, or even fading them in and out) won't force the views to be redrawn. Most of the time this means our view will be drawn once when it is first created. It may be redrawn if our system runs low on memory while it's offscreen. Otherwise, the system will just continue to use the cached version.

DRAWING FOR THE RETINA DISPLAY

As you probably know, the iPhone's Retina display has a 960x640 display. This is four times the number of pixels as the 3GS and earlier models. This could result in a lot of complexity for developers—if we had to constantly test for the screen size and alter our drawing code to match. Fortunately, Apple has hidden much of this complexity from us.

All the native drawing functions (Core Graphics, UIKit, and Core Animation) use a logical coordinate system measured in points. A point is approximately 1/160 of an inch. It's important to note that these points may or may not be the same as the screen's pixels. Draw a 1-point-wide line on a regular display, and you get a 1-pixel-wide line. Draw the same line on a Retina display, and it is now 2 pixels wide. This also means a full-screen frame is the same size, regardless of the display type. We still have three screen sizes to deal with: iPhone 3.5-inch, iPhone 4-inch, and iPad. But, three is better than five or six.

A device's scale factor gives us the conversion between points and pixels. You can access the scale property from the UIScreen, UIView, UIImage, or CALayer classes. This allows us to perform any resolution-dependent processing. However, we actually get a lot of support for free.

- All standard UIKit views are automatically drawn at the correct resolution.

- Vector-based drawings (e.g., UIBezierPath, CGPathRef, and PDFs) automatically take advantage of the higher resolution to produce smoother lines.

- All text is automatically rendered at the higher resolution.

There are, however, some steps we still need to take to fully support multiple screen resolutions. One obvious example occurs when loading and displaying images and other bitmapped art. We need to create higher-resolution copies of these files for the Retina display. Fortunately, UIKit supports automatically loading the correct resolution from the assets category.

Let's say you have a 20-pixel by 30-pixel image named stamp.png. You also need to create a Retina version that is 40 x 60 pixels. Now open the Images.xcassets. The catalog editor has two parts: a list of all your assets on the left and a detail view on the right.

Drag and drop your original image into the assets list. Xcode will automatically make a new entry for it called stamp. Now select the stamp entry. The detail view will show you the 1x version of your image, with a placeholder for the 2x. Drag the Retina version into the 2x position. The image is now ready to use. You just need to request the image by the asset's name, as shown here:

```
UIImage* stampImage =
[UIImage imageNamed:@"stamp"];
```

UIKit will automatically load the correct version for your device.

Similarly, if we are creating bitmaps programmatically, we will want to make sure we give them the correct scale factor. The UIGraphicsBeginImageContext function creates a bitmap-based graphics context with a 1.0 scale factor. Instead, use the UIGraphicsBeginImageContextWithOptions function and pass in the correct scale (which you can access by calling [[UIScreen mainScreen] scale]).

Core Animation layers may also need explicit support. Whenever you create a new CALayer (one that is not already associated with a view), it comes with a default scale value of 1.0. If you then draw this layer onto a Retina display, it will automatically scale up to match the screen. You can prevent this by manually changing the layer's scale factor and then providing resolution-appropriate content.

Finally, OpenGL ES also uses a 1.0 scale by default. Everything will still draw on the Retina display, but it will be scaled up and may appear blocky (especially when compared to properly scaled drawings). To get full-scale rendering, we must increase the size of our render buffers. This, however, can have severe performance implications. Therefore, we must make these changes manually. Changing a view's contentScaleFactor will automatically alter the underlying CAEAGLLayer, increasing the size of the render buffers by the scale factor.

It is also important to test your drawing code on all the devices you intend to support. Drawing a 0.5-point-wide line may look fine on a retina display but appear large and fuzzy on a regular display. Similarly, higher-resolution resources use more memory and may take longer to load and process. This is particularly true for full-screen images.

Even with all these exceptions and corner cases, iOS's logical coordinate system greatly simplifies creating custom drawing code that works across multiple resolutions. Most of the time we get automatic Retina support without doing anything at all.

SUBPIXEL DRAWING

All of our drawing routines use `CGFloat`, `CGPoint`, `CGSize`, and `CGRect`, and all of these use floating-point values. That means we can draw a 0.34-pixel-wide line at y = 23.428. Obviously, however, our screen cannot display partial pixels.

Instead, our drawing engine simulates subpixel resolutions using anti-aliasing—proportionally blending the drawn line with the background color in each partial pixel. Anti-aliasing makes lines look smoother, especially curved or diagonal lines. It fills in the otherwise harsh, jagged edges. Unfortunately, it can also make our drawings appear softer or somewhat fuzzy.

By default, anti-aliasing is turned on for any window or bitmap context. It is turned off for any other graphics contexts. However, we can explicitly set our context's anti-aliasing using the `CGContextSetShouldAntiAlias()` function.

It's also important to realize that the graphics context's coordinates fall in between the pixels, and the drawing engine centers the lines on their endpoints. For example, if you draw a 1-point-wide horizontal line at y = 20, on a non-Retina display (iPad 2 or iPad mini, for example), the line will actually be drawn half in pixel row 19 and half in row 20. If anti-aliasing is turned on, this will result in two rows of pixels, each with a 50 percent blend. If anti-aliasing is off, you will get a 2-pixel-wide line. You can fix this by offsetting the drawing coordinates by half a point (y = 20.5). Then the line will fall exactly along the row of pixels.

For a Retina display, the 1-point line will result in a 2-pixel line that properly fills both rows on either side of the y-coordinate. A 0.5 pixel-wide line, though, will similarly need to be offset by 0.25 pixels. For more information on how Retina displays and scale factors work, see the "Drawing for the Retina Display" sidebar.

Additionally, when the system does ask us to draw or redraw a view, it typically asks us to draw the entire view. The rect passed into `drawRect:` will be equal to the view's bounds. The only time this isn't true is when we start using tiled layers or when we explicitly call `setNeedsDisplayInRect:` and specify a subsection of our view.

NOTE: We should never call `drawRect:` directly. Instead, we can force a view to redraw its contents by calling `setNeedsDisplay` or `setNeedsDisplayInRect:`. This will force the view to be redrawn the next time through the run loop. `setNeedsDisplay` will update the entire view, while `setNeedsDisplayInRect:` will redraw only the specified portion of the view.

Drawing is expensive. If you're creating a view that updates frequently, you should try to minimize the amount of drawing your class performs with each update. Write your `drawRect:` method so that it doesn't do unnecessary drawing outside the specified rect. You should also use `setNeedsDisplayInRect:` to redraw the smallest possible portion. However, for Health Beat, our views display largely static data. The graph is updated only when a new entry is added. As a result, we can take the easier approach, disregard the rect argument, and simply redraw the entire view.

Implement drawRect: as shown here:

```objc
- (void)drawRect:(CGRect)rect
{
    CGFloat width = CGRectGetWidth(self.bounds);
    CGFloat height = CGRectGetHeight(self.bounds);

    UIBezierPath *path = [UIBezierPath bezierPath];
    path.lineWidth = self.gridLineWidth;

    CGFloat x = self.gridXOffset;
    while (x <= width)
    {
        [path moveToPoint:CGPointMake(x, 0.0)];
        [path addLineToPoint:CGPointMake(x, height)];
        x += self.gridSpacing;
    }

    CGFloat y = self.gridYOffset;
    while (y <= height)
    {
        [path moveToPoint:CGPointMake(0.0, y)];
        [path addLineToPoint:CGPointMake(width, y)];
        y += self.gridSpacing;
    }

    [self.gridLineColor setStroke];
    [path stroke];
}
```

We start by using some of the CGGeometry functions to extract the width and height from our view's bounds. Then we create an empty UIBezierPath.

Bezier paths let us mathematically define shapes. These could be open shapes (basically lines and curves) or closed shapes (squares, circles, rectangles, and so on). We define the path as a series of lines and curved segments. The lines have a simple start and end point. The curves have a start and end point and two control points, which define the shape of the curve. If you've ever drawn curved lines in a vector art program, you know what I'm talking about. We can use our UIBezierPath to draw the outline (stroking the path) or to fill in the closed shape (filling the path).

FIGURE 4.1 Our back-
ground view

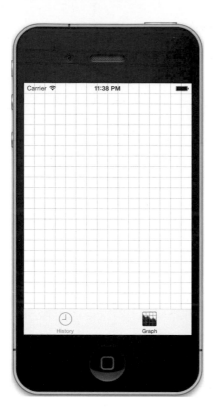

UIBezierPath also has a number of convenience methods to produce ready-made shapes. For example, we can create paths for rectangles, ovals, rounded rectangles, and arcs using these convenience methods.

For our grid, the path will just be a series of straight lines. We start with an empty path and then add each line to the path. Then we draw it to the screen.

Notice, when we create the path, we set the line's width. Then we create a line every 20 points, both horizontally and vertically. We start by moving the cursor to the beginning of the next line by calling `moveToPoint:`, and then we add the line to the path by calling `addLineToPoint:`. Once all the lines have been added, we set the line color by calling `UIColor`'s `setStroke` method. Then we draw the lines by calling the path's `stroke` method.

We still need to tell our storyboard to use this background view. Open `Main.storyboard` and zoom in on the Graph View Controller scene. Select the scene's `view` object (either in the Document Outline or by clicking the center of the scene), and in the Identity inspector, change Class to **BackgroundView**.

Just like in Chapter 3, the class should be listed in the drop-down; however, sometimes Xcode doesn't correctly pick up all our new classes. If this happens to you, you can just type in the name, or you can quit out of Xcode and restart it—forcing it to update the class lists.

Run the application and tap the Graph tab. It should display a nice, graph paper effect (**Figure 4.1**).

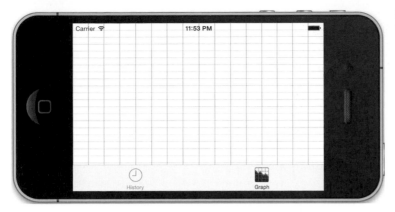

FIGURE 4.2 The background view is stretched when rotated.

There are a couple of points worth discussing here. First, notice how our drawing stretches up under the status bar. Actually, it's also stretched down below the tab bar, but the tab bar blurs and fades the image quite a bit, so it's not obvious.

One of the biggest changes with iOS 7 is the way it handles our bars. In previous versions of iOS, our background view would automatically shrink to fit the area between the bars. In iOS 7, it extends behind the bars by default.

We can change this, if we want. We could set the view controller's edgesForExtended Layout to UIRectEdgeNone. In our view, this would prevent our background view from extending below the tab bar. It will also make the tab bar opaque. However, this won't affect the status bar.

We actually want our background view to extend behind our bars. It gives our UI a sense of context. However, we want the actual content to be displayed between the bars. To facilitate this, we will draw our actual graph in a separate view, and we will use auto layout to size that view properly between the top and bottom layout guides.

Also notice, the status bar does not have any background color at all. It is completely transparent. We can set whether it displays its contents using a light or a dark font—but that's it. If we want to blur or fade out the content behind the bar, we need to provide an additional view to do that for us. However, I will leave that as a homework exercise.

There is one slight problem with our background view, however. Run the app again and try rotating it. When we rotate our view, auto layout will change its frame to fill the screen horizontally. However, as I said earlier, this does not cause our view to redraw. Instead, it simply reuses the cached version, stretching it to fit (**Figure 4.2**).

We could fix this by calling setNeedsDisplay after our view rotates—but there's an easier way. Open BackgroundView.m again. Find setDefaults, and add the following line after self.opaque = YES:

```
self.contentMode = UIViewContentModeRedraw;
```

The content mode is used to determine how a view lays out its content when its bounds change. Here, we are telling our view to automatically redraw itself. We can still move the view, rotate it, fade it in, or cover it up. None of that will cause it to redraw. However, change the size of its `frame` or bounds, and it will be redrawn to match.

Run the app again. It will now display correctly as you rotate it.

DRAWING THE LINE GRAPH

Now let's add the line graph. Let's start by creating a new `UIView` subclass named `GraphView`. Place this in the Views group with our other views.

Before we get to the code, let's set up everything in Interface Builder. Open `Main.storyboard`. We should still be zoomed into the Graph View Controller scene.

Drag a new view out and place it in the scene. Shrink it so that it is a small box in the middle of the scene and then change its Class to **GraphView** and its background to **lightGray**. This will make it easier to see (**Figure 4.3**).

We want to resize it so that it fills the screen from left to right, from the top layout guide to the bottom. However, it will be easier to let Auto Layout do that for us. With the graph view selected, click the Pin tool. We want to use the Add New Constraints controls to set the constraints shown in **Table 4.1**. Next, set Update Frames to **Items of New Constraints**, and click the Add 4 Constraints button. The view should expand as desired.

Run the app and navigate to our graph view. It should fill the screen as shown in **Figure 4.4**. Rotate the app and make sure it resizes correctly.

TABLE 4.1 Graph View's Constraints

SIDE	TARGET	CONSTANT
Left	Background View	0
Top	Top Layout Guide	0
Right	Background View	0
Bottom	Background View*	49*

* Ideally, we would like to pin the bottom of our graph view to the Bottom Layout Guide with a spacing constant of 0. This should align the bottom of our graph view with the top of the tab bar. If the tab bar's height changes or if we decide to remove the tab bar, the Bottom Layout Guide would automatically adjust.

However, as of the Xcode 5.0 release, there is a bug in the Bottom Layout Guide. When the view first appears it begins aligned with the bottom of the background view, not the top of the tab bar. If you rotate the view, it adjusts to the correct position. Unfortunately, until this bug is fixed, we must hard-code the proper spacing into our constraints. That is the only way to guarantee that our graph view gets laid out properly.

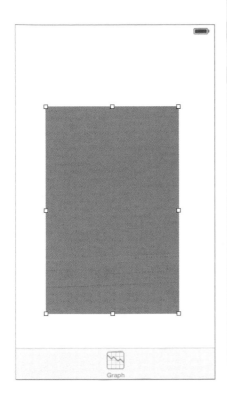

FIGURE 4.3 Adding the view

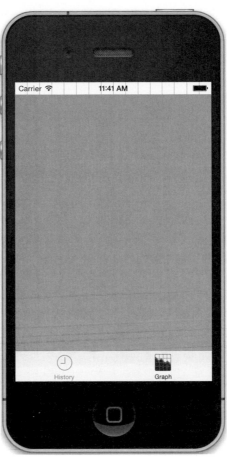

FIGURE 4.4 The properly sized graph view

There's one last step before we get to the code. We will need an outlet to our graph view. Switch to the Assistant editor, Control-drag from the graph view to GraphViewController.m's class extension, and create the following outlet:

```
@property (weak, nonatomic) IBOutlet GraphView *graphView;
```

Unfortunately, this creates an "Unknown type name 'GraphView'" error. We can fix this by scrolling to the top of GraphViewController.m and importing GraphView.h.

Now, switch back to the Standard editor, and open GraphView.h. We want to add a number of properties to our class. First, we need an NSArray to contain the weight entries we intend to graph. We also need to add a number of properties to control our graph's appearance. This will follow the general pattern we used for the background view.

Add the following properties to GraphView's public header:

```objc
// This must be an array sorted by date in ascending order.
@property (strong, nonatomic) NSArray *weightEntries;

@property (assign, nonatomic) CGFloat margin;

@property (assign, nonatomic) CGFloat guideLineWidth;
@property (assign, nonatomic) CGFloat guideLineYOffset;
@property (strong, nonatomic) UIColor *guideLineColor;

@property (assign, nonatomic) CGFloat graphLineWidth;
@property (assign, nonatomic) CGFloat dotSize;
```

Notice that we're assuming our weight entries are sorted in ascending order. When we implement our code, we'll add a few sanity checks to help validate the incoming data—but we won't do an item-by-item check of our array. Instead, we will assume that the calling code correctly follows the contract expressed in our comment. If it doesn't, the results will be unpredictable.

We've seen this methodology before. Objective-C often works best when you clearly communicate your intent and assume other developers will follow that intent. Unfortunately, in this case, we don't have any syntax tricks that we can use to express our intent. We must rely on comments. This is, however, an excellent use case for documentation comments. I'll leave that as an exercise for the truly dedicated reader.

Switch to GraphView.m. Just like our background view, we want the pair of matching init... methods, with a private setDefaults method. The init... methods are shown here:

```objc
- (id)initWithFrame:(CGRect)frame
{
    self = [super initWithFrame:frame];
    if (self) {
        [self setDefaults];
    }
    return self;
}


- (id)initWithCoder:(NSCoder *)aDecoder
{
    self = [super initWithCoder:aDecoder];
    if (self) {
        [self setDefaults];
    }
    return self;
}
```

And, at the bottom of the implementation block, add the setDefaults method.

```
#pragma mark - Private Methods

- (void)setDefaults
{
    self.contentMode = UIViewContentModeRedraw;
    self.backgroundColor = [UIColor clearColor];
    self.opaque = NO;

    self.margin = 20.0;

    if (self.contentScaleFactor == 2.0)
    {
        self.guideLineYOffset = 0.0;
    }
    else
    {
        self.guideLineYOffset = 0.5;
    }

    self.guideLineWidth = 1.0;
    self.guideLineColor = [UIColor darkGrayColor];

    self.graphLineWidth = 2.0;
    self.dotSize = 4.0;
}
```

This code is almost the same as our background view. Yes, the property names and values have changed, but the basic concept is the same. Notice that we are using a clear backgroundColor, letting our background view show through. We have also set the opaque property to YES.

Additionally, since our graph line's width is an even number of pixels, we don't need to worry about aligning it to the underlying pixels. If it's drawn as a vertical or horizontal line, it will already correctly fill 1 pixel above and 1 pixel below the given coordinates (in a non-Retina display). By a similar logic, the 1-point guidelines need to be offset only in non-Retina displays.

The app should successfully build and run. However, notice that our previously gray graph view has completely vanished. Now we just need to add some custom drawing, to give it a bit of content.

For the purpose of this book, we want to keep our graph simple. So, we will just draw three horizontal guidelines with labels and the line graph itself. Also, we're not trying to match the graph with the background view's underlying graph paper. In a production app, you would probably want to add guidelines or labels for the horizontal axis, as well as coordinate the background and graph views, giving the graph paper actual meaning.

PASSING THE DATA

The graph will be scaled to vertically fill our space, with the maximum value near the top of our view and the minimum near the bottom. It will also horizontally fill our view, with the earliest dates close to the left side and the latest date close to the right.

But, before we can do this, we need to pass in our weight entry data. Open `GraphViewController.m`. First things first—we need to import `WeightHistoryDocument.h`. We already added a forward declaration in the `.h` file, but we never actually imported the class. It hasn't been necessary, since we haven't used it—until now.

Then, add a `viewWillAppear:` method, as shown here:

```
- (void)viewWillAppear:(BOOL)animated
{
    [super viewWillAppear:animated];

    self.graphView.weightEntries =
    [[[self.weightHistoryDocument allEntries]
        reverseObjectEnumerator] allObjects];
}
```

As our `GraphView`'s comments indicated, we want to pass our weight entries in ascending order. However, our document stores them in descending order. So, we have to reverse this array.

We grab all the entries from our weight history document. We then access the reverse enumerator for these entries. The reverse enumerator lets us iterate over all the objects in the reverse order. Finally we call the enumerator's `allObjects` method. This returns the remaining objects in the collection. Since we haven't enumerated over any objects yet, it returns the entire array. This is a quick technique for reversing any array.

Of course, we could have just passed the entire weight history document to our graph view, but isolating an array of entries has several advantages. First, as a general rule, we don't want to give any object more access to our model than is absolutely necessary. More pragmatically, writing the code this way gives us a lot of flexibility for future expansions. We could easily modify our code to just graph the entries from last week, last month, or last year. We'd just need to filter our entries before we passed them along.

Unfortunately, there is one small problem with this approach. `WeightHistoryDocument` doesn't have an `allEntries` method. Let's fix that. Open `WeightHistoryDocument.h` and declare `allEntries` just below `weightEntriesAfter:before:`.

```
- (NSArray *)allEntries;
```

Now switch to `WeightHistoryDocument.m`. Implement `allEntries` as shown here:

```
- (NSArray *)allEntries
{
    return [self.weightHistory copy];
}
```

Here, we're making a copy of our history array and returning the copy. This avoids exposing our internal data, and prevents other parts of our application from accidentally altering it.

> **NOTE:** We have two options when it comes to returning our internal array. We could create an immutable copy of our array and return it, as shown here. This is the safest approach. Unfortunately, it can get very expensive, especially once our array grows quite large. Alternatively, we could just return the `weightHistory` array unmodified. While this may seem risky, our method signature says that we're returning an `NSArray`. Therefore, anyone calling this method should treat the returned value as an immutable array. Calling `NSMutableArray` methods on it would violate our contract. Since we call this method only once, when our view appears, the more secure approach is probably better. However, if we had to call this method multiple times in a tight loop, we might want to switch and just return our internal data directly. As always, if you have doubts, profile your application and base your decision on hard data.

Now, switch back to `GraphView.m`. There are a number of private properties we want to add. Some of these will hold statistical data about our entries. Others will hold layout data—letting us easily calculate these values once and then use them across a number of different drawing methods.

At the top of `GraphView.m`, import `WeightEntry.h`, and then add a class extension as shown here:

```
#import "WeightEntry.h"

@interface GraphView ()

@property (assign, nonatomic) float minimumWeight;
@property (assign, nonatomic) float maximumWeight;
@property (assign, nonatomic) float averageWeight;
@property (strong, nonatomic) NSDate *earliestDate;
@property (strong, nonatomic) NSDate *latestDate;

@property (assign, nonatomic) CGFloat topY;
@property (assign, nonatomic) CGFloat bottomY;
@property (assign, nonatomic) CGFloat minX;
@property (assign, nonatomic) CGFloat maxX;

@end
```

Now, let's add a custom setter for our `weightEntries` property. This will set the statistical data any time our entries change.

```
#pragma mark - Accessor Methods

- (void)setWeightEntries:(NSArray *)weightEntries
{
    _weightEntries = weightEntries;

    if ([_weightEntries count] > 0)
    {
        self.minimumWeight =
        [[weightEntries valueForKeyPath:@"@min.weightInLbs"] floatValue];

        self.maximumWeight =
        [[weightEntries valueForKeyPath:@"@max.weightInLbs"] floatValue];

        self.averageWeight =
        [[weightEntries valueForKeyPath:@"@avg.weightInLbs"] floatValue];

        self.earliestDate =
        [weightEntries valueForKeyPath:@"@min.date"];

        self.latestDate =
        [weightEntries valueForKeyPath:@"@max.date"];

        NSAssert([self.latestDate isEqualToDate:
                    [[self.weightEntries lastObject] date]],
                  @"The weight entry array must be "
                  @"in ascending chronological order");

        NSAssert([self.earliestDate isEqualToDate:
                    [self.weightEntries[0] date]],
                  @"The weight entry array must be "
                  @"in ascending chronological order");
    }
    else
    {
        self.minimumWeight = 0.0;
        self.maximumWeight = 0.0;
        self.averageWeight = 0.0;
```

```
        self.earliestDate = nil;
        self.latestDate = nil;
    }


    [self setNeedsDisplay];
}
```

Ideally, nothing in this method comes as a surprise. We assign the incoming value to our property. Then we check to see whether our new array has any elements. If it does, we set up our statistical data. Here, we're using the KVC operators we used in the "Updating Our View" section of Chapter 3. Notice that we can use them for both the weight and the date properties. @min.date gives us the earliest date in the array, while @max.date gives us the latest. We also check the first and last object and make sure the first object is our earliest date and the last object is our latest date. This acts as a quick sanity check. Obviously it won't catch every possible mistake—but it is fast, and it will catch most obvious problems (like forgetting to reverse our array). As a bonus, it works even if our array has only one entry.

If our array is empty (or has been set to nil), we simply clear out the stats data.

Now, let's draw the graph. Drawing code can get very complex, so we're going to split it into a number of helper methods.

Start by adding methods to calculate our graph size. We'll be storing these values in instance variables. I'm always a bit uncomfortable when I store temporary data in an instance variable. I like to clear it out as soon as I'm done—preventing me from accidentally misusing the data when it's no longer valid. So, let's make a method to clean up our data as well.

Add these private methods to the bottom of our implementation block:

```
- (void)calculateGraphSize
{
    CGRect innerBounds =
    CGRectInset(self.bounds, self.margin, self.margin);
    self.topY = CGRectGetMinY(innerBounds) + self.margin;
    self.bottomY = CGRectGetMaxY(innerBounds);
    self.minX = CGRectGetMinX(innerBounds);
    self.maxX = CGRectGetMaxX(innerBounds);
}


- (void)clearGraphSize
{
    self.topY = 0.0;
    self.bottomY = 0.0;
    self.minX = 0.0;
    self.maxX = 0.0;
}
```

The `calculateGraphSize` shows off more of the `CGGeometry` functions. Here, we use `CGRectInset` to take a rectangle and shrink it. Each side will be moved in by our margin. Given our default values, this will create a new rectangle that is centered on the old one but is 40 points shorter and 40 points thinner.

You can also use this method to make rectangles larger, by using negative inset values.

Then we use the `CGRectGet…` methods to pull out various bits of data. The `topY` value deserves special attention. We want the top margin to be twice as big as the bottom, left, and right. Basically, we want all of our content to fit inside the `innerBounds` rectangle. We will use the `topY` and `bottomY` to draw our minimum and maximum weight guidelines. However, the top guideline needs a little extra room for its label.

The `clearGraphSize` method is much simpler; we just set everything to `0.0`.

Now, let's add a private `drawGraph` method.

```
- (void)drawGraph
{
    // if we don't have any entries, we're done
    if ([self.weightEntries count] == 0) return;

    UIBezierPath *barGraph = [UIBezierPath bezierPath];
    barGraph.lineWidth = self.graphLineWidth;

    BOOL firstEntry = YES;
    for (WeightEntry *entry in self.weightEntries) {

        CGPoint point =
        CGPointMake([self calculateXForDate:entry.date],
                    [self calculateYForWeight:entry.weightInLbs]);

        if (firstEntry)
        {
            [barGraph moveToPoint:point];
            firstEntry = NO;
        }
        else
        {
            [barGraph addLineToPoint:point];
        }

        if (entry.weightInLbs == self.maximumWeight)
        {
```

```
        [self drawDotForEntry:entry];
    }

    if (entry.weightInLbs == self.minimumWeight)
    {
        [self drawDotForEntry:entry];
    }
}

[self.tintColor setStroke];
[barGraph stroke];
}
```

We start by checking to see whether we have any entries. If we don't have any entries, we're done. There's no graph to draw.

If we do have entries, we create an empty Bezier path to hold our line graph. We iterate over all the entries in our array. We calculate the correct x- and y-coordinates for each entry, based on their weight and date. Then, for the first entry we move the cursor to the correct coordinates. For every other entry, we add a line from the previous coordinates to our new coordinates. If our entry is our minimum or maximum value, we draw a dot at that location as well. Finally we draw the line. This time, we're using our view's tintColor. We discussed tintColor in the "Customizing Our Appearance" section of Chapter 3. Basically, graphView's tintColor will default to our window's tint color—but we could programmatically customize this view by giving it a different tintColor.

Let's add the methods to calculate our x- and y-coordinates. Start with the x-coordinate.

```
- (CGFloat) calculateXForDate:(NSDate *)date
{
    NSAssert([self.weightEntries count] > 0,
            @"You must have more than one entry "
            @"before you call this method");

    if ([self.earliestDate compare:self.latestDate] == NSOrderedSame )
    {
        return (self.maxX + self.minX) / (CGFloat)2.0;
    }

    NSTimeInterval max =
    [self.latestDate timeIntervalSinceDate:self.earliestDate];

    NSTimeInterval interval =
```

```
        [date timeIntervalSinceDate:self.earliestDate];

        CGFloat width = self.maxX - self.minX;
        CGFloat percent = (CGFloat)(interval / max);
        return percent * width + self.minX;
    }
```

We start with a quick sanity check. This method should never be called if we don't have any entries. Then we check to see whether our earliest date and our latest date are the same. If they are (for example, if we have only one date), they should be centered in our graph. Otherwise, we need to convert our dates into numbers that we can perform mathematical operations on. The easiest way to do this is using the `timeIntervalSinceDate:` method. This will return a double containing the number of seconds between the current date and the specified dates.

We can then use these values to calculate each date's relative position between our earliest and latest dates. We calculate a percentage from 0.0 (the earliest date) to 1.0 (the latest date). Then we use that percentage to determine our x-coordinate.

Note that our literal floating-point values and our time intervals are doubles. If we compile this on 32-bit, we want to convert them down to `float`s. If we compile on 64-bit, we want to leave them alone. We can accomplish this by casting them to `CGFloat`—since its size changes with the target platform.

Now, let's calculate the y-values.

```
- (CGFloat)calculateYForWeight:(CGFloat)weight
{
    NSAssert([self.weightEntries count] > 0,
            @"You must have more than one entry "
            @"before you call this method");

    if (self.minimumWeight == self.maximumWeight)
    {
        return (self.bottomY + self.topY) / (CGFloat)2.0;
    }

    CGFloat height = self.bottomY - self.topY;
    CGFloat percent = (CGFloat)1.0 - (weight - self.minimumWeight) /
    (self.maximumWeight - self.minimumWeight);

    return height * percent + self.topY;
}
```

The Y value calculations are similar. On the one hand, the code is a little simpler, since we can do mathematical operations on the weight values directly. Notice, however, that the math to calculate our percentage is much more complicated. There are two reasons for this. First, in our dates, the earliest date will always have a value of 0.0. With our weights, this is not true. We need to adjust for our minimum weight. Second, remember that our y-coordinates increase as you move down the screen. This means our maximum weight must have the smallest y-coordinate, while our minimum weight has the largest. We do this by inverting our percentage, subtracting the value we calculate from 1.0.

Now, let's add the method to draw our dots.

```
- (void)drawDotForEntry:(WeightEntry *)entry
{
    CGFloat x = [self calculateXForDate:entry.date];
    CGFloat y = [self calculateYForWeight:entry.weightInLbs];
    CGRect boundingBox =
    CGRectMake(x - (self.dotSize / (CGFloat)2.0),
               y - (self.dotSize / (CGFloat)2.0),
               self.dotSize,
               self.dotSize);

    UIBezierPath *dot =
    [UIBezierPath bezierPathWithOvalInRect:boundingBox];

    [self.tintColor setFill];
    [dot fill];
}
```

Here we get the x- and y-coordinates for our entry and calculate a bounding box for our dot. Our bounding box's height and width are equal to our dotSize property, and it is centered on our x- and y-coordinates. We then call bezierPathWithOvalInRect: to calculate a circular Bezier path that will fit inside this bounding box. Then we draw the dot, using our view's tint color as the fill color.

Now, we just need to call these methods. Replace the commented out drawRect: with the version shown here:

```
- (void)drawRect:(CGRect)rect
{
    [self calculateGraphSize];
    [self drawGraph];
    [self clearGraphSize];
}
```

FIGURE 4.5 A graph
with four entries

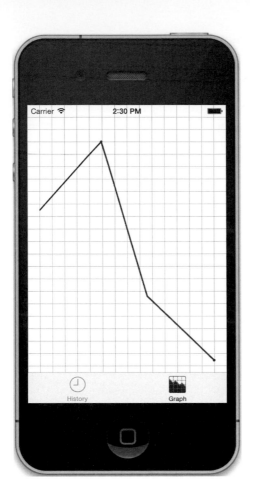

Build and run the application. When it has zero entries, the graph view is blank. If you add one entry, it will appear as a dot, roughly in the center of the screen. Add two or more entries, and it will draw the graph's line (**Figure 4.5**). Rotate it, and the graph will be redrawn in the new orientation.

Now we just need to add our guidelines. Let's start by making a private method to draw a guideline.

```
- (void)drawGuidelineAtY:(CGFloat)y withLabelText:(NSString *)text
{
    UIFont *font =
    [UIFont preferredFontForTextStyle:UIFontTextStyleCaption1];

    NSDictionary *textAttributes =
    @{NSFontAttributeName:font,
      NSForegroundColorAttributeName:self.guideLineColor};
```

```
    CGSize textSize = [text sizeWithAttributes:textAttributes];
    CGRect textRect = CGRectMake(self.minX,
                                 y - textSize.height - 1,
                                 textSize.width,
                                 textSize.height);

    textRect = CGRectIntegral(textRect);

    UIBezierPath *textbox = [UIBezierPath bezierPathWithRect:textRect];
    [self.superview.backgroundColor setFill];
    [textbox fill];

    [text drawInRect:textRect withAttributes:textAttributes];

    CGFloat pattern[] = {5, 2};

    UIBezierPath *line = [UIBezierPath bezierPath];
    line.lineWidth = self.guideLineWidth;
    [line setLineDash:pattern count:2 phase:0];

    [line moveToPoint:CGPointMake(CGRectGetMinX(self.bounds), y)];
    [line addLineToPoint:CGPointMake(CGRectGetMaxX(self.bounds), y)];

    [self.guideLineColor setStroke];;
    [line stroke];
}
```

We start by getting the Dynamic Type font for the Caption 1 style. Then we create a dictionary of text attributes. These attributes are defined in NSAttributedString UIKit Addons Reference. They can be used for formatting parts of an attributed string; however, we will be using them to format our entire string. We're setting the font to our Dynamic Type font and setting the text color to the guideline color.

Once that's done, we use these attributes to calculate the size needed to draw our text. Then we create a rectangle big enough to hold the text and whose bottom edge is 1 point above the provided y-coordinate. Notice that we use CGRectIntegral() on our rectangle. This will return the smallest integral-valued rectangle that contains the source rectangle.

The sizeWithAttributes: method typically returns sizes that include fractions of a pixel. However, we want to make sure our rectangle is properly aligned with the underlying pixels. Unlike the custom line drawing, when working with text, we should not offset our rectangle—the text-rendering engine will handle that for us.

We first use the `textRect` to draw a box using our `BackgroundView`'s background color. This will create an apparently blank space for our label, making it easier to read. Then we draw our text into the same rectangle.

Next, we define our line. Again, we start with an empty path. We set the line's width, and we set the dash pattern. Here, we're using a C array. This is one of the few places where you'll see a C array in Objective-C. Our dashed line pattern will draw a segment 5 points long, followed by a 2-point gap. It then repeats this pattern.

We draw this line from the left edge of our view to the right edge of our view along the provided y-coordinate. This means our line will lay just below the bottom edge of our text's bounding box. Finally, we set the line color and draw the line.

Now we need to create our guidelines. We will have three: one for the max weight, one for the minimum weight, and one for the average weight. Add the following method to our implementation file:

```objc
- (void) drawLabelsAndGuides
{
    if ([self.weightEntries count] == 0) return;

    WeightUnit unit = getDefaultUnits();

    if (self.minimumWeight == self.maximumWeight)
    {
        float weight = [self.weightEntries[0] weightInLbs];

        NSString * weightLabel =
        [NSString stringWithFormat:@"Weight: %@",
         [WeightEntry stringForWeightInLbs:weight inUnit:unit]];

        [self drawGuidelineAtY:[self calculateYForWeight:weight]
                withLabelText:weightLabel];
    }
    else
    {
        NSString *minLabel =
        [NSString stringWithFormat:@"Min: %@",
         [WeightEntry stringForWeightInLbs:self.minimumWeight
                                    inUnit:unit]];

        NSString *maxLabel =
```

```
[NSString stringWithFormat:@"Max: %@",
 [WeightEntry stringForWeightInLbs:self.maximumWeight
                            inUnit:unit]];

NSString *averageLabel =
[NSString stringWithFormat:@"Average: %@",
 [WeightEntry stringForWeightInLbs:self.averageWeight
                            inUnit:unit]];

[self drawGuidelineAtY:self.topY
         withLabelText:maxLabel];

[self drawGuidelineAtY:self.bottomY
         withLabelText:minLabel];

[self drawGuidelineAtY:
 [self calculateYForWeight:self.averageWeight]
         withLabelText:averageLabel];
    }
}
```

In this method, we simply check to see whether we don't have any entries. If there are
no entries, then we don't need to draw any guidelines, so we just return. Next, we check to
see whether all of our entries have the same weight (either because we have only one entry
or because the user entered the same weight for all entries). If we have only one weight
value, we create a single weight label and draw our line at the calculated y-coordinate (which
should be the vertical center of the graph). Our line should match up with the dot or line that
we drew in our drawGraph method.

If we have more than one weight value, we create a minimum, maximum, and average
strings and then draw lines corresponding to the appropriate values.

Now, add this method to drawRect: as shown here:

```
- (void)drawRect:(CGRect)rect
{
    [self calculateGraphSize];
    [self drawGraph];
    [self drawLabelsAndGuides];
    [self clearGraphSize];
}
```

FIGURE 4.6 Our completed graph view

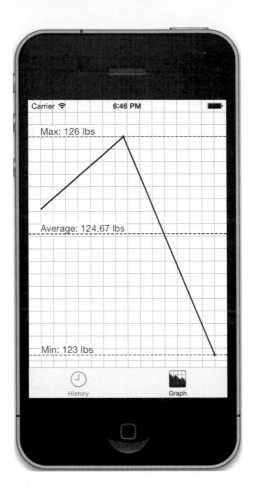

Run the application. With no entries, the graph view is still blank. Add a single entry. This will appear in roughly the middle of the screen, with a guideline running right through our dot. Add multiple lines. You should see the Max, Average, and Min guidelines (**Figure 4.6**).

Our graph is almost done. We just need to update the fonts when the user changes them. We will use the same basic procedure we used in the previous chapter for our history and entry detail views.

Open `GraphViewController.m` and import `UIViewController+HBTUpdates.h`. Now we need to override our `HBT_updateFonts` method as shown here:

```
- (void)HBT_updateFonts
{
    [super HBT_updateFonts];
    [self.graphView setNeedsDisplay];
}
```

If the user changes the font size, this method will mark our graph view as needing to be redrawn. The next time through the run loop, the system will redraw the graph, picking up the new fonts in the process.

Run the app. It will now update correctly when the user changes the font size.

Now, as you can see, there's a lot of room for improvement in this graph. Ideally, however, you've learned a lot along the way. We've covered drawing lines (the grid, graph, and guide lines), shapes (the dots), and text. There are similar methods for drawing images as well—though, it is often easier to just insert a `UIImageView` into your application. The `UIImageView`'s drawing code is highly optimized, and you're unlikely to match its performance.

You should be able to use these, and the other UIKit drawing methods, to create your own custom views. However, it doesn't end here. There are a couple of other graphic techniques worth considering.

OTHER GRAPHICS TECHNIQUES

Under the hood, all of the UIKit drawing methods are actually calling Core Graphics methods. Core Graphics is a low-level C-based library for high-performance drawing. While, most of the time, we can do everything we want at the UIKit level—if you need special features (e.g., gradients or shadows), you will need to switch to Core Graphics.

All core graphics functions take a `CGContextRef` as their first argument. The context is an opaque type that represents the drawing environment. Our UIKit methods also draw into a context—however, the context is hidden from us by default. We can access it, if we need, by calling `UIGraphicsGetCurrentContext()`. This lets us freely mix UIKit and Core Graphics drawing code.

In the `drawRect:` method, our code is drawn into a context that is then displayed on the screen, we can also create graphics contexts to produce JPEG or PNG images or PDFs. We may even use graphics contexts when printing.

However, custom drawing isn't the only way to produce a custom user interface. We can also drop bitmap images into our layout. There are two main techniques for adding bitmaps. If it's simply artwork, we can just place a `UIImageView` in our view hierarchy and set its `image` property. If, however, our image needs to respond to touches, we can place a custom `UIButton` and then call its `backgroundImageForState:` method (or set the background image in Interface Builder).

Bitmaps are often easier than custom drawing. You simply ask your graphic designer to create them for you. You place them in the assets catalog, and you drop them into your interface.

However, custom drawn interfaces have a number of advantages. The biggest is their size. Custom drawn views require considerably less memory than bitmaps. The custom drawn views can also be redrawn to any arbitrary size. If we want to change the size of a bitmapped image, we usually need to get our graphic designer to make a new one. Finally, custom drawn views can be dynamically generated at runtime. Bitmaps can only really present static, unchanging pieces of art.

Often, however, we can get many of the advantages of bitmaps while sidestepping their weaknesses by using resizeable images or image patterns. For more information, check out -[UIImage resizableImageWithCapInsets:], +[UIColor colorWithPatternImage:}, and the Asset Catalog Help.

NOTE: When using bitmapped images, you should always use PNG files, if possible. Xcode will optimize the PNG files for the underlying iOS hardware during compile time. Other formats may require additional processing at runtime, which may cause noticeable sluggishness or delays, especially for large files.

UPDATING OUR DRAWING WHEN THE DATA CHANGES

There's one last modification to our graph view. We need to make sure our graph is updated whenever our data changes. This isn't so important now, but it will become extremely important once we implement iCloud syncing.

To do this, we need to listen for our model's notifications. However, unlike our history view, we don't need to track each change individually. Instead, we will update our entire graph once all the changes are complete. This means we need to track only a single notification.

Open GraphViewController.m. In the class extension, add the following property:

```
@property (strong, nonatomic) id modelChangesCompleteObserver;
```

Now, add a dealloc method just below initWithNibName:bundle:.

```
- (void)dealloc
{
    NSNotificationCenter *center = [NSNotificationCenter defaultCenter];

    if (self.modelChangesCompleteObserver)
    {
        [center removeObserver:self.modelChangesCompleteObserver];
    }
}
```

Next, let's set up our observer. Since there's only one and the code is so simple, let's just put this in viewDidLoad:.

```
- (void)viewDidLoad
{
    [super viewDidLoad];
    self.tabBarItem.selectedImage =
    [UIImage imageNamed:@"graph_selected"];
```

```
NSNotificationCenter *center = [NSNotificationCenter defaultCenter];
NSOperationQueue *mainQueue = [NSOperationQueue mainQueue];
__weak GraphViewController *_self = self;

self.modelChangesCompleteObserver =
[center
 addObserverForName:WeightHistoryDocumentChangesCompleteNotification
 object:self.weightHistoryDocument
 queue:mainQueue
 usingBlock:^(NSNotification *note) {
     _self.graphView.weightEntries =
     [[[_self.weightHistoryDocument allEntries]
       reverseObjectEnumerator] allObjects];
 }];
}
```

This just resets our graph view's weight entry array whenever our document changes. Unfortunately, there's no way to test this code yet. We will get a chance to test it later this chapter, however.

CUSTOM TRANSITIONS

iOS 7 provides classes and methods to support adding custom transitions to our scenes. Specifically, we can customize the transitions when presenting modal views, when switching between tabs, when pushing or popping views onto a navigation controller, and during layout-to-layout transitions between collection view controllers.

In this chapter, we will look at custom transitions when presenting view controllers and when switching between tabs.

For modal segues, the transitions give us a lot of control beyond just modifying the transition's animation. We can also define the final shape and size of our presented view. Since the presented view no longer needs to cover the entire screen, our presenting scene remains in the view hierarchy. We may even be able to interact with any exposed portions of that original scene.

This is an important change, especially for the iPhone. In previous versions of the iOS SDK, presented views had to fill the entire screen on the iPhone (we had a few additional options on the iPad, but they were still relatively limited).

The ability to modify the tab bar animation is also a nice improvement. Before iOS 7, tab bar controllers could not use any animation at all. Touching a tab bar would instantaneously change the content.

However, we're not just going to add an animation sequence between our tabs; we will also create an interactive transition, letting the users drive the transition using a pan gesture. As the user slides her finger across the screen, we will match the motion, sliding from one tab to the next.

Before we can do any of this, however, we need to understand how Core Animation works. Core Animation is the underlying technology behind all of our transitions.

CORE ANIMATION

I won't lie to you: Core Animation is a rich, complex framework. Entire books have been written on this topic. There are lots of little knobs to tweak. However, UIKit has implemented a number of wrapper methods around the basic Core Animation functionality. This lets us easily animate our views, without dropping into the full complexity of the Core Animation framework.

The bad news is UIKit actually exposes two different animation APIs. The old API consists of calling a number of UIView methods. However, these methods must be called in the correct order or you will get unexpected behaviors. Furthermore, coordinating between different animations proved difficult.

While these methods have not been officially deprecated yet, their use is no longer recommended for any applications targeting iOS 4.0 or beyond. Since our minimum deployment target is iOS 4.3, there is no good reason to use these methods anymore.

Instead, we want to use UIView's block-based animation API. UIKit provides a number of class methods in the block-based animation API. Some of these let us animate our views—moving them, resizing them, and fading them in and out. Others let us transition between views. They will remove a view from the view hierarchy, replacing it with a different view.

All UIViews have a number of animatable properties. These include frame, bounds, center, transform, alpha, backgroundColor, and contentStretch. To animate our view, we call one of the animation methods. Inside the animation block, we change one or more of these properties. Core Animation will then calculate the interpolated values for that property for each frame over the block's duration—and it will smoothly animate the results.

If I want to move the view, I just change the frame or the center. If I want to scale or rotate the view, I change the transform. If I want it to fade in or fade out, I change the alpha. Everything else is just bells and whistles.

UIView's animation methods are listed here:

- animateWithDuration:animations: This is the simplest animation method. We provide a duration and the animation block. It animates our changes over the given duration.
- animateWithDuration:animations:completion: This adds a completion block. This block runs after our animation has ended. We can use this to clean up resources, set final positions, trigger actions, or even chain one animation to the next.

- `animateWithDuration:delay:options:animations:completion:` This is the real work-horse. It provides the most options for simple animations. We can set the duration, a delay before the animation begins, a bitmask of animation options, our animation block, and a completion block.

- `animateWithDuration:delay:usingSpringWithDamping:initialSpringVelocity:options:animations:completion:` This is a newer animation method. It's used to create simple, spring-like effects. If you want to give the animation a slight bounce before it settles into the final state, this is your method. You can control the spring's behavior by modifying the dampening and initial velocity arguments. We will look at other techniques for creating realistic, physics-based animations when we talk about UIDynamics in Chapter 8.

- `animateKeyframesWithDuration:delay:options:animations:completion:` We can use this method to run keyframe animations. These are more complex animations tied to specific points in time. To set up keyframe animations, you must call `addKeyframeWithRelativeStartTime:relativeDuration:animations:` inside this method's animation block.

- `addKeyframeWithRelativeStartTime:relativeDuration:animations:` Call this method inside `animateKeyframesWithDuration:delay:options:animations:completion:`'s animation block to set up keyframe animations.

- `performSystemAnimation:onViews:options:animations:completion:` This method lets us perform a predefined system animation on an array of views. We can also specify other animations that will run in parallel. At this point, this lets us only delete views. The views are removed from the view hierarchy when the animation block is complete.

- `transitionWithView:duration:options:animations:completion:` We can use this method to add, remove, show, or hide subviews of the specified container view. The change between states will be animated using the transition style specified in the options. This gives us more flexibility than `transitionFromView:toView:duration:options:completion:`, but it requires more work to set up properly.

- `transitionFromView:toView:duration:options:completion:` This method replaces the "from view" with the "to view" using the transition animation specified in the options. By default the "from view" is removed from the view hierarchy, and the "to view" is added to the view hierarchy when the animation is complete.

- `performWithoutAnimation:` You can call methods that include animation blocks inside this method's block. The changes in those animation blocks will take effect immediately with no animation.

AUTO LAYOUT AND CORE ANIMATION

The easiest way to move views around using animation is to modify the view's `frame` or `center` inside an animation block. This works fine as long as our view only has implicit auto layout constraints. In other words, we added a view to our view hierarchy, either programmatically or using Interface Builder, but we don't provide any constraints for that view.

As long as a view has implicit constraints, we can continue to programmatically alter its position and size using the `frame` and `center` properties. However, once we start adding explicit constraints, things get more difficult. We can no longer think in terms of the `frame` or the `center`. If we try, we may get the view to move, but Auto Layout and Core Animation code will eventually fight for control over the view's position. This can result in unexpected results. The animation may run to completion, only to have the view snap back to its original position. The animation may seem to work properly, only to revert after our device rotates or after some other call updates our constraints. Sometimes it can even cause views to flicker back to an old position briefly at the end of the animation. It all depends on the exact nature of the animation and the timing of the updates.

So, if we want to animate changes in size or position of a view with explicit constraints, we have two options.

- We can modify one of the existing constraints inside the animation block. This is the easiest option, but it is also more limited. We can change only the constraint's `constant` property. Nothing else.

- We can remove the old constraint, add a new constraint, and then call `layoutIfNeeded` inside the animation block. This lets us make any arbitrary changes to our constraints but requires more work.

For the purpose of the Health Beat project, we will perform animation on views only with implicit constraints. These are easier to write and easier to understand. I recommend shying away from animating Auto Layout constraints until you have gotten very comfortable with both Core Animation and Auto Layout.

CUSTOMIZING VIEW PRESENTATION

When creating our own transitions, we have two options: custom transitions and interactive transitions. Custom transitions work like most transitions we've seen. We trigger the transition, and then it automatically runs to completion. Most transitions occur rather rapidly, usually in 0.25 seconds.

On the other hand, the user drives interactive transitions. Before iOS 7, we had only one example of an interactive transition—the `UIPageViewController`. This is the controller behind iBook's page flip animation. As you drag your finger across the screen, the page seems to curl, following your finger. You can move the finger forward or backward. You can stop, speed up, or slow down. The animation follows along. Lift your finger and the page either flips to its original position or continues to flip to the new page.

We will start with a custom transition since it is simpler. The actual transition isn't too difficult—though it does have a number of moving parts to keep track of. However, it radically changes the behavior of our application, which will require some additional work to support.

CUSTOMIZING OUR ADD ENTRY VIEW'S TRANSITION

Our application presents our Add Entry View controller as a modal view. It slides in from the bottom and then slides back out again when we are done. We want to change this. Instead of covering the entire screen, we'd like to cover just a small rectangle in the center. We'd also like to fade in and out, instead of sliding.

Doing this requires three steps.

1. We set the presented controller's `modalPresentationStyle` to `UIModalPresentationCustom`.

2. We provide a transitioning delegate.

3. The transitioning delegate creates an object, which implements the actual animation sequences for us. It will actually provide two separate animation sequences: one to present our view, one to dismiss it.

Open `HistoryTableViewController.m` and add the following code to the bottom of its `prepareForSegue:sender:` method. This should go after the `if` block but before the closing curly bracket.

```
if ([segue.identifier isEqualToString:@"Add Entry Segue"])
{
    UIViewController *destinationController =
    segue.destinationViewController;

    destinationController.modalPresentationStyle =
    UIModalPresentationCustom;

    destinationController.transitioningDelegate = self;
}
```

Next, we need to have our history table view controller adopt the `UIViewController TransitioningDelegate` protocol. Scroll up to the top of the file, and modify the class extension's declaration as shown here:

```
@interface HistoryTableViewController ()
<UIViewControllerTransitioningDelegate>
```

This should get rid of our errors, but if you run the app and bring up the add entry view, you'll see that nothing has changed. Actually, the rotations no longer work properly—so things are worse than before.

We need to implement two of `UIViewControllerTransitioningDelegate`'s methods: `animationControllerForPresentedController:presentingController:sourceController:` and `animationControllerForDismissedController:`. However, before we do this, we need to create our animation controller class.

ANIMATOR OBJECT

We need to create an object, which will manage our transition's animation. In the Controller's group, create a new Objective-C class named AddEntryAnimator. It should be a subclass of NSObject. Open AddEntryAnimator.h, and modify it as shown here:

```
@interface AddEntryAnimator : NSObject <UIViewControllerAnimatedTransitioning>
@property (assign, nonatomic, getter = isPresenting) BOOL presenting;
@end
```

We're simply adopting the UIViewControllerAnimatedTransitioning protocol and declaring a presenting property.

Our AddEntryAnimator will be responsible for actually animating the appearance and disappearance of our Add Entry view. To do this, we must implement two methods: animateTransition: and transitionDuration:.

Switch to AddEntryAnimator.m. At the top of the file, let's import AddEntryViewController.h. Next, let's define a constant value before the @implementation block.

```
static const NSTimeInterval AnimationDuration = 0.25;
```

This is the duration we will use for our animations. We can now implement the transitionDuration: method as shown here:

```
- (NSTimeInterval)transitionDuration:
(id<UIViewControllerContextTransitioning>)transitionContext
{
    return AnimationDuration;
}
```

This method just returns our constant.

Now, let's look at animateTransition: method. This method takes a single argument, our transition context. This is an opaque type, but it adopts the UIViewController ContextTransitioning protocol. As we will see, the context provides a wide range of important information about our transition. This includes giving us access to our view controllers, the beginning and ending frames for their views (if defined by the transition), and our container view.

Our views and view controller hierarchies must be in a consistent state before our transition begins. They must also return to a consistent state after our transition ends. However, during the transition, they may pass through a temporary inconsistent state. To help manage this, we use a container view. The system will create the container and add it to our view hierarchy. It then acts as our superview during our animation sequence.

> **NOTE:** When presenting view controllers, the container view is always full screen and in portrait orientation. If you are animating views in landscape orientation, you will need to make any necessary conversions to the coordinates to get the desired results.

As part of `animateTransition:`, we need to perform the following steps:

1. Make sure both views have been added to the container view.

2. Animate the transition from one view to the next.

3. Make sure each view is in its final position, if defined.

4. Call `completeTransition:` to end the transition and put things back into a consistent state.

Since we are using the same animator for both presenting and dismissing our views, our `animateTransition:` method must handle both cases. To simplify things, we will do some preprocessing in `animateTransition:`, but then call separate private methods to handle the actual animations.

Add the `animateTransition:` method, as shown here:

```
-(void)animateTransition:
(id<UIViewControllerContextTransitioning>)transitionContext
{
    id fromViewController =
    [transitionContext viewControllerForKey:
     UITransitionContextFromViewControllerKey];

    id toViewController =
    [transitionContext viewControllerForKey:
     UITransitionContextToViewControllerKey];

    UIView *containerView = [transitionContext containerView];

    if (self.presenting)
    {
        [self
         presentAddEntryViewController:toViewController
         overParentViewController:fromViewController
         usingContainerView:containerView
         transitionContext:transitionContext];
    }
    else
    {
        [self
         dismissAddEntryViewController:fromViewController
         fromParentViewController:toViewController
         usingContainerView:containerView
         transitionContext:transitionContext];
    }
}
```

We start by requesting the "from" and "to" view controllers from our transition context. Then we ask for our container view. We check to see whether we're presenting or dismissing our Add Entry view, and then we call the corresponding helper method.

When presenting view controllers, the from- and to-controllers can be a common source of confusion and errors. When our Add Entry View is appearing, the from-controller will be our RootTabBarController. This is the presenting view controller as defined by our current presentation context. The to-controller is our AddEntryViewController. However, when we're dismissing the Add Entry View, these roles are reversed.

This means, sometimes our AddEntryViewController is the to-controller. Sometimes it's the from-controller. By using helper functions, we can pass the toViewController and fromViewController in as more clearly named arguments. This lets us work with the parentController and addEntryController—instead of trying to remember which is "from" and which is "to" in each particular case.

Next, add the presentAddEntryViewController:overParentViewController: usingContainerView:transitionContext: method as shown here:

```
#pragma mark - private


- (void) presentAddEntryViewController:
(AddEntryViewController *)addEntryController
overParentViewController:(UIViewController *)parentController
usingContainerView:(UIView *)containerView
transitionContext:
(id<UIViewControllerContextTransitioning>)transitionContext
{

    [containerView addSubview:parentController.view];
    [containerView addSubview:addEntryController.view];

    UIView *addEntryView = addEntryController.view;
    UIView *parentView = parentController.view;
    CGPoint center = parentView.center;

    UIInterfaceOrientation orientation =
    parentController.interfaceOrientation;
    if (UIInterfaceOrientationIsPortrait(orientation))    {
        addEntryView.frame = CGRectMake(0.0, 0.0, 280.0, 170.0);
    }
    else
    {
```

```
        addEntryView.frame = CGRectMake(0.0, 0.0, 170.0, 280.0);
    }

    addEntryView.center = center;
    addEntryView.alpha = 0.0;

    [UIView
     animateWithDuration:AnimationDuration
     animations:^{
         addEntryView.alpha = 1.0;
     }
     completion:^(BOOL finished) {
         [transitionContext completeTransition:YES];
     }];
}
```

We start by adding both views to the container view. We want to make sure the parent view is added first, so our Add Entry view appears above it when drawn. According to the documentation, the system usually adds the from-controller to the container for us, but we typically have to add the to-controller ourselves. Personally, I find it easiest to just add both views. This won't hurt anything, and it guarantees that both views are properly added and that they will be added in the correct order.

Next, we need to make sure our views end up in the proper position. Since we are presenting a view controller (instead of using the navigation controller or tab bar), our to-controller doesn't have a preset destination. We get to define its final size and location. However, our parent view controller must not move. We could verify this by calling our transition context's initialFrameForViewController: and finalFrameForViewController: methods for both view controllers. If it has a required position, it will return the frame for that location. If not, it returns CGRectZero instead—freeing us to do whatever we want.

We're going to make our Add Entry view 280 points wide and 170 points tall. We are also going to center it in its superview. However, we need to make sure all of these coordinates are in the container view's coordinate system, which is always in a portrait orientation.

Finally we perform the actual animation. We set our view's alpha to 0.0, making it invisible. Then we use an animation block to fade it in, by setting the alpha to 1.0 inside the animation block. When the animation is complete, we call completeTransition:. This puts our view and view controller hierarchies into their final state and performs other cleanup tasks.

NOTE: completeTransition:'s argument should be YES if our transition completed successfully, NO if the animation was canceled. Most custom transitions cannot be canceled, so we almost always just pass YES. However, this argument becomes more important when writing interactive transitions.

As you will see, the dismissal code is similar but much simpler. Add the following method, as shown here:

```objc
- (void) dismissAddEntryViewController:
(AddEntryViewController *)addEntryController
fromParentViewController:(UIViewController *)parentController
usingContainerView:(UIView *)containerView
transitionContext:
(id<UIViewControllerContextTransitioning>)transitionContext
{
    [containerView addSubview:parentController.view];
    [containerView addSubview:addEntryController.view];

    [UIView
     animateWithDuration:AnimationDuration
     animations:^{
         addEntryController.view.alpha = 0.0;
     } completion:^(BOOL finished) {
         [transitionContext completeTransition:YES];
     }];
}
```

This time, we don't need to worry about calculating anyone's frame. Again, the parent view should not move, while the Add Entry view will be removed from the view hierarchy and deallocated. So, we can safely ignore both of their frames.

We just add both views to the container view and then create our animation block. This time, we just set the Add Entry view's alpha to 0.0 inside the animation block and then call completeTransition: in the completion block.

IMPLEMENTING THE DELEGATE METHODS

Now, open HistoryTableViewController.m and import AddEntryAnimator.h. Then add the following methods after the storyboard unwinding methods:

```objc
#pragma mark - UIViewControllerTransitioningDelegate Methods

- (id<UIViewControllerAnimatedTransitioning>)
animationControllerForPresentedController:(UIViewController *)presented
presentingController:(UIViewController *)presenting
sourceController:(UIViewController *)source
{
    AddEntryAnimator *animator = [[AddEntryAnimator alloc] init];
    animator.presenting = YES;
```

```
        return animator;
}


- (id<UIViewControllerAnimatedTransitioning>)
animationControllerForDismissedController:(UIViewController *)dismissed
{
    AddEntryAnimator *animator = [[AddEntryAnimator alloc] init];
    animator.presenting = NO;
    return animator;
}
```

The first method is called when performing the modal segue to our AddEntryView
Controller. The second is called when our segue unwinds and our AddEntryViewController
is dismissed. In both cases, we instantiate an animator. We set its presenting property, and
we return the animator. The animator does all the real work.

Run the application, and display our Add Entry view. As you can see, there are a couple
of problems. Our keyboard covers our view. Our weight label is truncated—we really want
our text fields to shrink instead. Our view is not easy to see against the background. It does
not rotate properly. When the Cancel or Save button is pressed, it is not dismissed. And, we
can still use the controls of our background view. Click the Graph tab or the Edit button, and
they operate normally.

As you can see, switching from presenting a modal view to presenting a custom pop-up
can involve quite a few changes to our code.

GENERAL CLEANUP

Let's fix the easy things first. For whatever reason, when we use the regular modal presentation style, the segue unwinding methods will automatically dismiss our presented view controller. We didn't have to do anything. However, with the custom presentation style, we need
to programmatically dismiss our presented controller.

Still in HistoryTableViewController.m, navigate to our segue unwinding methods. Add
the following line to the bottom of both addNewEntrySaved: and addNewEntryCanceled::

```
[self dismissViewControllerAnimated:YES completion:nil];
```

Our Add Entry view will now be properly dismissed whenever the Save or Cancel button
is tapped.

Next, open Main.storyboard and zoom in on the Add Entry View Controller scene. Our
Auto Layout constraints did not work as we expected. Our labels are supposed to remain the
same size, while our text fields grow and shrink. This worked properly when we expanded
the view, but didn't work now that we shrunk the view.

There were no unusual warnings in the console, so either we have a bug in our constraint
logic or we have managed to create an ambiguous constraint. According to Interface Builder,
everything's OK, so let's take a look at the compression resistance and hugging priorities for
our labels and text fields.

Our labels have a content hugging of 251 and a compression resistance of 750. Our text fields have a content hugging of 100 and a compression resistance of 750. We reduced their content hugging to make sure they stretched when the view grew wider during rotations; however, we never thought about our views becoming smaller. Both the text field and the label have a content hugging of 750, which means we have an ambiguous layout. The system doesn't know which element to shrink.

Drop the Horizontal Compression Resistance on both text fields to 100. This breaks the tie. Now, when we run the app, our text fields shrink instead of our labels.

NOTE: Interface Builder did not alert us to this ambiguous layout, because typically the view's width typically expands only from its portrait orientation. Interface Builder does not check every possible change—just the most common ones.

This, however, introduces another problem. Our text fields are now too small for our date. Open AddEntryViewController.m and modify updateDateText as shown here:

```
- (void)updateDateText
{
    if (self.date == nil)
    {
        self.dateTextField.text = @"";
    }
    else
    {
        self.dateTextField.text =
        [NSDateFormatter
         localizedStringFromDate:self.date
         dateStyle:NSDateFormatterShortStyle
         timeStyle:NSDateFormatterShortStyle];

        self.dateTextField.textColor =
        [UIColor darkTextColor];
    }
}
```

Now, back in Main.storyboard, select the date text field, and change its Min Font Size attribute to **12**. That should both give us more space, and let the font shrink if necessary.

While we're in Interface Builder, let's do something about our view's appearance. Select the View, and then click the Background attribute. In the pop-up menu, select Other.... This brings up the color picker. I want a very light blue—almost, but not quite, white. Select the Color

Sliders tab, and set it to **RGB Sliders**. Set the Red to **240**, Green to **245**, and Blue to **255**. Then close the color picker. This will help our Add Entry view stand out against the background.

Finally, let's fix the rotation. Switch back to `AddEntryViewController.m` and add the following method just under `HBT_updateFonts`:

```
- (void)willAnimateRotationToInterfaceOrientation:
(UIInterfaceOrientation)toInterfaceOrientation
duration:(NSTimeInterval)duration
{
    [self centerViewInParent];
}
```

This method is called from within our rotation's animation block, so any animatable properties that we change here will be animated along with the rotation. We will be updating our view's position in a few different methods, so we should extract that code into its own, private method. Add the `centerViewInParent` method to the bottom of our private methods, just before the @end directive.

```
- (void)centerViewInParent
{
    UIView *parentView = self.view.superview;
    CGPoint center = parentView.center;
    center = [parentView convertPoint:center
                             fromView:parentView.superview];
    self.view.center = center;
}
```

Here, we calculate our center's new position. Again, we grab the superview's center and then convert it to the correct coordinate system. Finally, we assign it to our view.

This will cause our view's location to update properly when rotated.

AVOIDING THE KEYBOARD

We need to listen to the keyboard notifications and move out of the way of our incoming keyboard. We also need to adjust our position if the keyboard is being displayed when a new text field is selected or when we rotate. This means we need to know the keyboard's state.

Let's start by listening to some of the keyboard appearance and disappearance notifications. Open `AddEntryViewController.m`. In the class extension, we need to add two properties for our observers. We also need a property to hold our keyboard's frame and a property to record whether it's currently being displayed.

```
@property (strong, nonatomic) id keyboardWillAppearObserver;
@property (strong, nonatomic) id keyboardWillDisappearObserver;
@property (assign, nonatomic) CGRect keyboardFrame;
@property (assign, nonatomic) BOOL keyboardIsShown;
```

Now, after `initWithNibName:bundle:`, add a dealloc method to remove these observers.

```
- (void)dealloc
{
    NSNotificationCenter *center = [NSNotificationCenter defaultCenter];

    if (self.keyboardWillAppearObserver)
    {
        [center removeObserver:self.keyboardWillAppearObserver];
    }

    if (self.keyboardWillDisappearObserver)
    {
        [center removeObserver:self.keyboardWillDisappearObserver];
    }
}
```

Most of the time, we've removed our observers just because it's a good habit to get into. However, since the view controllers in question would last throughout our application's entire life cycle, it was not vital. In this case, however, it is required. Our Add Entry View Controller will be deallocated after it is dismissed. We must make sure it removes all its observers before it disappears.

Now, navigate to `viewDidLoad:` We're going to add the following line to the bottom of the method (just after the call to `setupInputAccessories`):

```
[self setupNotifications];
```

Next, we need to implement this method. Add `setupNotifications` just after our `centerViewInParent` method:

```
- (void)setupNotifications
{
    NSNotificationCenter *center = [NSNotificationCenter defaultCenter];
    NSOperationQueue *mainQueue = [NSOperationQueue mainQueue];
    UIWindow *window =
    [[[UIApplication sharedApplication] delegate] window];

    __weak AddEntryViewController *_self = self;

    self.keyboardWillAppearObserver =
    [center
     addObserverForName:UIKeyboardWillShowNotification
```

```
    object:nil
    queue:mainQueue
    usingBlock:^(NSNotification *note) {
        _self.keyboardIsShown = YES;
        CGRect frame =
        [note.userInfo[UIKeyboardFrameEndUserInfoKey] CGRectValue];
        frame = [window convertRect:frame fromWindow:nil];
        frame = [_self.view.superview convertRect:frame fromView:window];
        _self.keyboardFrame = frame;

        NSTimeInterval duration =
        [note.userInfo[UIKeyboardAnimationDurationUserInfoKey]
         doubleValue];

        [UIView animateWithDuration:duration animations:^{
            [_self placeFirstResponderAboveKeyboard];
        }];
    }];


    self.keyboardWillDisappearObserver =
    [center
     addObserverForName:UIKeyboardWillHideNotification
     object:nil
     queue:mainQueue
     usingBlock:^(NSNotification *note) {
        _self.keyboardIsShown = NO;
        _self.keyboardFrame = CGRectZero;

        NSTimeInterval duration =
        [note.userInfo[UIKeyboardAnimationDurationUserInfoKey]
         doubleValue];

        [UIView animateWithDuration:duration animations:^{
            [_self centerViewInParent];
        }];
    }];
}
```

When the keyboard appears, we set `keyboardIsShown` to `YES`, and then we grab the keyboard's end frame from the notification's `userInfo` dictionary. We convert it into our superview's coordinate system. Then we call a private method to update our position relative to the keyboard. We do the update in an animation block and set the animation duration to our keyboard's appearance duration—this helps match our keyboard's animation.

When the keyboard will disappear notification is received, we set `keyboardIsShown` to `NO`. We set the keyboard's frame to all zeros, and we center our view in the frame. Again, we use an animation block to sync with our keyboard's disappearance.

We still need to implement `placeFirstResponderAboveKeyboard`. Add this after our `setupNotifications` method.

```
- (void)placeFirstResponderAboveKeyboard
{
    UIView *parentView = self.view.superview;
    CGPoint currentCenter = self.view.center;

    UIView *firstResponder = [self.dateTextField isFirstResponder] ?
    self.dateTextField : self.weightTextField;

    CGRect textFrame = [parentView convertRect:firstResponder.frame
                                      fromView:self.view];

    // our superview is always in portrait orientation
    UIInterfaceOrientation orientation = self.interfaceOrientation;
    if (UIInterfaceOrientationIsPortrait(orientation))
    {
        CGFloat textBottom = CGRectGetMaxY(textFrame);
        CGFloat targetLocation =
        CGRectGetMinY(self.keyboardFrame) - (CGFloat)8.0;
        currentCenter.y += targetLocation - textBottom;
    }
    else if (orientation == UIInterfaceOrientationLandscapeLeft)
    {
        CGFloat textBottom = CGRectGetMaxX(textFrame);
        CGFloat targetLocation =
        CGRectGetMinX(self.keyboardFrame) - (CGFloat)8.0;
        currentCenter.x += targetLocation - textBottom;
    }
    else
    {
```

```
    CGFloat textBottom = CGRectGetMinX(textFrame);
    CGFloat targetLocation =
    CGRectGetMaxX(self.keyboardFrame) + (CGFloat)8.0;
    currentCenter.x += targetLocation - textBottom;
  }

  self.view.center = currentCenter;
}
```

We start by grabbing our parent view and our current center. We want to make sure that all coordinates are in our parent view's coordinate system, so we will convert our coordinates when necessary.

Next, we determine who our first responder is. Here, we use C's ternary operator. Basically, it has three parts. It checks to see whether the first part (before the question mark) is true. If it is true, it returns the second part (between the question mark and the colon). If it's not true, it returns the third part (after the colon).

We can then convert our first responder's frame to the parent view's coordinate system and calculate the distance we need to move our view. This gets a bit complicated, as you can see.

Here's the problem. You might think that our Add Entry view's superview would be the presenting controller's view (e.g., the RootTabBarController's view). This is not the case. It's actually kept in the container view from our transition. And, just like inside our transition, the container view is always kept in portrait orientation. This means we have to adjust our coordinates appropriately.

Conceptually, we get the bottom of the selected text view and the top of our keyboard. We calculate the difference between them, adding in an 8-point margin. Then we offset our view's center by that difference. Of course, the details vary depending on our current orientation.

This will shift our view so that the currently selected text field is just above the keyboard. Notice that it also works when we rotate, since our keyboard is removed and re-added during rotations.

Now, our keyboard moves out of the way—most of the time. However, there's a problem when our view first appears. The keyboard appears as well, but the timing doesn't quite work. The simplest solution is to move our call to becomeFirstResponder from viewWillAppear: to viewDidAppear:. This delays the appearance of our keyboard, making sure our view can move out of the way as expected.

Delete the following line from viewWillAppear::

```
[self.weightTextField becomeFirstResponder];
```

And, just after that method, implement `viewDidAppear:` as shown here:

```
- (void)viewDidAppear:(BOOL)animated
{
    [super viewDidAppear:animated];
    [self.weightTextField becomeFirstResponder];
}
```

One last tweak. If we are currently editing one text field and we select the other text field, our view should shift appropriately. Let's start by adding an action method that the views can trigger when they begin editing.

Add this method right after the `unitButtonTapped` method:

```
- (IBAction)textFieldSelected:(id)sender {
    if (self.keyboardIsShown)
    {
        [UIView animateWithDuration:0.25 animations:^{
            [self placeFirstResponderAboveKeyboard];
        }];
    }
}
```

Here, we just check to make sure the keyboard is already showing. If it is, we adjust our view's positioning inside an animation block with a quarter-second duration.

> **NOTE:** If in doubt, use a quarter-second animations. These usually match the system animations nicely.

Now, let's switch to `Main.storyboard`. Control-click the weight text field to bring up its connections HUD. Drag from Editing Did Begin to our Add Entry View Controller, and select textFieldSelected:. Do the same thing for our date text field.

> **NOTE:** We could have used the Assistant editor to Control-drag between the UI and code—however, I find that connecting a second control to an existing action is often tricky in the Assistant editor. One of the keys to enjoying Interface Builder is to realize that there are multiple ways to achieve most tasks. If one approach isn't working, try another.

That's it. Our pop-up view now automatically adjusts its positioning relative to the keyboard. Run the app and test it. It would be nice to have a Next button in our toolbar to toggle between the text fields, but I'll leave that as an exercise for the reader.

ROTATING THE CONTAINER VIEW

The fact that the container view is always in portrait orientation may seem odd—but it makes sense once we dig a bit deeper. Remember, our transition's container view acts as the superview for both our presenting and our presented view controller. And, as we saw, the presenting view controller is our RootTabBarController.

Now, before the transition began, the RootTabBarController's superview was our window, and the window is always displayed as full screen and in portrait orientation, so the container view simply matches that.

While this makes sense, it's often harder to work with. Ideally we would like to rotate the container view to the interface's current orientation and just present our view controllers inside it. This is possible, but it may be more work than is worth.

The basic procedure is simple. Grab the transform from the from-controller. Assign that to the container view. Then set the transform for both the from-controller and the to-controller to CGAffineTransformIdentity. Update the frames as necessary.

The code should look like the following:

```
// Adjust the coordinate system of all three views

containerView.transform = fromViewController.view.transform;

containerView.frame = window.bounds;


fromViewController.view.transform = CGAffineTransformIdentity;

fromViewController.view.frame = containerView.bounds;


toViewController.view.transform = CGAffineTransformIdentity;
```

This, however, isn't enough. The system expects our views to be in the original orientation. It will also "helpfully" reset some (but not all) of the transforms. To make things work completely correctly, you'll need to set everything up before each animation block and then reset it during the completion handler. That also means we'd have to do a similar shuffle-and-reset in our placeFirstResponderAboveKeyboard method.

However, if all of that is done correctly, we wouldn't need to check the orientation and modify our math. Of course, I think the modified math is simpler—but your mileage may vary.

MAKING THE VIEW MODAL AGAIN

Currently, the users can interact with the scenes behind our Add Entry view. This doesn't cause any real problems. You can actually use this to make sure our graph view is updating properly. With the History view showing, bring up the Add Entry view. Then tap the Done button to dismiss the keyboard. With our Add Entry view still showing, select the Graph tab. Now enter a weight. It should appear on the graph.

While this is somewhat interesting, I'd rather make our Add Entry scene behave like a modal view again. I think that would be less surprising and confusing to the users. Fortunately, this is rather easy to do. However, the solution is not obvious or intuitive.

We just need to modify the way our Add Entry view performs hit testing.

When a finger touches the screen, the system uses hit testing to determine exactly which element was touched. For each touch event, it asks the window if the touch was within its bounds. If it was, the window asks all of its children. If the touch was within any of their bounds, they ask all their children. This repeats all the way down the view hierarchy.

The system does this using the `hitTest:withEvent:` method. By default, if the touch event is outside the receiver's bounds, it returns `nil`. Otherwise, it calls `hitTest:withEvent:` on all of its subviews. If any of them return a non-`nil` value, it returns the results from the subview at the highest index (the one that would lie on top of all the others). Otherwise, it returns itself.

So, we've already seen that our Add Entry view's superview is our transition's container view. This view fills the entire screen. So, no matter where the user touches on the screen, it will be inside the container's bounds. The container will then call our view's `hitTest:withEvent:` method. We just need to guarantee that our view never returns `nil`. This will allow our view to grab all the touch events whenever it is displayed.

So, let's start by adding a new `UIView` subclass to the Views group. Name this class `AddEntryView`. Then open `AddEntryView.m`. We don't need the `initWithFrame:` or the commented-out `drawRect:` methods. Delete them both. Then add the following method:

```
- (UIView *)hitTest:(CGPoint)point withEvent:(UIEvent *)event
{
    UIView *view = [super hitTest:point withEvent:event];
    if (view == nil) return self;
    return view;
}
```

Here, we call super's `hitTest:withEvent:`. If this returns a value, we simply pass that value along. Otherwise, we return self. This lets our view's subviews continue to respond to touch events but grabs and ignores all other touch events.

Now, open `Main.storyboard`. Zoom in on the Add Entry View Controller scene. Select the scene's view, and in the Identity inspector, change its class to **AddEntryView**.

Run the application. When you bring up the Add Entry view, you can no longer touch any of the controls below our view. However, the keyboard still works, since it is displayed above our view.

LAST THOUGHTS ON PRESENTING CUSTOM VIEWS

The actual custom animation had a number of cogs and gears that needed to be connected correctly, but it really wasn't that hard. We spent most of our time writing custom code to deal with the fact that our Add Entry view was no longer a full-screen, modal view.

In fact, we've written all of the custom code with the basic assumption that our Add Entry View Controller will always be presented using the UIModalPresentationCustom presentation style.

If we ever plan on pushing this controller onto a navigation stack, adding it to our tab bar, or even presenting it full screen using the UIModalPresentationFullScreen style, we would need to check and see how our view is being displayed and then enable or disable the code as appropriate.

We could use our view controller's presentingViewController, navigationController, tabBarController, modalPresentationStyle, and similar properties to determine this. However, going through all the different corner cases gets quite involved.

The good news is if you mess this up, it will be immediately, visibly obvious. This is not one of those bugs that can sneak up and bite you unexpectedly.

INTERACTIVE TRANSITIONS

Now, let's look at interactive transitions.

There's good news, bad news, and good news again. Interactive transitions build upon everything we learned about custom transitions. They are a bit more complex, since we have to sync them with a gesture (or really anything that can programmatically drive our percentages). We also need to determine whether our transition is finished or whether it has been canceled.

Fortunately, we are just adding animation and a bit of additional interactivity to the tab bar controller—we're not making fundamental changes to the way these scenes are presented, like we did with our Add Entry scene. So, once the animation is working, we're done.

When presenting a view controller, we had to set the controller's transitioningDelegate. Fortunately, when customizing the transitions for tab bars or navigation bars, the animation methods have already been added to the UITabBarControllerDelegate and UINavigationControllerDelegate protocols. So, we just need to create an object that adopts UITabBarControllerDelegate. Assign it as our tab bar's delegate and implement the animation methods

Just like before, our delegate will return an animator object that adopts the UIViewControllerAnimatedTransitioning protocol. This will manage the noninteractive portions of our animation; for example, if you select a new tab, the animator object will automatically animate the transition from one scene to the next.

If we want to add interactivity, we also need to return an object that adopts the UIViewControllerInteractiveTransitioning protocol. This is responsible for the interactive portion. Interactively driving the animation could get quite complex. Fortunately, UIKit provides a concrete implementation, UIPercentDrivenInteractiveTransition, that handles most of the details for us.

The percent-driven interactive transition will actually use our animator object. It can access the frames that the animator object produces and display the correct frame based on the interaction's current state.

While driving the animation interactively, we just change the percentage, and the animation updates appropriately. If we cancel the interaction, it will use the animator to roll back the animation to its beginning state. If we finish the interaction, it will use the animator to complete any remaining animation, bringing the views to their correct, final position.

Strictly speaking, we don't need to subclass `UIPercentDrivenInteractiveTransition`, but I find that it usually simplifies our application's logic. It also lets us combine our `UIPercentDrivenInteractiveTransition` and our `UITabBarControllerDelegate` into a single object.

CREATING THE ANIMATOR OBJECT

So, let's start with our animator object. In the Controllers group, create a new `NSObject` subclass named `TabAnimator`.

Now that we have a couple of animators, let's give them their own group. Select `TabAnimator.h`, `TabAnimator.m`, `AddEntryAnimator.h`, and `AddEntryAnimator.m`. Control-click them and select "New Group from Selection" from the pop-up menu. Name the group **Animators**.

In my mind, these objects belong with the controllers, so I will leave this group inside the Controllers group. However, you could drag it up to the top level or into one of the other groups, if you wanted.

Now, select `TabAnimator.h`. Modify it as shown here:

```
@interface TabAnimator : NSObject <UIViewControllerAnimatedTransitioning>
@property (weak, nonatomic) UITabBarController *tabBarController;
@end
```

We are simply adopting the `UIViewControllerAnimatedTransitioning` protocol and adding a property that will refer back to our tab bar controller.

Switch to `TabAnimator.m`. At the top of the file, before the beginning of our `@implementation` block, we need to declare a constant for our duration. Add the following line of code:

```
static const NSTimeInterval AnimationDuration = 0.25;
```

Now, we can define our methods. As before, we have to implement only two methods. The first is `transitionDuration:`.

```
-(NSTimeInterval)transitionDuration:
(id<UIViewControllerContextTransitioning>)transitionContext
{
    return AnimationDuration;
}
```

Just like our AddEntryAnimator, this method returns our constant. After this, add the animateTransition: method.

```objc
-(void)animateTransition:
(id<UIViewControllerContextTransitioning>)transitionContext
{
    UIViewController *fromViewController =
    [transitionContext viewControllerForKey:
     UITransitionContextFromViewControllerKey];

    UIViewController *toViewController =
    [transitionContext viewControllerForKey:
     UITransitionContextToViewControllerKey];

    NSUInteger fromIndex =
    [self.tabBarController.viewControllers
     indexOfObject:fromViewController];

    NSUInteger toIndex =
    [self.tabBarController.viewControllers
     indexOfObject:toViewController];

    BOOL goRight = (fromIndex < toIndex);

    UIView *container = [transitionContext containerView];

    CGRect initialFromFrame =
    [transitionContext initialFrameForViewController:fromViewController];

    CGRect finalToFrame =
    [transitionContext finalFrameForViewController:toViewController];

    CGRect offscreenLeft =
    CGRectOffset(initialFromFrame,
                 - CGRectGetWidth(container.bounds),
                 0.0);


    CGRect offscreenRight =
    CGRectOffset(initialFromFrame,
```

```
                CGRectGetWidth(container.bounds),
                0.0);

CGRect initialToFrame;
CGRect finalFromFrame;
if (goRight)
{
    initialToFrame = offscreenRight;
    finalFromFrame = offscreenLeft;
} else
{
    initialToFrame = offscreenLeft;
    finalFromFrame = offscreenRight;
}

fromViewController.view.frame = initialFromFrame;
toViewController.view.frame = initialToFrame;

[container addSubview:fromViewController.view];
[container addSubview:toViewController.view];

UIViewAnimationOptions options = 0;
if ([transitionContext isInteractive])
{
    options = UIViewAnimationOptionCurveLinear;
}

[UIView
 animateWithDuration:AnimationDuration
 delay:0.0
 options:options
 animations:^{
    toViewController.view.frame = finalToFrame;
    fromViewController.view.frame = finalFromFrame;
 } completion:^(BOOL finished) {
    BOOL didComplete = ![transitionContext transitionWasCancelled];

    if (!didComplete)
    {
```

```
            toViewController.view.frame = initialToFrame;
            fromViewController.view.frame = initialFromFrame;
        }


        [transitionContext completeTransition:didComplete];
    }];
}
```

Phew, that's a lot of code! Let's walk through it. Just as before, we start by grabbing our "from" and "to" view controllers. Since we are adding a custom transition to a tab bar, we don't have the same confusion we did with the custom presentation. We are always moving explicitly from one controller to another controller. The from-controller is the controller we started with. The to-controller is the new tab's controller. We may not make it. Our transition may get canceled. But it is our intended destination.

Even if the interactive portion gets canceled, it doesn't change these objects—our interactive transition will simply run this animation in reverse.

Next, we calculate the tab index of our from- and to-controllers, and we determine whether we are sliding to the right or to the left.

We grab our container and request the initial frame for our from- and the final frame for our to-controller. In theory, these should be the same frame, since our final view is replacing our initial view. However, I like to grab them as separate local variables—just in case something changes in future implementations.

Also, notice that, unlike the presentation transition, the transitionContext defines a final frame for our to-controller. This means our to-controller's view must be in the specified position when the animation ends. However, the context does not specify a starting position for our to-controller. It also does not specify an ending position for our from-controller. Since we're sliding views in and out, we'd like the to-controller to start just offscreen and the from-controller to end just off the opposite side. Whether they are sliding from the left or right edge depends on the transition's direction.

Returning to our code, we take the from-controller's initial frame and use CGRectOffset() to create new frames that are shifted horizontally just past the edge of the screen. These are our offscreenLeft and offscreenRight rectangles.

Notice that, unlike the presenting transition, the container view will rotate to match our tab bar's orientation. This means we don't need to modify our math based on our orientation.

Next, we use the offscreen rectangles to set our to-controller's initial frame and our from-controller's final frame. We make sure our views are in the correct starting position, and we add them to our container view.

There's one last pretransition check. We see whether our animation is interactive. If it is, we're going to set the animation curve to linear. If not, we will use the default curve.

By default, our animations are not displayed at a linear speed. Rather, they ease in and ease out. This means they start at a complete stop. They accelerate up to speed, and then they decelerate back to a stop. This gives the animation a nice appearance that mimics the way physical objects move. However, the ease-in-out animation curve is not always appropriate, so we can change the animation curve by passing the correct option to the relevant animation methods.

In this case, when we are presenting an interactive animation, we want to make sure our view stays under the user's finger. That means we must use a linear animation. Otherwise, the view and finger will move at different rates.

Finally, we perform our animation. We have to use the longer animateWithDuration:delay:options:animations:completion: method, since we may be changing our animation's curve.

In the animation block, we simply update the frames for both our "to" and "from" view controllers. In the completion block, we check to see whether the animation was canceled. If it was, we reset the frames to their initial positions. Finally, we call completeTransition:. We pass YES if the transition completed and NO if it was canceled. This should close out the transition and move the view and view controller hierarchies into their final states.

NOTE: In theory, we shouldn't need to reset the frames in our completion handler. The transition should reset the frames automatically if the transition is canceled. Unfortunately, as of the iOS 7.0 release, in some cases, the frames do not reset properly. This can result in the system having a completely black screen after a transition is canceled. Programmatically resetting the frames fixes this problem.

BUILDING TABINTERACTIVETRANSITION

Now let's create our UIPercentDrivenInteractiveTransition subclass. This object will also act as our UITabBarControllerDelegate. Create a new Objective-C class in the Animators group. Name it TabInteractiveTransition and make it a subclass of UIPercentDrivenInteractiveTransition.

Next, open TabInteractiveTransition.h. We want to adopt the UITabBarControllerDelegate property and declare a public method, as shown here:

```
@interface TabInteractiveTransition : UIPercentDrivenInteractiveTransition
<UITabBarControllerDelegate>
- (id)initWithTabBarController:(UITabBarController *)parent;
@end
```

Switch to TabIntractiveTransition.m, and import TabAnimator.h. And create a class extension with the following properties:

```
@interface TabInteractiveTransition ()
@property (assign, nonatomic, getter = isInteractive) BOOL interactive;
@property (weak, nonatomic) UITabBarController *parent;

@property (assign, nonatomic) NSUInteger oldIndex;
@property (assign, nonatomic) NSUInteger newIndex;
@end
```

The `interactive` property will track whether we're currently in an interactive transition. The `parent` property will hold a reference to our tab bar controller. Finally, the `newIndex` and `oldIndex` properties will hold the starting and ending tab indexes for the duration of our transition.

Now, add our `init…` methods. These go just after the `@implementation` line.

```
- (id)initWithTabBarController:(UITabBarController *)parent
{
    self = [super init];
    if (self) {
        _parent = parent;
        _interactive = NO;
    }
    return self;
}


- (id)init
{
    [self doesNotRecognizeSelector:_cmd];
    return nil;
}
```

`initWithTabBarController` is our designated initializer. It just sets the `parent` property and starts with `interactive` set to `NO`. Then, as always, we override the designated `init` method of its superclass. This time, we throw an exception if this method is called. This forces us to always use our designated initializer.

Now, we have two animation methods from `UITabBarControllerDelegate` that we need to implement. The first returns our animation object.

```
#pragma mark = UITabBarControllerDelegate Methods


-(id<UIViewControllerAnimatedTransitioning>)tabBarController:
(UITabBarController *)tabBarController
animationControllerForTransitionFromViewController:
(UIViewController *)fromVC
toViewController:(UIViewController *)toVC
{
    TabAnimator *animator = [[TabAnimator alloc] init];
    animator.tabBarController = self.parent;
    return animator;
}
```

Here, we just instantiate `TabAnimator`, set its `tabBarController` property and return it.

TESTING THE CUSTOM ANIMATION

Before we wire in our interactivity, let's test the custom animation. Switch to RootTabBar Controller.m, and import TabInteractiveTransition.h. Then add the following property to the class extension:

```
@property (strong, nonatomic) TabInteractiveTransition
*interactiveTransition;
```

This will hold our interactive transition object.

Finally, at the bottom of viewDidLoad, add the following two lines of code:

```
self.interactiveTransition =
[[TabInteractiveTransition alloc] initWithTabBarController:self];

self.delegate = self.interactiveTransition;
```

Here, we instantiate our TabInteractiveTransition object and assign it to our interactiveTransition property. We also assign it to our delegate property. This may seem like unnecessary duplication, but both steps are important.

We need to assign our object to our delegate property, since that's where the real work is done. Unfortunately, delegate properties are almost always weak. This helps prevent retain cycles. Unfortunately, this also means that the delegate property, alone, won't keep our TabInteractiveTransition object in memory. If we want it to last beyond this method, we need to assign it to a strong property as well. The interactiveTransition property simply exists to keep our TabInteractiveTransition object alive.

Run the application and tap the tab bars. Our custom animation will now slide between the History and Graph views.

ADDING INTERACTIVITY

We have a custom animation, but it's not yet interactive. Let's fix that.

Open TabInteractiveTransition.h and declare two additional methods.

```
- (void)handleLeftPan:(UIPanGestureRecognizer *)recognizer;
- (void)handleRightPan:(UIPanGestureRecognizer *)recognizer;
```

We will connect these to our gesture recognizer in a minute.

Switch to TabInteractiveTransition.m. We still have one more delegate method to implement.

```
- (id<UIViewControllerInteractiveTransitioning>)tabBarController:
(UITabBarController *)tabBarController
interactionControllerForAnimationController:
(id<UIViewControllerAnimatedTransitioning>)animationController
{
    if (self.interactive)
    {
```

```
        return self;
    }


    return nil;
}
```

If we want to produce an interactive transition, we must implement both
`tabBarController:animationControllerForTransitionFromViewController:`
`toViewController:` and `tabBarController:interactionControllerForAnimation`
`Controller:`. The interaction controller method will not be called unless the animation
controller returns a valid object.

In this case, we simply return `self` if we're in an interactive state. Otherwise, we return
`nil`. Or, to put it more simply, if the user starts the animation with a gesture, this method
will return `self`, and the animation will proceed interactively. If the user simply taps one of
the tabs, it will return `nil`, and the animation will complete automatically.

Now, all we need to do is set up a gesture recognizer to drive the interactive transition.

GESTURE RECOGNIZERS
There are two ways to handle touch events. First, we could use low-level touch handling to
monitor each and every touch. Alternatively, we could use higher-level gesture recognizers
to recognize and respond to common gestures.

Let's look at the low-level approach first.

Whenever the user's finger touches the screen, this creates a touch event. The system
uses hit testing to determine which view was tapped. That view is then sent the touch event.
If it doesn't respond, the touch event is passed up the responder chain, giving others a
chance to respond.

UIResponder defines a number of methods that we can override to respond to
touch events. These include `touchesBegan:withEvent:`, `touchesMoved:withEvent:`,
`touchesEnded:withEvent:`, and `touchesCanceled:withEvent:`. Both our views and our view
controllers inherit from `UIResponder`, so we can implement these methods in either place.

If you want to receive the event and not let it pass on up the responder chain, you must
implement all four methods, and you should not call super. If you want to just peek at the
event and then place it back on the responder chain (possibly letting others respond to it as
well), you can just implement the methods you are interested in—but you must call super
somewhere inside your method.

While this lets us easily receive simple touch information, tracking touches over time
to detect more-complex gestures gets very complex. Even something as simple as distinguishing between a single tap, a double tap, and a long press would involve a fair bit of code.
Worse yet, if developers create their own, custom algorithms to recognize each gesture, different applications may respond slightly differently to different gestures.

To solve both of these problems, the iOS SDK provides a set of predefined gesture recognizers. Each gesture recognizer has a number of properties and methods and can be used
either to request information from the recognizer or to fine-tune the recognizer's behavior.

The recognizers are listed in **Table 4.2.** We can also create our own, custom gesture recognizers—though that is an advanced topic and beyond the scope of this book.

TABLE 4.2 Gesture Recognizers

GESTURE RECOGNIZER	DESCRIPTION
UITapGestureRecognizer	Triggers an action once the tap gesture is recognized. You can set both the number of fingers and the number of taps, letting you distinguish between, say, a one-finger tap and a four-finger quadruple-tap.
UIPinchGestureRecognizer	Returns continuous pinch data. This is typically used to modify something's size.
UIRotationGestureRecognizer	Returns continuous rotation data. This is typically used to rotate objects.
UISwipeGestureRecognizer	Triggers an action when the swipe gesture is recognized. You can set the direction and the number of fingers for the gesture.
UIPanGestureRecognizer	Returns continuous location data as the finger is moved around the screen. You can set the minimum and maximum number of fingers.
UIScreenEdgePanGestureRecognizer	Like the pan gesture, but it recognizes only the gestures that originate from the edge of the screen. This gesture is new with iOS 7. We can set the edges that the gesture will monitor.
UILongPressGestureRecognizer	Triggers an action when the user presses and holds a finger on the screen. We can set the duration, the number of fingers, the number of taps before the hold, and the amount of motion allowed. While this is primarily used to trigger actions, it will return continuous data as well.

In many cases, we can set up our gesture recognizers in Interface Builder. We can drag them out and drop them onto a view. Then we can select the gesture recognizer icon to set its attributes. Finally, we can Control-drag from the icon to our code in the Assistant editor to create a method that will be called whenever the recognizer fires.

For discrete gesture recognizers, this method is called once, when the gesture is recognized. For continuous recognizers, it is called when the gesture begins, again for each update, and then when the gesture is canceled or ends. Our method will need to check the recognizer's state and respond accordingly.

We're going to add screen edge pan recognizers to all the view controllers managed by our tab bar. This is a continuous gesture, so we can monitor how far the user has moved their finger across the screen.

We could do this in Interface Builder; however, the screen edge pan recognizer has not been added to the library yet. So, we cannot just drag and drop it in place. More importantly, we will want to automate adding these gesture recognizers based on the tab's index; that way the gesture recognizers will be added correctly even if we end up adding or removing tabs later.

Open RootTabBarController.m. Add the following method to the bottom of the private methods:

```
- (void)addPanGestureRecognizerToViewController:
(UIViewController *)controller
forEdges:(UIRectEdge)edges
{
    NSParameterAssert((edges == UIRectEdgeLeft)||
                      (edges == UIRectEdgeRight));
    SEL selector;

    if (edges == UIRectEdgeLeft)
    {
        selector = @selector(handleRightPan:);
    }
    else
    {
        selector = @selector(handleLeftPan:);
    }

    UIScreenEdgePanGestureRecognizer *panRecognizer =
    [[UIScreenEdgePanGestureRecognizer alloc]
     initWithTarget:self.interactiveTransition
     action:selector];

    panRecognizer.maximumNumberOfTouches = 1;
    panRecognizer.minimumNumberOfTouches = 1;
    panRecognizer.edges = edges;
    [controller.view addGestureRecognizer:panRecognizer];
}
```

Here we start with a parameter assert. This is just like a normal NSAssert, but it's specifically designed for checking incoming parameter values. It's also easier to use, since the system automatically generates the error message for us. In this case, we just want to verify that we are setting our recognizer to watch either the left or right edge (not the top, bottom, or multiple edges).

Next, we determine the selector for the method that should be called when the gesture is triggered. If we're panning from the left to the right, it's the handleRightPan: method. If we're panning from the right to the left, it's the handleLeftPan: method. The *right* or *left* in the handler's name refers to the direction of motion—not the starting position.

We then create our gesture recognizer, passing in our interactive transition as the target, and our selector as the action. When the recognizer is triggered, it will call the specified method on our interactive transition object.

Finally, we set it to respond to one, and only one finger, from the specified edge. Then we add it to our container's view.

Now we need to call this method once for each view controller. Add the following method right before addPanGestureRecognzierToViewController:forEdges::

```objc
- (void)setupEdgePanGestureRecognizers
{
    NSUInteger count = [self.viewControllers count];
    for (NSUInteger index = 0; index < count; index++)
    {
        UIViewController *controller = self.viewControllers[index];

        if (index == 0) {
            [self addPanGestureRecognizerToViewController:controller
                    forEdges:UIRectEdgeRight];
        }
        else if (index == count - 1)
        {
            [self addPanGestureRecognizerToViewController:controller
                    forEdges:UIRectEdgeLeft];
        }
        else {
            [self addPanGestureRecognizerToViewController:controller
                    forEdges:UIRectEdgeRight];

            [self addPanGestureRecognizerToViewController:controller
                    forEdges:UIRectEdgeLeft];
        }
    }
}
```

This method iterates over all our view controllers. This time, we don't use fast enumeration, since we actually need the index number. If it's the first tab, we add a gesture recognizer on the right edge. If it's the last tab, we add a gesture recognizer on the left edge. If it's somewhere in the middle, we add them to both edges.

Now, add the following line to the bottom of viewDidLoad:

```objc
[self setupEdgePanGestureRecognizers];
```

This sets up our gesture recognizers when our tab bar controller loads.

Now we just need to implement handleRightPan: and handleLeftPan:. Switch to TabInteractiveTransition.m and add the following method to the bottom of the @implementation block:

```
- (void)handleLeftPan:(UIPanGestureRecognizer *)recognizer
{
    CGPoint translation = [recognizer translationInView:self.parent.view];

    CGFloat percent =
    -translation.x / CGRectGetWidth(self.parent.view.bounds);

    percent = MAX(percent, 0.0f);
    percent = MIN(percent, 1.0f);

    if (recognizer.state == UIGestureRecognizerStateBegan)
    {
        NSAssert(self.oldIndex == 0, @"We shouldn't already have an "
                @"old index value");
        NSAssert(self.newIndex == 0, @"We shouldn't already have a "
                @"new index value");

        self.oldIndex = self.parent.selectedIndex;
        NSAssert(self.oldIndex != NSNotFound,
                @"Interactive transitions from the "
                @"More tab are not possible");

        self.newIndex = self.oldIndex + 1;
        NSAssert(self.newIndex < [self.parent.viewControllers count],
                @"Trying to navigate past the last tab");

    }

    [self handleRecognizer:recognizer
      forTransitionPercent:percent];
}
```

We start by getting the translation from our gesture recognizer. This is the amount our finger has moved from the original point of contact. We then convert this to a percentage. As a safety step, we clamp this value so that it cannot be lower than 0.0 or higher than 1.0. These values will make sense only during change notifications—not when the recognizer began, ended, or was canceled—but we're going to precalculate them anyway, making the rest of our code easer to read. If it's not a change notification, the percent will simply get ignored.

Next, if this is a begin notification, we save our new and old index. Then we call handleRecognzier:forTransitionPercent:.

handleRightPan: is largely the same. The math for calculating our percentage is a little different, since the gesture is moving in the opposite direction.

```
- (void)handleRightPan:(UIPanGestureRecognizer *)recognizer
{
    CGPoint translation = [recognizer translationInView:self.parent.view];

    CGFloat percent =
    translation.x / CGRectGetWidth(self.parent.view.bounds);

    percent = MAX(percent, 0.0f);
    percent = MIN(percent, 1.0f);

    if (recognizer.state == UIGestureRecognizerStateBegan)
    {
        NSAssert(self.oldIndex == 0, @"We shouldn't already have an "
                @"old index value");
        NSAssert(self.newIndex == 0, @"We shouldn't already have a "
                @"new index value");

        self.oldIndex = self.parent.selectedIndex;
        NSAssert(self.oldIndex != NSNotFound,
                @"Interactive transitions from the "
                @"More tab are not possible");

        self.newIndex = self.oldIndex - 1;
        NSAssert(self.newIndex >= 0,
                @"Trying to navigate past the first tab");

    }

    [self handleRecognizer:recognizer
      forTransitionPercent:percent];
}
```

Finally, add the handleRecognzier:forTransitionPercent: method after the other two.

```objc
- (void)handleRecognizer:(UIPanGestureRecognizer *)recognizer
    forTransitionPercent:(CGFloat)percent
{
    switch (recognizer.state)
    {
        case UIGestureRecognizerStateBegan:
            self.interactive = YES;
            self.parent.selectedIndex = self.newIndex;
            break;

        case UIGestureRecognizerStateChanged:
            [self updateInteractiveTransition:percent];
            break;

        case UIGestureRecognizerStateCancelled:
            self.completionSpeed = 0.5;
            [self cancelInteractiveTransition];
            self.interactive = NO;
            self.newIndex = 0;
            self.oldIndex = 0;
            break;

        case UIGestureRecognizerStateEnded:
            self.completionSpeed = 0.5;
            if (percent > 0.5)
            {
                [self finishInteractiveTransition];
            }
            else
            {
                [self cancelInteractiveTransition];
            }
            self.newIndex = 0;
            self.oldIndex = 0;
            self.interactive = NO;
            break;
```

```
    default:
        NSLog(@"*** Invalid state found %@ ***", @(recognizer.state));
    }
}
```

Since the edge pan recognizer is a continuous recognizer, it will send us updates as our finger moves across the screen. This method checks the recognizer's state and responds appropriately.

If the recognizer has just begun, it places us in interactive mode and then changes the tab bar's index to the new index.

Every time we get a change update, it updates our animation percentage by calling UIPercentDrivenInteractiveTransition's updateInteractiveTransition: method.

If the recognizer is canceled, we cancel the transition, clear our index properties, and set interactive to NO.

Finally, if the gesture ends normally (because the user lifts his finger or runs past the edge of the screen), it checks to see how much we have completed. If it is greater than 50 percent, it finishes the transition. The animation will automatically complete. If it is less than 50 percent, it cancels the transition. The animation will automatically roll back to the initial state.

NOTE: There appears to be a bug with the iOS 7.0 release. If you cancel an interactive transition, you will often see a flash of black where the to-controller should be. Fortunately, slowing down the animation seems to fix this. In the sample code, we set the completion speed to 0.5 both when the gesture is canceled and when the gesture completes. Obviously, this shouldn't be necessary. In fact, we should use the completion speed to speed up our slow down our animation, usually based on our own aesthetics, but perhaps to match the gesture's velocity or some other value.

That's it. Run the app. You can now swipe your finger from the edge of the screen to trigger the transition.

WRAPPING UP

In this chapter, we examined a number of techniques that will be helpful when building your own custom views and custom controls. This includes custom drawing, custom transitions, and tracking user interaction through gesture recognizers.

We will take this a step further in Chapter 8, when we look at advanced user interface techniques. In the meantime, Chapter 5 will look at saving our application's data. Chapter 6 will look at syncing that data using iCloud, and Chapter 7 will look at replacing our custom model with Core Data.

OTHER RESOURCES

- **Quartz 2D Programming Guide**

  OS Developer's Library

  This is the complete guide for using Core Graphics. If you want to go beyond the basics, you should definitely read through this programming guide.

- **PaintCode**

  www.paintcodeapp.com

  This is a third-party application for creating custom-drawn interfaces. PaintCode is an illustrator-like drawing tool—but it saves the graphics as Objective-C Code. We can then take that code and paste it into our application. Sometimes the code can be used as-is. Sometimes it needs to be cleaned up or refactored. Regardless, it can save a significant amount of time over coding everything by hand.

  While the application may be a bit pricy, I highly recommend downloading and playing around with the demo. If nothing else, it's a great tool for learning how to generate a wide range of visual effects with Core Graphics.

- **Event Handling Guide for iOS**

  iOS Developer's Library

  This guide provides detailed information about all aspects of iOS event handling. This includes low-level event handling, hit testing, gesture recognizers, and even handling motion or remote control events.

- **Core Animation Programming Guide**

  iOS Developer's Library

  This guide provides a detailed discussion of Core Animation. Note that this goes very deep into a fairly complex topic—however, most of the time we can add a touch of animation to our user interface without getting bogged down in the Core Animation framework itself. Still, if you run into a situation where your animation isn't behaving quite the way you expect, this is a good resource to have in your back pocket.

- **Custom Transitions Using View Controllers**

  2013 WWDC Videos

  Currently, this is the only source of information about custom transitions from Apple. This presentation covers both custom transitions and interactive transitions. While this provides a nice, high-level explanation of the API, it often feels frustratingly thin on details. Hopefully Apple will supplement this presentation with either sample code or a Custom Transition Programming Guide in the near future.

CHAPTER 5

Loading and Saving Data

This chapter will focus on loading and saving data. We will begin with a brief discussion on living within the iOS file system. Working on an iOS device is different from working on a desktop machine. The most obvious change is, of course, the added security. We, as developers, are severely limited as to where we can save, open, or modify files. But, the differences go much deeper. For example, we need to make sure our application's data plays nicely with the app's updates and backups. We even need to rethink the way we handle UI design. In the typical iOS application, there are no save buttons and no folders or files to search through. We need to make the whole procedure more transparent and more natural to our users.

Finally, we will look at the different ways to store data, from storing preferences in the user defaults to serializing complete object graphs.

THE iOS FILE SYSTEM

Always remember, iOS is not a desktop operating system. Some of the things we take for granted on desktop machines become impossible, inappropriate, or at least very difficult in iOS. The file system is a great example. Where the desktop often displays dialog boxes to open and save files, forcing the user to search through a forest of directories, iOS goes to great lengths to hide the underlying file system, both from the user and from the applications.

This provides two main benefits. For the user, this greatly simplifies the experience. You don't need to worry about where files are stored or how to find them. Your application handles all of this for you.

For the applications, limiting access to the file system improves system security. Each application is limited to its own sandbox. The application can freely open and save files within this sandbox, but it cannot touch anything outside these carefully defined boundaries. This protects both your data and the system files from accidental (or worse yet, malicious) alterations. Unfortunately, it also makes sharing files between applications somewhat difficult. The communication channels between applications remain both limited and tightly controlled.

SANDBOX BASICS

Each iOS application is given its own sandbox. This is a unique directory that can be accessed only by that application. The sandbox contains both the application bundle and all of its data. It also acts as the home directory for our application. With rare exceptions, our application cannot access any part of the file system outside our sandbox. Even data inside the sandbox may be tightly controlled.

By default, iOS organizes the sandbox into a number of well-known directories. Each directory has its own intended use. When our application saves its data, we need to make sure we store its information in the correct location. **Figure 5.1** shows the common directories.

FIGURE 5.1 The sandbox and its directories

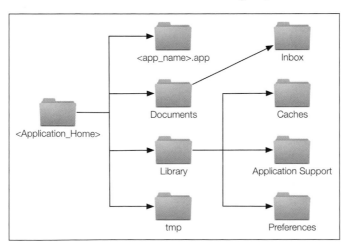

ACCESSING THE SANDBOX

Working with the file system in iOS often feels like we are poking around in the dark. Sometimes it helps to just pry open the sandbox and rummage around inside.

Fortunately, we can do this. There are two ways to glimpse behind the curtain. If you're running an app in the simulator, you can access the simulator's file system at ~/Library/ Application Support/iPhone Simulator/7.0/Applications/. This directory will have all the sandboxes for the iOS 7.0 simulator. Different simulators will have slightly different paths.

We can also view, download, and upload data to the sandbox on a test device.

1. Plug a test device into your computer.

2. Inside Xcode, select the Window > Organizer menu item.

3. In the Organizer window, select the Devices tab.

4. In the navigation bar, expand the selected device, and select the Applications option.

5. Select the application you want to explore.

The Organizer will display its sandbox (everything except the application bundle) at the bottom of the screen (**Figure** 5.2). Click the download button to save a copy of the app's data. This wlll be saved as a data bundle. Control-click the bundle and select Show Package Contents to explore it. We can also use the Upload button to upload custom, test data to our device—which can be quite helpful during testing and debugging.

FIGURE 5.2 Viewing the application's sandbox

Not all of these directories are created when the application is installed. The Application Bundle, Documents, Library, Caches, and Temporary folders will all exist by default. The system may create the others, as it needs them.

A brief description of each directory is listed below:

- **Application Bundle (<app_name>.app):** When our application is compiled, the executable and all the resources are placed in our application bundle. The bundle is then cryptographically signed. The system checks this signature before running the application. If anything has changed, the signature will not match, and the application will not run.

  The bundle is (obviously) read-only. Any resources that we add to our project will be included in the application bundle. We can load these resources from the bundle; however, we cannot add, modify, or delete anything inside the bundle.

  Bundles are just folders that OS X treats as files. If you want to view the contents of an application bundle, locate the bundle in the Finder. Then Control-click the bundle and select Show Package Contents. This will open the bundle's contents in a separate window.

- **Documents:** As the name implies, this is where we store our documents. Here, the word *documents* has a very specific meaning. We are referring to any file that contains user-generated data.

  For example, when writing a text editor, this is where we save the user's text files. When designing a game, this is where we store the saved game files. For Health Beat, this is where we save our `WeightHistoryDocument`.

  Files in the Documents directory are backed up. They are transferred to the new sandbox when our app upgrades, and they can be shared with iTunes. This means we need to think carefully about every file we place in the Documents directory.

- **Documents/Inbox:** The Inbox directory will store files that were sent to our app by outside applications. For example, if the user tells the Mail application to send a file extension to our application, that file will be saved here. Other document interaction controllers may also place files here.

  Our application can read and delete files in this folder, but we cannot create new files or modify the existing files. If the user needs to edit the file, we should move it from the Inbox to the Documents directory and then open it.

- **Library:** This is the root directory for all application support files. It contains our Caches, Application Support, and Preferences directories. We don't typically use this directory directly. Instead, we will request one of the subdirectories. However, we can create our own subdirectories here as well. This can be particularly useful for files that we don't want to expose to the user.

  Everything in the library directory is transferred to the new application sandbox when an app is upgraded. All of its contents, except the Caches directory, are also backed up.

- **Temporary (tmp):** The Temporary directory provides a handy location for storing information that does not need to survive past the current session. This often includes scratch space needed for large calculations and similar transient uses.

If possible, we should delete our temporary files when they are no longer needed; however, the system will periodically clear out the Temporary directory when our application is not running.

Data in the temporary directory is not backed up. It is also not transferred to the new sandbox when our app is upgraded

- **Caches:** The Caches directory also stores temporary information; however, this directory focuses on caching data to improve performance. Most of the time this means saving information that we may need to reuse later. This includes any resources that we download or any derived data that takes a long time or a lot of computational effort to re-create.

  The Caches directory differs from the Temporary directory in one important aspect— items in the Caches directory typically persist beyond the current session. In fact, they may stay around indefinitely. The system begins clearing the Caches directory only when the device starts to run out of storage space. Unfortunately, this means anything we place in the Caches directory could be deleted at any time—so we must check and re-download or re-create the files, if necessary.

- **Application Support:** We can use this directory to hold any data files that the application needs to run but that aren't created by the user. This often includes modified copies of resources from our application bundle.

  The Application Support directory is both backed up and transferred to the new sandbox when updating. Note, however, that the system does not create this directory by default. We will need to create it before we can use it.

- **Preferences:** This directory is used to store our preferences. We don't typically interact directly with this directory. Instead, we use the `NSUserDefaults` API to save and load preference data. That data is then stored in this directory in as a plist file.

  Preference data is both backed up and transferred to the new sandbox when updating. We will look at using `NSUserDefaults` in the "Managing User Preferences" section later this chapter.

In addition to these directories, our iOS application can create its own subdirectories in either the Library or Documents directory. We can do this to provide additional organization to our data, as necessary.

BACKING UP OUR DATA

iOS devices can back up their data in one of two ways. They can back up to iTunes when plugged into a computer, or they can back up wirelessly to iCloud.

With a few specific exceptions, the system backs up everything inside the Documents and Library directories (including Application Support and Preferences).

The Caches and Temporary directories are not backed up. Furthermore, we can apply the `com.apple.MobileBackup` extended attribute to any files or directories to exclude them from the backup.

We need to carefully think about which files get backed up. From the beginning, Apple encouraged developers to make sure the backed-up data was as lean and streamlined as possible—but in the age of iCloud backups, this has become even more important.

Most people have only 5GB in their iCloud account. You don't want to be responsible for chewing through a large chunk of that storage space. Specifically, any file that can be downloaded or generated again should be excluded from the backup. Either place the file in the Caches Directory or use NSURL's setResourceValue:forKey:error: method to exclude the file or directory, as shown here:

```
[URL setResourceValue:@YES
            forKey:NSURLIsExcludedFromBackupKey
           error: &error];
```

NOTE: Be extra, double careful when it comes to downloaded content like video or audio files. Apple will reject apps that place files like these in the backup. You have been warned.

SHARING WITH ITUNES

If the UIFileSharingEnabled key is set in the application's Info.plist, then everything inside the Documents directory appears in iTunes. Users can add or delete files from iTunes, modifying the content stored on their device.

Unfortunately, many applications produce or consume files that are intended for sharing (PDFs, text files, image files, and so on) but may store their internal state in a proprietary binary format. Typically, we don't want to share these proprietary files with iTunes.

Ideally, we should save this private data in another location. If it is simply application data (not a user document), then we can stash it in the Application Support directory. If, on the other hand, it really is a private version of the user's document, then we probably want to create a custom directory to hold it. Apple recommends creating a <Application_Home>/Library/Private Documents directory for these cases.

The system does not share anything within the Temporary, Caches, or Application Support directories with iTunes.

UPGRADING OUR APPLICATION

When upgrading an app, the system starts by creating a new sandbox for our application. It then downloads the new application bundle into that sandbox.

Once downloaded, the system validates the application bundle. If everything looks good, it copies the entire contents of the Documents and Library directories. It then deletes the old application sandbox only after everything has finished transferring successfully.

Anything that is not in the Documents or Library directory (including subdirectories such as Caches, Preferences, or Application Support) cannot be copied to the new version and can be deleted when the application updates. Since applications are automatically updated in the background in iOS 7, this could happen at any time.

This, obviously, becomes a rather strong argument against making random directories inside your application's sandbox. As much as possible, use the common directories, and use them for their intended purposes.

BEYOND THE SANDBOX

There are a few ways to reach beyond the sandbox. If we're accessing a public system resource—such as our address book, our calendar, our photo album, or our music—we can access that data through the appropriate framework. Each framework defines the API used to access, create, modify, or delete those resources.

Note, each API will limit exactly which data we can access and what we can do with it. For example, we can add images to the photo library, but we cannot delete images. Additionally, to help prevent privacy violations, many of these frameworks will ask the user for permission before we can access them.

We can also use the UIDocumentInteractionController to send files to other applications that support the same file type or use the UIActivityViewController to send our data to various standard services: copying to the pasteboard, posting to social media sites, sending by email, and others.

Next, iCloud extends the sandbox, as we will see in Chapter 6, "iCloud Syncing."

Finally, the Security framework provides methods for reading and writing data to the keychain. A *keychain* is an encrypted storage for passwords and other secret information. It is intended only for storing small pieces of data, such as passwords, API keys, and the like, and should not be used for encrypting and storing general data.

The keychain's data is stored outside the apps sandbox. This means it is not deleted when the application is deleted. If you want your application to clear its keychain data whenever it's deleted and reinstalled, you will need to do so programmatically the first time the application launches.

Keychain data is backed up by iTunes. A keychain item that is password protected can be restored onto a different device only if its accessibility is not set to kSecAttAccessible AlwaysThisDeviceOnly. With iOS 7, keychain data can also be synced to iCloud. Keychain data is not affected by application updates in any way.

ACCESSING COMMONLY USED DIRECTORIES

The iOS SDK gives us a number of methods for accessing the common directories. Some methods return the path to the directory as an NSString. Others return NSURL objects. We can easily convert between paths and URLs using NSURL's URLWithString: and path methods.

In general, I try to use NSURLs whenever possible. Most methods that deal with files have both a path and a URL version—however, there are a few methods that exist in only one version or the other.

- NSHomeDirectory(): This function returns the path to our application's home directory (a.k.a. our application's sandbox) as an NSString.
- NSTemporaryDirectory(): This function returns the path to our temporary directory as an NSString.

- `NSFileManager`: This class represents our basic interface with the file system. We will use it to create directories, as well as moving, renaming, examining, and deleting files. Two methods, in particular, can help us retrieve the URL for our Documents, Library, Caches, or Application Support directories.

- `URLsForDirectory:inDomains:` returns an array of URLs. This method was originally designed for OS X, so it has a number of options that simply don't work in iOS. For our purposes, we can use `NSDocumentDirectory`, `NSLibraryDirectory`, `NSCachesDirectory`, or `NSApplicationSupportDirectory` for the search path. We always use `NSUserDomainMask` for the domain mask. This will return an array with one item.

- `URLForDirectory:inDomain:appropriateForURL:create:error:` can be used to locate or create the specified directory. When simply looking up the known directories, the directory and domain arguments are the same as `URLsForDirectory:inDomains:`, and the `appropriateForURL:` argument should be nil. We also pass a `BOOL` value, indicating whether we want the method to create the directory for us, if it doesn't already exist. Finally, in case something goes wrong, we have an error output argument.

  We can also use this method to create a new, temporary directory for us. In this case, we pass `NSItemReplacementDirectory` as the directory argument and then provide a valid parent directory as the `appropriateForURL:` argument.

  This method returns a single `NSURL` object. In some ways, that makes it easier to use, since we don't need to pull the URL from the array. However, we also have to deal with a few extra parameters, so pick your poison. Note that this method can be particularly handy when accessing the Application Support directory, since it can create that directory for us automatically.

- `NSBundle`: We can call `[NSBundle mainBundle]` to get an object for our application's bundle. We can then use this object to access resources in the bundle. The `NSBundle` class defines a number of methods that return both URLs and paths, as in `URLForResource:withExtension:`. We pass in the filename (without the extension) and the extension, and we get back an `NSURL` for that file.

  This works for any resource file that we've added to our project. By default, they are stored in the root of our application's bundle. However, we can also organize our resources into directories. If we do, we must call `URLsForResourcesWithExtension:subdirectory:` and pass in the directory name as well.

  Some other classes also support loading data directly from the bundle. `UIImage`'s `imageNamed:` method will automatically search for the given image in the application bundle. Similarly, `UINib` and `UIViewController` can search for and load nib files.

USING PATHS

Once you have the path to a file or directory, what can you do with it?

Well, `NSString` has a number of methods for manipulating paths. For example, `stringByAppendingPathComponent:` adds a subdirectory or filename to an existing path. `stringByDeletingLastPathComponent:` lets us move back up the directory tree. `NSURL` has a set of parallel methods, letting us easily manipulate URLs as well.

NSFileManager also provides a number of useful methods for querying and manipulating the file system. For example, the following code explores a given path. If it points to a file, it will print out information about that file. If it points to a directory, it will get a list of the entire directory's contents and then recursively explore each item in the list.

```
- (void)explorePath:(NSString*)path
{
    // Access singleton file manager.
    NSFileManager* fileManager = [NSFileManager defaultManager];
    BOOL isDirectory;

    // If the file doesn't exist, display an error
    // message and return.
    if (![fileManager fileExistsAtPath:path
                           isDirectory:&isDirectory])
    {
        NSLog(@"%@ does not exist", path);
        return;
    }

    // If it's not a directory, print out some
    // information about it.
    if (!isDirectory)
    {
        [self printFileInformationForPath:path];
        return;
    }

    // If it is a directory, print out the full path and then
    // recurse over all its children.
    NSLog(@"Directory: %@", path);

    NSArray* childPaths =
    [fileManager contentsOfDirectoryAtPath:path error:nil];

    for (NSString* childPath in childPaths)
    {
        [self explorePath:
         [path stringByAppendingPathComponent:childPath]];
    }
}
```

We start by getting a reference to the default file manager. Then we check to see whether a file or directory exists at the provided path. If we have a regular file, we call our printFileInformationForPath: method.

If it's a directory, we call contentsOfDirectoryAtPath:error: to get an array containing the directory's contents. This performs a shallow search. It gives us the names of all the subdirectories, files, and symbolic links within the provided directory; however, it does not return the contents of those subdirectories, traverse the links, or return the current (.) or parent (..) directories.

We then iterate over this array, recursively calling explorePath: on each entry. Note that the strings in the array represent just the file and directory names, not the complete path. We must append these names to our path to create each child path.

```
- (void)printFileInformationForPath:(NSString*)path
{
    NSFileManager* fileManager = [NSFileManager defaultManager];
    NSString* fileName = [path lastPathComponent];

    NSMutableArray *permissions = [NSMutableArray array];

    if ([fileManager isReadableFileAtPath:path])
    {
        [permissions addObject:@"readable"];
    }
    if ([fileManager isWritableFileAtPath:path])
    {
        [permissions addObject:@"writeable"];
    }
    if ([fileManager isExecutableFileAtPath:path])
    {
        [permissions addObject:@"executable"];
    }
    if ([fileManager isDeletableFileAtPath:path])
    {
        [permissions addObject:@"deletable"];
    }

    NSString *permissionString;
    if ([permissions count] == 0)
    {
        permissionString = @"none";
```

```
    }
    else
    {
        permissionString = [permissions componentsJoinedByString:@", "];
    }

    NSLog(@"File: %@ Permissions: %@", fileName, permissionString);
}
```

In `printFileInformationForPath:` we extract the filename from the path and then query the file manager about the file's permissions: Can we read, write, execute, or delete the file? Once we're done, we print out this information.

Note that we're using `NSArray`'s `componentsJoinedByString:` method to combine an array of our permission strings into a single, comma-separated string. This is a simple, elegant way to solve this problem, ensuring that we get a comma between each permission but nothing after the last entry.

Now, we can use this method to explore our entire application's sandbox by calling it as shown here:

```
[self explorePath:NSHomeDirectory()];
```

I highly recommend reading through the full documentation for `NSFileManager` before doing any serious file system work. There are a wide range of methods to help you move, delete, and even create files, links, and directories.

> **NOTE:** While `explorePath:` demonstrates a number of `NSFileManager`, `NSArray`, and `NSString` methods, it is not really the best way to iterate over a deep set of nested directories. For production code, I recommend using `enumeratorAtPath:` or `enumeratorAtURL:includingPropertiesForKeys:options:errorHandler:` instead.

While file manipulation and exploration is fun, ultimately we want to use these paths to save or load our data. Cocoa provides a number of options for us. Many classes have methods both for initializing objects from a file and for saving objects directly to a file. This includes `NSString` (for text files) and `UIImage` (for image files), as well as many of the collection classes (for collections of supported objects) and even `NSData` (for raw access to a file's bits).

These methods are often useful for quick tasks; however, saving an entire application's state typically requires something a bit more robust. Here, we could use one of `NSCoder`'s subclasses to save and load entire hierarchies of objects. Our only restriction is that all the objects in the hierarchy must adopt the `NSCoding` protocol. Typically this means using the `NSKeyedArchiver` and `NSKeyedUnarchiver` classes to perform our serialization, while adding the `initWithCoder:` and `encodeWithCoder:` methods to our custom classes.

Alternatively, we can use database technologies to persist our application's data. For on-device storage, these include using either SQLite or Core Data with an SQLite-based store. While NSCoding forces us to save and load an entire file at a time, SQLite and Core Data let us work with smaller, discrete chunks of data. Core Data, in particular, has a number of features to help us manage and greatly reduce our application's memory footprint. Of course, this comes at a cost. These technologies tend to be a bit more complex. Still, we will look at Core Data in more depth in Chapter 7, "Core Data."

MANAGING USER PREFERENCES

Preferences are special. They define the customizable portions of the application. How loud are the sound effects? Have you watched this video before? If so, how far did you get? Or, in the case of Health Beat, do you want to measure the weights in pounds or kilograms?

While the users may change these values, the application needs a default value to start with. As a result, we often refer to preferences as *defaults* (or, to be more precise, user defaults).

Typically, applications save their preferences separately from the rest of their data. This means we can change the sound effect volume without affecting our saved games. More importantly, when you switch from one saved game to another, the volume probably shouldn't change.

Furthermore, preferences can represent both the explicit and implicit settings for our application. Explicit preferences are exposed to the user, either in the Settings app or through settings controls in our application. For example, if users want to change the sound effect volume, we present a slider and let them adjust it as they want.

Implicit preferences, on the other hand, are inferred from the user's actions. In most cases we simply watch what the user is doing and record it. This could include recording the last site visited in a web view or the last paragraph read in an e-book reader.

In theory, implicit data could include the current state of the user interface. What tab did the user have open the last time she used the application? If they were filling in a form, what data had they entered so far? However, iOS provides a separate API for saving and restoring the user interface's state. You can find more information about this in the "State Persistence and Restoration" bonus chapter.

As we saw earlier, iOS has a specific directory for saving preferences, the Library/Preferences directory. However, we usually don't touch this directory directly. Instead, we should use the NSUserDefaults class (or, alternatively, Core Foundation's CFPreferences API) to store and load our preference data.

NSUserDefaults gives us programmatic access to the defaults database. This stores information in key-value pairs. To use this class, access the shared object using the standardUserDefaults class method. Then we can call a variety of methods to set and retrieve values for the specified keys.

All of the changes are cached locally to improve performance. We can call the synchronize method to force updates. This both writes local changes to disk and updates the in-memory values from disk. However, the system will automatically synchronize itself periodically, including saving before the app goes to the background. So, we need to call synchronize only when we want to programmatically force an update.

But wait, there's more. The NSUserDefaults interface is only the beginning. We can also add a Settings.bundle to our application. This allows us to configure a custom preferences page in the device's Settings application. This page uses the same defaults database as the NSUserDefaults class, allowing us to freely mix both in-app and Settings-based preferences.

The Settings application provides a convenient, centralized location for many preferences. In many ways, it is better than designing your own in-application settings. You don't need to build the interface or find a way to fit it into the application's workflow. You just configure the Settings.bundle's .plist file, and iOS handles the rest.

Unfortunately, Settings pages have a serious drawback: They aren't part of the application, so it's easy for users to forget about them. I can only speak for myself, but I'd like to think I'm reasonably technically savvy. Still, I rarely remember to check Settings after installing a new app. When I do remember, it's only after I've wasted hours searching for an in-app way to change the default behavior.

General wisdom says that the Settings app should be used for settings that the user makes once and then largely leaves alone. In-app settings should be used for things the user often changes while working with the app. However, there is no clear dividing line between these two. In practice, the Settings app has a relatively limited range of controls. This may force the decision for us. In addition, in-app settings can be easier for users to find and use. Of course, that relies on your ability to add them to your application's interface in a manner that is both unobtrusive and helpful, and that's often easier said than done.

ADDING PREFERENCES TO HEALTH BEAT

We have only a single preference value for Health Beat, our default units. Our font size is already handled through Dynamic Type, and the user interface's state should really be handled using State Preservation and Restoration. Still, we need some way to store and load our default units, and NSUserDefaults is the best fit, by far.

We already have a function to get the default weight. Let's create a function to save the defaults. Open WeightUnits.h and add the following function declaration at the bottom of the file. Be sure to add a blank line after the function, or you will receive a compiler warning.

```
void setDefaultUnits(WeightUnit defaultUnit);
```

Switch to `WeightUnits.m`. Add a static string constant to use as our unit default key, and then modify `getDefaultUnits` as shown here:

```
static NSString * const WeightUnitsDefaultUnitsKey =
@"WeightUnitsDefaultUnitsKey";

WeightUnit getDefaultUnits(void)
{
    return (WeightUnit)[[NSUserDefaults standardUserDefaults]
                        integerForKey:WeightUnitsDefaultUnitsKey];
}
```

Here, instead of simply returning LBS, we grab the current value from our user preferences. We will use the `WeightUnitsDefaultUnitsKey` string to both get and set this value. If the value has not been set yet, this will default to 0, which happens to be LBS. That is exactly what we want.

In your own projects, you may have to check whether a value has been set for a given key and return an appropriate default value if it has not. You can also bulk-set the default values for your keys by calling `registerDefaults:`. This lets you specify the value that is returned whenever we do not have a specific value stored for that key. Note, the values set by `registerDefaults:` are not saved to disk, so you need to call this method every time your application launches—often in `application:didFinishLaunchingWithOptions:`.

Now, let's add our `setDefaultUnits()` function.

```
void setDefaultUnits(WeightUnit defaultUnit)
{
    [[NSUserDefaults standardUserDefaults]
     setInteger:defaultUnit
     forKey:WeightUnitsDefaultUnitsKey];
}
```

Here, we simply use our key to store the provided unit value.

> **NOTE:** I strongly recommend wrapping all calls to `NSUserDefaults` behind a custom interface. Here, we use simple C functions. For more complex applications, you may want to create your own singleton class.
>
> Keeping all the `NSUserDefault` code in one place will make the rest of our application cleaner and easier to maintain. We can properly type our accessor methods. Plus, this will make adopting iCloud Key-Value syncing much, much easier, as we will see in Chapter 6. Using a custom singleton class has the added advantage of letting us customize our change notifications as well.

We're going to treat this as an implicit property. When the user changes the units in the Add Entry scene, we will update the default units to match. So, open `AddEntryViewController.m`.

We no longer need a property to store our units, so at the top of the file, delete the units property declaration. This should create several errors in the file. We will fix them as we go along.

Scroll down to viewDidLoad and remove the line that assigns the default units to our unit property. Next, scroll down to the unitButtonTapped: method. Modify it as shown here:

```
- (IBAction)unitButtonTapped:(id)sender {

    if (getDefaultUnits() == LBS)
    {
        setDefaultUnits(KG);
    }
    else
    {
        setDefaultUnits(LBS);
    }

    NSString *unitString = [WeightEntry stringForUnit:getDefaultUnits()];
    [self.unitButton setTitle:unitString forState:UIControlStateNormal];
}
```

Finally, scroll down to setupInputAccessories and change the following line:

```
NSString *unitString = [WeightEntry stringForUnit:getDefaultUnits()];
```

That should fix all the warnings—unfortunately, we're not done yet. Switch to AddEntryViewController.h and delete the unit property from there as well. That creates more warnings. Open HistoryTableViewController.m and navigate to the addNewEntrySaved method. Modify this method as shown here:

```
- (IBAction)addNewEntrySaved:(UIStoryboardSegue *)segue
{
    AddEntryViewController *controller = segue.sourceViewController;

    WeightEntry *entry = [WeightEntry entryWithWeight:controller.weight
                                           usingUnits:getDefaultUnits()
                                              forDate:controller.date];

    [self.weightHistoryDocument addEntry:entry];
    [self dismissViewControllerAnimated:YES completion:nil];
}
```

Now we're done. Build and run the application. Open the Add Entry view, and change the units to KG. Cancel the Add Entry view and open it again. Notice that the system is still using KG for the units. Try entering a number of weights with different units. Notice that the history view is not updating properly. We end up with different rows displaying different units. Instead, the application should update the entire table every time our default units change.

To do this, we need to listen for the `NSUserDefaultsDidChangeNotification`. However, much like our font changes, the user default change is something that will affect a significant portion of our application. While we could let each individual view controller listen and respond to the notification on their own, that results in a lot of code to write, test, and maintain. Instead, let's do the same thing we did for our font changes. We'll let the app delegate listen for the changes, and then it will dispatch an update method down our entire view controller hierarchy.

Open `UIViewController+HBTUpdates.h`. We need to declare our new update method as shown here:

```
- (void)HBT_updateUserDefaults;
```

Now, switch to `UIViewController+HBTUpdates.m`. We could just implement this method—but it's going to look a lot like our existing `HBT_updateFonts` method. In fact, dispatching messages down the view controller hierarchy is a general problem. Let's extract it into its own method.

At the bottom of the `@implementation` block, just before the `@end` directive, add the following private method:

```
#pragma mark - Private Methods


- (void)HBT_updateWithSelector:(SEL)selector
{
    for (UIViewController *controller in self.childViewControllers)
    {
#pragma clang diagnostic push
#pragma clang diagnostic ignored "-Warc-performSelector-leaks"
        [controller performSelector:selector];
#pragma clang diagnostic pop
    }


    if (self.presentedViewController.presentingViewController == self)
    {
#pragma clang diagnostic push
#pragma clang diagnostic ignored "-Warc-performSelector-leaks"
        [self.presentedViewController performSelector:selector];
#pragma clang diagnostic pop
    }
}
```

This follows the same general pattern as our HBT_updateFonts method. However, in this case, we are passing in the selector that we want to call; then we're indirectly calling that selector using the performSelector: method.

There is one small catch. ARC doesn't know anything about our selector, so it has no idea how to handle the memory management. This will cause the compiler to raise warnings.

We know that our selector refers to a method that doesn't return any objects, so there are no memory management issues. This means we can safely ignore this warning. To do that, we have to tell our compiler to temporarily turn off that particular warning. We do this using the #pragma directives as shown.

With this in place, our HBT_updateFonts and HBT_updateUserDefaults methods become simple.

```
-(void)HBT_updateFonts
{
    [self HBT_updateWithSelector:_cmd];
}


-(void)HBT_updateUserDefaults
{
    [self HBT_updateWithSelector:_cmd];
}
```

In both cases, we're just calling updateWithSelector: and passing _cmd. _cmd is one of the two hidden arguments to every method. It holds the selector for the current method.

Now we have to set up our application delegate. Open AppDelegate.m. In the class extension, add the following property:

```
@property (strong, nonatomic) id userDefaultsChangeObserver;
```

Then, modify the dealloc method to remove our new observer. We're also moving our notification center to a local variable, so each if statement can access it.

```
- (void)dealloc
{
    NSNotificationCenter *center = [NSNotificationCenter defaultCenter];

    if (self.fontChangeObserver)
    {
        [center removeObserver:self.fontChangeObserver];
    }

    if (self.userDefaultsChangeObserver)
    {
```

```
        [center removeObserver:self.userDefaultsChangeObserver];
    }
}
```

Finally, we modify the application:didFinishLaunchingWithOptions: method to set up our notifications. Again, I am extracting many of the common data elements into local variables, to make it easier to use them for both notifications.

```
- (BOOL)application:(UIApplication *)application
didFinishLaunchingWithOptions:(NSDictionary *)launchOptions
{
    self.window.tintColor =
    [UIColor colorWithRed:0.5 green:0.0 blue:0.0 alpha:1.0];

    UIViewController *rootViewController = self.window.rootViewController;
    NSNotificationCenter *center = [NSNotificationCenter defaultCenter];
    NSOperationQueue *mainQueue = [NSOperationQueue mainQueue];

    self.fontChangeObserver =
    [center
     addObserverForName:UIContentSizeCategoryDidChangeNotification
     object:[UIApplication sharedApplication]
     queue:mainQueue
     usingBlock:^(NSNotification *note) {
         [rootViewController HBT_updateFonts];
     }];

    self.userDefaultsChangeObserver =
    [center
     addObserverForName:NSUserDefaultsDidChangeNotification
     object:[NSUserDefaults standardUserDefaults]
     queue:mainQueue
     usingBlock:^(NSNotification *note) {
         [rootViewController HBT_updateUserDefaults];
     }];

    return YES;
}
```

That's it. Our entire view controller hierarchy will now be notified whenever the user defaults change. Now we just need to override HBT_updateUserDefaults in each of our controllers, to update their content.

Open HistoryTableViewController.m and override HBT_updateUserDefaults just under HBT_updateFonts.

```
- (void)HBT_updateUserDefaults
{
    [super HBT_updateUserDefaults];
    [self.tableView reloadData];
}
```

This is the same as our update fonts method. We just tell the table to reload all its data. This will update all the unit values and labels.

Next, open EntryDetailViewController.m. Again, override HBT_updateUserDefaults just under HBT_updateFonts.

```
- (void)HBT_updateUserDefaults
{
    [super HBT_updateUserDefaults];
    [self updateUI];
}
```

This time, we're just calling our updateUI method. This will reset all the text field contents, updating our weights and units.

Repeat this procedure for GraphViewController.m. This time we're going to call graph view's setNeedsDisplay to force the view to redraw itself. As before, this will update all the weights and unit labels.

```
- (void)HBT_updateUserDefaults
{
    [super HBT_updateUserDefaults];
    [self.graphView setNeedsDisplay];
}
```

Finally, open AddEntryViewController.m. This one requires a bit more work. First, since our view will automatically update anytime the defaults change, we no longer need to modify our button text in unitButtonTapped:. Navigate to unitButtonTapped: and delete the following lines of code:

```
NSString *unitString = [WeightEntry stringForUnit:getDefaultUnits()];
[self.unitButton setTitle:unitString forState:UIControlStateNormal];
```

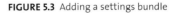

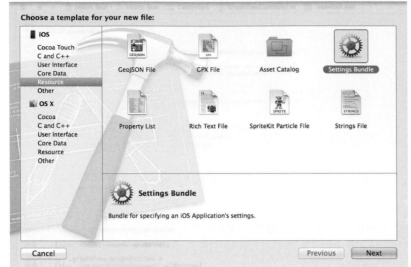

FIGURE 5.3 Adding a settings bundle

FIGURE 5.4 Settings.bundle's contents

Then move that code to our HBT_updateUserDefaults method.

```
- (void)HBT_updateUserDefaults
{
    [super HBT_updateUserDefaults];
    NSString *unitString = [WeightEntry stringForUnit:getDefaultUnits()];
    [self.unitButton setTitle:unitString forState:UIControlStateNormal];
}
```

That's it. Our entire user interface should update correctly whenever we change the default units. Run the application. Try changing the defaults using the Add Entry scene, and then cycle through the other scene and make sure they're picking up the change.

Now, before you get too excited, the sad truth is, most of the scenes would have updated themselves automatically during their viewDidAppear: method anyway. So, our code isn't really helping that much yet. But it will...oh, yes...it will.

Once we add a custom preference page for our application, the default values can be changed at any time in the background. Then our updates become very, very important.

ADDING SYSTEM SETTINGS SUPPORT

Adding a custom preferences page to the Systems application is not too difficult. Control-click the Supporting Files group and select New File. Under iOS > Resource, select Settings Bundle and click Next (**Figure 5.3**). Make sure the file is named Settings, and click Create.

This adds the Settings.bundle file to your application. If you expand this bundle, you will see that it contains an English-language localization folder (en.lproj) with a strings file, and it contains a file named Root.plist (**Figure 5.4**).

Key		Type	Value
▼ iPhone Settings Schema		Dictionary	(2 items)
▼ Preference Items		Array	(4 items)
▼ Item 0 (Group – Group)		Dictionary	(2 items)
Title		String	Group
Type		String	Group
▼ Item 1 (Text Field – Name)		Dictionary	(8 items)
Autocapitalization Style		String	None
Autocorrection Style		String	No Autocorrection
Default Value		String	
Text Field Is Secure		Boolean	NO
Identifier		String	name_preference
Keyboard Type		String	Alphabet
Title		String	Name
Type		String	Text Field
▼ Item 2 (Toggle Switch – Enabled)		Dictionary	(4 items)
Default Value		Boolean	YES
Identifier		String	enabled_preference
Title		String	Enabled
Type		String	Toggle Switch
▼ Item 3 (Slider)		Dictionary	(7 items)
Default Value		Number	0.5
Identifier		String	slider_preference
Maximum Value		Number	1
Max Value Image Filename		String	
Minimum Value		Number	0
Min Value Image Filename		String	
Type		String	Slider
Strings Filename		String	Root

FIGURE 5.5 Exploring Root.plist

We've brushed up against property lists (or plists) a few times. Basically, these files store key-value pairs. However, since the values can include arrays and dictionaries, we can use them to manage complex data structures. Property list files are commonly used to configure applications in both iOS and Mac OS X.

Xcode displays property lists using a property list editor. Under the surface, however, plists may be saved in a variety of formats, including a JSON-like format, an XML format, and a binary format. For more information, check out Apple's Property List Programming Guide.

The default Root.plist defines a sample preferences page. If you expand all the elements, you will see that it has a single group of settings, somewhat simplistically titled Group. Next, we have three controls: a text field titled Name, a toggle switch titled Enabled, and an untitled slider. Each of these controls also has an identifier field (name_preference, enabled_preference, and slider_preference). This value should match the keys used to access these values from NSUserDefaults (**Figure 5.5**).

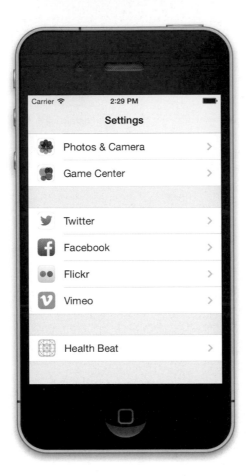

FIGURE 5.6 Our Health Beat entry in the Settings app   **FIGURE 5.7** Health Beat's settings page

Let's see this preferences sheet in action. Run the application. This will compile a new copy of your app that includes the Settings.bundle and then upload it to the simulator or device. Once the application launches, tap the home button to send it to the background. Switch to the Settings application. You should now see an entry for Health Beat's settings (**Figure 5.6**).

Tap the Health Beat row to open the custom preferences page. It has a single group with three controls, just as we expected (**Figure 5.7**).

Of course, this isn't what we want. We really need a single group named Units, with a single multivalue item that will allow us to choose between pounds and kilograms. Edit the property list file so that it matches the settings shown in **Figure 5.8**.

I find it easiest to just delete the four existing items and start fresh. Select the Preference Items key. Plus and minus buttons will appear next to the key name. Press the plus button twice. This will add two new items to the Preference Items array. Expand Item 0. Change Type to **Group**, and change Title to **Units**.

Key	Type	Value
▼ iPhone Settings Schema	Dictionary	(2 items)
▼ Preference Items	Array	(2 items)
▼ Item 0 (Group – Units)	Dictionary	(3 items)
Type	String	Group
Title	String	Units
Key	String	
▼ Item 1 (Multi Value – Weight)	Dictionary	(6 items)
Type	String	Multi Value
Title	String	Weight
Identifier	String	WeightUnitsDefaultIUnitsKey
▼ Values	Array	(2 items)
Item 0	Number	0
Item 1	Number	1
▼ Titles	Array	(2 items)
Item 0	String	lbs
Item 1	String	kg
Default Value	Number	0
Strings Filename	String	Root

FIGURE 5.8 Health Beat's finished `Root.plist` file

FIGURE 5.9 Health Beat's final preference page

Next, expand Item 1. Change Type to **Multi Value**, Title to **Weight**, and Identifier to **WeightUnitsDefaultUnitsKey**. For this to work correctly, the Identifier entry must match the key we use to access our `NSUserDefaults` values. In our case, it must match the `WeightUnitsDefaultUnitsKey` constant we defined at the top of `WeightUnits.m`.

Now select the Identifier row, and press the plus button three times. It should automatically add the Default Value, Titles, and Values entries. If not, rename them as needed.

For Default Value, set Type to **Number** and Value to **0**. For Values, expand it, and then press its plus button twice to add two new items to our Values array. Item 0 should be of type **Number** and Value **0**. Item 1 should also be of type **Number**, with a value of **1**. Do the same thing to Titles, but make its item types **String** with values of **lbs** and **kg**.

Run the application again. Add weights, and open the graph view. Now put the app in the background and open the Settings app. Navigate to the Health Beat settings (**Figure 5.9**). Change the default units. Move back to Health Beat. The graph should have automatically changed to match the value in our Settings app. Repeat this test for the other scenes: History, Entry Detail, and Add Entry.

In each case, the NSUserDefaultsDidChangeNotification is being sent as soon as our application returns from the background. Our app delegate receives the notification and sends the HBT_updateUserDefaults message down the view controller hierarchy, and everything is correctly updated. It's an elegant solution to managing global changes.

SAVING THE WEIGHT HISTORY DOCUMENT

When it comes to saving and loading custom data objects, we will be using two different tools: NSCoding and NSCoder. NSCoding is a protocol that our custom data objects must implement. It defines two methods. initWithCoder: is called to load the object, while encodeWithCoder is called to save the object.

NSCoder is an abstract superclass. It defines a number of methods to save and load data. We cannot instantiate NSCoder directly; instead, we will use one of its concrete subclasses. Typically we use NSKeyedArchiver to save our data and NSKeyedUnarchiver to load it.

These archivers support both saving to in-memory archives (storing our object graph as an NSData) and serializing the archive directly to disk. Often we use a two-step process, first creating the in-memory archive and then saving the archive. This lets us more easily separate archiving/unarchiving errors from disk read/write errors. As we will see, it also lets us perform the in-memory archive tasks on the main thread and the disk I/O tasks in the background.

While we could use these archivers directly, there's actually a better way. We will create a subclass of UIDocument, which will handle many of the details involved in saving and loading our data automatically.

NOTE: While we use NSKeyedArchiver and NSKeyedUnarchiver in this example, NSCoder also has an older set of concrete subclasses: NSArchiver and NSUnarchiver. These archives do not use keys to save and load their objects and values. Instead, they must load the data in the same order they saved it. In general, you should avoid using these whenever possible. They have been replaced by the keyed archives for iOS and all versions of Mac OS X 10.2 and newer.

USING A UIDOCUMENT

UIDocument is also an abstract subclass. To use it, we must subclass it and implement the contentsForType:error: and loadFromContents:ofType:error: methods. In our MVC design pattern, UIDocument (and our subclasses) are a type of model object controller. This gives us two, different types of controllers.

UIViewControllers are tightly bound with a particular set of views. Similarly, the UIDocument is more tightly bound with our model. This gives us a Model – Model Controller – View Controller – View design.

USING KEYED ARCHIVES

When using NSKeyedArchiver or NSKeyedUnarchiver, all the objects and values are given a key to identify them. These keys must be unique within the scope of the current object being saved or loaded. Therefore, if you are creating a public class that might be subclassed in the future, you should add a prefix to your keys to prevent collisions with any possible future subclasses. Additionally, you should avoid starting your keys with $, NS, or UI, since these are used by the system. Apple's documentation recommends appending the full class name to the front of the key.

While the keys add a little complexity, they give us considerable flexibility when loading our data. We can load the data in any order and even selectively choose which data to load. This gives us better support for forward and backward compatibility should our data structure change, letting us easily add or remove keyed values from our archives.

Keyed archives are also easy to use. You can store an object hierarchy into an NSData object by calling the NSKeyedArchiver's archivedDataWithRootObject: class method. You save it to disk by calling archiveRootObject:toFile: instead.

The system will take your root object and call its encodeWithCoder: method, passing in a properly formatted NSKeyedArchiver object. The keyed archive contains a number of methods that you can use to store raw C values (e.g., encodeBool:forKey:, encodeInt:forKey:, and encodeFloat:forKey:). It also includes a method for encoding other objects, unsurprisingly named encodeObject:forKey:. These children objects must also adopt the NSCoding protocol. The system then calls their encodeWithCoder: method, passing along the keyed archive, until the entire object graph is saved.

Unarchiving works the same way. Simply call NSKeyedUnarchiver's unarchiveObject WithData: or unarchiveObjectWithFile: method. This will build the object hierarchy, calling initWithCoder: on each object, and then return the root object.

The archivers are smart enough to notice when your object graph has multiple references to the same object, and they will correctly save or load just one version of the object with all the references properly linking to that object. This means we can make our object graph as complex as we like. We don't need to worry about loops or circular references.

However, for the sake of performance, we want to minimize the number of objects we save and load. Unless the operations are computationally intense, you should manually set, calculate, or create any values that you can, and then save and load only those values that you absolutely must.

UIDocument was originally designed to support iCloud syncing. However, as you will see, it provides a wide range of useful features, even when used on its own. I highly recommend using UIDocument, even if you never plan on turning on iCloud.

Specifically, UIDocument provides the following:

- Asynchronous background reading and writing of our data.

- Coordinated reads and writes, letting multiple processes safely access our data files. While this is not particularly useful for most iOS applications, because of the sandbox's limitations, it will become very important once we start using iCloud syncing.

- Safe, atomic write operations, by saving the document to a temporary file first and then moving it to the final location.

- Automatically saving the document as the user changes it.

Of these, the automatic background saves are particularly important. To help keep the user interface as responsive as possible, we should avoid doing any tasks that take a considerable amount of time on the main thread. In particular, this means we should avoid any file read/write operations or any network operations on the main thread. While NSOperationQueue makes dispatching tasks to a background relatively safe and easy, I'm not going to complain about getting the background disk I/O for free.

ADDING A UIDOCUMENT SUBCLASS TO HEALTH BEAT

Instead of creating a new class, we're going to change our WeightHistoryDocument into a UIDocument subclass. Open WeightHistoryDocument.h.

Let's start by changing WeightHistoryDocument's superclass to UIDocument. Modify the @interface line as shown here:

```
@interface WeightHistoryDocument : UIDocument
```

Next, let's declare a few public class methods. We will use these to get the URL for our local document and to check whether the document exists yet. Add the following declarations to the bottom of the @interface block, just before the @end directive:

```
+ (NSURL *)localFileURL;
+ (BOOL)localFileExists;
```

Now, switch to WeightHistoryDocument.m. At the top of the file, just below the other constants, add the following constant definition:

```
// Used to create our file URLs
static NSString * const WeightHistoryDocumentFileName =
@"WeightHistoryDocument.data";
```

We will use this constant when creating URLs for our document file.

NOTE: There's nothing special about this particular filename or extension. You're free to pick any filename and extension you want. However, I would shy away from common extensions with known document types (such as .txt, .doc, and .jpg).

Next, we have to modify the `init` method. Since we're no longer subclassing `NSObject`, `init` is no longer our superclass's designated initializer. Instead, it's `initWithFileURL:` Let's change our custom `init` method so that it's overriding `initWithFileURL:` instead.

Navigate to the `init` method and modify it as shown here:

```
- (id)initWithFileURL:(NSURL *)url
{
    self = [super initWithFileURL:url];
    if (self) {
        _weightHistory = [NSMutableArray array];
    }
    return self;
}
```

Now, let's add our class methods. Scroll down to the end of the public methods, and add the following:

```
#pragma mark - Public Class Methods

+ (NSURL *)localFileURL
{
    NSArray *urls = [[NSFileManager defaultManager]
                    URLsForDirectory:NSDocumentDirectory
                    inDomains:NSUserDomainMask];

    NSURL *documentURL = [urls lastObject];
    return [documentURL URLByAppendingPathComponent:
            WeightHistoryDocumentFileName];
}
```

Here, we use the file manager's `URLsForDirectory:inDomains:` method to request our Documents directory. As we saw before, this method returns an array. On the desktop, this array could have multiple matches, especially when searching across multiple domains. However, on iOS, this will have only one entry, so we can safely grab the last (or first) entry.

Then we create a new URL by adding our document filename as a path component to the end of our directory's URL. This will automatically insert the slash between the directory and our file's name.

Now, let's add our `localFileExists` method.

```
+ (BOOL)localFileExists
{
    NSFileManager *manager = [NSFileManager defaultManager];
    BOOL isDirectory;
```

```
    BOOL fileExists = [manager fileExistsAtPath:[[self localFileURL] path]
                                   isDirectory:&isDirectory];
    return fileExists || (!isDirectory);
}
```

Here, we get a reference to the default file manager. Then we call the file manager's `fileExistsAtPath:isDirectory:` method. The second argument of this method is an out argument. We need to pass it a pointer to a `BOOL` variable. If the file exists and it is a directory, the method will set our `BOOL` variable to `YES`. If it's a regular file, the method will set it to `NO`.

The local file exists if it is both present and if it is not a directory.

With the preliminaries out of the way, we're ready to start working with our `UIDocument` subclass. The following are the tasks we must perform to get it up and running:

1. Add code to load or create our document.

2. Override `contentsForType:error:` to create a snapshot of our document's data so that the system can save it in the background.

3. Override `loadFromContents:ofType:error:` to extract our document's data from the content loaded in the background.

4. Respond to document state changes.

5. Let our `UIDocument` subclass know when changes have occurred so it can trigger automatic background saves.

LOADING AND CREATING OUR DOCUMENT

Open `RootTabBarController.m`, and navigate to the `viewDidLoad` method. We're going to extract the code to set up our document into a private method. So, change `viewDidLoad` as shown here:

```
- (void)viewDidLoad
{
    [super viewDidLoad];
    [self setupDocument];
    self.interactiveTransition =
    [[TabInteractiveTransition alloc] initWithTabBarController:self];
    self.delegate = self.interactiveTransition;
    [self setupEdgePanGestureRecognizers];
}
```

Now, at the top of the private methods, add our `setupDocument` method.

```
- (void)setupDocument
{
    NSURL *fileURL = [WeightHistoryDocument localFileURL];
    self.weightHistoryDocument = [[WeightHistoryDocument alloc]
                                  initWithFileURL:fileURL];
```

```
[self.weightHistoryDocument addSubscriber:self];
//    [self addMocData];
[self documentReady];

if ([WeightHistoryDocument localFileExists])
{
    [self loadFileAtURL:fileURL];
}
else
{
    [self createNewFileAtURL:fileURL];
}
}
```

Here, we get the URL for our local file. We use that to instantiate our weight history document. Then we add the tab controller as a subscriber, and we call the documentReady method. Next, we check to see whether the local file exists. If it does, we load the file. If it doesn't, we create a new, empty file. The document will actually be loaded or created on a background thread and will send a state change notification once it is open and ready to use.

There's only one small problem with this. The documentReady method's name doesn't really seem appropriate anymore. Let's refactor this.

We could just change the method name both where it is defined and where it is used. However, that could be a lot of work, especially if a method ends up being called many times in many different files. Instead, let's use the refactoring tool.

Navigate to the documentReady method, and select the method name. Then Control-click the method name and select Refactor > Rename.... In the pop-up sheet, change the name to **passDocumentToViewControllers** and press Preview.

The preview page will show us all the changes that the refactoring tool will make throughout our document. In this case, it is both modifying the method call inside our setupDocument method and changing the method's declaration. Click Save to make the changes.

Xcode might ask about enabling snapshots before making this change. That is usually a good idea. I typically enable snapshots before refactoring, so I can automatically revert to my original code if something goes horribly wrong.

NOTE: Occasionally you may receive the following warning when trying to refactor code, "The selection is not a type that can be renamed. Make a different selection and try again." Providing your selection was correct—method, class, property, and variable names should all work—then Xcode's index has probably become corrupted. To fix this, quit out of Xcode and delete the entire derived data directory (by default it's located at ~/Library/Developer/Xcode/DerivedData). When you relaunch Xcode, it will rebuild its index, and refactoring should work as expected.

Next, add `loadFileAtURL:` after our newly renamed `passDocumentToViewControllers` method.

```objc
- (void)loadFileAtURL:(NSURL *)fileURL;
{
    NSLog(@"Loading File");
    __weak RootTabBarController *_self = self;
    [self.weightHistoryDocument
    openWithCompletionHandler:^(BOOL success) {
        if (!success)
        {
            NSLog(@"*** Corrupt file at %@, "
                @"attempting to delete it and create a new "
                @"data file. ***",
                fileURL);

            [[NSFileManager defaultManager] removeItemAtURL:fileURL
                                                error:nil];

            [_self setupDocument];
            return;
        }
        else
        {
            NSLog(@"File Loaded");
        }
    }];
}
```

Here, we call `UIDocument`'s `openWithCompletionHandler:` method. This method should be called on the main thread. It will load our data file on a background thread and then call our completion handler on the main thread once the file is open.

Notice that we don't get a very verbose error message. Either the file successfully loads or it doesn't. We checked to make sure the file existed before calling this method—so if we cannot load the file, we must assume it's corrupt. Let's delete the corrupted file and create a new one. The easiest way to do this is to just call our `setupDocument` method again.

Yes, this is a bit heavy-handed as far as error management goes, but it's better than nothing. Still, you'll probably want to replace it in production code. We should at least ask the user before deleting their document. However, I'll leave that as an extra-credit exercise.

Next, let's add the `createNewFileAtURL:` method.

```objc
- (void)createNewFileAtURL:(NSURL *)fileURL
{
    NSLog(@"Creating New File");
    [self.weightHistoryDocument
     saveToURL:fileURL
     forSaveOperation:UIDocumentSaveForCreating
     completionHandler:^(BOOL success) {
         if (!success)
         {
             NSString *message =
             [NSString stringWithFormat:
              @"Unable to create a new file at %@", fileURL];

             NSLog(@"*** Error: %@ ***", message);

             [NSException
              raise:NSInternalInconsistencyException
              format:@"Error Creating UIDocument: %@", message];
         }
         else
         {
             NSLog(@"File Created");

         }
     }];
}
```

Again, we call UIDocument's `saveToURL:forSaveOperation:completionHandler:`
method, and again, this is an asynchronous, block-based method that should be called from
the main thread. It will save a new document on a background thread. Once the document is
ready for use, it calls our completion handler on the main thread.

Most of the time, this method should fail because of a developer error. Therefore, we'll
use very minimal error checking here. If something goes wrong, we simply log a message to
the console, and then throw an exception. This will crash the application, letting us know
there is a problem.

While this is fine for development, it's not so great for production. There are legitimate
reasons why this could fail in the real world. The most obvious example is that the user's
device simply does not have enough storage space left to save our file. We should, therefore,
replace this with user-friendly error handling before we ship.

The UIDocument class is an excellent object lesson in concurrent iOS programming. The basic assumption is that our application should access its data only on the main thread. If we need to process that data on a background thread (to save it, send it across the network, or perform long and costly calculations on it), we should create a copy of that data and pass the copy to the background thread. Then, when the background thread is done, it passes the results back to the main thread, and we can safely update our data.

When done right, there's no need for locks, semaphores, or other synchronization. There's no risk of deadlocks or race conditions. Our multithreaded code is more robust and usually faster than traditional threaded code.

However, we must be careful to create deep copies of our data before moving it to the background. Simply calling the copy method on an NSArray, for example, will create a shallow copy. This could introduce race conditions, since we may have two different threads reading and modifying the same objects at the same time.

Often, the easiest way to make a deep copy is to archive the data, just as we do in contentsForType:error:.

High-level threading operations are typically handled using the NSOperationQueue class. A simple demo is shown here:

```
NSOperationQueue *backgroundQueue = [[NSOperationQueue alloc] init];
backgroundQueue.name = @"Calculation Background Queue";
[backgroundQueue setMaxConcurrentOperationCount:1];
self.backgroundQueue = backgroundQueue;
```

First we create our operation queue. By default this will run on one or more background threads. Operations are processed first-in, first-out. However, the queue may process multiple operations at once—the system will choose the exact number of threads to allocate to a queue based on its current load and the resources available.

However, I often use code like this, even during the late beta testing period. This code forces a hard crash when something goes wrong. My testers will definitely notice and report the crash. Even more importantly, I can have the testers send me a copy of their crash logs.

This is particularly useful if you know something might fail but you're not exactly sure how it could fail. By gathering crash logs from beta testers, you will quickly get a list of the most common errors, and then you can write code to specifically handle those situations.

Also notice that in both our loadFile... and createFile... methods, we are using a lot of logging to help peek into UIDocument's inner workings. The one problem with UIDocument is that it can be rather opaque at times. I find that adding a little extra logging can really help when it comes to debugging problems later, especially timing issues.

If we run the application, you will see that it logs the Creating New File message and then crashes with the following exception:

```
The default implementation of -[UIDocument writeContents:toURL:
forSaveOperation:originalContentsURL:error: only understands contents
of type NSFileWrapper or NSData, not (null). You must override one of
the write methods to support custom content types
```

In the sample, we give the queue a name. This isn't required but can make debugging easier. We also limit the number of concurrent operations to 1, forcing the queue to perform its actions serially. Then we assign the queue to an instance variable.

We need to make sure our queue survives for the entire lifetime of the tasks assigned to it. Often the easiest way to do this is to create an instance variable to hold the queue. Create the queue when we first create our owning object. As long as the owning object exists, the queue exists, and we can assign tasks to it as needed.

There is a simple block-based API to add operations to a queue:

```
[self.backgroundQueue addOperationWithBlock:^{
    NSLog(@"printed from a background thread!");
}];
```

We can also explicitly create NSBlockOperation objects and add them to the queue. This lets us customize the operation: adding dependencies, priorities, or completion blocks. We can also cancel operations or wait for them to complete.

iOS also supports low-level concurrent programming through the Grand Central Dispatch (GCD) framework. This is a block-based C framework. NSOperationQueues are actually implemented using GCD. While NSOperationQueues add a few high-level features (such as dependencies), they also lack other features, such as barrier-blocks. Also, GCD has a slightly lower overhead than NSOperationQueues—which can be important in high-performance code.

Finally, a growing number of block-based asynchronous APIs are showing up scattered throughout iOS's frameworks. All of these are built upon NSOperationQueues and GCD.

OVERRIDING CONTENTSFORTYPE:ERROR:

Whenever our UIDocument subclass tries to save its data, it will call the contentsForType:error: method. We must override this method, making and returning a snapshot of our current data. UIDocument supports using either NSData or NSFileWrapper for the document's contents. The difference is that the system saves NSData objects as a single file, while NSFileWrappers are saved as a hierarchy of directories and files.

If possible, applications should try to use NSFileWrappers, breaking up their data into natural, independent chunks. This lets the application selectively save and load only those files that have actually changed. This is especially true once we start syncing this data with iCloud. However, Health Beat stores all of its data in a single array. Trying to partition this across multiple files is more trouble than it's worth. As a result, we're going to store everything inside a single NSData object.

The snapshotting procedure is done on the main thread. This is an in-memory procedure, so there's no risk of slowing down the user interface. The system then saves the data to disk on a background thread—taking as much time as it needs.

Open WeightHistoryDocument.m and implement contentsForType:error: after the public class methods as shown here:

```
#pragma mark - UIDocument Methods


- (id)contentsForType:(NSString *)typeName
              error:(NSError *__autoreleasing *)outError
{
    NSLog(@"Saving our data...");
    return [NSKeyedArchiver
         archivedDataWithRootObject:self.weightHistory];
}
```

Here, we simply log the fact that we're saving our data (again, helping us peek behind the scene); then we archive our array to an NSData object and return it.

Note that we aren't doing any error handling here. If an error occurs, we could create an error object, assign it to the outError pointer, and return nil. However, this is rarely worth the effort. archivedDataWithRootObject: almost always fails because of developer error. In those cases, it throws an exception, which we should discover and fix during development.

Actual runtime errors should occur only when the system is experiencing a catastrophic failure—in which case there probably isn't anything useful we can do.

> **NOTE:** If you want to provide more robust error messages from either contentsForType:error: or loadFromContents:ofType:error:, you also need to override handleError:userInteractionPermitted: to handle those errors. Otherwise, they will be silently swallowed by the system.

OVERRIDING LOADFROMCONTENTS:OFTYPE:ERROR:

Our loadFromContents:ofType:error: method is almost as simple.

```
- (BOOL)loadFromContents:(id)contents
                 ofType:(NSString *)typeName
                  error:(NSError *__autoreleasing *)outError
{
    NSParameterAssert([contents isKindOfClass:[NSData class]]);
    NSLog(@"Loading our data...");
    @try {
        self.weightHistory =
        [NSKeyedUnarchiver
         unarchiveObjectWithData:contents];
    }
    @catch (NSException *exception) {
        NSLog(@"*** An Exception Occurred: %@ ***", exception);
```

```
            self.weightHistory = nil;
        }
        @finally {
            return self.weightHistory != nil;
        }
    }
}
```

Here, the system will load our data file in the background and then will call this method on the main thread, passing us either an NSData or an NSFileWrapper. Since we're saving NSData objects, we should get NSDatas back. So, the first thing we do is check the contents argument and make sure it is an NSData object.

Then we have an Objective-C try/catch block. We rarely use try/catch blocks, but this is one of the few exceptions.

unarchiveObjectWithData: is almost as robust as archiveDataWithRootObject:; however, there is one case where it could fail. If the file becomes corrupt, unarchiveObject WithData: will throw an exception. Now, corrupt files should be exceedingly rare—especially given all the safeguards UIDocument provides. Between its safe, atomic writes and the file system coordination—not to mention the closed nature of the app sandbox—there aren't that many ways for our app to shoot its data in the foot. Still, flash drives do occasionally fail, and you never know when a rogue gamma ray might strike. So, corrupted files will always remain an unfortunate possibility.

In the rare case when unarchiveObjectWithData: throws an exception, we simply set our weight history to nil. And, if our weight history is nil, we return NO. Otherwise, everything is good and we return YES.

Again, we could create an NSError object and pass it through the out argument—but, unless we're planning to override handleError:userInteractionPermitted: to explicitly handle this error, it's not going to make any difference.

Furthermore, since handleError:userInteractionPermitted: has a tendency to silently swallow our error messages, I often find it useful to override it as well. Here, we're just going to log the error message—giving us yet another peek inside UIDocument's black box.

```
- (void)handleError:(NSError *)error
userInteractionPermitted:(BOOL)userInteractionPermitted
{
    NSLog(@"*** A WeightHistoryDocument error occurred: %@ ***",
        [error localizedDescription]);

    [super
     handleError:error
     userInteractionPermitted:userInteractionPermitted];
}
```

If we've done our job correctly, we shouldn't ever see this message in our console. Still, when things don't work quite right, it's always nice to have every clue possible.

Now, when we run the application, you will see that it successfully creates the document the first time we launch it. It also loads the document every time after that. However, we're not actually saving any data yet. We have a few more steps before saving and loading is completely enabled.

RESPONDING TO DOCUMENT STATE CHANGES

Unfortunately, before we actually start saving data, we have to respond to document state changes. UIDocument has five different states.

- UIDocumentStateNormal: The document is open and ready to be used.
- UIDocumentStateClosed: The document either has not been opened yet or has been closed.
- UIDocumentStateInConflict: This will occur only when syncing with iCloud. It indicates that the system has detected conflicting edits to our document.
- UIDocumentStateSavingError: The document experienced an error while trying to save its state. We need to communicate this to the user.
- UIDocumentStateEditingDisabled: Again, this is typically seen only with iCloud. Document editing may be temporarily disabled while the file is syncing, as well as during other errors.

The document starts in the UIDocumentStateClosed state. We want to make sure the user cannot make any changes until it has successfully opened. We also want to disable the Add Entry button whenever our document is closed, in conflict or if editing is disabled. Additionally, we want to dismiss the Add Entry scene, if it is being presented when we enter any of these states.

Furthermore, since the document is automatically saving in the background, we need to alert the user whenever any saving errors occur.

And, finally, we want to reload our history and graph scenes whenever our document enters the UIDocumentStateNormal and UIDocumentStateClosed states. This will let us set up our scenes when our document first loads and clear the scenes if it closes.

Unlike our earlier example, we need to observe these changes in only three places: our RootTabBarController (to display our save error alert, no matter which scene is currently displayed), our HistoryTableViewController, and our GraphViewController.

We could use the same approach we did for our fonts and user defaults and pass the notification down our view controller hierarchy—however, that leaks information about our model a little more broadly than I'm comfortable with.

We could also have each individual view controller listen for the notification directly— like we did for the notifications about the document's contents. That's a perfectly valid solution, even if it does end up being a lot of repetitive code.

However, I'd like to use this as an opportunity to show you yet another technique for passing information from one part of our application to another. We've already used delegates; this time we'll create our own delegate API, or, rather, a delegate-like API.

In this case, instead of having a single delegate, our document object will be able to have a collection of observing objects. Furthermore, these objects won't be able to modify the document's behavior; they will just receive information about the changes to the document. To avoid confusion, let's call these observing objects *subscribers*.

There are three steps to creating delegate-like APIs.

1. Create the protocol that the delegate must adopt.

2. Create the API for setting the delegate object.

3. Have the delegating object call the methods defined in our protocol on its delegate.

Open `WeightHistoryDocument.h`. Now, we have a bit of a chicken-and-the-egg problem here. We need to declare a protocol that our subscribers must implement. This protocol needs to refer to our `WeightHistoryDocument` class, so the class must be declared first. However, our `WeightHistoryDocument`'s interface will also need to refer to this protocol, so the protocol needs to be declared first. Fortunately, we can cut through this Gordian knot with a simple forward declaration.

At the top of the file, just below the `@class WeightEntry` forward declaration, add a second forward declaration for our property.

```
@protocol WeightHistoryDocumentSubscriber;
```

Then, at the bottom of the file, just below the `@interface` block's `@end` directive, add the full protocol declaration. Be sure to add a blank line after the last `@end` as well.

```
@protocol WeightHistoryDocumentSubscriber <NSObject>
- (void)weightHistoryDocument:(WeightHistoryDocument *)document
              stateDidChange:(UIDocumentState)state;
@end
```

One of the advantages of a delegate-like approach is that we can make the communication channel as rich and as complex as we like. We can create as many methods as we want. Each method can have any number of arguments. We can even make the methods optional or required—whatever best fits our situation.

In this case, we're just creating a single method. By tradition, these methods always return the sender as their first argument. Here, we're sending the new state as our second. We're also making this a required method. There's no point in adopting the `WeightHistoryDocumentSubscriber` protocol unless you also implement this method.

Now, we just need to add the methods to set and change our subscribers. For a traditional delegate or data source, you would just create a public property. However, in our case we don't just want a single subscriber—we want to be able to add an arbitrary number of subscribers. Therefore, we'll create methods to add and remove our subscribers.

Add the following two methods to the @interface block. I placed them between the `allEntries` method declaration and the class method declarations.

```
- (void)addSubscriber:(id <WeightHistoryDocumentSubscriber>)subscriber;
- (void)removeSubscriber:(id <WeightHistoryDocumentSubscriber>)subscriber;
```

Now we need to add a property to hold our subscribers. In theory, an `NSMutableArray` would work. An `NSMutableSet` would be even better, since it would let us have only one copy of each object. That would keep our subscriber from receiving duplicate methods if we accidentally added it twice.

However, both of these have a problem. These containers hold a strong reference to any objects they contain. When storing delegate-like objects, we always want to use a weak reference, to avoid potential retain cycles. So, we need a collection object that uses weak references.

Enter `NSHashTable`. The `NSHashTable` class is based loosely on the `NSSet` class, with a number of subtle differences. First, it is always mutable. There is no immutable version. Second, we can define how it stores the objects it contains. It can create strong references, it can copy the objects, and it can create weak references. We can even use it to store nonobject pointers.

Switch to `WeightHistoryDocument.m` and add the following property to the class extension:

```
@property (strong, nonatomic)NSHashTable *subscribers;
```

Then, modify `initWithFileURL:` as shown here:

```
- (id)initWithFileURL:(NSURL *)url
{
    self = [super initWithFileURL:url];
    if (self) {
        _weightHistory = [NSMutableArray array];
        _subscribers = [NSHashTable hashTableWithOptions:
                        NSHashTableWeakMemory];

        [self setupDocumentNotifications];
    }
    return self;
}
```

This creates a hash table that will store its objects with weak references. Here, our weak references will actually play two roles. First, like with all delegate-like objects, they help prevent retain cycles. Second, since they're zeroing weak references, the system will automatically set the subscriber to `nil` whenever it is deallocated. This means, unlike the notification center or KVO, our subscribers won't need to unsubscribe before they are deleted. The weak reference effectively lets them unsubscribe automatically.

Ignore the `setupDocumentNotifications` method for now. We will implement it in a bit. Instead, implement the following two methods just before our public class methods:

```
- (void)addSubscriber:(id<WeightHistoryDocumentSubscriber>)subscriber
{
    [self.subscribers addObject:subscriber];
}
```

```objc
- (void)removeSubscriber:(id<WeightHistoryDocumentSubscriber>)subscriber
{
    [self.subscribers removeObject:subscriber];
}
```

Now, we just need to have our WeightHistoryDocument call the subscriber notification method. We want to do this whenever the document's state changes. Somewhat unintuitively, the easiest way to do this is to have our WeightHistoryDocument listen for its own notifications.

Add another property to the class extension. This one will hold our notification observer.

```objc
@property (strong, nonatomic) id documentStateObserver;
```

Next, add a dealloc method to remove our observer. I usually place these under the init... methods.

```objc
-(void)dealloc
{
    if (self.documentStateObserver)
    {
        [[NSNotificationCenter defaultCenter]
         removeObserver:self.documentStateObserver];
    }
}
```

And, finally, we need to register for our notifications. We've already added the call to setupDocumentNotifications—now we just need to implement that method. Place this at the end of our Private methods.

```objc
- (void)setupDocumentNotifications
{
    __weak WeightHistoryDocument *_self = self;
    self.documentStateObserver =
    [[NSNotificationCenter defaultCenter]
     addObserverForName:UIDocumentStateChangedNotification
     object:self
     queue:[NSOperationQueue mainQueue]
     usingBlock:^(NSNotification *note) {
         for (id <WeightHistoryDocumentSubscriber> subscriber
              in _self.subscribers)
         {
             [subscriber weightHistoryDocument:_self
                             stateDidChange:_self.documentState];
         }
     }];
}
```

Here, we simply register for the document state changed notification. When we receive that notification, we iterate over all our subscribers and call the `weightHistoryDocument:stateDidChange:` method on each one.

Now, we need to have our view controllers adopt the `WeightHistoryDocumentSubscriber` protocol and implement the `weightHistoryDocument:stateDidChange:` method. Then we need to add them as subscribers to the document.

Open `RootTabBarController.m` and modify the class extension's `@interface` line as shown here:

```
@interface RootTabBarController () <WeightHistoryDocumentSubscriber>
```

Then add the `WeightHistoryDocument:StateDidChange:` method, right before the private methods.

```
#pragma mark - WeightHistoryDocumentSubscriber Methods


- (void)weightHistoryDocument:(WeightHistoryDocument *)document
            stateDidChange:(UIDocumentState)state {

    if (state == UIDocumentStateSavingError)
    {
        NSString *title = @"Error Saving Weight History";
        NSString *message = @"Unable to save the weight history at this "
        @"time. Please free up some drive space on your device "
        @"and try again.";

        UIAlertView *alertView =
        [[UIAlertView alloc] initWithTitle:title
                                   message:message
                                  delegate:nil
                         cancelButtonTitle:@"OK"
                         otherButtonTitles:nil];

        [alertView show];
    }
}
```

Here, we check to see whether the state is UIDocumentStateSavingError. If it is, we present an alert view, letting users know we cannot save their changes.

Finally, modify the setupDocument method as shown here:

```
- (void)setupDocument
{
    NSURL *fileURL = [WeightHistoryDocument localFileURL];
    self.weightHistoryDocument = [[WeightHistoryDocument alloc]
                                  initWithFileURL:fileURL];

    [self.weightHistoryDocument addSubscriber:self];

    //    [self addMocData];
    [self passDocumentToViewControllers];

    if ([WeightHistoryDocument localFileExists])
    {
        [self loadFileAtURL:fileURL];
    }
    else
    {
        [self createNewFileAtURL:fileURL];
    }
}
```

Next, open HistoryTableViewController.m. In the class extension, have it adopt the WeightHistoryDocumentSubscriber protocol.

```
@interface HistoryTableViewController ()
<UIViewControllerTransitioningDelegate, WeightHistoryDocumentSubscriber>
```

Then, we need an outlet to our Add Entry button. Switch to the Main.storyboard and open the Assistant Editor. Zoom in on the History Table View Controller scene, and then Control-drag from the + button in the navigation bar to the class extension. Create an outlet as shown here:

```
@property (weak, nonatomic) IBOutlet UIBarButtonItem *addButton;
```

Now, switch back to the Standard editor and open HistoryTableViewController.m. Add the weightHistoryDocument:stateDidChange: method. I placed this just after the accessor methods.

```
#pragma mark - WeightHistoryDocumentStateObserver Methods

- (void)weightHistoryDocument:(WeightHistoryDocument *)document
            stateDidChange:(UIDocumentState)state
{
    if ((state == UIDocumentStateNormal) ||
        (state == UIDocumentStateClosed))
    {
        [self.tableView reloadData];
    }

    if (state != UIDocumentStateNormal)
    {
        if ([self.presentedViewController
             isKindOfClass:[AddEntryViewController class]])
        {
            [self dismissViewControllerAnimated:YES completion:nil];
        }
    }

    [self updateAddButton];
}
```

If our state is either UIDocumentStateNormal or UIDocumentStateClosed, we reload the table. If our state is not UIDocumentStateNormal and we are presenting an AddEntryViewController, then we dismiss the view. Finally, we update our add button's state.

Next, add the updateAddButton method to the bottom of our private methods, as shown here:

```
- (void)updateAddButton
{
    if (self.weightHistoryDocument.documentState == UIDocumentStateNormal)
    {
        self.addButton.enabled = YES;
    }
    else
    {
```

```
        self.addButton.enabled = NO;
    }
}
```

This checks the document's state. If it's UIDocumentStateNormal, we enable the button. Otherwise, we disable the button. We also want to call this method in our viewWill Appear: method to set the button's state whenever our view is displayed. Override viewWillAppear: just under our viewDidLoad method.

```
- (void)viewWillAppear:(BOOL)animated
{
    [super viewWillAppear:animated];
    [self updateAddButton];
}
```

If you run the code now, you will see that the add button is disabled. It never becomes enabled. This is because we haven't registered as a subscriber yet. Navigate to the setWeightHistoryDocument: method, and modify it as shown here:

```
- (void)setWeightHistoryDocument:
(WeightHistoryDocument *)weightHistoryDocument
{
    if (_weightHistoryDocument)
    {
        [self removeNotifications];
    }

    [weightHistoryDocument addSubscriber:self];
    _weightHistoryDocument = weightHistoryDocument;
    [self setupNotifications];
}
```

If everything is correct, when we run the application now, the button will work as before. At this point, the file should load so quickly our button instantly appears enabled, especially if you're testing in the simulator.

Let's slow things down to actually see it appear. Open RootTabBarController.m and navigate to the setupDocument method. Make the following changes:

```
if ([WeightHistoryDocument localFileExists])
{
//  [self loadFileAtURL:fileURL];
    [self performSelector:@selector(loadFileAtURL:)
            withObject:fileURL
            afterDelay:2.0];
```

```
}
else
{
//  [self createNewFileAtURL:fileURL];
    [self performSelector:@selector(createNewFileAtURL:)
            withObject:fileURL
            afterDelay:2.0];
}
```

This will create a two-second delay between when our document is created and passed to the other view controllers and when our document is loaded (or created) and its UIDocumentNormal state is set. When you run the application, the Add Entry button should start disabled but should become enabled after two seconds.

Once you're convinced that the code is working properly, change RootTableView Controller's setupDocument method back to the original code.

We just need to update our graph view controller. Open GraphViewController.m. Again, use the class extension to adopt the WeightHistoryDocumentSubscriber protocol.

```
@interface GraphViewController () <WeightHistoryDocumentSubscriber>
```

Next, we need to add the graph view controller as a subscriber. The easiest way to do this is to create a custom setter for our weightHistoryDocument property, as shown. I added this to the end of the @implementation block, just before the @end directive.

```
#pragma mark - Accessor Methods

- (void)setWeightHistoryDocument:
(WeightHistoryDocument *)weightHistoryDocument
{
    _weightHistoryDocument = weightHistoryDocument;
    [weightHistoryDocument addSubscriber:self];
}
```

And then we just need to implement the subscriber method. Implement the following method just below our accessor method:

```
#pragma mark - WeightHistoryDocumentStateObserver methods

- (void)weightHistoryDocument:(WeightHistoryDocument *)document
            stateDidChange:(UIDocumentState)state
{
    if ((state == UIDocumentStateNormal) ||
        (state == UIDocumentStateClosed))
    {
```

```
        self.graphView.weightEntries =
        [[[self.weightHistoryDocument allEntries]
            reverseObjectEnumerator] allObjects];
    }
}
```

Here, we check to see whether our state is either UIDocumentStateNormal or UIDocumentStateClosed. In either case, we reload our graph data. This will force our graph to redraw itself.

That's it. Our application should be responding to all the relevant state changes. We'll do some additional work with state changes once we add iCloud syncing in Chapter 6. In particular, we will need to resolve conflicts as they arise. However, we don't have to worry about that in a self-contained app.

TRIGGERING AUTOMATIC BACKGROUND SAVES

The UIDocument will save our data automatically—but, for this to happen we need to let it know that a change has occurred. We can do this either by calling its updateChangeCount: method or by setting an undo action with the document's undoManager.

In general, you should always try to go through the undo manager. This not only triggers our automatic background saves but lets us add undo and redo support to our application.

Adding undo actions is easy. We simply call the undo manager's prepareWithInvocation Target: method. This method then returns a proxy for our target. We can call any methods we want on that proxy, and the undo manager will record them and invoke them on the target when the undo action is triggered.

To register our undo actions, open WeightHistoryDocument.m and navigate to the addEntry: method. Add the following code to the end of the method, just before its closing curly bracket:

```
[[self.undoManager prepareWithInvocationTarget:self]
 deleteEntryAtIndexPath:indexPath];


[self.undoManager setActionName:
 [NSString stringWithFormat:@"Do you want to remove the %@.",
  weightEntry]];
```

The first expression simply tells the undo manager to call deleteEntryAtIndexPath: with the given index path whenever this undo action is triggered. The second expression sets the action name for the undo action.

Action names are used by OS X to display contextual information in the Edit menu. For example, if I check my word processor's Edit menu right now, it gives me the option to Undo Typing or to Redo Typing. "Typing" is the current action name.

Unlike desktop applications, iOS apps shouldn't have a Save button. Instead, the application automatically saves its state at the appropriate times. Of course, that raises the question, what are the appropriate times?

Traditionally, there have been two basic approaches. The first involves waiting and saving the application's entire state (or at least all the changes) just before it goes into the background or terminates. The second involves saving each change as soon as the user makes it. They both have their advantages and disadvantages.

It is often simpler to wait and save everything at once. This can greatly reduce the number of times you need to write to disk, and it can streamline and simplify your code. This is especially true when you are using NSCoding to persist a large object hierarchy. You cannot save just part of the object hierarchy—it's an all-or-nothing procedure, and you probably don't want to save your whole data file every time you make a tiny little change.

On the other hand, iOS applications need to be able to transition quickly to the background. In general, we have about five seconds to save our data before the system kills our application. In practice, we want to stay well short of that. We don't want to accidentally lose user data because it took a fraction of a second longer than we expected. If our application needs to save a large amount of data, we may need to find ways to split it up and save off portions as the application is running, rather than leaving everything until the end.

Additionally, even though well-made iOS applications tend to be more reliable than their desktop counterparts, they still crash. If you're bulk-saving your application's data, your users will lose all their work from the current session.

Saving as you go helps to spread the computational cost over the application's entire life cycle. In general, this prevents any noticeable lags as the application stops to load or save a large chunk of its data.

iOS does not use the action name directly. However, we can hijack this feature and use it as a convenient place to stash additional context information about our undo action. We will then use this context information when confirming the undo action.

Now, add the following code to the beginning of the deleteEntryAtIndexPath: method. In this case, it's important that we grab the entry before we delete it.

```
WeightEntry *entry = [self entryAtIndexPath:indexPath];
[[self.undoManager prepareWithInvocationTarget:self] addEntry:entry];
[self.undoManager setActionName:
 [NSString stringWithFormat:@"Do you want to restore the %@.", entry]];
```

With this code in place, our application should save its data correctly. Run the application. Add some data. Press the home button to send it to the background (or just wait, it will automatically save eventually).

However, instead of seeing the Saving our data... message in the console, our application crashes. What went wrong?

If you scroll to the top of the exception, you should see something similar to the following:

```
-[WeightEntry encodeWithCoder:]: unrecognized selector sent to instance 0x8a18ad0
```

In practice, this can be harder to achieve. We often intend to load only one or two entries—but if they refer to other entries, which refer to still other entries, we may accidentally pull in a lot more data than we expect.

You will typically need to use some sort of database or database-like technology to support a save-as-you-go approach. I highly recommend using Core Data, but SQLite is also well supported. You can also find a number of third-party solutions that are worth considering.

On the downside, loading and saving as you go can easily become more complex and harder to maintain, especially if your persistence code ends up scattered throughout your application rather than concentrated in a couple of methods.

Additionally, you need to make sure your application's data does not end up in an inconsistent state if your application stops unexpectedly. For example, if a typical task involves several steps, you might want to wait until the entire task is finished before saving your application. If your application crashes in the middle of a task, saving after each step could leave a half-finished, malformed task in your database.

Fortunately, UIDocument simplifies all of this. We no longer need to worry about when our document will be saved. UIDocument handles this for us. We simply tell the document about any changes we make to the file, and it decides when to save the file. UIDocument won't necessarily save the document immediately. For performance reasons, it will collect a number of changes and then save all of them at once. However, it always saves before the application goes into the background.

When testing, it's important to always send the application to the background before closing it. Xcode's stop button does not terminate the application in a nice, orderly manner. It kills the app immediately. By sending it to the background first, we force the app to save its data.

When we use the NSKeyedArchiver to convert our array into an NSData object, the array calls encodeWithCoder: on all of the objects that the array contains. The array should be filled with our WeightEntry objects. Unfortunately, our WeightEntry class doesn't yet adopted the NSCoding protocol. That means they don't have an encodeWithCoder: method. Let's fix that.

IMPLEMENTING NSCODING

If we want to save or WeightEntrys, they need to adopt the NSCoding protocol. As we've already seen, NSCoding declares only two methods: initWithCoder: and encodeWithCoder:. Both are required.

Open WeightEntry.m. Let's start by declaring a couple of constants at the top of the file. Place the following two lines right after our number formatter constant:

```
static NSString * const WeightEntryWeightInLbsKey =
@"WeightEntryWeightInLbsKey";
static NSString * const WeightEntryDateKey = @"WeightEntryDateKey";
```

These are the keys we will use to save and load our data. Next, add the following two methods just before our public methods:

```
#pragma mark - NSCoding Methods

- (id)initWithCoder:(NSCoder *)aDecoder
{
    self = [super init];
    if (self)
    {
        _weightInLbs =
        [aDecoder decodeFloatForKey:WeightEntryWeightInLbsKey];

        _date = [aDecoder decodeObjectForKey:WeightEntryDateKey];
    }
    return self;
}


- (void)encodeWithCoder:(NSCoder *)aCoder
{
    [aCoder encodeFloat:self.weightInLbs
              forKey:WeightEntryWeightInLbsKey];

    [aCoder encodeObject:self.date forKey:WeightEntryDateKey];
}
```

initWithCoder: follows the same general pattern we've seen in all our init… methods. However, there's one small change. If our superclass adopts the NSCoding protocol, we should call [super initWithCoder:], just like we did in our BackgroundView and GraphView classes in Chapter 4, "Custom Views and Custom Transitions."

WeightEntry is a subclass of NSObject. Since NSObject doesn't adopt the NSCoding protocol, we cannot call [super initWithCoder:]. Instead, we'll call the superclass's designated initializer—just to make sure we don't skip any important initialization code.

Inside initWithCoder:'s if block, we use our keys to pull our values out of the archive and assign them to our instance variables. In encodeWithCoder: we do the opposite. We take the values from our instance variables and use the keys to save them in the archive.

If our superclass adopted the NSCoding protocol, we would have to call super somewhere in this implementation. However, even in that cases, we don't have to worry about reassigning self or making sure that self != nil. That's only for the init… methods. Just call [super encodeObject:] somewhere in your implementation, and you're good to go.

There is another important point here. Notice that we're explicitly saving and loading our weightInLbs as floats, regardless of the underlying architecture. While it's tempting to update all data types to their 64-bit versions for the new 64-bit devices, we need to make sure we're using a common format when we save and load our data. Since our weight values won't ever need the extra range or precision that the double provides, the easiest solution is to just use float on both platforms.

That's it. Run the app again. Create a new weight. Press the home button to put the app in the background. You should see the "Saving our data..." message appear in the console. Kill the application and run it again. It should load the data successfully.

ADDING AN UNDO ACTION

Since we're registering undo actions, we may as well use them. iOS often uses the shake gesture to trigger undo. However, it's easy to accidentally shake the device, so let's ask users before we change their data.

Let's start by making our HistoryTableViewController respond to the shake gesture. Now, our controller inherits from UIResponder, and UIResponder has a number of motion event methods we can implement to receive this notification.

Typically, if we're going to respond to UIResponder's event messages, we need to decide whether we're going to grab the event and keep it or whether we're going to peek at the event and then pass it up the responder chain.

In the first case, we need to implement all the responder methods, but we shouldn't call super inside our implementation. This will prevent the event from proceeding up the responder chain. No one else will ever know it existed.

In the second case, we just need to implement the method we're interested in, but we must call super somewhere inside our implementation. This will pass the event back up the responder chain, and other responders may also see and react to it.

Either approach is fine. For this project, let's go ahead and grab the event.

Open HistoryTableViewController.m, and start by adopting the UIAlertViewDelegate protocol. This will allow us to respond to button presses in any alert views we show.

At the top of the file modify the class extension's @interface line as shown here:

```
@interface HistoryTableViewController ()
<UIViewControllerTransitioningDelegate, WeightHistoryDocumentSubscriber,
UIAlertViewDelegate>
```

Next, let's add the following methods after our navigation methods:

```
#pragma mark - UIResponder Methods

- (void)motionBegan:(UIEventSubtype)motion withEvent:(UIEvent *)event
{
}

- (void)motionEnded:(UIEventSubtype)motion withEvent:(UIEvent *)event
```

```
{
    if (motion == UIEventSubtypeMotionShake)
    {
        if (![self.weightHistoryDocument.undoManagercanUndo]) return;

        UIAlertView *alertView =
        [[UIAlertView alloc]
         initWithTitle:@"Confirm Undo"
         message:[self.weightHistoryDocument.undoManager undoActionName]
         delegate:self
         cancelButtonTitle:@"Undo"
         otherButtonTitles:@"Cancel", nil];

        [alertView show];
    }
}


- (void)motionCancelled:(UIEventSubtype)motion withEvent:(UIEvent *)event
{
}
```

Notice that `motionBegan:withEvent:` and `motionCancelled:withEvent:` are simply stubs. They don't do anything. We implement them only to grab the events and prevent them from passing up the responder chain.

In `motionEnded:withEvent:`, we start by making sure our motion event is a shake event. Currently, there is only one type of motion event, so this will always be true—but a little bit of future proofing never hurts.

Then, we check to see whether our undo manager has any undo actions in its stack. If it doesn't, we just return.

If we can undo the user's last action, we display an AlertView. We set the alert's title to "Confirm Undo." For the message, we grab the undo action name that we set earlier. Then we set our history table view as the delegate, and we give it two buttons, an OK button and a Cancel button.

The arguments get a little odd here. The cancel button is actually the first button— or the leftmost button. The other button appears to the right. Now, normally we want to have the default action on the right, since that's the easiest button to accidentally hit with your thumb. Most of the time, that will be the action button—but when you're doing a potentially destructive action (like undoing someone's entry), you should err on the side of caution. So, despite the names, we're placing our cancel button on the right.

Finally, we display the alert view.

This doesn't do anything yet. We're just asking the user if we should actually undo the latest change.

Next, add the following method, just below our motion methods:

```
#pragma mark - UIAlertViewDelegate Methods

- (void)alertView:(UIAlertView *)alertView
willDismissWithButtonIndex:(NSInteger)buttonIndex
{
    if (buttonIndex == 0)
    {
        [self.weightHistoryDocument.undoManager undo];
    }
}
```

This method is called whenever a button is pressed in our alert view. We check to see whether it's the first button (our OK button). If it is, we simply tell the undo manager to undo the last registered action.

Run the application. Add some data. Now shake the device (in the simulator, use ^ ⌘Z). And...nothing happens.

That's because there's a catch. Our view controller will respond to motion events only if it is the first responder. But, calling becomeFirstResponder won't work either (OK, there are two catches). Currently, our controller's canBecomeFirstResponder method returns NO. We need to override it to return YES. Then we need to become the first responder. And finally, we can respond to motion events.

Add the following method immediately before our table view data source methods:

```
- (BOOL)canBecomeFirstResponder
{
    return YES;
}
```

This lets us become first responder. Now, we need to request first responder status in two places: first, when our view first appears, and second, whenever we dismiss a modal view.

Start by calling becomeFirstResponder at the bottom of viewWillAppear:.

```
- (void)viewWillAppear:(BOOL)animated
{
    [super viewWillAppear:animated];
    [self updateAddButton];
    [self becomeFirstResponder];
}
```

Then add it to our storyboard unwinding methods as well.

```
- (IBAction)addNewEntrySaved:(UIStoryboardSegue *)segue
{
    AddEntryViewController *controller = segue.sourceViewController;

    WeightEntry *entry = [WeightEntry entryWithWeight:controller.weight
                                            usingUnits:getDefaultUnits()
                                               forDate:controller.date];

    [self.weightHistoryDocument addEntry:entry];
    [self dismissViewControllerAnimated:YES completion:nil];
    [self becomeFirstResponder];
}

- (IBAction)addNewEntryCanceled:(UIStoryboardSegue *)segue
{
    [self dismissViewControllerAnimated:YES completion:nil];
    [self becomeFirstResponder];
}
```

Run the application again. Add some data. Shake the device and undo the action. Remove some data. Shake the device and undo the action. Everything should work as expected.

WRAPPING UP

This chapter covered a lot of ground. We learned about the limits of the iOS file system and how to work within our application's sandbox. We saw a number of methods for saving and loading our document's data, from storing user preferences using the NSUserDefaults API to saving document data using a UIDocument subclass. We looked at different techniques for sending notifications to broad sections of our application, and we glimpsed a bit at concurrent programming. Finally, we learned how to restore our user interface's state so users can launch our application and continue working exactly where they left off.

But, saving and loading data doesn't end here. In the next chapter, we are going to sync both our application's preferences and our document's data using iCloud. Then, in Chapter 7, we will replace our current WeightHistoryDocument with Core Data.

OTHER RESOURCES

- **Keychain Services Programming Guide**

  iOS Developer's Library

  This programming guide explains how to use the keychain service to save passwords and other secret information. This is definitely a must-read guide, if your application handles passwords or other sensitive information.

- **Preferences and Settings Programming Guide**

  iOS Developer's Library

  This guide gives more information on using NSUserDefaults and the Settings bundle. It includes discussions on what type of preferences we should save. How to provide an in-app interface for our preferences. And more details on setting up the Settings bundle and working with iOS's Settings app.

- **File System Programming Guide**

  iOS Developer's Library

  If you're looking for more information on iOS's file system, this should be your first stop. Note, however, that this covers both the OS X and the iOS file systems, so you have to read it somewhat carefully. Much of what you see will only be appropriate on OS X.

- **Concurrency Programming Guide**

  iOS Developer's Library

  This guide covers all the concurrent programming technologies available for iOS development. This includes detailed information about both NSOperationQueues and Grand Central Dispatch, and beyond.

- **iOS App Programming Guide: State Preservation and Restoration**

  iOS Developer's Library

  While the entire iOS App Programming Guide is worth reading, the section on State Preservation and Restoration provides detailed information about the State Preservation and Restoration process.

CHAPTER 6

iCloud Syncing

iCloud is an umbrella term used to refer to a broad range of technologies. If you want to leave your music, movies, or TV shows on the iTunes servers, downloading them only as you need them, that's iCloud. If you want to automatically stream your photos to your Apple TV, that's iCloud. If you want to back up your iOS device wirelessly to the cloud, that's also iCloud.

However, when developers talk about iCloud, we're really talking about Documents in the Cloud, or—to step away from Apple's marketing language—iCloud syncing. This is the only part of iCloud that we, as developers, can touch.

The idea is simple enough. Users should be able to access their data on all their devices. They can start writing a letter on their laptop, edit it during lunch on their iPad, and then review and send it from their iPhone as they walk back to the office.

From the user's perspective, all the data transfers and syncing should be handled automatically and transparently. They open their application, and their data is already waiting for them.

WHAT IS iCLOUD SYNCING?

Before we dig into the details, it's important to understand what iCloud syncing is—or, more importantly—what it isn't.

Specifically, iCloud is not the following:

- Remote storage
- A communication channel between different users
- A general communication channel between different applications
- A cross-platform syncing solution

iCloud syncing lets us sync all of our data and documents from one application (or a tightly integrated suite of applications) among all the devices owned by a single user. That's it. Period.

We cannot use iCloud to create the next Twitter. We cannot build a suite of collaborative editing tools on iCloud. We can't even use it to share data among different applications from different developers.

iCloud syncing may let us save a little storage space, since we can evict old documents and redownload them the next time we need them. But, we always work off a locally stored copy.

It may also provide a light backup for our documents. If someone drops their phone in the toilet, they could redownload all the files onto their new device. However, this isn't a replacement for proper backups. For example, we can download only the current version of our data from iCloud. If that data were to become corrupt or to accidentally get overwritten or erased, we're out of luck.

Finally, iCloud syncing works best for users who live and work entirely within Apple's walled garden. While it can offer some Windows support, it cannot be used to sync to Android or other OSs.

A number of third-party solutions provide cross-platform document syncing to a greater or lesser degree. However, for iOS and OS X applications, iCloud syncing provides the most convenient, most transparent syncing solution for the broadest range of users.

iCLOUD APIS

iCloud syncing provides three different APIs: Key-Value Storage, Document Storage, and Core Data Storage. We will examine both Key-Value and Document Storage in this chapter. Core Data Storage will wait until we discuss Core Data in Chapter 7.

KEY-VALUE STORAGE

iCloud Key-Value Storage provides a simple interface for saving data in the cloud. It is designed to store small, discrete values. In many ways, it parallels the `NSUserDefaults` API. In fact, we will typically use it to sync users preferences across multiple devices.

Unfortunately, Key-Value Storage is also more restricted than the other syncing APIs. It can only store a limited amount of data, 1MB per user, divided among up to 1,024 unique keys. Furthermore, it stores only `property-list` data types: `NSNumber`, `NSDate`, `NSString`, `NSArray`, `NSDictionary`, and `NSData`. Finally, it does not have any conflict resolution—the last save always wins.

On the plus side, Key-Value Storage does not count toward the user's iCloud storage space, so there's no reason not to use it.

Before we can use Key-Value Storage, we must enable iCloud in our project. This involves changing the settings both in our application's entitlements and in the App ID. Furthermore, changing the App ID often requires creating and downloading new provisioning profiles. Fortunately, Xcode 5's new Capabilities tool handles all of this for us. We simply turn on iCloud support and make sure the key-value store is enabled. Then we're ready to go.

With the store enabled, we can access the shared `NSUbiquitousKeyValueStore` object. This object defines a number of methods we can use to read and write our data. The store initially caches all our changes in memory, saving them to disk as needed.

Just like the `UIDocument` or the `NSUserDefaults`, the system will always save before going to the background. Once the changes are saved to disk, the system will alert the iCloud server, which will upload the change to the cloud, and then push the update to all our other devices.

We don't even need to worry about whether the user is logged into iCloud. If the user is not logged in, iCloud Key-Value Storage continues to save a local version of the data. Then, once iCloud becomes available, it will sync its most recent data with the cloud.

> **NOTE:** Syncing the `NSUbiquitousKeyValueStore` does not force the system to upload its changes to iCloud immediately. Indeed, the system may deliberately delay uploading, especially when our application makes frequent changes. The more frequent the updates, the longer the delay.
>
> In older versions of iOS, this made testing key-value syncing something of a challenge. You could get only two or three changes to sync before the system started throttling. Then, suddenly, key-value syncing stopped working.
>
> Now, however, the thresholds are much higher—approximately 15 requests every 90 seconds before throttling kicks in. So, you're unlikely to accidentally trigger throttling with anything except the extreme stress testing.

Since the Key-Value Storage API so closely resembles `NSUserDefaults`, it's tempting to just use Key-Value Storage as a drop-in replacement. Resist this temptation.

The best approach involves using `NSUserDefaults` to manage the application's preferences locally and using Key-Value Storage to sync these preferences across multiple devices.

This two-stage setup is both more robust and more flexible. For example, we can compare incoming values from the cloud with what we've stored in the user defaults. This lets us create our own, custom update rules.

Key-Value Storage's last-save-wins approach works fine for many types of data. If we're tracking the last video that a user watched, last-save-wins works fine. If we're tracking the current default units in a weight-tracking app, again last-save-wins seems perfectly acceptable.

We always need to think about what, exactly, we're saving in iCloud. In general, we want to minimize the amount of data we send and receive. However, there are a few, specific types of data we should always watch out for.

- **Passwords or other secrets:** Sensitive data should be stored in the keychain, never in the cloud.

- **Device-specific data such as view size or scroll position:** These details may not have the same meaning on different devices. An iPhone's scroll position will be vastly different than an iPad's.

- **Data that can cause "sync storms":** Things like last-modified timestamps should not be synced. Otherwise, an incoming update will modify the data, changing the timestamp and triggering another sync. That will then update the data on another device, changing its timestamp and triggering another sync. Repeat until we've used up our entire monthly data plan.

- **Device-specific data:** For example, iOS uses a `UIImage` object to hold image data. OS X uses an `NSImage`. These objects are not compatible. If you want to sync between iOS and the desktop, you need to save the image in a common format (such as PNG or JPEG).

- **Data that makes assumptions about the device's bit size:** We cannot assume that all our devices use either 32- or 64-bit processors. Our code must either translate the data or save it in a common format. See the "Supporting 64-Bit Code" sidebar in the "Objective-C" bonus chapter for more information.

- **Data that can be re-created or downloaded easily:** To help minimize the amount of data being sent to iCloud, do not sync anything that can be easily recreated by the application, either by recalculating it or by downloading it again.

- **SQLite databases:** SQLite databases are not designed to be modified by multiple processes concurrently. Syncing an SQLite directly using iCloud is guaranteed to corrupt the database. It's not a question of *if*, it's a question of *when*. As we will see next chapter, Core Data solves this problem by keeing the database out of the Ubiquity Container, and syncing the transaction logs.

However, if we want to sync a game's high score across all our apps, we really need to make sure the incoming value is actually higher than the current value in our user defaults. If it is not higher, we should save the actual high score back out into the cloud instead.

DOCUMENT STORAGE

iCloud Document Storage lets us sync any files or file packages we want. We are limited only by the amount of available storage space in the user's iCloud account. However, since most users have only the free 5GB account and much of that space may be used to back up their devices, we need to be a little careful about how much we sync to the cloud.

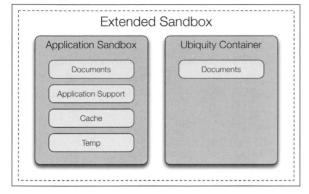

FIGURE 6.1 The extended sandbox

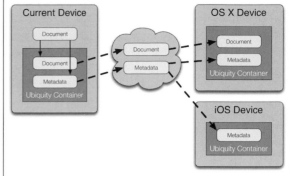

FIGURE 6.2 The flow of data and metadata

At its most basic, iCloud Document Storage creates a specially blessed directory on our drive. We call this the Ubiquity Container. This container lies outside our application's regular sandbox. When we set up our application for iCloud, we will extend the application sandbox to include this directory (**Figure 6.1**).

When we save a document to the Ubiquity Container, the system actually saves two pieces of data. It saves metadata about the document, and it saves the document's data.

The iCloud service monitors our Ubiquity Container and automatically uploads any changes to the cloud. From there, iCloud automatically pushes the metadata to all our devices (**Figure 6.2**); however, iOS devices will not download the document data. Instead, the application must request the download. Of course, once an iOS device has downloaded the document, it will continue to automatically download any further updates.

Most of the time the data is transparently downloaded when the application tries to load the file; however, iCloud provides API to both monitor and trigger the download of nonlocal files. This is particularly useful when dealing with large files. You don't want to surprise the user with unexpectedly long load times as the application struggles to download a 2GB file. Often, it's better to explicitly show whether the document is local or in the cloud and let the user explicitly download it before trying to open it.

iOS applications may also evict data from the Ubiquity Container. While we can do this programmatically, the system will automatically evict data when the device runs low on storage space, beginning with applications that have not been opened recently. After all, the application can always download the data from iCloud if necessary.

This design has a number of advantages. Since we are always modifying a local file, we can work offline. The iCloud service will simply wait and sync our document once the Internet becomes available. It also minimizes bandwidth and data usage. All devices are notified of any changes, but iOS devices download only the data they're actually using.

OS X, on the other hand, acts as the greedy partner. As long as it has an active iCloud connection, it will always download everything. This includes iCloud data for iOS-only applications. Furthermore, OS X iCloud data is never evicted. This means our OS X machine should have a reasonably up-to-date copy of every document we have stored in the cloud.

If you open the Finder and go to `~/Library/Mobile Documents/`, you will see a list of all the Ubiquity Containers for all the iCloud-enabled applications associated with your account. We can also add and remove documents from these folders using the Finder. These changes will be synced back to our iOS devices. This can be useful when setting up test data.

Also, notice that non-Apple containers begin with a ten-digit developer team ID. We can create a Ubiquity Container that is shared among different applications from the same team—but we cannot share with other applications from a different team. Still, shared containers can be particularly useful, especially when creating free and paid versions of an application. You don't want someone to lose their iCloud data just because they upgraded.

Also, we can create whatever subdirectories we need inside the Ubiquity Container; however, there is one special subdirectory that we must be aware of. Any files or file packages placed inside the `Documents` directory will be displayed to the user by name. The user can select and delete these documents individually. All the files placed outside the `Documents` directory are combined and listed as "Documents & Data." Users cannot see or delete the individual files. However, they can delete all the data, if they want.

Therefore, we have to be careful about where we save our files. As much as possible, we should try to save our data into the `Documents` directory. This gives users the most fine-grained control over their iCloud storage space. However, we need to make sure that deleting just one of the files won't put our application into a bad state. If you have multiple files that must be deleted as a group, either place them together in a file package or store them outside the `Documents` directory.

To manage iCloud documents, on OS X open the Systems Preferences. Select the iCloud preferences and then click the "Manage..." button in the bottom-right corner. This will bring up a list of all the applications saving data to iCloud. Select an application to see its documents and data. On iOS, open the Settings app and select iCloud > Storage & Backup > Manage Storage. Again, select an application to see its documents and data.

Finally, remember, the truth is always in the cloud. If you really want to see exactly what's in your iCloud storage, you should log into `http://developer.icloud.com`. This site lets us browse through and (in some cases) download the data directly from the iCloud servers.

IMPLEMENTATION DETAILS

While the theory sounds relatively simple, once we get into the implementation details, things begin to get complicated.

To enable document storage, we must add identifiers for our Ubiquity Containers to our application's entitlements. These identifiers define the different containers available to our application. We can have as many containers as we want, but the first container is somewhat special. Its identifier must be the bundle identifier for the current target or the bundle identifier for another app that has already been submitted to the App Store using the same Team ID. Again, Xcode 5 handles all of this through the Capabilities tool.

iCloud also tries to minimize the amount of data it needs to upload and download. It will automatically break our application's data into chunks and—when possible—upload and download only the chunks that have actually changed. iCloud will also transmit data peer-to-peer across the local Wi-Fi network when it can. Still, as developers, we need to be careful with both the amount of data we store and the amount of bandwidth we consume.

We also need to consider other things that the users might do to our data. Here are a few key issues we must remember when working with iCloud storage:

- Users may not have an active iCloud account.
- Users can log out of their iCloud account or log into another account at any point.
- Users can deactivate or reactivate document storage at any point.
- Users can delete any file or file package inside the Documents folder at any point.
- Users can also delete all the documents and data outside the Documents folder.
- The iCloud server may download updates and modify our document at any point. Our application must listen for and respond to these changes.
- Conflicts are a part of iCloud life. We must detect and resolve all conflicts as they occur.

To do this, we must perform the following steps:

1. Call `ubiquityIdentityToken` early in our application's launch cycle. This will tell us whether the user is logged into iCloud.

2. Listen and respond to the `NSUbiquityIdentityDidChangeNotification`. This will tell us when the user logs in, logs out, or changes iCloud accounts.

3. Get the URL for the Ubiquity Container by calling `URLForUbiquityContainerIdentifier:`. As a side effect, this also extends the application's sandbox to include the Ubiquity Container. This means we must call this method before we do any read or write operations inside the container. It also means we often need to call this for its side effect long before we need the actual URL.

4. Move a document to the Ubiquity Container by calling `setUbiquitous:itemAtURL: destinationURL:error:`. Typically, we will create a file in the sandbox, letting the user use it immediately, and then we will move it to the Ubiquity Container on a background thread.

5. Search for documents in the Ubiquity Container using `NSMetadataQuery`. This lets us know if a document exists, even if it has not been downloaded yet. Since other copies of our application might rename or move files, we should never store the URL or file path to anything in the Ubiquity Container. Even if we know our application never moves the file, it's always best to search for files. We never know how our application may change in the future.

6. Since we have two different processes accessing files in the Ubiquity Container (our application and the iCloud service), we must perform all file read and write operations using an `NSFileCoordinator`.

7. Whenever we display document data to users, we must adopt the `NSFilePresenter` protocol. This protocol allows us to monitor the data's state and respond to changes as needed. This includes loading a new version of the data whenever the iCloud server downloads an update or managing conflicting versions as they are detected.

Of these, the `NSFileCoordinator` and `NSFilePresenters` are worth a little additional attention.

FILE COORDINATORS

File coordinators perform two main functions. First, they act as a blocking mechanism, making sure no one else is reading a file while you are writing it, or vice versa. Second, they coordinate reading and writing across multiple processes. By default, a coordinated read action will cause all other processes to write any unsaved data they have to that file before the read operation can begin.

File coordinators allow any number of simultaneous read operations; however, they will allow only one write operation at a time. Furthermore, new read operations will block until the current write operation has completed. A new write operation will also block until all the current read or write operations have ended.

As far as the implementation goes, file coordinators use a block-based API. We will perform the actual reading and writing operations inside the block that we pass to the coordinator.

There are five main methods that we will use to perform coordination.

- `coordinateReadingItemAtURL:options:error:byAccessor:` This is the basic coordinated read operation. We use it to read from a single URL.

- `coordinateWritingItemAtURL:options:error:byAccessor:` This is the basic coordinated write operation. We use it to write to a single URL.

- `coordinateReadingItemAtURL:options:writingItemAtURL:options:error:byAccessor:` This method lets us coordinate reading from one URL and writing to another URL. We typically use this to copy a file or directory from one location to another.

- If we are reading and writing to the same URL, we can often perform both the read and the write inside a single coordinated write operation instead, since writing is stricter than reading.

- There may be times, however, where we want to specify particular options for both the reading and the writing operation. You can use this method to handle those cases as well.

- `coordinateWritingItemAtURL:options:writingItemAtURL:options:error:byAccessor:` This method lets us coordinate writing at two different URLS. We typically use this to move a file or directory from one location to another.

- `prepareForReadingItemsAtURLs:options:writingItemsAtURLs:options:error:byAccessor:` This lets us batch process a number of read and write operations. This is often faster than performing the individual coordinated reads and writes. Note, however, that this method does not handle the actual coordination. We must still call the appropriate coordinated read and write methods inside this block.

All of these methods share a number of noteworthy features.

First, the blocks on these methods are all performed synchronously. Up until now, most of the block-based APIs have been asynchronous. When we pass a block to an asynchronous method, the system goes off and does some processing and then calls our block at some undetermined time in the future (if the block is ever called at all).

With the file coordinator blocks, on the other hand, we are guaranteed that our block will run before the coordination method finishes. This makes using the coordinators a little bit easier.

Additionally, these methods will block the thread they are called on. And, since the file coordinator may need to wait until other operations are finished, the thread could block for an indeterminate amount of time. Therefore, we should never call these methods from the main thread.

Finally, the file coordinator will always provide us with a new URL to use inside our reading and writing blocks. This is important, since another coordinated write operation could move the files, changing their URLs.

FILE PRESENTERS

File coordinators work hand-in-hand with file presenters. NSFilePresenter is a protocol that we can implement to enable low-level monitoring of our files and directories. We will receive notifications whenever a coordinated write modifies, moves, or deletes a file. We may also be asked to save any pending changes we have for a file. Finally, other file coordinators can ask us to temporarily relinquish control over the file that we're monitoring.

Any time we are presenting an iCloud document's data to the user, we must implement a file presenter for that document, and we need to respond to the notification methods as appropriate.

The need to use file coordinators and presenters makes reading and writing to the Ubiquity Container considerably more difficult than normal file I/O. Fortunately, UIDocument manages a lot of this complexity for us. In particular, it already adopts the NSFilePresenter protocol. It also automatically uses NSFileCoordinators during its standard load and save operations.

The rest, however, is still up to us.

FILE VERSIONING

Before we add iCloud Document Storage to our application, we need to make sure our data files have some type of versioning built in. This can be as simple as adding a version number to the document—of course, if we add a version number, that implies we're also prepared to handle changes to that version number.

The basic issue is as follows. As we continue to enhance our application and release updates, we may reach a point where we want to change the format of our data files. Maybe we want to add additional data. Maybe we want to move away from a single array of WeightEntry objects, to something more complex. Unfortunately, as soon as we change our data's format we will have two (or more) possible document types floating around. Our application needs some way to identify the different document types and respond appropriately.

Versioning is always a good idea; however, with iCloud syncing enabled, it becomes a lot more serious. Newer versions of our application should be able to detect and handle old file formats with little difficulty. The real problem is when old versions of the app get ahold of newer documents. Fortunately, given the fact that our files are hidden away from the users, and the way that the App Store and iOS handle updates, it would be difficult, if not impossible, for someone to accidentally open a newer document with an older app.

However, as soon as we enable iCloud Document Storage, this is no longer true. Users will be accessing the same file on multiple devices, and they may not update all their devices at the same time.

iOS 7 partially solves the problem, since applications now update automatically. However, what if the user turns off automatic updates? Or, what if he's accidentally left the device in airplane mode, and hasn't yet received the update? Or what happens if we release separate iPhone and iPad versions of our app? Even if we try to release the updates at the same time, one might be held up in Apple's review process.

Bottom line, if something can happen it will happen. We should always assume that the user could be running different versions of our app on different devices. Therefore, our syncing needs to take this into account.

When we detect different versions of our application, we have four basic options:

1. We could open the document and convert the data to the current version. If the user makes changes, we save the document in the current version. This is the easiest option to develop, but it has a few risks. If a newer version of the application opens an old document, the converted document may not be readable by the old app. Similarly, if an old version of the application opens and saves the document, it will undoubtedly erase any new data that was added to the file format.

2. We could open the document and convert the data to the current version; however, when we save changes, we save them back as the old version. Obviously, this is only an option for newer versions of our application. An old version of the application has no idea what the new data format should look like. Also, newer versions of our app may lose data when they save to the older format.

3. We could open the document read-only, letting the user view the data but not save changes.

4. We could refuse to open the document at all.

In addition, we need to decide how much information we're going to pass on to the user. In many cases it's best to silently upgrade file formats without ever notifying the user. However, we should always alert the user if there's a chance of data getting lost—possibly giving him a choice on how he wants to proceed.

iCLOUD DOCUMENT STORAGE STRATEGIES

There are three main strategies for iCloud-enabled applications.

The simplest solution is to always use iCloud when it's available and fall back to the sandbox only if the user has either disabled document syncing or is not logged into an iCloud account.

Alternatively, we can ask users if they want to use iCloud the first time it becomes available. We then save either to iCloud or the sandbox based on their decision. In this case, we probably want to give the users some way to change their mind.

We also need to decide how changing from the sandbox to iCloud, or back, affects the currently saved documents. The simplest approach is to just leave the documents where they are. If users switch between the sandbox and iCloud, we just give them a new, blank slate to work with.

Moving documents from the sandbox to iCloud isn't the problem. It's moving files back from iCloud where things get sticky. Unfortunately, there are a number of situations where we simply cannot migrate the data back before it becomes unavailable. If the user is toggling a control that we provide, then we can move the documents, no problem. But, if she disables document syncing or logs out of iCloud, she will instantly lose access to anything in the cloud. We won't have a chance to move the documents before they become unavailable.

The last iCloud strategy involves letting the user choose on a file-by-file basis. In this case, we typically provide some mechanism for moving files into and out of iCloud. This is, by far, the most complex approach. Additionally, we still have problems moving documents back from iCloud. If the user logs out or disables document syncing, she will lose access to anything stored in the cloud. She'll have to log back in or reenable document syncing, transfer the files, and then log out again.

Picking the correct strategy is not easy, however, consider the following. In iOS 7, users have the option to disable document syncing on an application-by-application basis. This means they can disable document syncing for our application, even if we use the simplest approach. And, arguably, using Apple's controls for disabling and enabling syncing gives all the applications a common look and feel.

So, unless you're working with very large files, I recommend taking the simplest approach. It's the easiest to implement, easiest for users to understand, the most consistent, and the most robust.

If, however, you are saving significant amounts of data, you really should ask users before eating into their iCloud storage. In this case, pick either the second or third approach, based on the needs of your application.

ADDING KEY-VALUE SYNCING TO HEALTH BEAT

We need to start by enabling iCloud for our application. Click the blue Health Beat icon in the Project navigator, and then click the Capabilities tab. This page lists a variety of features we can enable for our application, including iCloud, Game Center, Passbook, In-App Purchases, and others.

If we expand the iCloud capabilities, we can see that enabling it will add the iCloud entitlement to our App ID, and it will add the iCloud container identifiers to our entitlements (**Figure 6.3**).

In the past, this was a lot of work. We would typically create a new App ID specifically for our application. This meant we would also need to create and download a new provisioning profile. Then we'd need to go into our project's build settings and set it to use our new provisioning profile. Finally, we'd need to create the entitlements file and set the proper iCloud key-value pairs.

FIGURE 6.3 The iCloud capabilities

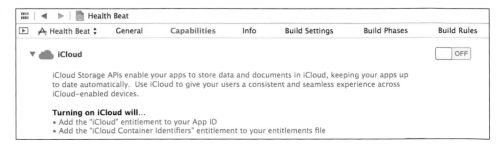

FIGURE 6.4 iCloud capabilities enabled

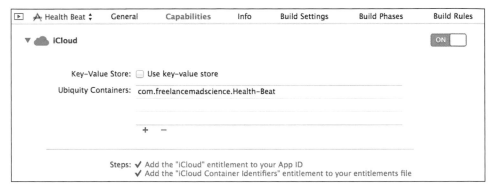

Fortunately, Xcode 5 simplifies this to the flick of a single switch. It has also simplified the backend, letting us continue to use the Generic App ID and team profile, which vastly cuts down on the number of IDs and profiles that get linked to our developer account.

Somewhat ironically, turning on the iCloud capabilities won't actually prepare our application's key-value store, but it gets our app into a state where we can enable it.

Click the iCloud Capabilities switch to turn it on. The interface should change to something similar to **Figure 6.4**. Your Ubiquity Container ID will be different, but everything else should be the same.

We don't actually need the Ubiquity Container ID yet, but let's leave it. We'll use it in the next section. For the current task at hand, check the "Use key-value store" box to enable key-value syncing.

The Capabilities tool lets us turn key-value syncing only on and off, and by default it will use the current target's bundle ID to set up our syncing. This is fine for stand-alone apps, like Health Beat. However, if you want to share key-value syncing across multiple apps (for example, syncing between a free and a paid version of your app), you must manually edit your entitlements file. You can find detailed instructions in Apple's iCloud Design Guide.

Since we already have our user defaults working, we just need to add the code to sync them. There are four basic steps:

1. Whenever the user changes our defaults, we need to update the key-value store.

2. We need to listen for updates from the store.

3. As soon as we're listening for updates, we should sync our store to download the current value.

4. When an update occurs, we need to decide whether we should update our user defaults or whether we should keep the user defaults and change the value in the store.

We can do step 1 with our existing framework easily enough. However, only objects can listen for notifications. Our current defaults implementation just uses C functions. So, we'll need to move our code into an object—and a singleton object at that.

Create a new subclass of NSObject named CloudManager. Then open CloudManager.h. Modify the header file as shown here:

```objc
#import <Foundation/Foundation.h>
#import "WeightUnits.h"

@interface CloudManager : NSObject
+ (instancetype)sharedManager;
@property (assign, nonatomic) WeightUnit defaultWeightUnits;
@end
```

Here, we're just importing the WeightUnits.h file and then declaring our sharedManager class method and our defaultWeightUnits property.

Switch to CloudManager.m. Let's start by implementing the sharedManager class method as shown here:

```objc
+ (instancetype)sharedManager
{
    static CloudManager *sharedManager = nil;
    static dispatch_once_t onceToken;
    dispatch_once(&onceToken, ^{
        sharedManager = [[self alloc] init];
    });

    return sharedManager;
}
```

Here, we're using Grand Central Dispatch's dispatch_once method to create a thread-safe singleton instance. The sharedManager and dispatch_once variables are static local variables. This means they are declared at compile time. In the case of sharedManager, its initial value is set to nil. Each time this method is called, it will reuse the same variables; however, these variables can be accessed or modified only inside this method. Also, the declaration lines are not called at runtime, so we do not reset the sharedManager's value to nil. They will continue to hold whatever value was last assigned.

The dispatch_once method will execute the given block of code once and only once in the entire lifetime of our application. If it is called simultaneously from multiple threads, all the calls will wait synchronously until the block has completed. Then they will all return.

In this case, we use it to create our shared manager and assign it to the static variable. Then our class method simply returns that shared manager.

So, the first time this method is called, the `dispatch_once` block will run, creating the shared manager; assign it to our static variable; and return the manager. The next time it's called, `dispatch_once`'s block won't run. Instead, we just return the instance stored in our static variable. This lets us create the shared instance once but access it as many times as we want.

Now, we need to create custom accessors for our `defaultWeightUnits` property. These are going to be copied from `WeightUnit`'s `getDefaultUnits()` and `setDefaultUnits()`—with a few modifications to support iCloud syncing.

First, move the `WeightUnitsDefaultUnitsKey` constant from `WeightUnits.m` to the top of `CloudManager.m`. We also need to define `DefaultWeightUnitsKey` as shown here:

```
static NSString * const WeightUnitsDefaultUnitsKey =
@"WeightUnitsDefaultUnitsKey";

static NSString * const DefaultWeightUnitsKey =
@"defaultWeightUnits";
```

Notice that the second string value does not match the constant's name. Instead, it must match our `defaultWeightUnits` property.

Next, in `CloudManager.m` define the `defaultWeightUnits` method and move the `getDefaultUnits()` implementation inside it as shown here:

```
#pragma mark - Accessor Methods

- (WeightUnit)defaultWeightUnits
{
    return (WeightUnit)[[NSUserDefaults standardUserDefaults]
                    integerForKey:WeightUnitsDefaultUnitsKey];
}
```

Do the same thing for `setDefaultWeightUnits:`; however, this time we're going to add a bit of code to sync the change to the iCloud key-value store.

```
- (void)setDefaultWeightUnits:(WeightUnit)defaultUnit
{
    [[NSUserDefaults standardUserDefaults]
     setInteger:defaultUnit
     forKey:WeightUnitsDefaultUnitsKey];

    [[NSUbiquitousKeyValueStore defaultStore]
     setLongLong:defaultUnit
     forKey:WeightUnitsDefaultUnitsKey];
}
```

We start by changing the value in our user defaults. This is copied from our setDefaultUnits() method. Then, we update the value stored in the key-value store. Notice that while the NSUbiquitousKeyValueStore API roughly mirrors the NSUserDefaults API, it doesn't have quite as many options. In fact, the only option we have for integer data is to store our default units as a long long.

Let's switch back to WeightUnits.m for a second. Let's modify getDefaultUnits() and setDefaultUnits() to use our new singleton. Start by importing CloudManager.h at the top of the file. Then modify the two functions as shown here:

```
WeightUnit getDefaultUnits(void)
{
    return [[CloudManager sharedManager] defaultWeightUnits];
}


void setDefaultUnits(WeightUnit defaultUnit)
{
    [[CloudManager sharedManager] setDefaultWeightUnits:defaultUnit];
}
```

With this in place, we won't need to change our code anywhere else in our application. The underlying implementation has changed, but the interface remains the same. All of our existing code will continue to work as expected.

> **NOTE:** I often like to provide a C function interface to access data in my singleton objects. Both C functions and singleton objects are global in scope—but the C functions often feel more concise.

Now we need to listen for updates from the cloud. Switch back to CloudManager.m. Let's add a class extension at the top of the file, just below the constants. Inside the extension, declare a property to hold our observer.

```
@interface CloudManager ()
@property (strong, nonatomic) id ubiquitousStoreChangeObserver;
@end
```

Next, let's override the init method as shown here:

```
- (id)init
{
    self = [super init];
    if (self) {
        [self setupCloudStore];
    }
    return self;
}
```

This simply calls setupCloudStore, which does the real work. We will also need a dealloc method to remove our observer.

```
- (void)dealloc
{
    if (self.ubiquitousStoreChangeObserver)
    {
        [[NSNotificationCenter defaultCenter]
          removeObserver:self.ubiquitousStoreChangeObserver];
    }
}
```

Next, let's implement setupCloudStore as a private method at the bottom of the @implementation block.

```
#pragma mark - Private Methods

- (void)setupCloudStore
{
    NSUbiquitousKeyValueStore *cloudStore =
    [NSUbiquitousKeyValueStore defaultStore];

    self.ubiquitousStoreChangeObserver =
    [[NSNotificationCenter defaultCenter]
     addObserverForName:
     NSUbiquitousKeyValueStoreDidChangeExternallyNotification
     object:cloudStore
     queue:[NSOperationQueue mainQueue]
     usingBlock:^(NSNotification *note) {

         NSArray *effectedKeys =
         note.userInfo[NSUbiquitousKeyValueStoreChangedKeysKey];

         for (NSString *key in effectedKeys)
         {
             [self updateKey:key];
         }
    }];

    [cloudStore synchronize];
    //   [self eraseCloudKeyValueStorage];
}
```

This code gets a reference to our default key-value store object. Then we register for the NSUbiquitousKeyValueStoreDidChangeExternallyNotification notification. When this notification is called, we grab an array of the affected keys from the notification's userInfo dictionary. Then, for each key, we call our yet-undefined updateKey: method. Finally, we synchronize the key-value store, forcing the system to download the current values from the cloud.

Also, notice the commented-out code at the bottom of the method. This is our emergency escape hatch. It's not uncommon to accidentally store invalid data into iCloud during development. Having a "delete all" method like this is helpful. If things start acting in unexpectedly bizarre ways, uncomment this method. Run the app once to clear out the key-value store. Quit the app as soon as it launches. Then comment out this line again.

> **NOTE:** You need to make sure a weight unit is displayed to ensure this code runs. If your history is empty, click the plus button to bring up the AddEntry ViewController. Then you can quit the application.

Now, let's define updateKey: just below setupCloudStore.

```objc
- (void)updateKey:(NSString *)key
{
    NSUbiquitousKeyValueStore *cloudStore =
    [NSUbiquitousKeyValueStore defaultStore];

    NSUserDefaults *userDefaults =
    [NSUserDefaults standardUserDefaults];

    if ([key isEqualToString:WeightUnitsDefaultUnitsKey])
    {
        NSInteger weightValue =
        (NSInteger)[cloudStore longLongForKey:key];

        [self willChangeValueForKey:DefaultWeightUnitsKey];
        [userDefaults setInteger:weightValue forKey:key];
        [self didChangeValueForKey:DefaultWeightUnitsKey];
        return;
    }

    NSLog(@"*** Unrecognized Key: %@ ***", key);
    [NSException raise:NSGenericException
                format:@"Unrecognized key: %@", key];
}
```

Here, we grab references to both our key-value store and our user defaults. Then we check the key; if it is equal to our `WeightUnitsDefaultUnitsKey`, we grab the current value from the iCloud store and assign it to our user defaults. It's important that we bracket this change with the KVO `willChange...` and `didChange...` notifications, since we're not going through the property's setter.

Additionally, we're not doing any additional processing or comparisons. We're simply adopting the key-value store's last-save-wins approach. We just use whatever value iCloud gives us.

If the key does not match our default unit key, we log an error message and throw an exception.

We've made our new `defaultWeightUnit` property mostly KVO compliant. However, there's still one edge case to deal with. What happens if the user changes our default units using the settings app?

Open `AppDelegate.m`. Import `CloudManager.m` and add the static string for our `defaultWeightUnits` key as shown here:

```
#import "CloudManager.h"
static NSString * const DefaultUnitWeightsKey = @"defaultWeightUnits";
```

Now, navigate to the `application:didFinishLaunchingWithOptions:` method. Modify our user defaults change observer.

```
self.userDefaultsChangeObserver =
[center
 addObserverForName:NSUserDefaultsDidChangeNotification
 object:[NSUserDefaults standardUserDefaults]
 queue:mainQueue
 usingBlock:^(NSNotification *note) {
     [[CloudManager sharedManager]
      didChangeValueForKey:DefaultUnitWeightsKey];
     [rootViewController HBT_updateUserDefaults];
 }];
```

Here, we call `didChange...` after we receive notification of a change. However, for this to work, we need to also call `willChange...` before the change occurs. If the system doesn't see both of these, it will not send out the KVO notifications.

The easiest way to do this is to call `willChange...` in `applicationDidEnterBackground:` as shown here:

```
- (void)applicationDidEnterBackground:(UIApplication *)application
{
    [[CloudManager sharedManager]
     willChangeValueForKey:DefaultUnitWeightsKey];
}
```

Here, `willChange…` will be called every time our application goes to the background. However, since it won't have any effect unless the completing `didChange…` method is also called. Therefore, we won't send out KVO notifications unless the user actually modified the default weight units in the Settings app.

Finally, let's implement `eraseCloudKeyValueStorage`. Ideally we won't ever need to run this code, but it's nice to have, just in case. Open `CloudManager.m` and add this method to the end of the private methods.

```
- (void)eraseCloudKeyValueStorage
{
    NSUbiquitousKeyValueStore *cloudStore =
    [NSUbiquitousKeyValueStore defaultStore];

    NSArray *keys = [[cloudStore dictionaryRepresentation] allKeys];
    for (NSString *key in keys)
    {
        [cloudStore removeObjectForKey:key];
    }

    [cloudStore synchronize];
}
```

This starts by getting an `NSDictionary` representation of everything in our iCloud key-value store. Then we grab all the keys from the dictionary. We iterate over the keys, removing each one from the store, and then we force synchronize our store.

> **NOTE:** Neither deleting the application from the device nor deleting all the data from iCloud storage using the System Preferences or Settings app will clear out the key-value store. Additionally, we cannot see the contents of the key-value store at `http://developer.icloud.com`. The only way to clear the store (or to explore its contents) is to do so programmatically, as shown in our `eraseCloudKeyValueStore` method.

That's it. Let's test our code. It's easiest to test iCloud syncing with two physical devices. However, with Xcode 5, it's possible to do some testing in the simulator. However, you will need to use the Debug > Trigger iCloud sync menu item to download the new data from iCloud.

Launch two different copies of the application. Change the units on one device. Then send the application in the background to force the key-value store to sync. The change should appear on the other device within a few seconds (maybe up to a minute, if you're working at a café with a bad Wi-Fi connection). Make sure that changes work in both directions.

As a second test, change the default units to kilograms, and sync the change to the cloud. Then close the application on all your devices. Delete the application from one of the devices. This will remove the user defaults from that device. Run the app again on that device. It will start with an empty history. Click the plus button to bring up the `AddEntryViewController`. Notice that it initially says pounds for the units. Let it sit for a few seconds. The units should automatically change to kilograms—as it downloads the default values from iCloud and updates the user defaults.

As you can see, the iCloud key-value syncing is relatively painless to implement. It has also proven remarkably stable across a wide range of production code. In my opinion, there is no reason not to implement it in your own applications.

ADDING DOCUMENT SYNCING TO HEALTH BEAT

The good news is that `UIDocument` is designed to support iCloud Document Storage. The bad news is there's still a lot of work to get everything set up properly.

We can divide this work into two main tasks. The first task involves modifying how our document is loaded or created. The second task involves managing conflicts when they arise.

However, before we begin either of those tasks, let's talk a bit about file versioning.

FILE VERSIONING IN HEALTH BEAT

Since Health Beat uses a single file to store its data, we are effectively using the most primitive type of versioning—the file name. If we change our data format, we can always change our file name. That way older versions of the application won't see or even know about the new files. New versions of the app, however, can still look for and upgrade older documents.

This is a simple and effective solution. However, we may want something a little more robust. In that case, we really need to build versioning in from the very beginning.

One option would be to change the way `WeightHistoryDocument` saves its data. Instead of saving the `weightHistory` array directly, we could create an object to represent our file format. This object would have one property representing the actual data, and additional properties to manage various pieces of metadata. At a minimum, I'd recommend having a version number and a minimum value to read. This object would also need to adopt the `NSCoding` protocol, letting it load and save its properties.

Our file format object could then check the metadata before loading the actual data. If the application's file version is equal to the document's file version, we simply load the data normally. If the application's version is lower than the document's version, but equal to or higher than the minimum read value, we load the data, but we open the document as read-only and alert the user. If the application's file version is lower than the minimum read value, we don't even try to load the data; we just alert the user.

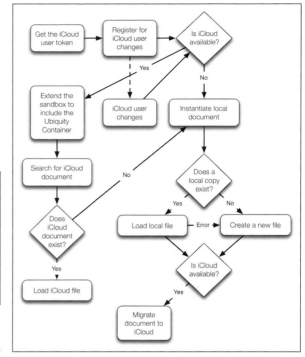

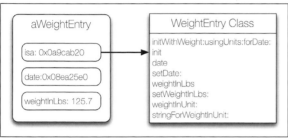

FIGURE 6.5 Original document start-up sequence

FIGURE 6.6 iCloud document start-up sequence

For this to work, we need to build the entire framework into the initial version of our application. Obviously, there's a fourth case that we will eventually have to deal with, when the application's version is higher than the document's version, but we wouldn't need that in our initial release.

Having said all of this, I'm going to leave robust versioning as an exercise for the truly dedicated reader. For this project, simple filename-based versioning is sufficient.

MODIFYING OUR DOCUMENT'S START-UP SEQUENCE

Currently, when our document starts up, we instantiate our document object, then we check to see if a local copy exists. If it does, we load it. If not, we create a new file. This start-up sequence is shown in **Figure 6.5**.

However, to support iCloud Document Syncing, we must use a somewhat more complex start-up sequence, as shown in **Figure 6.6**.

If the user is not logged into iCloud, we will create a local file for them. If they are logged into the cloud, we will search for an existing iCloud file. If we cannot find one, we will either create or load a local file and then migrate it to the cloud.

This has a number of nice features. As we discussed earlier, creating a local file is much faster than creating a file in the Ubiquity Container, since the Ubiquity Container's file coordination can cause the code to block as other read-write operations are performed. By creating a local file and migrating it, we let our user start working with the application as quickly as possible.

Additionally, if users have been working with the application for a while before they sign up for iCloud, it will transparently move their existing document to the cloud for them. They won't lose any of their data.

However, the move to the cloud is a one-way operation. Once the data is moved to the cloud, if users log out or disable document storage, their data will disappear. They will need to reenable the iCloud account before they can access their data.

To break this down into code, our CloudManager will be responsible for determining whether iCloud is available and tracking user changes. Our WeightHistoryDocument will extend the sandbox to include the Ubiquity Container and will migrate the document to the Ubiquity Container. Finally, our RootTabBarController will handle the iCloud search and will manage the overall workflow.

MONITORING THE iCLOUD USER

Open CloudManager.h. At the top of the file, declare an external constant string for our user changed notification and a C function to check and see whether iCloud is available.

```
extern NSString * const CloudManagerUserChangedNotification;

BOOL isCloudAvailable(void);
```

Then, in the @interface block, add the following property:

```
@property (nonatomic, readonly, getter = isCloudAvailable)
BOOL cloudAvailable;
```

Just like our default weight units, we will use this virtual property to check our current iCloud status, while the isCloudAvailable() function will be a thin wrapper around this property.

Now switch to CloudManager.m and add the following code, right before the class extension:

```
NSString * const CloudManagerUserChangedNotification =
@"CloudManagerUserChangedNotification";

BOOL isCloudAvailable(void)
{
    return [[CloudManager sharedManager] isCloudAvailable];
}
```

Here, we're defining our notification constant, while our isCloudAvailable() function calls our singleton's isCloudAvailable method.

Now, we need to add the following two properties to our class extension:

```
@property (strong, nonatomic) id ubiquityIdentityChangeObserver;
@property (strong, nonatomic) id <NSObject, NSCopying, NSCoding>
identityToken;
```

In the dealloc method, remove our new ubiquityIdentityChangeObserver.

```
if (self.ubiquityIdentityChangeObserver)
{
    [[NSNotificationCenter defaultCenter]
     removeObserver:self.ubiquityIdentityChangeObserver];
}
```

Next, at the bottom of our Accessor methods, add the accessor and KVO methods for our cloudAvailable property.

```
- (BOOL)isCloudAvailable
{
    return (self.identityToken != nil);
}


+ (NSSet *)keyPathsForValuesAffectingCloudAvailable
{
    return [NSSet setWithObject:@"identityToken"];
}
```

Notice that we renamed the getter to isCloudAvailable in the property declaration. So, our custom getter method must use that method name. However, the property's key is still "cloudAvailable," so we use keyPathsForValuesAffectingCloudAvailable, not keyPathsForValuesAffectingIsCloudAvailable.

The logic here is pretty simple. If we have a valid user identity token, then iCloud is available. Similarly, changes to the token may indicate a change in iCloud's availability.

Now, implement the following method at the end of our private methods:

```
- (void)setupCloudUserMonitoring
{
    NSFileManager *defaultFileManager =
    [NSFileManager defaultManager];

    self.identityToken = [defaultFileManager ubiquityIdentityToken];
    __weak CloudManager *_self = self;

    self.ubiquityIdentityChangeObserver =
    [[NSNotificationCenter defaultCenter]
     addObserverForName:NSUbiquityIdentityDidChangeNotification
     object:nil
     queue:[NSOperationQueue mainQueue]
```

```
usingBlock:^(NSNotification *note) {
    _self.identityToken =
    [defaultFileManager ubiquityIdentityToken];

    [[NSNotificationCenter defaultCenter]
    postNotificationName:CloudManagerUserChangedNotification
    object:_self];
}];
}
```

We start by getting a reference to the default file manager. Then we use this reference to get our current ubiquity identity token. This will be a unique token for the current user logged into iCloud. If the user isn't currently logged into iCloud or if he's disabled document syncing, this will return nil. We then assign that value to our identityToken property.

Next, we set up a notification to listen for changes to the iCloud user. This notification will be triggered whenever the user performs an action that might affect iCloud's availability: logging out, logging in, disabling document syncing, or reenabling document syncing.

When a change has occurred, we update our identityToken property, and then we send out our own CloudManagerUserChangedNotification. On the surface, sending our own notification looks like a waste of time and effort. After all, anyone can just listen for NSUbiquityIdentityDidChangeNotification directly. However, using our own notification has a distinct advantage.

When you have more than one observer listening to the same notification, there's no guarantee on which order the observer blocks will run. This means other observers could run before we've had a chance to update our identityToken property (and therefore our cloudAvailable property). And, if this observer triggers code that calls isCloudAvailable() or checks our manager's cloudAvailable property, it may get an incorrect value.

By listening to the CloudManagerUserChangedNotification notification, we can guarantee that our observer's block is called after our identityToken and cloudAvailable properties have been properly updated.

> **NOTE:** The NSUbiquityIdentityDidChangeNotification is smart enough to filter out cases where nothing has actually changed. If the user logs out and then immediately logs back into the same account or disables and then immediately reenables Document Storage, no notification methods are sent.

Finally, we need to call `setupCloudUserMonitoring`. Navigate back up to our `init` method and modify it as shown here:

```
- (id)init
{
    self = [super init];
    if (self) {
        [self setupCloudStore];
        [self setupCloudUserMonitoring];
    }
    return self;
}
```

EXPANDING THE SANDBOX

Next, we need a way to expand our sandbox to include the Ubiquity Container. We do this by calling the file manager's `URLForUbiquityContainerIdentifier:` method. This method takes a single argument, which is the fully qualified container identifier for the container we want to use. This ID uses the format <team_id>.<container_id>, where the team ID is our team's ten-digit ID and the container ID is one of the values from the Ubiquity Containers list in our iCloud Capabilities settings.

Fortunately, if we just pass `nil`, the system will automatically use the fully qualified container identifier for the first Ubiquity Container in our list. That means we need to worry only about passing in the ID if we have more than one container.

Additionally, this method must always be called from a background thread. Setting up the container, especially if the container does not yet exist, can require a significant amount of time.

This means we will need to create an asynchronous method with a callback handler.

Open `WeightHistoryDocument.h`. Let's start by declaring a `CallbackHandler` block type, just under our `EntryEnumeratorBlock` block type.

```
typedef void (^CallbackHandler) (BOOL success);
```

Then declare the following class method, just after the other class methods:

```
+ (void)setupCloudContainer:(CallbackHandler)callbackHandler;
```

Now, switch to `WeightHistoryDocument.m`. Before we can do anything else, we need to set up our background queue. Declare the following static variable just before the class extension:

```
static NSOperationQueue *WeightHistoryDocumentBackgroundQueue;
```

Then, right at the top of our @implementation block, define an initialize method to set up the queue.

```
+ (void)initialize
{
    if (self == [WeightHistoryDocument class])
    {
        WeightHistoryDocumentBackgroundQueue =
        [[NSOperationQueue alloc] init];

        [WeightHistoryDocumentBackgroundQueue
          setName:@"Weight History Document Background Queue"];

        [WeightHistoryDocumentBackgroundQueue
          setMaxConcurrentOperationCount:1];
    }
}
```

Like all initialize methods, we start by checking to make sure this is being called by our WeightHistoryDocument class and not a subclass. Then, we instantiate our background queue, give it a name, and set it to process our operations serially.

Now, we can finally implement our setupCloudContainer method. Add the following to the end of our public class methods:

```
+ (void)setupCloudContainer:(CallbackHandler)callbackHandler
{
    [WeightHistoryDocumentBackgroundQueue addOperationWithBlock:^{

        NSURL *url = [[NSFileManager defaultManager]
                     URLForUbiquityContainerIdentifier:nil];

        BOOL success = (url != nil);

        [[NSOperationQueue mainQueue]
         addOperationWithBlock:^{
             callbackHandler(success);
         }];
    }];
}
```

We start by adding an operation block to our background queue. Inside this block, we request the Ubiquity Container URL from the default file manager. We're not particularly interested in the URL itself; we really just want to trigger the side effect, extending our container.

However, we do use the URL to determine whether the operation was a success. If we receive a valid URL, then iCloud is available and ready to use. If not, then the sandbox has not been extended, and we cannot use iCloud syncing.

Finally, we create a new operation block on our main thread. Inside the operation block, we call our callback handler, passing it our success value. This way, the callback handler always runs on the main thread.

MIGRATING THE DOCUMENT

Now, let's add a method to let us migrate the document to iCloud. Switch back to `Weight HistoryDocument.h` and declare the following method immediately before our class methods:

```
- (void)migrateToCloud;
```

Now, switch back to `WeightHistoryDocument.m` and import `CloudManager.h`. Next, add the `migrateToCloud` method to the end of our public methods.

```
- (void)migrateToCloud
{
    NSAssert(self.documentState == UIDocumentStateNormal,
            @"We must be open and ready to use "
            @"before we can migrate to the cloud");

    NSAssert(isCloudAvailable(),
            @"iCloud storage must be available before we can migrate");

    NSLog(@"Migrating to iCloud...");
    NSURL *fileURL = self.fileURL;
    [WeightHistoryDocumentBackgroundQueue addOperationWithBlock:^{

        NSURL *cloudFileURL;
        cloudFileURL = [self createCloudURL];

        if (!cloudFileURL)
        {
            NSLog(@"*** Unable to access ubiquity container ***");
            return;
        }

        NSError *migrationError;
        BOOL success =
        [[NSFileManager defaultManager] setUbiquitous:YES
                                        itemAtURL:fileURL
```

```
                              destinationURL:cloudFileURL
                                        error:&migrationError];

        if (success)
        {
            NSLog(@"Migration Complete!");
        }
        else
        {
            NSLog(@"*** Unable To migrate: %@ ***",
                    [migrationError localizedDescription]);
        }
    }];
}
```

Here, we start by performing a couple of sanity checks. We should call this method only if our document is open and ready to use and if our user is logged into iCloud and document syncing is turned on.

If it passes those checks, we log a quick message at the console. Again, a lot happens asynchronously or behind the scenes, so I like to add a few logging messages, just to help me track the progress a bit more clearly.

Next, we get our file URL, and then we create an operation on the background queue. Inside that operation, we calculate the cloud URL and check to make sure we have access to the Ubiquity Container. Finally, we call the file manager's setUbiquitous:itemAtURL: destinationURL:error: method.

Since setUbiquitous… performs coordinated writes, it could block. Therefore, we should always call it on a background thread. To call this method, we tell it whether we're moving into or out of the Ubiquity Container. Then we give it the current URL, the new URL, and the address of an error object.

After this method returns, we do some light error checking. Again, the error handling in this implementation is not what I'd call "production quality" error handling. At this point, it's more of a developer tool, designed to provide us with additional information if something unexpected happens.

The documentation doesn't really give us any clues as to why this method may fail, leaving us to either guess or discover the errors on our own. Personally I often use this style error checking through the beta testing process—slowly replacing it with more robust error checking based on the actual errors uncovered by my testers.

We still need to implement the createCloudURL method. The idea is fairly straightforward. We will ask the file manager for the Ubiquity Container's URL (this time, we want the URL, not the side effect). We want to place our document inside the Documents subfolder. This will let the System Preferences and Settings app display our document as an individual file. However, this means we may need to create the `Documents` folder. Then, we build our cloud URL by appending the `Documents` folder and our file name to the container URL.

The problem is, we must coordinate any write operations in the Ubiquity Container. That includes creating our `Documents` folder. So, the final code ends up being a bit complex.

Add the method to the bottom of our private methods as shown here:

```
- (NSURL *)createCloudURL
{
    NSAssert(![[NSThread currentThread] isEqual:[NSThread mainThread]],
             @"This must be called on a background queue.");

    NSFileManager *defaultManager =
    [NSFileManager defaultManager];

    NSURL *ubiquityContainer =
    [defaultManager URLForUbiquityContainerIdentifier:nil];

    if (!ubiquityContainer) return nil;

    NSURL *cloudDocumentDirectory =
    [ubiquityContainer URLByAppendingPathComponent:@"Documents"];

    NSFileCoordinator *coordinator =
    [[NSFileCoordinator alloc] initWithFilePresenter:nil];
    __block BOOL success = YES;
    NSError *coordinatorError = nil;
    [coordinator
     coordinateWritingItemAtURL:cloudDocumentDirectory
     options:0
     error:&coordinatorError
     byAccessor:^(NSURL *newURL) {
         if (![defaultManager fileExistsAtPath:[newURL path]])
         {
             NSError *createDirectoryError;
             BOOL created =
             [defaultManager createDirectoryAtURL:newURL
                     withIntermediateDirectories:YES
                                      attributes:nil
                                           error:&createDirectoryError];
```

```
                if (!created)
                {
                    NSLog(@"*** Unable to create the Documents "
                          @"directory: %@ ***",
                          [createDirectoryError localizedDescription]);

                    success = NO;
                }
            }
        }];

        if (!success) return nil;

        return [cloudDocumentDirectory URLByAppendingPathComponent:
                WeightHistoryDocumentFileName];
}
```

We start with a quick sanity check. This method should be called only from a background thread.

Next, we grab a reference to the default file manager and use that to get our Ubiquity Container's URL. If this does not return a valid URL, then our Ubiquity Container is not available, and we should just return `nil`.

Assuming we have a valid URL, we append "Documents" to it, creating the URL for our `Documents` directory. Then we create a file coordinator. Since we are not yet presenting a document to the user, we can simply pass in `nil` for the file presenter. Once we have the coordinator, we can perform a coordinated write at our `Documents` directory's URL.

The actual write operation is performed inside the block that we pass to the coordinator. Notice that the coordinator will pass us a new URL. We should always use that URL to perform our write operations.

Inside the write block, we check to see whether the `Documents` directory exists. Technically this is a read operation—but since it takes place inside the coordinated write block (and since write blocks are more strict than read blocks), this is OK. We don't need a separate read block.

If the directory does not exist, we ask the file manager to create the `Documents` directory. Again, we're using light error checking, in case something unexpected happens, but this should almost never fail.

Also notice that our write block is performed synchronously. This lets us create a `success` variable before we call the block and modify `success`'s value inside the block, and it will have the correct value by the time `coordinateWritingItemAtURL:options:error:byAccessor` method returns.

If we cannot successfully create the directory, we just return `nil`. Otherwise, we append our file name to the end of the `Documents` directory and return the resulting URL.

UPDATING OUR START-UP SEQUENCE

Now, all the pieces are in place. We just need to modify our workflow. That will be RootTabBarController's job. Open RootTabBarController.m and import CloudManager.h.

Add a new observer property to the class extension, as shown here:

```
@property (strong, nonatomic) id cloudUserChangeObserver;
```

And, of course, we need to add a dealloc method to unregister this observer.

```
- (void)dealloc
{
    if (self.cloudUserChangeObserver)
    {
        [[NSNotificationCenter defaultCenter]
          removeObserver:self.cloudUserChangeObserver];
    }
}
```

Next, in viewDidLoad, add a call to a yet-undefined setupNotifications method.

```
- (void)viewDidLoad
{
    [super viewDidLoad];
    [self setupNotifications];
    [self setupDocument];
    self.interactiveTransition =
    [[TabInteractiveTransition alloc] initWithTabBarController:self];
    self.delegate = self.interactiveTransition;
    [self setupEdgePanGestureRecognizers];
}
```

Then, at the top of our private methods, implement setupNotifications.

```
- (void)setupNotifications
{
    [[NSNotificationCenter defaultCenter]
      addObserverForName:CloudManagerUserChangedNotification
      object:[CloudManager sharedManager]
      queue:[NSOperationQueue mainQueue]
      usingBlock:^(NSNotification *note) {
          [self setupDocument];
      }];
}
```

Now, the obvious explanation for this code is that we're registering for the CloudManagerUserChangedNotification. When we receive that notification, we call setupDocument to create a new document. However, there's a lot going on under the surface. This call to [CloudManager sharedManager] should be the first time we reference our shared cloud instance in this app. That means our sharedManager method will alloc and init a new CloudManager object. The init method will, in turn, check to see whether we have an iCloud user logged in and set the CloudManager to observe changes to the iCloud user.

Next, scroll down to the setupDocument method. This is where things really start to change. Replace the current setupDocument method with the following implementation:

```objc
- (void)setupDocument
{
    if (isCloudAvailable())
    {
        __weak RootTabBarController *_self = self;
        [WeightHistoryDocument setupCloudContainer:^(BOOL success) {

            if (success)
            {
                [_self searchForCloudDocument];
            }
            else
            {
                NSLog(@"Unable to open the cloud container!");
                [_self searchForLocalDocument];
            }
        }];
    }
    else
    {
        [self searchForLocalDocument];
    }
}
```

The logic here should be relatively straightforward. We check to see whether iCloud is available. If it is, we try to set up our cloud container. Remember, this is an asynchronous call, so we don't know how long it will take. If everything is successful, we search for a document in iCloud. Otherwise, we search for a local document.

Obviously, there are a number of new, private methods we need to add. Let's start by adding createWeightHistoryForURL: right after setupDocument.

```objc
- (void)createWeightHistoryForURL:(NSURL *)fileURL
{
    self.weightHistoryDocument = [[WeightHistoryDocument alloc]
                                  initWithFileURL:fileURL];

    [self.weightHistoryDocument addSubscriber:self];
    [self passDocumentToViewControllers];
}
```

Most of this code was taken from our old setupDocument method. Here, we simply instantiate a new document using the provided URL. Then we add ourselves as a subscriber. Finally, we pass this document to all of our child view controllers.

I think UIDocument's handling of URLs is somewhat awkward. For example, we can create a new document at any arbitrary URL, but we can load documents only from the URL we provided when the document object was first instantiated.

Additionally, we cannot use the same document object to open different files. We must create a new document any time we want to open (or create) a new file. Since we may be loading documents from different URLs (one in the sandbox, one in the Ubiquity Container), and since we often need to create new documents, breaking these out to their own method will help save a lot of time and effort.

Next, let's implement our searchForCloudDocument method.

```objc
- (void)searchForCloudDocument
{
    NSLog(@"Searching for cloud documents...");
    NSURL *localFileURL = [WeightHistoryDocument localFileURL];
    NSString *fileName = [localFileURL lastPathComponent];

    // Search for the file in the cloud
    NSMetadataQuery* query = [[NSMetadataQuery alloc] init];

    [query setSearchScopes:
     [NSArray arrayWithObject:NSMetadataQueryUbiquitousDocumentsScope]];

    // get all files
    [query setPredicate:[NSPredicate predicateWithFormat:@"%K like %@",
                         NSMetadataItemFSNameKey,
                         fileName]];
```

```
    __weak NSNotificationCenter *center =
    [NSNotificationCenter defaultCenter];
    __weak RootTabBarController *_self = self;
    __block id searchObserver =
    [center
     addObserverForName:NSMetadataQueryDidFinishGatheringNotification
     object:query
     queue:[NSOperationQueue mainQueue]
     usingBlock:^(NSNotification *note) {
         [query disableUpdates];
         [center removeObserver:searchObserver];
         [_self processQuery:query];
         [query stopQuery];
     }];

    [query startQuery];
}
```

We start by grabbing the local file URL, and then we get the file name by extracting the last path component from that URL.

Next, we instantiate our NSMetadataQuery. We set it to search our Ubiquity Container, and we set the search predicate. In this case, we're using the predicate format string syntax to look for a file whose name matches our data file's name.

I'm not going to talk about predicates and the predicate format string syntax here. We'll cover it in detail in Chapter 7, "Core Data."

Once we have the query ready to go, we register for the NSMetadataQueryDid FinishGatheringNotification. When we receive this notification, we will call the processQuery method.

This notification-handling code should look different from most of the notifications we've created so far. In this case, we want the block to fire only once. Then we want it to dispose of all its resources.

To do this, we're keeping all of our resources strictly local. The observer is a local, block variable. We let the notification block capture both the observer and our query object, keeping them in memory until the notification block is destroyed. Then, inside the block, we remove the notification observer and stop our query. This will cause the notification block to be deallocated, releasing the values that it had captured. Our observer and query objects will then get deallocated as well.

The metadata query operates in two stages. First is the initial gathering phase. This is relatively fast and looks for any existing files that match our query. We might not have downloaded the file yet—but we will still have access to its metadata.

Once this search is done, the query enters the live-update phase. Here, the query will continue to monitor the file system and will alert us to any additional matches.

In Health Beat, we're interested only in the gathering phase. So, we disable and dismiss the query as soon as that phase is complete.

Next, add the processQuery: method.

```objc
- (void)processQuery:(NSMetadataQuery*)query {

    NSUInteger fileCount = [query resultCount];
    id result;
    NSURL *cloudFileURL;

    switch (fileCount) {
        case 0:

            NSLog(@"No Cloud Documents found");
            [self searchForLocalDocument];
            break;

        case 1:

            NSLog(@"Loading a cloud document");

            result = [query resultAtIndex:0];
            cloudFileURL =
            [result valueForAttribute:NSMetadataItemURLKey];

            [self createWeightHistoryForURL:cloudFileURL];
            [self loadFile];
            break;

        default:

            // We should never have more than 1 file. If this
            // occurs, it's due to a bug in our code that needs
            // to be fixed.

            [NSException
             raise:NSInternalInconsistencyException
             format:@"NSMetadata should only find a "
```

```
                  @"single file, found %@",
                  @(fileCount)];
              break;
      }
}
```

Here, we determine how many files our query found, and then we pass that value to a switch statement.

- If we found zero files, then we perform a local search.
- If we find one file, we get its URL, create our document, and load it.
- If we find more than one file, an error has occurred.

We should never find more than one file. Even if our document has conflicts, it will return only a single file, containing the most current version. So, if an error occurs, we throw an exception, which will kill our application, forcing us to come back and find and fix the problem.

Next, implement searchForLocalDocument as shown here:

```
- (void)searchForLocalDocument
{
    NSURL *fileURL = [WeightHistoryDocument localFileURL];
    [self createWeightHistoryForURL:fileURL];

    //    [self addMocData];
    if ([WeightHistoryDocument localFileExists])
    {
        [self loadFile];
    }
    else
    {
        [self createNewFileAtURL:fileURL];
    }
}
```

This is, basically, the second half of our original setupDocuments method. Here, we get the local file URL and create our document based on that URL. Then we check to see whether the local file exists. If it does, we load it; otherwise, we create a new file.

Now, modify loadFile as shown here:

```
- (void)loadFile
{
    NSLog(@"Loading File");
    __weak RootTabBarController *_self = self;
    [self.weightHistoryDocument
```

```
    openWithCompletionHandler:^(BOOL success) {

        NSFileManager *fileManager = [NSFileManager defaultManager];
        NSURL *fileURL = _self.weightHistoryDocument.fileURL;

        if (!success)
        {
            NSLog(@"*** Corrupt file at %@, "
                    @"attempting to delete it and try again. ***",
                    fileURL);

            NSFileCoordinator *coordinator =
            [[NSFileCoordinator alloc] initWithFilePresenter:nil];

            [coordinator
             coordinateWritingItemAtURL:fileURL
             options:NSFileCoordinatorWritingForDeleting
             error:nil
             byAccessor:^(NSURL *newURL) {
                 [fileManager removeItemAtURL:newURL
                                        error:nil];
             }];

            [_self searchForLocalDocument];
            return;
        }
        else
        {
            NSLog(@"File Loaded");

            if (isCloudAvailable())
            {
                if (![fileManager isUbiquitousItemAtURL:fileURL])
                {
                    [self.weightHistoryDocument migrateToCloud];
                }
            }
        }
    }];
}
```

Here, we delete the corrupted file using a coordinated write, since we may be deleting the file from the Ubiquity Container. Then, instead of calling setupDocument, we call searchForLocalDocument to explicitly start looking for a local copy—if this fails, it will create a local copy.

Additionally, once the file loads, we check to see whether iCloud is enabled. If it is, we check to see whether our file is stored in the Ubiquity Container. If it is not, we migrate it to the Ubiquity Container.

And finally, we need to make one small change to createNewFileAtURL:. Add the following code:

```
else
{
    NSLog(@"File Created");
    if (isCloudAvailable())
    {
        [self.weightHistoryDocument migrateToCloud];
    }
}
```

Much like our loadFile method, once we successfully create the file, we want to check and see whether iCloud is available. If it is, we want to migrate our file to the cloud. This time, however, we don't need to check and see whether it's already inside the Ubiquity Container, since we always create our files in the local sandbox.

That's it. You can test the syncing, if you want. Add or remove weights and send the application to the background. That will force it to save the changes, which will then be synced by the iCloud server.

However, we haven't implemented any conflict resolution system yet—so it may stop syncing correctly at any point. Let's fix that next.

RESOLVING CONFLICTS

There's a simple rule. If you're using iCloud storage, then you must be prepared to handle conflicts. Conflicts occur when the cloud storage receives contradicting updates. This typically happens when one device saves a change, and then a second device saves a different change before receiving the first update.

In most cases, this should rarely occur. Sure, I want to have the same data on my iPhone, my iPad, and my Mac—however, I'm probably not going to run the same application on two different devices at the same time. If I make a change on my phone, there should be plenty of time for the update to reach my Mac before I open the file there.

However, remember how iCloud works. Each application saves and reads to a local file. The system then syncs this file with the cloud. There may be times when the system is unable to sync these changes—for example, if the device is in airplane mode or if it's located in the Wi-Fi–less sub-basement of an office building. In both cases, the user can still access and edit any documents on his device. Any changes he makes will be saved locally but won't be synced until he gets an active Internet connection. Furthermore, devices can be shut off. They can run out of power. There are any number of reasons why an update may be delayed, creating ample opportunities for conflicts.

Most importantly, if it can happen, it will happen—guaranteed. So, we have to be prepared to handle it.

There are three basic approaches to managing conflicts. The simplest is to let the last change win. From a developer's standpoint, this is by far the easiest solution. We mark all the conflicting versions as resolved and then delete them. Done and done. However, it has a rather large downside. While this may work fine in many cases, we risk accidentally deleting some of our user's data. That would be a bad thing.

The second approach involves showing the users all the different versions and let them select the one to use. This has one major advantage—the users are in complete control. They get to decide exactly what happens to their data. However, it has several significant problems as well. First, it's much harder to design. In some cases, it may be extremely difficult to display the differences in a meaningful way. Also, it requires user intervention, and that means our users are wasting their time getting our app to work, instead of getting work done. Finally, we still risk losing user data. Anytime we pick one version over another, something may get lost.

The best approach is to automatically merge all the conflicting versions into a complete, final version. Unfortunately, this may not be possible for all documents in all situations—but if you can do it, you probably should. In our case, merging is relatively easy. We can simply take the union of all the entries across all versions. Yes, this may cause a deleted weight entry to reappear—but we're not going to lose any information. The user can always delete the data again.

Unfortunately, as we will soon see, relatively easy is not the same as easy.

Open WeightHistoryDocument.m and navigate to the setupDocumentNotifications method. Modify the code as shown here:

```
- (void)setupDocumentNotifications
{
    __weak WeightHistoryDocument *_self = self;
    self.documentStateObserver =
    [[NSNotificationCenter defaultCenter]
     addObserverForName:UIDocumentStateChangedNotification
     object:self
     queue:[NSOperationQueue mainQueue]
     usingBlock:^(NSNotification *note) {

        if (_self.documentState == UIDocumentStateInConflict)
        {
            NSLog(@"*** Conflicting Documents found ***");
```

```
            [_self resolveConflicts];
        }

        for (id <WeightHistoryDocumentSubscriber> subscriber
            in _self.subscribers)
        {
            [subscriber weightHistoryDocument:_self
                              stateDidChange:_self.documentState];
        }

    }];
}
```

Here, we check to see whether we're in a conflicting state. If we are, we call resolve Conflicts. Now we just need to implement resolveConflicts.

Resolving conflicts often requires a lot of file system work. Unfortunately, UIDocument doesn't provide automated support for us here, so we need to create our own file coordinators. This makes the code a bit more cumbersome than it would be otherwise.

Having said that, let's add the resolveConflicts method to the end of our private methods.

```
- (void)resolveConflicts
{
    NSURL *currentURL = self.fileURL;

    NSFileVersion *currentVersion =
    [NSFileVersion currentVersionOfItemAtURL:currentURL];

    NSMutableArray *currentHistory =
    [self loadHistoryArrayFromURL:currentVersion.URL];

    NSArray *unresolvedVersions =
    [NSFileVersion unresolvedConflictVersionsOfItemAtURL:currentURL];

    for (NSFileVersion *version in unresolvedVersions)
    {
        NSMutableArray *oldHistory =
        [self loadHistoryArrayFromURL:version.URL];

        currentHistory =
        [self mergeCurrentHistory:currentHistory
                    withOldHistory:oldHistory];
```

```
    }

    self.weightHistory = currentHistory;
    __weak WeightHistoryDocument *_self = self;

    [self
     saveToURL:currentURL
     forSaveOperation:UIDocumentSaveForOverwriting
     completionHandler:^(BOOL success) {

      if (success)
      {
          [_self removeConflictedVersions];
      }
      else
      {
          NSLog(@"*** Unable to save resolved data ***");
      }
    }];
}
```

Here's the basic idea. We get the current version of our document by calling +[NSFileVersion currentVersionOfItemAtURL:]. Then we get an array containing all the unresolved, conflicting versions by calling +[NSFileVersion unresolvedConflictVersions OfItemAtURL:].

We can get the URL for each version. This lets us load the weight history array for each version directly. We then merge these all with our current version.

Once we're done, we set our weightHistory property to the merged version, and we save the document. If the save is successful, we remove all the conflicting versions.

Most of the real work is done in loadHistoryArrayFromURL:, mergeCurrentHistory: withOldHistory: and removeConflictedVersions. Let's implement them next, starting with loadHistoryArrayFromURL:.

```
- (NSMutableArray *)loadHistoryArrayFromURL:(NSURL *)url
{
    NSFileCoordinator *coordinator =
    [[NSFileCoordinator alloc] initWithFilePresenter:self];

    __block NSData *data = nil;
    NSError *coordinatorError = nil;
```

```
[coordinator
 coordinateReadingItemAtURL:url
 options:0
 error:&coordinatorError
 byAccessor:^(NSURL *newURL) {
     data = [NSData dataWithContentsOfURL:url];
 }];

if (coordinatorError)
{
    NSLog(@"*** Unable to perform a coordinated read on %@: %@ ***",
        url, [coordinatorError localizedDescription]);

    return nil;
}


return [NSKeyedUnarchiver unarchiveObjectWithData:data];
}
```

Most of this code is just setting up the coordinated read block. Now, we know that our document data is just an NSData object containing our weight history array. Therefore, inside the read block, we use +[NSData dataWithContentsOfURL:] to create an NSData object from the specified file.

Then, after the coordinated read has completed, we use +[NSKeyedUnarchiver unarchiveObjectWithData:] to convert our data back to a mutable array, and we return the results.

Next, let's implement mergeCurrentHistory:withOldHistory:.

```
- (NSMutableArray *)mergeCurrentHistory:(NSMutableArray *)currentHistory
                   withOldHistory:(NSArray *)oldHistory
{

    NSUInteger currentIndex = 0;
    NSUInteger currentCount = [currentHistory count];
    NSUInteger oldIndex = 0;
    NSUInteger oldCount = [oldHistory count];

    NSMutableArray *mergedArray =
    [NSMutableArray arrayWithCapacity:currentCount + oldCount];
```

```
while ((currentIndex < currentCount) && (oldIndex < oldCount))
{
    WeightEntry *current = currentHistory[currentIndex];
    WeightEntry *old = oldHistory[oldIndex];

    if ([current isEqual:old])
    {
        [mergedArray addObject:current];
        currentIndex ++;
        oldIndex ++;
    }
    else if ([current.date compare:old.date] == NSOrderedDescending)
    {
        [mergedArray addObject:current];
        currentIndex ++;
    }
    else
    {
        [mergedArray addObject:old];
        oldIndex ++;
    }
}

for (; currentIndex < currentCount; currentIndex++)
{
    [mergedArray addObject:currentHistory[currentIndex]];
}

for (; oldIndex < oldCount; oldIndex ++)
{
    [mergedArray addObject:oldHistory[oldIndex]];
}

return mergedArray;
}
```

Here, the logic gets a little more complex. We want to make sure our merge code does the following:

1. We want the union of both arrays.

2. We don't want any duplicate entries.

3. We want to make sure all the entries remain in descending order.

We could use the `@distinctUnionOfObjects` KVC collection operator to quickly merge the arrays and then sort the final results. This could be accomplished with very little code—however, it ignores the fact that our code is already sorted. Sorting can be very expensive, so I prefer to avoid it if possible.

If we just take the most recent object from the front of either array and dispose of any duplicates, we should be able to very quickly and efficiently merge the arrays without requiring a separate sort operation. Unfortunately, there are a lot of corner cases that we need to take into account.

We start by creating variables to indicate our current position in both arrays. We also grab the count of both arrays, since we will frequently use those values.

Next, we create a mutable array that is large enough to hold all the elements from both arrays.

Then, we perform our `while` loop as long as both the indices are lower than their relative count. Inside the `while` loop, we grab the `WeightEntry` at the current indices. If the weight entries are equal, we add one copy to the new array and increment both indices. Otherwise, we add the most recent entry to the new array and increment its index.

Once the while loop is done, we've reached the end of one or both of our arrays. However, one of the arrays may have a few leftover values. So, we simply check to see whether either array has any remaining entries. If it does, we add those to the end of our new array in order.

When that is done, we can finally return the new array.

Finally, we need to implement `removeConflictedVersions`.

```
- (void)removeConflictedVersions
{
    NSURL *currentURL = self.fileURL;

    NSArray *unresolvedVersions =
    [NSFileVersion unresolvedConflictVersionsOfItemAtURL:currentURL];

    for (NSFileVersion *version in unresolvedVersions)
    {
        NSLog(@"Resolving version %@", version);
        version.resolved = YES;
    }
```

```objc
    __block NSError *clearOldVersionsError = nil;
    NSError *coordinatedWriteError = nil;

    NSFileCoordinator *coordinator =
    [[NSFileCoordinator alloc] initWithFilePresenter:self];

    __block BOOL removed = NO;

    [coordinator
     coordinateWritingItemAtURL:currentURL
     options:NSFileCoordinatorWritingForDeleting
     error:&coordinatedWriteError
     byAccessor:^(NSURL *newURL) {
         removed = [NSFileVersion
                    removeOtherVersionsOfItemAtURL:currentURL
                    error:&clearOldVersionsError];
     }];

    if (coordinatedWriteError)
    {
        NSLog(@"*** unable to perform a coordinated write to %@ ***",
            currentURL);
    }

    if (removed)
    {
        NSLog(@"All Conflicts Resolved");
    }
    else
    {
        NSLog(@"*** Unable to remove conflicting versions: %@ ***",
            [clearOldVersionsError localizedDescription]);
    }
}
```

This looks like a lot of code, but it's mostly the write coordinator and our error handling. We start by getting all the unresolved conflicting versions, just like we did in `resolveConflicts`. We then iterate over all the conflicting versions, setting their `resolved` property to YES.

Next, we call `+[NSFileVersion removeOtherVersionsOfItemAtURL:error:]`. Unfortunately, this must be called from within a coordinated write block. Like much of our file coordination code, we end up with multiple error objects: one for the coordinated block and one for the actual write operation. This makes for somewhat complicated error handling code.

Once this method has been added, our project should build without any errors—but it's not quite correct yet. In our merge code, we use `isEquals` to compare our `WeightEntry` objects. Unfortunately, the default implementation compares the object's pointer values.

Obviously, objects that we loaded from separate data files will have completely different pointers, but they might have the same underlying data. We need to override `WeightEntry`'s `isEqual:` method so that it compares the object's `date` and `weightInLbs` properties instead.

Open `WeightEntry.m` and implement `isEqual:` right after the `description` method.

```
- (BOOL)isEqual:(id)object
{
    if (![object isKindOfClass:[WeightEntry class]]) return NO;
    WeightEntry *test = object;

    return (self.weightInLbs == test.weightInLbs) &&
            [self.date isEqual:test.date];
}
```

This checks to make sure the `object` argument is a `WeightEntry` instance (or a subclass of `WeightEntry`). If it's not, it returns NO.

Then we check both the `weightInLbs` and the `date` properties. We're combining them using an AND operation. So, if they both match we return YES; otherwise, we return NO.

However, we cannot override the `isEqual:` method without also overriding the `hash` method.

```
- (NSUInteger)hash
{
    NSUInteger weight = (NSUInteger)floor(self.weightInLbs * 100);
    return ([self.date hash] << 12) ^ weight;
}
```

Good hash methods are hard to write. If two objects are equal, their hash value needs to also be equal. Nonequal objects can have the same hash value—but we should make that as rare as possible. Also, the performance of data structures, like Dictionaries, can be impacted by the quality of the hashes.

A full description of hash methods is well beyond the scope of this book; however, the implementation shown here should be good enough. We take the weight, shift it two decimal places, and convert it to an integer. Then we combine this with the date's hash value, shifting the date 12 spaces so the two pieces of data don't overlap. We'll lose the top 12-bits of the date hash, but—if Apple has implemented it reasonably—we will capture the most significant bits. That should be more than sufficient.

That's it. Run the app on two devices. Make changes to the content on one device. Send the application to the background, and watch for the changes to appear on the other. Changes can take several seconds to sync. They shouldn't take longer than 15 to 30 seconds over a good Wi-Fi and will usually be much faster.

You also want to test the conflict resolution. The easiest way to generate a conflict is to put one device in airplane mode. Make changes on both devices. Put the app into the background on both devices, saving the changes. Then take the device out of airplane mode. It should now try to sync its changes.

One of the two devices will detect the conflict and will resolve it. The other device will simply get an update message once the conflict is resolved.

iCloud Document Syncing is very robust and stable. Apple uses it for its iWork applications, so it has been well tested. However, implementing document syncing is nontrivial. It's easy to forget a minor detail (such as file coordination) that can lead to odd and intermittent bugs.

I generally recommend that developers try to add Document Syncing to their applications—but only once they understand how much work it is likely to be.

DEBUGGING iCLOUD DOCUMENT STORAGE

As we have seen, iCloud Document Storage can be somewhat opaque. Fortunately, with Xcode 5, Apple provides a great set of tools to help us see exactly what's going on, helping us find and fix problems.

When running Health Beat, either on a tethered device or on the simulator, switch to the Debug navigator. In the Navigator area, you will see three rows for each copy of the app that is currently being debugged: a CPU row, a Memory row, and an iCloud row. In each row, there's a bar graph that shows a quick overview of that resource's usage over time.

However, we can get more detailed information by clicking one of the rows. If you click the iCloud row, it will bring up the iCloud Usage display (**Figure 6.7**).

The detailed data can be divided into three sections. The top shows general information: the Ubiquity Container ID, the amount of iCloud storage space available, the amount used, and the length of time since the last update.

The middle displays the actual transfers. Green bars show when the iCloud service uploaded data to the cloud. Blue lines show when it downloaded data.

FIGURE 6.7 iCloud usage details

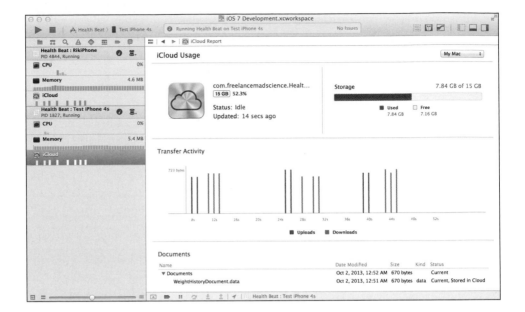

Finally, the bottom shows the contents of our Ubiquity Container. It also tells us the time and date of the file's last update and its current status. "Current" means the most recent version has been downloaded from iCloud. "Stored in Cloud" means it has been uploaded successfully to the cloud.

Note that the status messages represent the device's understanding of its own state. If another device has uploaded a change but this device has not yet received the metadata, it will still list the file as "Current." So, you usually need to look at the modification date when considering the status.

NOTE: While the iCloud Usage display is a fantastic tool with a lot of promise, the Xcode 5.0 implementation still seems to get confused or lost on occasion. If it's showing clearly old or outdated information—or if it's not showing any useful information at all—you may need to quit Xcode and relaunch it. This seems to fix the problem.

Additionally, we can download the iCloud Logging Profile from http://developer .apple.com/downloads. If we install this profile on one of our test devices, that device will generate additional iCloud logging data. This is primarily used when reporting a bug to Apple. Install the profile, duplicate the bug, and attach the log file to your bug report. This gives the Apple engineers a lot of additional information, which can help them debug the problem.

WRAPPING UP

In this chapter, we implemented both key-value and document syncing. iCloud's Key-Value Storage is easy to use but provides a limited set of features. It works best as a technique for syncing user defaults between devices.

iCloud Document Syncing has more features but is much harder to implement. There is good news, however. In the next chapter we will look at syncing Core Data documents using iCloud. With Core Data, Apple automates away almost all of the issues we had to deal with here.

Of course, iCloud Core Data syncing has traditionally been a bit buggy and unreliable. We will talk about that next chapter as well.

As difficult as it can be to set up correctly, when you have iCloud syncing working, it's almost like magic. You're data just appears on all of your devices, ready and waiting for you to use. In my opinion, it's well worth the effort.

OTHER RESOURCES

- **iCloud Design Guide**

  iOS Developer's Library

  This guide covers all three iCloud APIs. I would highly recommend reading through it before implementing iCloud Document Storage. It's a complex enough topic, so it's worth hearing more than just one take on the subject.

- **Storing Documents in iCloud Using iOS 5**

  WWDC 2011 Videos

  Though a bit old, this is still one of the primary sources for iCloud Document Storage. Honestly, iCloud Document Storage hasn't really changed at all since iOS 5—though some of the details have been clarified in later documentation. Still, this presentation will give you a good overview on using UIDocument. Its biggest problem is that it over-simplifies the subject, ignoring several important steps that developers must perform. Still, it's well worth watching.

- **Taking Advantage of File Coordination**

  WWDC 2011 Videos

  File presenters and file coordinators were introduced for Mac OS 7 and iOS 5, and they have not changed substantially since then. This video describes file coordination in detail. It is well worth watching, especially if you have to do a lot of file system work in the Ubiquity Container, or if you're considering implementing your own file presenter.

CHAPTER 7

Core Data

Core Data is, in many ways, a replacement for our application's model layer. It is much more than just storage; it also manages the life cycles of our data objects, tracks and validates any changes to our data, provides effortless undo support, and, yes, saves our data to disk. Furthermore, the `UIManagedDocument` class simplifies and improves on Core Data by automatically setting up our Core Data stack, performing file read and writes on background threads, and adding simple iCloud Document syncing.

In this chapter, we will look at the technologies underlying both Core Data and `UIManagedDocument`. Then we will replace Health Beat's entire model layer with a `UIManagedDocument`-based model. As you will see, this provides a much simpler model than our previous custom-built approach.

INTRODUCING CORE DATA

The Core Data framework provides support for automatically managing many common model layer tasks. We have already seen how Xcode simplifies our application's view layer. With Interface Builder, we can draw our application's scenes. The built-in guidelines ensure that our application follows Apple's Human Interface Guidelines, but it goes beyond that. We can draw connections between our view and controllers, linking objects to outlets and events to actions. With storyboards, we can link scenes with segues, letting us rapidly sketch out the entire application's workflow. With a few clicks of the mouse, Xcode helps us build complex structures that would normally require a considerable amount of boilerplate code.

Core Data brings a similar magic to our model. For most applications, the models share a number of features. This includes one or more object graphs. These graphs define both the content and the relationships in our application's data. Applications need to manage the life cycles of these object graphs, adding, modifying, and deleting objects in the graphs. They also need to validate the graphs and save and load them to disk. Undo and redo support would also be nice. Furthermore, if the format of our data changes, we need to migrate our saved data from one schema to the next.

Core Data provides all of these features and more. In many cases, it can perform these tasks automatically. In others, it presents a rich API for expanding and customizing its behavior. It is also tightly integrated with Xcode's tool chain. Core Data is mature, well tested, and highly optimized. It is used by millions of customers across thousands of applications. While we could try to build a custom solution to better fit our specific needs, it would require a considerable amount of effort to match the performance and stability already provided by Core Data. In most cases, it's more cost effective to just use Core Data and to focus the developer effort on other areas.

And, yes, we can even graphically lay out our object graphs.

This chapter will start with a quick overview of Core Data's architecture, to give you an idea of how it works and how you might use it for other projects. Then we will convert our Health Beat application from a custom model to Core Data. Along the way, we will look at many of the tricks and tips (and possible traps) involved in using Core Data.

ARCHITECTURE OVERVIEW

Our Core Data model can be divided into two parts. The managed object model defines our data's schema, describing how our data is organized. We also have the Core Data stack. This combines both the managed object context (our application's live data) and the persistence stack (for saving and loading our entities to disk).

MANAGED OBJECT MODEL

The NSManagedObjectModel object defines the structure of our data. It describes what type of data we can store and how the individual pieces of data relate. We do this by creating one or more entity descriptions. The managed object model then maintains the mapping between these descriptions and the corresponding NSManagedObject objects in our Core Data stack.

We can create managed object models programmatically at runtime, but we generally use Xcode's Data Model Design tool to graphically lay out our schema.

ENTITY DESCRIPTIONS

Core Data uses the NSEntityDescription class to define our model's entities. At a minimum, this description includes a unique name for the entity and the name of the managed object class that will be instantiated in the Core Data stack (either NSManagedObject or a custom subclass). Most entities also have one or more properties.

Properties represent the type of data stored in our entity. They become our instance variables when we instantiate objects for our entities. All Core Data properties are completely key-value compliant; Core Data automatically defines the equivalent Objective-C properties for us. Finally, Core Data supports three types of properties: attributes, relationships, and fetched properties. Each specifies a different relationship between the entity and its data.

Attributes are the simplest Core Data property. They represent values stored within the entity itself. Unfortunately, we are somewhat limited in the type of attributes that we can use. **Table 7.1** shows the complete list of Core Data attribute types and their corresponding Objective-C and scalar data types.

TABLE 7.1 Core Data Attribute Types

ATTRIBUTE TYPE	OBJECTIVE-C TYPE	SCALAR TYPE
Undefined	*unknown*	
Integer 16	NSNumber	int16_t
Integer 32	NSNumber	int32_t
Integer 64	NSNumber	int64_t
Decimal	NSDecimalNumber	
Double	NSNumber	double
Float	NSNumber	float
String	NSString	
Boolean	NSNumber	BOOL
Date	NSDate	NSTimeInterval
Binary Data	NSData	
Transformable	id	

Some of these deserve a little special attention. Let's take the easiest one first. Internally, Core Data saves date attributes as the number of seconds since the reference date (January 1, 2001 GMT). It doesn't store the time zone. Internally, NSDate operates the same way—however, NSDate will implicitly use the device's default time zone. This means our date values will appear in PST when saved in Los Angeles and in EST when read in New York. If we need to save the time zone information, we must explicitly create a separate attribute to store it.

Next, let's look at the undefined attribute type. This type can be used only with transient attributes (attributes that are not saved to the persistent store but whose changes are monitored, allowing undo/redo support). Any Objective-C object can be assigned to an undefined attribute. As we will see in the "Managed Objects" section, undefined attributes are often used to provide a friendly Objective-C wrapper around more primitive Core Data types.

Finally, we have the transformable data type. This type uses an NSValueTransformer object to convert the attribute to and from an instance of NSData. By default, Core Data will use NSKeyedUnarchiveFromDataTransformerName. In practice, this means we can assign any Objective-C object that adopts the NSCoding protocol to a transformable attribute, without requiring any additional work on our part. Of course, if we're feeling ambitious, we could always select a different NSValueTransformer or even write our own custom transformer to handle various special cases.

Attributes also have a number of settings. They can be optional, transient, or indexed.

- **Optional:** The attribute can have a nil value. More specifically, if the optional setting is turned off, we must assign a non-nil value before we can save the entity.

- **Transient:** Core Data does not save or load the attribute's value from the persistent store. It will still track the value, however, for undo, redo, and validation.

- **Indexed:** This attribute is important when searching through a list of entities. Persistent stores may use indexed attributes to improve search performance on fetch requests. This is particularly true of SQLite-backed stores.

Additionally, each attribute type has a number of validation settings. For numeric attributes, we can assign minimum, maximum, and default values. For strings, we can set the minimum length, maximum length, default value, and regular expression that the string must match.

Relationships represent the second property type. Core Data uses relationships to define connections between entities. We will typically define both sides of a relationship. For example, if our Department entity has a Manager relationship, then the Manager entity should have a matching Department relationship. Furthermore, the Manager's relationship should be assigned as the Department's inverse relationship.

> **NOTE:** While inverse relationships are not required, they are highly recommended. Core Data uses this information to ensure that the object graph remains consistent as the application makes changes. If we do not use inverse relationships, then we are responsible for ensuring the consistency, tracking changes, and managing the undo support. See the "Unidirectional Relationships" section of the Core Data Programming Guide for more information.

Relationships can be either to-one or to-many. To-one references are modeled using a pointer to the target object. Most of the time, to-many relationships are modeled using NSSets. The relationship did not have any inherent order; however, it could be sorted based on any of the values from the entities.

We can, optionally, use an NSOrderedSet for our to-many relationships. This allows us to place our entities into any arbitrary order we want without regard to the entities' values. However, this is not generally recommended. Ordered relationships often impose a heavy performance hit on our application. In addition, ordered relationships are not supported by iCloud Document syncing. In general, it is better to add an index attribute to the entities and then sort them by their indices.

MANY-TO-MANY RELATIONSHIPS

Relationships are implicitly either one-to-one or one-to-many. It's possible to create a many-to-many relationship—but this requires a bit more work.

There are two recommended approaches. We can just make sure both ends are set as to-many relationships and set them as the inverse of each other. If we save these objects to an SQLite-based store, Core Data will automatically build the join table for us. Alternatively, we can explicitly build a join entity that represents these relationships. See the "Many-to-Many Relationships" section of the Core Data Programming Guide for more information.

Like attributes, relationships support optional and transient settings. For to-many relationships, we can also set the minimum and maximum number of entities in the relationship. Finally, we can specify a delete rule. Delete rules describe what happens to the relationship when we delete our entity. The different options are listed here:

- **Cascade:** Deleting the source object also deletes all the objects at the relationship's destination. For example, deleting a Course object also deletes all its Students.

- **Deny:** If there is at least one object at the relationship's destination, then the source object cannot be deleted. If we want to delete a Course entity, we must first remove all its Students.

- **Nullify:** Sets the inverse relationship for any entities at the destination to nil. Deleting the Course entity sets all the Students' Course relationship to nil.

- **No Action:** The entity at the other end remains unchanged. In general, this should be used only for unidirectional relationships. If it has an inverse relationship, that relationship now points to an entity that no longer exists. For example, our Students will still think they're registered for the now-nonexistent Course.

Fetched properties are similar to relationships, but they are used to model weak one-way connections between entities. As the name suggests, the fetched property's value is calculated using a fetch request. We will discuss fetch requests in more detail later this chapter, but basically fetch requests let us look up entities that match a given entity description. We can also apply a predicate to filter our results and then sort them according to a set of sort descriptors. For example, we could create a fetch request that returns all students (entity description) who are taking more than 18 credit hours (predicate), and then we could sort them by descending GPA (sort description).

Fetched properties use lazy initialization. The actual fetch is not performed until the property's value is accessed. However, once the value is calculated, it is cached for future use. Our system models fetch properties using arrays, not sets, since fetched properties have a defined sort order. Additionally, fetched properties are the only way to model cross-store relationships. Normal relationship properties can refer only to objects saved in the same persistent store.

In many ways, an entity description is similar to a class. It is a blueprint used to instantiate managed objects—and, like classes, entity descriptions support inheritance. If we have a number of similar entities, we can factor out the common properties into a super-entity. We can even explicitly declare abstract entities (something not explicitly supported by the Objective-C object model).

However, there are a few important differences between entity inheritance and object inheritance. Remember, the entities describe how our data is organized. We use the entities to create objects—but the resulting object inheritance tree is separate from our entity inheritance tree. For example, we will often use NSManagedObjects for all of our entities—superclasses and subclasses alike. If we are creating custom classes for our entities, we probably want the model's inheritance tree to match our entities—but that's not required, and it's something we will have to manage by hand.

Most importantly, however, entity inheritance can have unexpected performance implications. If we save our entities in an SQLite-based store, then the database will place our entire hierarchy in a single table. It will create a column for each property, requiring a table large enough to contain all the properties from all the different subentities.

If we have a large number of subentities and our subentities each add a significant number of unique properties, we may end up with large, sparsely populated tables. This can affect both the amount of disk space we need to store our entities and the performance of our fetch requests.

MIGRATING DATA

Changes to the schema may make the model incompatible with previously created data stores. When this happens, we need to migrate the old stores before we can open them. By default, Core Data manages this with a three-step process:

1. Model versioning
2. Mapping model
3. Data migration

Core data lets us create multiple versions of our managed object model. We can add a new version by selecting our managed object model and then selecting Editor > Add Model Version.

FIGURE 7.1 Adding a mapping model

Choose a template for your new file:

iOS			
Cocoa Touch			
C and C++	Data Model	Mapping Model	NSManagedObject
User Interface			subclass
Core Data			
Resource			
Other			

Mapping Model

A Core Data mapping model file that allows you to define rules used in store migration.

Cancel   Previous   Next

The mapping model describes how to transform the data from one version to the next. Typically, we add a new mapping model to our project by selecting File > New File and then selecting iOS > Core Data > Mapping Model (**Figure 7.1**). Xcode's mapping model editor allows us to graphically set the transformations between the source and destination models.

Finally, we must migrate the existing data from our old model to our new one. Most of the time, we will perform automatic migration by calling addPersistentStoreWithType:con figuration:URL:options:error: to open our persistent store. For the options: parameter, pass in an NSDictionary containing the NSMigratePersistentStoresAutomaticallyOption key with an NSNumber object set to YES.

```
NSDictionary *options =
@{NSMigratePersistentStoresAutomaticallyOption:@YES};
if (![self.persistentStoreCoordinator
      addPersistentStoreWithType:NSSQLiteStoreType
      configuration:nil
      URL:storeURL
      options:options
      error:&error]) {

    NSLog(@"Unable to open persistent store at %@, %@: %@",
          storeURL, error, [error userInfo]);
    abort();
}
```

LIGHTWEIGHT MIGRATION

In the simplest cases, we may not need a mapping model. Core Data can often infer the differences between the source and destination models and automatically migrate our data. In particular, we can perform any of the following:

- Add, remove, or rename entities or properties
- Make a nonoptional property optional
- Make an optional property nonoptional as long as it has a default value
- Make a to-one relationship a to-many relationship
- Change a nonordered relationship into an ordered relationship
- Create new parent or child entities
- Move entities up or down the entity hierarchy

In this case, open our persistent store by calling `addPersistentStoreWithType:configuration:URL:options:error:` and setting both the `NSMigratePersistentStoresAutomaticallyOption` and `NSInferMappingModelAutomaticallyOption` keys to YES.

Not surprisingly, data migration gets quite complex. To help manage this, Core Data provides additional support for injecting custom code when detecting version skew and while performing the actual data migration. See Apple's Core Data Model Versioning and Data Migration Programming Guide for more information.

Remember, not all changes require migration. We can change an attribute's default value or validation constraints without altering the existing stores. Additionally, we will want to test our data migration very carefully. We don't want to corrupt or lose our user's data. If you've ever updated an app only to have it erase all your data, you know exactly what I mean.

SUPPORT DATA

Our models can also contain two types of support data: fetch requests and configurations. While the entities represent the actual data stored in Core Data, the fetch requests and configurations represent different ways of searching through or partitioning that data.

Fetch requests let us request all the entities that match a given specification. While we often create our fetch requests at runtime, we may want to build complex or commonly used fetch requests directly into our model.

Xcode's fetch request editor can be helpful when creating complex requests. By default, we can create a list of expressions and return the entities where All, Any, or None of the expressions are true. However, by holding down the Option key, we can add a subconditional expression, allowing us to specify a subgroup where All, Any, or None of those subexpressions must be true (**Figure 7.2**).

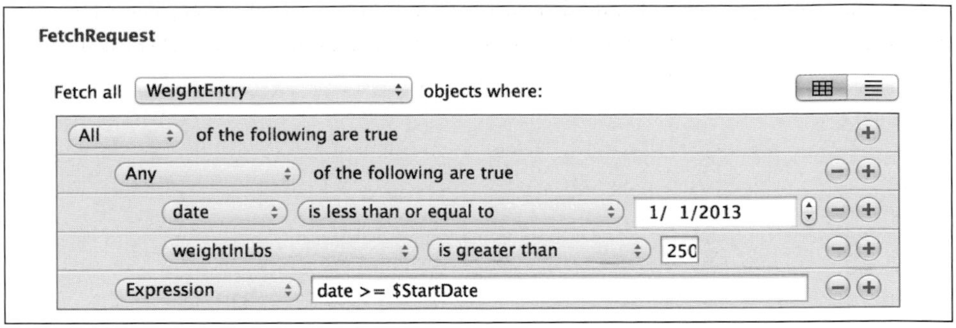

FIGURE 7.2 Creating
complex fetch requests

For each row, we can either select one of our attributes as the left expression and then specify a comparison operator and a constant value or select an expression type and provide a complex predicate expression, including substitution variables, using the predicate format string syntax (see the "Fetch Requests" section for more information on the predicate syntax).

When adding fetch requests to our model, there are a few limitations. As described earlier, we can include variables only in Expression lines. Additionally, we cannot add a sort description using the graphic interface. This isn't a huge problem, though, since we can use the editor to build the basic fetch request, and then we can add the sort descriptors at runtime, as necessary.

On the plus side, building the fetch request into our model can provide a significant performance increase over programmatically creating our fetched requests.

Next, we have configurations. Configurations are just arrays of entity descriptions. We access our configurations using NSManagedObjectModel's entitiesForConfiguration: and setEntities:forConfiguration: methods. We can then use the configurations to define subsets of our model. For example, a user logged in as an administrator may have access to a broader set of entities than someone logged in as a user.

Mostly, however, we use configurations when we want to split our model across several persistent data stores. In this case, we need to partition our model using configurations. Then we specify the correct configuration for each store as we add them to our persistent store coordinator. Core Data automatically saves each entity into the correct store.

MANAGED OBJECT CONTEXT

We now move from defining our data to actually managing it. The managed object context acts as a temporary scratch space. When we fetch objects from a persistent store, they are placed in the context. We can then manipulate them, change their properties, or even add or remove objects from the context. The managed object context monitors these changes, recording them and enabling undo/redo support. In addition, when we save these changes back to our persistent store, the context validates our objects, ensuring that everything remains in a valid state before committing the changes.

Each manage object context should be accessed only from a single thread. There are three different concurrency patterns that we can use to access our contexts. These can be passed to `initWithConcurrencyType:` when creating our context.

- `NSConfinementConcurrencyType:` This is the default concurrency type and is primarily used for backward compatibility. The developer is responsible for ensuring that the context is used only in the same thread that it was created in.

- `NSPrivateQueueConcurrencyType:` The context is created on a private queue. All access must be performed on that private queue.

- `NSMainQueueConcurrencyType:` The context is created on the main queue and can be accessed on the main queue. This can greatly simplify interactions between the context and the user interface.

Contexts using either private or main queue concurrency should be accessed using the `performBlock:` or `performBlockAndWait:` method. We call these methods on our context and pass in a block containing any other method calls on that context. This guarantees that the block of code will run on the correct queue.

We must use these block methods whenever we access a context with private queue concurrency—since we have no way of accessing the queue directly. If our context uses main queue concurrency and we're sure that our code will always run on the main queue, we can simply call the context's methods directly. However, it's generally recommended that we access a main queue context through the `performBlock...` methods as well.

We can open more than one managed object context at a time. In fact, an object in our persistent store may be modified by multiple contexts simultaneously. By default, the context will attempt to merge these changes, causing an error if there are conflicts. We can further control the merge process by changing the merge policy and by observing `NSManagedObjectContextObjectsDidChangeNotification` notifications. Note that the system may use its own managed object contexts internally, so we want to make sure we specify the correct context when we register as an observer. Otherwise, we may receive notifications from these system-level sources.

We can also create nested managed contexts, where each parent context may contain one or more child contexts. When connected this way, saving a child context merely pushes the changes up to the parent context. Data is not saved to the persistent store until the top-level context is saved. Fetch requests will pull data down through every context level, while `objectWithID:` will pull through the fewest number of contexts possible.

Nested contexts can greatly simplify a number of complex problems, including performing asynchronous saves on a background thread, sharing unsaved changes between different contexts, and even simplifying background fetching.

For example, to implement asynchronous saves, we simply need to create two managed object contexts with a simple parent-child relationship. Our application makes all its changes to the child context. When it wants to save, we start by saving the child context on the main queue. This creates a snapshot of our data—pushing our changes up to the parent context. Then we save the parent context on a private queue. As we will see, UIManagedDocument uses this technique when autosaving document data.

When creating hierarchies of managed object contexts, all parent contexts must use either private queue or main queue concurrency. The final child contexts can use any concurrency model.

NOTE: When creating a new project with Core Data enabled, the template's autogenerated code accesses the managed object context directly from the app delegate. This is somewhat unfortunate, since Apple's documentation recommends switching to a "pass the baton" approach, where the correct context is handed from object to object along the view controller hierarchy. This is especially true in any applications using multilayer contexts.

The template also creates the managed object context using confinement concurrency, instead of using the more modern private queue or main queue concurrency.

For these reasons, I do not recommend using the current Core Data templates unmodified. If you want to use the template, I'd definitely change the context's concurrency type. I'd also consider moving the core data stack out of the App Delegate.

MANAGED OBJECTS

All Core Data entities are instantiated as an NSManagedObject or one of its subclasses. Each managed object is associated with an entity description. This includes both the object's metadata and information about the managed object context where our object resides.

In many cases, we can simply use raw managed objects in our project. Each managed object will automatically generate both public and primitive accessors for all the modeled properties. For attributes and other to-one relationships, these follow the standard <key> and set<Key> naming conventions.

For to-many relationships, these accessors can be used to get and set the entire collection (as an NSSet or NSOrderedSet, depending on the type of to-many relationship). We can also request a mutable set using the mutableSetValueForKey: or mutableOrderedSetValueForKey: method. We can then add or remove entities from the mutable set—all changes will be made to the managed object context's object graph. Finally, we can use the dynamic relationship accessors add<Key>Object: and remove<Key>Object: (insertObject:in<Key>AtIndex: and removeObjectFrom<Key>atIndex: for ordered to-many relationships) to add or remove objects from the relationship directly.

NSManagedObject also creates primitive accessors. These take the form primitive<Key> and setPrimitive<Key>:. Unlike the public accessors, these do not trigger KVO notifications. We will typically use the primitive accessors when writing our own custom accessors. We will see some examples later.

While the autogenerated accessors are useful, they have a downside. Unfortunately, the compiler does not know about these methods, so it will generate warnings (and if you're following my advice, these warnings will be treated like errors, preventing your app from building successfully). There are a couple of ways around this. First, we can always use key-value coding to access data from raw managed objects. Alternatively, we could create a category on NSManagedObject that declares the properties and methods. Finally, we could create a custom subclass for our entity and explicitly declare these properties.

Making a custom subclass is easy—and, in my opinion, best expresses our intentions. Just select File > New > New File and select the iOS > Core Data > NSManagedObject subclass template. Xcode will automatically generate the properties for us and link our subclass to its entity in the managed object model.

Custom subclasses are particularly important when we need to implement custom accessors or validation methods, implement nonstandard attributes, specify dependent keys, calculate derived values, or implement other custom logic. However, there are a few points we should keep in mind when subclassing NSManagedObject.

- Core Data relies on NSManagedObject's implementation of these methods to function properly: primitiveValueForKey:, setPrimitiveValue:forKey:, isEqual:, hash, superclass, class, self, zone, isProxy, isKindOfClass:, isMemberOfClass:, conformsToProtocol:, respondsToSelector:, managedObjectContext, entity, objectID, isInserted, isUpdated, isDeleted, and isFault. We should never override any of these methods.

- We are discouraged from overriding the following methods: description, initWith Entity:insertIntoManagedObjectContext:, valueForKey:, and setValue:forKeyPath:. If they are not handled properly, they can cause unexpected results.

- We should invoke the superclass's implementation before executing our own code for the following methods: awakeFromInsert, awakeFromFetch, and validation methods like validateForUpdate:.

- We can override the awakeFromInsert and awakeFromFetch methods to perform any custom initialization when a new object is created or when an object is loaded from the persistent store, respectively.

- We should not provide instance variables for any properties in the model. Core Data will automatically manage the life cycles of these objects.

- The declaration for any object properties should use (nonatomic, retain). Alternatively, we can declare scalar properties for any data types that support scalar types (the various integer and floating-point numbers, as well as Booleans and Dates); these properties should be declared using (nonatomic). In both cases, we should use the @dynamic property implementation directive for all of these. NSManagedObject will create the correct accessors based on our declaration.

- If we create custom accessors for any modeled properties, we must manually trigger KVO access and change notifications by calling willAccessValueForKey:, didAccessValueForKey:, willChangeValueForKey:, didChangeValueForKey:, willChangeValueForKey:withSetMutation:usingObjects:, and didChangeValue ForKey:withSetMutation:usingObjects:, as appropriate. Core Data disables automatic KVO notification for any modeled properties.

NOTE: Even though we're using ARC, we can use `(nonatomic, retain)` to declare the properties generated by our managed object context. Actually, `(strong, nonatomic)` also works, but Xcode will use `(nonatomic, retain)` in its autogenerated code. Remember, Core Data manages the object's life cycle, so we don't need to think too hard about what it's doing behind the scenes.

NONSTANDARD ATTRIBUTES

We often create custom subclasses when we want to implement nonstandard attributes. There are two ways of doing this. The first is to set the attribute's type to transformable and then assign an `NSValueTransformer` that can convert the class to and from an `NSData` object. The vast majority of the time, we can simply use the default transformer—just make sure the properties adopt the `NSCoding` protocol. Everything will just work.

If we need more control, we can create custom accessors. Typically, we declare two attributes. One is the nonstandard attribute. We declare this as transient with an undefined type. The other attribute must be a standard, concrete type—this will hold the actual data that is saved to our persistent store. Then we write our accessor methods to convert our data back and forth between the two attributes.

Let's say we want to add a nonstandard `NSTimeZone` attribute to our entity. `NSTimeZone` adopts the `NSCoding` protocol, so the simplest approach is to just declare it as a transformable attribute. We can then declare the property in our custom subclass, as shown here:

```
@property (nonatomic, retain) NSTimeZone* timeZone;
```

Then, in the `@implementation` block, declare the property as dynamic. This tells the compiler that the accessors' implementations will be provided at runtime (if not earlier). Remember, `NSManagedObject` automatically creates these accessors for us.

```
@dynamic timeZone;
```

That's it. Core Data will automatically handle the conversion to and from an `NSData` object.

Next, let's look at implementing the same nonstandard attribute using custom accessors. This time add both a transient, undefined `timeZone` attribute and a string `timeZoneName` attribute. In our `NSManagedObject` subclass's `@interface`, declare the `timeZone` property as shown in the previous example. However, in the implementation file, start by declaring two private properties.

```
@interface MyManagedObject()
@property (nonatomic, retain) NSString * timeZoneName;
@property (nonatomic, retain) NSTimeZone* primitiveTimeZone;
@end
```

Then, in the implementation block, declare the two private properties as dynamic.

```
@dynamic timeZoneName;
@dynamic primitiveTimeZone;
```

Since we will be implementing our own custom accessors for the `timeZone` property, we don't need to call the @dynamic directive. Instead, just implement the methods as shown here:

```objc
- (NSTimeZone*)timeZone
{
    // Get transient value.
    [self willAccessValueForKey:@"timeZone"];
    NSTimeZone* timeZone = self.primitiveTimeZone;

    // If we have no transient value,
    // try to generate it from the persistent value.
    if (timeZone == nil)
    {
        // Get the persistent value.
        NSString* name = self.timeZoneName;
        if (name != nil)
        {
            timeZone = [NSTimeZone timeZoneWithName:name];
            // Set the transient value.
            self.primitiveTimeZone = timeZone;
        }
    }
    [self didAccessValueForKey:@"timeZone"];
    return timeZone;
}
- (void)setTimeZone:(NSTimeZone *)timeZone
{
    // Set transient value.
    [self willChangeValueForKey:@"timeZone"];
    self.primitiveTimeZone = timeZone;

    // Set persistent value.
    self.timeZoneName = [timeZone name];
    [self didChangeValueForKey:@"timeZone"];
}
```

The getter simply calls the autogenerated `primitiveTimeZone` method to access our transient attribute's current value. Remember, unlike the other attributes, timeZone is transient. Its value is not loaded from the persistent store. If we haven't programmatically set it, its value defaults to nil. In this case, we try to create a new NSTimeZone object using the value stored in our private timeZoneName attribute. We then set the timeZone's value and return that value. The next time we call `timeZone`, we will be able to pull the value directly from the `timeZone` attribute.

The setter is even simpler. Here, we first set our `timeZone` attribute, and then we set the underlying `timeZoneName` attribute. Remember, in both accessors we need to send out the proper KVO notifications.

These are probably the simplest implementations, but there are other possibilities. We could precalculate the `timeZone` attribute during the `awakeFromFetch` method, or we could delay setting the `timeZoneName` attribute until the `willSave` method is called. Both of these approaches are shown in the "Nonstandard Persistent Attributes" section of Apple's Core Data Programming Guide.

NOTE: Although we declared the `timeZoneName` attribute as private in our sample `NSManagedObject` subclass, this is not necessarily required. We could declare a public read-only property for `timeZoneName`. We could even declare it as publicly read/writeable—however, this complicates things. We would need to make sure our `timeZone` value is updated whenever the `timeZoneName` value is changed. We would also need to make sure our implementation is KVO compliant by declaring `timeZone` as a dependent key.

A hybrid approach is sometimes useful when trying to save nonobject values. This is especially true for structures that are supported by the `NSValue` class (for example, `CGPoint`, `CGRect`, and `CGSize`). Here, we simply define the attribute as a transformable type and then write custom accessors to convert the structs to and from an `NSValue` object.

However, while these approaches can simplify the interface, they are not generally recommended. Core Data tries to optimize its autogenerated accessors. The performance advantages gained by letting Core Data manage its own data usually outweigh any ease of use that is granted by dealing directly with the structs. This is especially true in data-intensive applications.

FETCH REQUESTS

We access our managed objects using an `NSFetchRequest`. We can create a fetch request in two basic ways: using `+[NSFetchRequest fetchRequestWithEntityName:]` to programmatically create a basic fetch of all the objects of a given entity type and then configuring and fine-tuning our request or loading a fetch request by calling either `-[NSManagedObjectModel fetchRequestTemplateForName:]` or `-[NSManagedObjectModel fetchRequestFromTemplate WithName:substitutionVariables:]`.

NOTE: `fetchRequestTemplateForName:` returns an immutable fetch request. If we want to modify it further (for example, adding sort descriptors), we need to copy it and modify the copy.

Once we have our fetch request, we call the `executeFetchRequest:error:`, which returns an array containing all instances of the entities matching our request, including any subentities of our named entity.

FORMATTING STRING PLACEHOLDERS VS. SUBSTITUTION VARIABLES

When dealing with predicate strings, we have two different types of variables. Substitution variables begin with a $. A predicate with one or more substitution variables is called a *predicate template*. We cannot use templates directly. Instead, we use it to create an actual predicate with actual values by calling methods like `predicateWithSubstitutionVariables:`.

We often use substitution variables when writing expressions in the fetch request editor. The variables are replaced when we load the fetch request from our model using `fetchReq uestFromTemplateWithName:substitutionVariables:`.

Format string placeholders also let us pass data into a predicate at runtime. They begin with a %. We use these placeholders when creating predicates programmatically using formatting strings. They are replaced immediately using the arguments that follow the formatting string. The values are placed into the string first, and the resulting string is parsed and converted to a predicate. This produces a ready-to-use predicate, but the placeholder values are now fixed and cannot be changed.

The fetch will return objects based on their state in the managed object context—even if these changes have not yet been saved. This means a fetch will return new objects added to the context and will not return any objects deleted from the context. Likewise, the system will evaluate predicates based on the object's in-memory state—not its saved state. Of course, if we haven't yet loaded the objects into managed object context, then the fetch request loads them from their persistent store.

We have a lot of control over which objects are returned and how they are organized. By adding an `NSPredicate` to our fetch request, we can set constraints on our request. Our fetch request will return only those entities that match our predicate. An array of `NSSortDescrip-tors` defines the order in which our objects are returned.

Predicates are a rich and complex topic. While Interface Builder's fetch request editor can help create complex fetch requests—we need to be comfortable writing our own predicate expressions if we want to use it effectively. This is particularly true, since the editor can be used only to create stored fetch requests, not fetched properties. This means we still need to learn how to write our own predicate expressions.

PREDICATES

Basically, a predicate is a logical operator. When the predicate is evaluated on an object, it performs the specified comparison and then returns YES or NO.

We can build our `NSPredicate` object using a combination of `NSComparisonPredicate`, `NSCompoundPredicate`, and `NSExpression` objects; however, it's usually easier to create our predicate using a formatting string. The `NSPredicate` class then parses this string and builds a predicate to match.

The predicate parser is whitespace insensitive. It is also case insensitive when it comes to keywords, and it supports nested parenthetical expressions. The simplest predicates have three parts: the left expression, a comparison, and the right expression.

These expressions can be constants, key paths, or variables. Most of the time, we will compare one of the object's key paths against a constant. String constants can be typed directly into the formatting string, but they must be surrounded by quotes (either double or single quotes work). Most of the other values (for example, NSDate or NSNumber) are passed in using the %@ formatting placeholder. We can even pass in string constants using %@, and the parser will automatically quote them for us.

The comparison includes most of what we expect: ==, <, >, <=, >=, and !=. The parser often understands common variations for these. For example, the following comparisons are also valid: =, =<, =>, and <>. The parser also adds the BETWEEN comparison—whose right side must be a two-value array, though it seems to work only with numeric data.

For strings, we have the BEGINSWITH, CONTAINS, ENDSWITH, LIKE, and MATCHES comparisons. Most of these should be relatively straightforward. LIKE simply checks to see whether the left string is equal to the right string. However, it supports the ? and * wildcards for matching a single character or zero or more characters. MATCHES, on the other hand, treats the right value as a regular expression. Appending [cd] to the end of the comparison makes it case and diacritic insensitive.

A few sample predicates are shown here:

```
// Determines if the object's lastName attribute equals @"Jones".
[NSPredicate predicateWithFormat:@"lastName LIKE 'Jones'"];
```

```
// Determines if the object's pubDate occurred before
// the given targetDate.
[NSPredicate predicateWithFormat:@"pubDate < %@", targetDate];
```

```
// Determines if the person is in our target demographics.
[NSPredicate predicateWithFormat:@"age BETWEEN %@",
 @[@18, @34]];
```

Note that we can also include literal array constants by placing a comma-separated list of values inside curly braces. This means that the target demographics example could also be written as shown here:

```
// Determines if the person is in our target demographics.
[NSPredicate predicateWithFormat:@"age BETWEEN {%@, %@}",
 @18, @34];
```

The key paths can even include to-many relationships. Often we will prefix these expressions with one of the aggregate operators, ANY, ALL, or NONE, as shown here:

```
// The target has at least one child under 18.
[NSPredicate predicateWithFormat:@"ANY children.age < 18"];
```

```
// All the target's children are under 18.
[NSPredicate predicateWithFormat:@"ALL children.age < 18"];
```

```
// None of the target's children are under 18.
[NSPredicate predicateWithFormat:@"NONE children.age < 18"];
```

We can also check the size of the to-many relationship by appending [size] to the key path.

```
// Determines if the target has at least 3 children.
[NSPredicate predicateWithFormat:@"children[size] < 3"];
```

Finally, we can combine simple comparisons using AND, OR, or NOT.

```
// Determines if the target has at least 3 children
// and all their children are above the specified age
[NSPredicate predicateWithFormat:
 @"(children[size] < 3) AND (NONE children.age < %@)", @(ageLimit)];
```

These formatting strings allow us to specify a wide range of predicates in a relatively compact format. Unfortunately, it's easy to accidentally misspell a key path or inadvertently pass in the wrong type of object. These mistakes will show up only as runtime errors. It is, therefore, important to test all our predicates.

Additionally, not all data sources support all of NSPredicate's features. This is particularly important for Core Data, since the predicate's behavior can change when we switch from one type of persistent store to another. This also means the behavior may change depending on whether we use the predicate in a fetch request or use it to filter the returned NSArray. We'll talk about these differences more in the "Persistent Stores" section, later in this chapter.

> **NOTE:** Each fetch request requires a round-trip to the persistent store. Therefore, if we need to get a subset of objects, it may be faster to filter an existing array than to perform a new fetch request. Additionally, we cannot perform fetch requests using predicates based on transient attributes, since these attributes are not saved to the persistent store. We can, however, use transient attributes when filtering arrays of objects in memory.

Finally, iOS provides additional support for Core Data–driven table views using the NSFetchedResultsController class. This class analyzes the results of a fetch request (including any predicate or sorting descriptors) and automatically maps the returned objects to their corresponding index paths. We can even specify a key path that will be used to partition the results into sections.

In addition, the NSFetchedResultsController monitors changes to the objects in its managed object context and reports these changes to its delegate. The controller also caches its results, improving performance if the table is redisplayed.

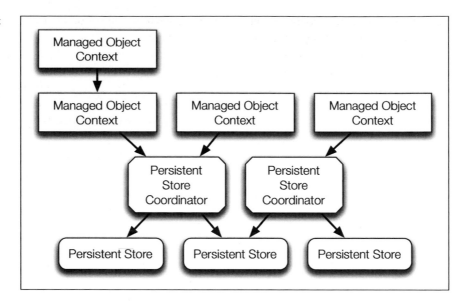

FIGURE 7.3 Persistent store coordinators in the Core Data stack

Managed Object Context

Managed Object Context

Managed Object Context

Managed Object Context

Persistent Store Coordinator

Persistent Store Coordinator

Persistent Store

Persistent Store

Persistent Store

PERSISTENT STORE COORDINATOR

Each managed object context has a single persistent store coordinator. This coordinator sits between the context and the stores. Each managed object context can have one and only one persistent store coordinator. The coordinator, however, can support more than one context. It can also connect to any number of persistent stores (**Figure 7.3**).

The persistent store coordinator primarily acts as a façade for a number of stores. We could have just a single persistent store, or we could have a hundred. As far as the managed object context is concerned, it doesn't matter. The persistent store coordinator provides a single, unified interface, presenting the union of all the data in all the provided stores.

The persistent store coordinator also serializes access to its stores. If multiple contexts are accessing the coordinator from different threads, they must lock and unlock the coordinator. If we want true multithreaded access, each thread should have its own persistent store coordinator. Therefore, we often create a separate store coordinator (and its corresponding managed object context) when we want to load or modify data in the background.

PERSISTENT STORES

Persistent stores act as a wrapper for a data source (usually a file saved to disk). The store is responsible for mapping objects in the managed object context to the data in the data source—both saving objects to disk and instantiating objects from disk. iOS supports three types of persistent stores: atomic, in-memory, and SQLite.

All three stores are fast, especially when compared to plists or other XML-based storage. The atomic format stores the object graph in a single binary file. As a result, the persistent store must load the whole object graph into memory at once. In most cases, however, this produces the smallest file size of any data store. As the name suggests, atomic stores also write out their data as an atomic action—either the entire file will be written or nothing will be written. We will never get corrupted data from a half-written file.

The in-memory store acts more like a virtual scratch space. It does not store the objects to disk; rather, it keeps them in active memory. Objects placed into an in-memory store benefit from Core Data features such as validation, change tracking, and undo support; however, if we want to persist this data, we would have to write additional code to load and save these objects outside Core Data.

Most of the time we will use the SQLite persistent stores. This has a significant advantage over the other stores: We do not need to load the entire object graph into memory. We load only the objects we actually intend to use.

By default, a fetch request to an SQLite-based store instantiates only the objects it returns. All the relationships for those objects are represented by faults. Basically, a fault is a placeholder for an object or array. If we access the fault, it fires, and Core Data uses lazy initialization to instantiate an actual copy of the object. Most of the time this occurs transparently behind the scenes. The NSFetchRequest class includes a number of methods to manage whether the request returns faults or objects, how many objects it returns, and whether any of the objects' relationships are also prefetched.

While faults help us save memory by letting us limit the number of objects we need to load, firing faults can be inefficient, particularly if we fire a number of faults in series. If we know we're going to need a large number of faulted objects, it is better to batch fire all the faults or prefetch all the objects.

To batch fire a number of faults, we just need to create a fetch request to load those objects. Of course, this means that all our faults must be of the same entity type. Simply build an array containing the faulted relationships, and then build a predicate using the IN operator as shown here:

```
NSArray* faults =@[fault1, fault2, fault3];
NSPredicate* predicate =
[NSPredicate predicateWithFormat:@"self IN %@", faults];
```

Alternatively, we can use NSFetchRequest's setRelationshipKeyPathsForPrefetching: method. This lets us set an array of key paths. All the relationships represented by those key paths are also instantiated as full objects when the fetch is executed. This lets us prefetch objects that we know we are going to need.

We have to be careful with this, however. It is easy to accidentally grab more memory than we originally intended. As always, it's a good idea to profile our code. Looking at actual performance numbers will help us find the right balance between runtime performance and memory usage.

We can also reduce memory overhead by refaulting individual objects. To do this, call the managed object context's refreshObject:mergeChanges: method. If the mergeChanges: flag is set to NO, then the object is converted back into a fault, and all pending changes are lost. In addition, all of the object's relationships are released—possibly trimming them from the in-memory object graph as well.

Faulting is just one of many differences between SQLite and other stores. With non-SQLite stores (and when working with NSArrays or other collections), the system executes both predicates and search descriptors in Objective-C. This means we have full access to NSStrings comparison methods. We can even incorporate our own Objective-C code by providing a custom selector or NSComparator block for our sort descriptor or by creating a predicate using the predicateWithBlock: method.

When using SQLite stores, however, the predicates and sort descriptors are translated into SQL and executed by the database. We cannot use predicates or sort descriptors that incorporate custom Objective-C code. SQLite supports only the following NSString sort selectors: compare:, caseInsensitiveCompare:, localizedCompare:, localizedCaseIn-sensitiveCompare:, and localizedStandardCompare:. Finally, key paths in predicates can include only a single to-many relationship. But we can string together any number of to-one relationships and attributes with the to-many relationship (**Table 7.2**).

TABLE 7.2 Sample Key Path Patterns

VALID	INVALID
<to_one>.<to_one>.<to_many>	<to_many>.<to_one>.<to_many>
<to_one>.<to_many>.<to_one>	<to_many>.<to_many>.<to_one>
<to_many>.<to_one>.<to_one>	<to_one>.<to_many>.<to_many>
<to_one>.<to_one>.<to_one>	<to_many>.<to_many>.<to_many>

Remember that if we need additional features, we can always perform a more general fetch request and then execute the custom sorting and filtering on the resulting array. This wastes memory, but sometimes you just gotta do what you gotta do.

NOTE: I lied. There is one other type of persistent store, the custom incremental stores. This lets us build our own stores. We create a subclass of NSIncrementalStore and override methods to support data access. This lets us build Core Data wrappers to data storage technology of our choice. It can provide a slick way to connect Core Data to a web service.

DATA PROTECTION

Persistent stores encrypt the data on disk. The persistent stores support a range of encryption options.

- `NSFileProtectionNone:` Turns off encryption.

- `NSFileProtectionComplete:` Provides the tightest security. The files can be accessed only after the device is authenticated and as long as the device is unlocked. Unfortunately, this can prevent our app from accessing the data while operating in the background.

- `NSFileProtectionCompleteUnlessOpen:` Prevents access to files unless the device is authenticated and unlocked. Our application can continue to access any open files while locked; however, we cannot open new files.

- `NSFileProtectionCompleteUntilFirstUserAuthentication:` Prevents access to files while the device is booting and until the user authenticates with her password. However, once the user authenticates, the files remain accessible, even if the device is later locked.

Core Data will use `NSFileProtectionCompleteUntilFirstUserAuthentication` by default. We can change the protection level by assigning a value to the `NSPersistentStore` `FileProtectionKey` when configuring our persistent store.

UIMANAGEDDOCUMENT

`UIManagedDocument` is a concrete subclass of `UIDocument` that is specifically designed for managing Core Data. `UIManagedDocument` greatly simplifies the setup of a Core Data model. It will automatically merge all model objects in the application bundle and then use the combined model to create and manage our complete Core Data stack. By default, this stack includes an SQLite-based persistent store, a persistent store coordinator, and a two-layer managed object context.

The two-level context helps support asynchronous background saves. The child layer uses main queue concurrency, letting us interact with this context directly on the main thread. `UIManagedDocument` monitors changes made to this context and automatically saves the changes at a convenient point during the application's run cycle.

When it decides to save changes, it starts by making a snapshot of the changes, by simply saving the child context. This pushes the current batch of changes up to the parent context. Then, the document saves the parent context on a private background queue. This actually saves the changes to disk.

Much of the time, we can use `UIManagedDocument` without further subclassing. We simply instantiate a new `UIManagedDocument` object and then set the options for the persistent store. Finally, we call `openWithCompletionHandler:` to open an existing document, or we call `saveToURL:forSaveOperation:completionHandler:` to create a new document. We will also want to listen for the document state change notifications.

We can subclass `UIManagedDocument` to further modify its default behaviors. For example, we can change the name of the persistent store in our document package. We can change the type of persistent store or modify how the document models or stores are created. We can even enable support for saving and loading data from outside Core Data.

Apple recommends using `UIManagedDocument` for all document-style Core Data applications. These are applications that can save or load multiple Core Data documents.

I actually recommend using `UIManagedDocument` for all Core Data applications, library- and document-style alike. It simplifies creating the Core Data stack, and I like the automatic background saves. Furthermore, as noted earlier, Xcode's Core Data application templates still use somewhat outdated code to set up and manage the Core Data stack. `UIManaged Document` provides a nice, concise alternative to the default templates.

CORE DATA PERFORMANCE

Core Data is a mature, efficient object graph management framework. Its classes have been highly optimized. For example, `NSManagedObject` instances use reflection to examine their internal data. The managed object then leverages this information to optimize access to this data. Therefore, accessing values from an `NSManagedObject` is often faster than comparable accessors on generic Objective-C objects.

SQLite-based persistent stores help us minimize the number of objects held in active memory, letting us fetch and hold only the objects we need. This is especially important for iOS applications, since memory management remains one of our key concerns.

Still, there are some key points to remember to avoid poor performance.

FETCH REQUESTS

Fetch requests are expensive. They start by accessing the data from the persistent store. Then they merge this data with the existing data in the managed object context. Most of the time, we want to reduce the total number of fetches. In general, this means combining groups of smaller fetches into a single larger fetch.

However, there are times when we want to quickly return a small subset of the data and then fill in the rest while the system is idle. We might do this, for example, when filling in a table view.

We can restrict the number of objects loaded into memory by setting either `setFetchLimit:` or `setFetchBatchSize:`. In both cases, the full fetch is calculated, and all the other objects are returned as faults. When calling `setFetchLimit:`, we can manually load the remaining objects by calling `setFetchOffset:` to the first fault and then setting the fetch limit to 0. A second fetch will then grab the remaining objects.

Setting the batch size, on the other hand, returns a proxy array that automatically faults new batches as needed. Each time it performs a fetch, it grabs another batch-sized group of objects.

FAULTING

When a fault fires, it acts like a fetch request, except only a single object is returned. This becomes very expensive if we accidentally iterate over an array of faults, firing each one individually. Instead, we need to batch fault or prefetch our data to reduce the total number of trips to the persistent store (see "Persistent Stores" for more information).

Note that we can safely call the following methods on a fault without causing it to fire: `isEqual:`, `hash`, `superclass`, `class`, `self`, `zone`, `isProxy`, `isKindOfClass:`, `isMemberOfClass:`, `conformsToProtocol:`, `respondsToSelector:`, `description`, `managedObjectContext`, `entity`, `objectID`, `isInserted`, `isUpdated`, `isDeleted`, and `isFault`.

Among other things, this means we can freely store faults into collections. However, we must treat these collections carefully. It is easy to accidentally trigger faults when calling the collection's methods. Anything that accesses the data stored in the collection or calls `valueForKey:` on the collection's objects will trigger faults—most likely triggering all the faults in the entire array.

REDUCING MEMORY OVERHEAD

In general, unless we have a good reason to do otherwise, we should always use an SQLite-based store. We should also avoid loading more objects into memory than is absolutely necessary. I also recommend saving changes as we go—rather than letting unsaved changes accumulate in the managed object context. This also helps free up memory and can help avoid problems with overly long save times.

By default, the Managed Object Context retains only the objects that have unsaved changes. All other objects have weak references. This means that just because we fetch an object doesn't mean the object will stick around. We need to make sure some other part of our application has a strong reference to the object, if we want it to stay in memory. For example, an `NSFetchedResultsController` will keep a strong reference to the objects it has fetched.

Managed objects also create strong references to all the objects in their relationships. Unfortunately, this can easily create retain cycles, which will prevent objects from being released from memory. If we find that we're unexpectedly accumulating a large number of objects in memory, we can break these cycles by refaulting the objects.

We can manually refault objects by calling the context's `refreshObject:mergeChanges:` method. We can also clear the entire managed object context by calling its `reset` method.

> **NOTE:** Calling `reset` on the managed object context will invalidate any objects currently in the context. Be sure to dispose of all references we have to these objects before resetting. Accidentally holding onto these references will produce dangling pointers, leading to errors that are bizarre, intermittent, and otherwise difficult to debug.

LARGE DATA OBJECTS

Adding large binary objects (that is, images, sounds, videos, and so on) to a persistent store can severely affect performance. Here we get into an area that's more art than science. How large is large? Well, the answer really depends on how our application uses the data. If we're loading only one or two objects into memory at a time, then large attributes may not be a problem. If we're loading hundreds or thousands, we really need to think things through.

In general there are three approaches. We can store the object directly in the Core Data store as an attribute. This is usually recommended only for small binary objects.

Next, we can create a separate entity for the data and refer to it using a to-one relationship. This can be particularly helpful if the binary data isn't always used. When our object is fetched, the to-one relationship will be a fault. Core Data won't load the binary data unless we actually need it. This is recommended for modestly sized data objects.

Finally, we can store the data object directly in the device's file system and save the path in the database. We then manually load the data when necessary. This is recommended for the largest objects.

As a rule of thumb, if your object is measured in kilobytes, it's probably modest; if it's measured in megabytes, it's large. However, this is an area where we definitely want performance testing. Just remember, the end users often use applications in unexpected ways. Don't be surprised when they add 100,000 entities to the persistent store or try to load a 10MB text file. Try to test these extremes, if possible.

Fortunately, Core Data can help simplify this. Binary data attributes now have an Allows External Storage checkbox. Simply select this when configuring the attribute. The system will heuristically decide whether to store our binary data directly in the database or to simply store a URL and load the file as needed. All of this is transparently handled behind the scenes. There is, however, one small restriction: Once external storage is enabled, we cannot use the binary data in our fetch request's predicate.

TOOLS

Performance testing is covered in more detail in the "Other Tools of the Trade" bonus chapter, which can be found at `www.freelancemadscience.com/creating-ios-7-apps-bonus-chap/`. However, it's worth noting that Instruments has a number of tools to help troubleshoot Core Data performance issues. These include instruments to track Core Data fetches, saves, faults, and cache misses. We will want to use these in conjunction with the regular allocations, leaks, and time profile when testing our application.

As always, we should focus on getting the application working properly first and then try to optimize the code based on actual performance data. Premature optimization often wastes time without producing any tangible results.

iCLOUD SUPPORT

Core Data provides easy integration with iCloud. The iCloud support focuses on managing many of the details that were dealt with in Chapter 6. If we're using a single centralized Core Data store—what the documentation refers to as a *library-style application*—then setup is simple: Set a single option when creating the persistent store coordinator and then listen and respond to a few notifications, and we're done. Everything else is handled automatically. There's no need to use NSMetadataQuery to search for the file, Core Data will track the database's location for us. Core Data will also merge our conflicts automatically. We won't even need to tell the application how to save and load our data. Core Data handles it all.

> **NOTE:** If our application lets users save multiple documents and each document is its own iCloud store, things get a tad bit more difficult. We will need NSMetadataQuery to search for DocumentMetadata.plist. This file will be inside each document package. We can then use NSPersistentStoreUbiquitousContentNameKey to request the content name for our store—and then use that value to open the store.

When using Core Data with SQLite stores, each application manages its own local database, and the database is never uploaded into iCloud storage. Instead, each database saves transaction log files and uploads the log files. Other copies of the application can then identify and download these log files, using them to update their local database. This also means the file is only uploading deltas—the differences between the files on a per-entry basis. This greatly minimizes the amount of data that Core Data transmits between the app and iCloud.

iCloud also uses three-way merges to automatically resolve conflicts on a per-entry basis. Here, the system compares both of the conflicting copies with the original. This allows for a much more accurate and autonomous merging.

For example, look at the two-way merge we implemented in Chapter 6. Imagine a case where a WeightEntry object is present in version A but missing from version B. Our two-way merge had no way of telling whether this entry had been added to A or deleted from B. So, we erred on the side of caution, always choosing to keep the mismatched entry.

A three-way merge, on the other hand, can positively identify whether the entry had been added or deleted. This means it can take the proper steps when merging. If the object had been added to A, it should be included in the merged version. If it had been deleted from B, it should be removed.

Core Data also manages our data's versions for us. It will only sync data between apps running the same model version. That means, if we change our data model in an app update, users won't be able to sync until they update all their devices. While that's a little inconvenient, it's actually much better than the alternative—which is having our devices pass two different versions of the data back and forth.

SETTING UP iCLOUD SYNCING

To set up a centralized Core Data store, we simply set the NSPersistentStoreUbiquitous-ContentNameKey. This is roughly equivalent to the store's file name. Each store, for each application, must have its own, unique name.

Next, we need to listen to the following notifications: NSPersistentStoreCoordinator StoresWillChangeNotification, NSPersistentStoreCoordinatorStoresDidChange Notification, and NSPersistentStoreDidImportUbiquitousContentChangesNotification.

NSPersistentStoreCoordinatorStoresWillChangeNotification is sent when the user logs out of iCloud, disables iCloud Document Storage, or logs in as a different user. At this point, we still have access to the old persistent store—but it is going away soon. We must save any changes and reset our managed object contexts.

Note that these saves are stored locally. We no longer have access to the Ubiquity Container, so they cannot be synced. However, the next time the account becomes available, they will be transferred and synced as normal.

Also, this notification is sent on a background thread, and everything we do must be done synchronously to guarantee that we will still have access to our old persistent store. The store will be deallocated once this method returns.

NSPersistentStoreCoordinatorStoresDidChangeNotification is sent once the new store is available. We can use this method to update our user interface, if necessary.

Finally, NSPersistentStoreDidImportUbiquitousContentChangesNotification is sent after importing updates from iCloud. We need to update our managed object context so that it has a current copy of the correct data.

iCLOUD AND THE FALLBACK STORE

Creating a persistent store and linking it to the Ubiquity Container can take a considerable amount of time. As we saw in the previous chapter, access to the Ubiquity Container could be blocked temporarily. In addition, the system will try to connect to the iCloud servers and make sure everything is in a valid state before setting up the final, iCloud store.

To solve this problem, iOS 7 will start by creating a fallback store. This is a purely local store that the user can interact with while the iCloud store is being set up. Then, once the Ubiquity Container is ready, it will automatically switch to the iCloud store.

You may recognize this design pattern. It's the same basic pattern that we used (some might say, stole) in the previous chapter. However, Core Data is able to integrate and manage things much more effectively under the hood.

For example, Core Data automatically manages the user's ID for us. It will create a separate fallback and iCloud store pair for each ID. Furthermore, if the user isn't logged into iCloud or if document storage is disabled, it will use a default "local" ID. We no longer need to worry about checking and tracking the IDs ourselves.

The fallback store is used only the first time the application is launched and in response to changes to the user ID. Otherwise, the iCloud store will open immediately.

NOTE: The iCloud store is a local SQLite database saved inside our application's sandbox. Only the transaction logs get synced to the Ubiquity Container. Unfortunately, this approach is considerably different from the recommended best practices for previous versions of iOS. For example, in iOS 6, Apple's documentation recommended saving the SQLite store inside a `.nosync` directory in our Ubiquity Container. You may still see this recommendation in online tutorials, and even in Apple's documentation. However, unless you are explicitly supporting iOS 6, it is no longer recommended. Instead, we should just let Core Data manage both the fallback and the iCloud store for us.

The first time we run the application on a device, we will see the following:

1. The Store Did Change notification is sent, indicating that our fallback store is available and ready to use.

2. The system will print a message to the console. It will look something like the following:

```
-[PFUbiquitySwitchboardEntryMetadata setUseLocalStorage:](754): CoreData:
→ Ubiquity: mobile~C9C8554A-BD44-43C3-AC54-603046EF0162:com~freelancemad
→ science~HealthBeat
Using local storage: 1
```

The most important part of the message is the last line. `Using local storage: 1` means we're currently running on the fallback store.

3. The system will set up the iCloud store in the background. This can take several minutes, especially if the system has a lot of cleanup work to do.

4. The persistent store coordinator sends a Store Will Change notification, letting us know we need to save all the changes to our fallback store.

5. The coordinator sends a Store Did Change notification, letting us know we can update our UI with the complete contents of our new iCloud store.

6. Finally, the system will print another message to the console. This time it will say `Using local storage: 0`, indicating that we are now running on the iCloud store.

The next time the application launches, we will just get a single Store Did Change notification, followed by the two log messages to the console, one right after the other. However, if the user logs out, disables iCloud Document Storage, or logs into a different account, we will see the following:

1. The system prints `Using local storage: 1`, indicating that we're back on our fallback store.

2. We get a Store Will Change notification, letting us save changes to the fallback store.

3. We get a Store Did Change notification, letting us know the old store is gone.

4. Then the system sets up our new store. If iCloud is not available, we will simply get a second Store Did Change notification, and we're up and running on a local store. If iCloud is available, we go through the entire first launch procedure again (setting up a fallback store and then switching to the iCloud store).

iCLOUD LIMITATIONS

Now for the bad news. Using Core Data on iCloud imposes the following restrictions:

- No support for ordered relationships.
- We cannot use mapping models to migrate our schema. Lightweight migration is still OK.
- When creating a new store, we should not populate it with a preexisting database file. If we need to seed some initial data, we should either programmatically create the data in code or use NSPersistentStoreCoordinator's `migratePersistentStore:toURL:options :withType:error:` to move the data from an existing store to our iCloud store.

iCLOUD'S RELIABILITY

Over the past two years, iCloud has received a lot of bad press in the Apple developer community. Most of this has focused on using iCloud to sync Core Data documents.

One of the biggest problems has been the system's opacity. It's hard to tell what's going on behind the scenes. As a result, when things don't work as expected, it's difficult to determine whether the problem is developer error or an actual bug in the framework. Worse yet, the more complex the data, the more likely the developers were to run into suspicious problems.

However, over the last few years Apple's engineers have worked hard to improve the system. They've removed a number of bugs, and they've tried to make the entire system more streamlined and more transparent. All of this hard work definitely shows.

The iOS 7 implementation of Core Data iCloud syncing is a lot easier to set up and is much more robust than any of the earlier versions—but does that mean it's good enough?

I've heard a lot of mixed reviews from developers. Many are using Core Data and iCloud with no problems. Others are still having issues—though again, the reports about the issues have been sketchy at best. So, it's hard to tell where the problems lie.

We probably won't know for sure, until big applications with complex data and hundreds of thousands of users try implementing Core Data's iCloud syncing. But, I'm tentatively hopeful.

In my own testing, I've found three issues that I'm going to label as bugs. These are either documentation bugs (meaning, there is an important step that will solve these issues but that has not been properly documented yet), or they are honest bugs in the framework. Fortunately, they are all easy to work around.

- If we use the default merge policy, then deleting an entity will cause a conflict when that change syncs to other devices. The delete operation will appear to sync successfully, but the next time the other device tries to save, we get an error.
- The system often seems to have trouble processing multiple delete operations at the same time. This is particularly true when it tries to merge large, conflicting changes that include multiple delete operations. Some of the deleted entities will still appear, even after the sync completes. However, they have been removed from the persistent store, and they will be properly deleted the next time the app runs.

- If the user deletes the application and then reloads and relaunches it, the application will take a long time to switch from the fallback store to the iCloud store. This, by itself, isn't a bug. Honestly, it's a good sign. It shows that the framework is dealing with all the old transaction logs in the Ubiquity Container before it tries to create a new iCloud store. However, when it does create the iCloud store, it may not update any fetched results controllers correctly. Again, everything works fine the next time the application launches.

We will look at the workarounds when we implement our Core Data model for Health Beat. However, I wouldn't let these "bugs" worry you too much. While I don't recommend using Core Data and iCloud when supporting iOS 5 and I hesitate to use it with iOS 6, it looks like a viable solution for iOS 7 and beyond. I threw some pretty nasty tests at it, and it rolled with the punches quite nicely. Of course, it may still require a bit of tweaking to get everything working just right. But, it's no longer a lost cause.

CONVERTING HEALTH BEAT

We're going to replace Health Beat's current model with one based on Core Data. At the same time, we will enable iCloud syncing, since it's relatively trivial once we have Core Data in place. Fortunately, our `WeightHistoryDocument` is fairly modular. We can replace it with few changes to our code. Most of those changes will be focused in the code that loads or creates our document in our `RootTabBarController`. Ironically, our new code to load or create the document will more closely resemble the pre-iCloud code from Chapter 5, "Loading and Saving Data."

The rest of the project will remain largely unchanged. We will have to listen to a couple of additional notifications, there's a new header to import, and one method call is altered—but no significant modifications to existing code.

DEFINING THE MANAGED OBJECT MODEL

Let's start by creating our managed object model. In the Project navigator, Control-click the Model group and select New File…. In the template chooser, select iOS > Core Data > Data Model. Save it as **HealthBeatModel**. This will create a `HealthBeatModel.xcdatamodeld` file. Select that file to bring up Xcode's manage object model editor (**Figure 7.4**).

Our data model is very simple. We have only one type of entity, our `WeightEntry`. Click the Add Entity button to add a new entry to our model. This will add an entry named Entity. Double-click its name, and change the name to **WeightEntry**.

Now we need to add our attributes. Make sure the editor is using the Table view (the ⊞ button). Then click the Add Attribute button. For the name, type in **weightInLbs**, and hit the Return key. Then click the type and set it to **Float**. Select the `weightInLbs` attribute, and open the Data Model Inspector (the 🗋 tab). In the Attributes settings, uncheck the Optional box. In the Validation settings, give it a Minimum of **0** and uncheck Default. This will force us to provide a valid date before saving.

FIGURE 7.4
The manage object
model editor

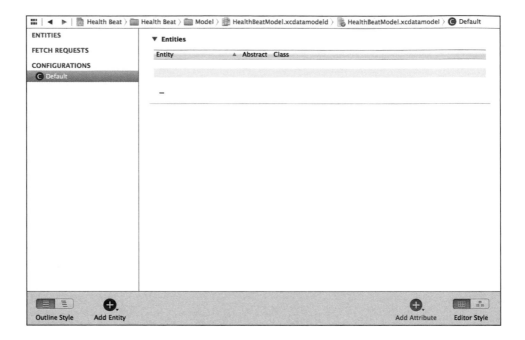

Next, add a second attribute. This should be named **date** with the type set to **Date**. We will be searching for weight entries based on this property, so make sure its Indexed attribute is checked and its Optional attribute is not checked. We also don't need a default value. Again, this will force us to provide a valid date before saving.

We need to be a little careful when adding attributes. As soon as we finish typing the name, the editor will alphabetically reorganize the attributes. It's important, therefore, to always hit Tab or Return after we're done typing the name. This triggers the reordering. If we simply use the mouse to click the Type setting without reordering the attributes first, the editor may reorder them out from under us. Eventually we will end up modifying the wrong attribute.

That's it for our entry. It should now match **Figure 7.5**.

Next, let's add a fetch request. We want to fetch all the WeightEntries between any two given dates, inclusively.

Click and hold the Add Entity button, and then select Add Fetch Request from the pop-up menu. Name the request **EntriesBetweenDates**. In the fetched request editor, make sure the "Fetch all" setting is set to **WeightEntry** (it should be our only choice). Next, make sure the Table view is selected and the first row says "All of the following are true."

Click the plus button at the end of the first row. This will add a new row to our request. Make sure it's an Expression and type **date >= $StartDate** in the text field. Then create a second Expression row and type **date <= $EndDate** in its text field. The EntriesBetweenDates request should now match **Figure 7.6**.

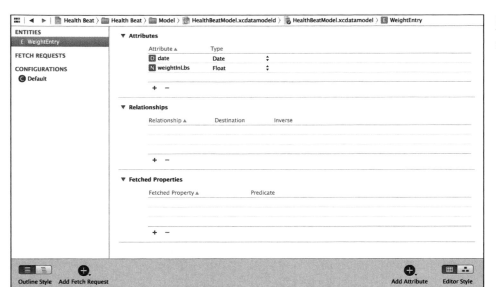

FIGURE 7.5
The completed
WeightEntry entity

FIGURE 7.6
The completed Entries-
BetweenDates fetch
request

Here, we are using predicate syntax expressions. We're just saying that our object's date attribute will be equal to or after the StartDate variable and our date will be equal to or earlier than the EndDate variable. When we load this request from the managed object model, we will need to provide both variables.

And that's it. We don't need any configurations or additional entities or fetched requests. Our model is very simple, just a collection of WeightEntries.

CREATING A NEW WEIGHTENTRY CLASS

Now that we have a model, we need to create a new WeightEntry class. This will be a subclass of NSManagedObject. Let's start by getting rid of our old WeightEntry class. However, we don't want to delete it just yet. We'll be scavenging some methods from it.

Instead, in the Project navigator click and hold slightly on WeightEntry.h's name. This should select the name and let us edit it. Change it to WeightEntry_old.h. Do the same thing for WeightEntry.m. Rename it WeightEntry_old.m. Also, for WeightEntry_old.m, open the File inspector and uncheck the Target Membership for Health Beat. That way, the old class will no longer be built into our application.

Now, let's generate our new WeightEntry class. Control-click the Model group and select New File.... Then select iOS > Core Data > NSManagedObject subclass and click Next. The next page should list all the models we can select from. We have only one, our HealthBeatModel. Make sure it is selected and click Next.

In the next page, we have a list of all the available entities. Again, we have only one choice, our WeightEntry. Check it and click Next.

Now, we have a choice to make. We can either turn the "Use scalar values for primitive data types" option on or off. If we turn it on, it will create simple C scalar accessors for many of our attributes. Unfortunately, it will do this for all the data types that have a C-scalar equivalent, including Date. That's not what we want. I wish there was a way to selectively choose which properties used objects and which used scalar types—but it's an all-or-nothing operation.

Fortunately, we can always modify the properties by hand, so let's just leave the box unchecked. In my opinion, it's slightly easier to turn objects in to scalars. Simply click Create to generate the class.

Now select WeightEntry.h. Our WeightEntry class is now a subclass of NSObject. It has only two properties, our weightInLbs and date. Also, for whatever reason, the generated code labels these as retain, not strong. I suspect this makes the generated code compatible with both ARC and non-ARC projects. However, I wouldn't be surprised if it changed sometime soon.

We want to tweak these properties slightly. First, we want weightInLbs to use a C scalar value. Second, we want them both to be read-only. Modify the code as shown here:

```
@property (nonatomic, readonly) float weightInLbs;
@property (nonatomic, retain, readonly) NSDate * date;
```

Now, let's look at WeightEntry.m. The implementation is empty except for the two @dynamic directives. These tell the compiler that someone (in this case, Core Data) will provide the accessor methods at runtime. They basically pat the compiler on its head and tell it not to worry about the missing accessor methods.

Now, we want to copy over many of the methods from our old WeightEntry class; however, we have a small problem.

When working with Core Data, we often end up making changes to the managed object model. When we do, we often need to regenerate our custom NSManagedObject subclasses.

Unfortunately, if we just create new subclasses, they will overwrite the existing files, deleting any custom changes that we've made.

Alternatively, we can make the modifications to our NSManagedObject subclass by hand, but this gets tedious and can be error prone, especially if we have a large number of changes.

The best solution involves creating a class category for our NSManagedObject subclass and placing our custom methods in that category. That way, we can freely update the class without touching our custom code. Yes, we will still need to tweak the properties each time, modifying the scalars and making them all read-only. However, that's relatively minor in comparison.

Let's create a category for our WeightEntry class. Control-click the Model group and select iOS > Cocoa Touch > Objective-C category. In the next sheet, make the Category **addons** and the "Category on" **WeightEntry**.

Create the category and then open WeightEntry+addons.h. Make sure both WeightEntry.h and WeightUnits.h are imported. Add the following method declarations to the @interface block.

```
+ (instancetype)entryWithWeight:(float)weight
                    usingUnits:(WeightUnit)unit
                       forDate:(NSDate *)date
                         inMOC:(NSManagedObjectContext *)moc;


+ (float)convertLbsToKg:(float)lbs;


+ (float)convertKgToLbs:(float)kg;


+ (NSString*)stringForUnit:(WeightUnit)unit;
+ (NSString*)stringForWeight:(float)weight ofUnit:(WeightUnit)unit;
+ (NSString*)stringForWeightInLbs:(float)weight inUnit:(WeightUnit)unit;


- (float)weightInUnit:(WeightUnit)unit;
- (NSString*)stringForWeightInUnit:(WeightUnit)unit;
```

We're adding an extra argument to entryWithWeight…, but other than that, all of these can be copied directly from WeightEntry_old.h.

> **NOTE:** It looks like we're breaking the rules here. I previously recommended that we always prefix all the methods in a category; however, that really applies only to categories on classes that we don't control. Here, we're creating a category on our own class, so we know exactly what methods it defines, including all its private methods. We also know that there are no other categories on this class. Bottom line, defining methods in this category is no different from defining the methods directly in WeightEntry itself, so there's no need to worry about prefixing these methods.

Now, let's switch to `WeightEntry+addons.m`. We're going to start by creating a private category that will redeclare our properties as read-write. Add the following code just after the `#import` directive:

```
@interface WeightEntry(private)
@property (nonatomic, assign, readwrite) float weightInLbs;
@property (nonatomic, retain, readwrite) NSDate * date;
@end
```

We're naming this category private, indicating that it's a collection of private methods. Note that we never actually implement any of these accessors. Core Data is already going to create them for us. This category simply declares them so that the compiler won't give us warnings when we try to use these properties.

Next, copy our constants from `WeightEntry_old.m`. Place them after the private category but before the `@implementation` block.

```
static const float LBS_PER_KG = 2.20462262f;
static NSNumberFormatter* formatter;
static NSString * const WeightEntryWeightInLbsKey =
@"WeightEntryWeightInLbsKey";
static NSString * const WeightEntryDateKey = @"WeightEntryDateKey";
```

Now, at the top of the `@implementation` block, let's set up our number formatter. In our old code, we did this in the `initialize` method. However, we shouldn't override `initialize` in a category. We should use `load` instead.

```
+ (void)load
{
    @autoreleasepool {
        if (self == [WeightEntry class])
        {
            formatter = [[NSNumberFormatter alloc] init];
            [formatter setNumberStyle:NSNumberFormatterDecimalStyle];
            [formatter setMinimum:[NSNumber numberWithFloat:0.0]];
            [formatter setMaximumFractionDigits:2];
        }
    }
}
```

As mentioned earlier, load runs very early—before our application is properly set up. Therefore, we need to provide our own autorelease pool. See the "Formatting Weight Strings" section of Chapter 3, "Developing Views and View Controllers," for more information on `load` and `initialize`.

Next, let's implement our new entryWithWeight:usingUnits:forDate:inMOC: method just after our load.

```objc
+ (instancetype)entryWithWeight:(float)weight
                     usingUnits:(WeightUnit)unit
                        forDate:(NSDate *)date
                          inMOC:(NSManagedObjectContext *)moc

{
    NSEntityDescription *description =
    [NSEntityDescription entityForName:NSStringFromClass(self)
             inManagedObjectContext:moc];

    WeightEntry *entry = [[WeightEntry alloc] initWithEntity:description
                        insertIntoManagedObjectContext:moc];

    if (unit == LBS)
    {
        entry.weightInLbs = weight;
    }
    else
    {
        entry.weightInLbs = [self convertKgToLbs:weight];
    }

    entry.date = date;

    return entry;
}
```

Creating a new NSManagedObject (or subclass) is somewhat complex. First, we need to get a copy of our entity's description. The entity descriptions store the name, properties, and classes of each entity in our managed object model.

We can request the description given the class name and a managed object context. While we could hard-code the class name as an NSString, here we're dynamically generating the class name. This is basically the same trick we saw in the main() function in Chapter 1, "Hello, iOS." It's a little more typing, but it also has a major advantage. If we refactor our code and change our class's name, this will automatically pick up on that change.

Once we have the description, we can alloc and init the class using initWithEntity:in sertIntoManagedObjectContext:. This will create the WeightEntry object and place it in the provided managed object context. This will also automatically create an undo event, which will trigger UIManagedDocument's automatic save.

Once we've created our `WeightEntry`, we set its `weightInLbs` and date properties, converting the weight argument if necessary.

That's it for new code. Now we just need to copy over the implementation for all the following methods: `convertLbsToKg:`, `convertKgToLbs:`, `stringForUnit:`, `stringForWeight:ofUnit:`, `stringforWeightInLbs:inUnit:`, `weightInUnit:`, and `stringForWeightInUnit:`.

> **NOTE:** Do not copy over any of the `init…` methods, the `NSCoding` methods or `description`, `isEqual:`, or `hash`. We need to use `NSManagedObject`'s `init` methods to properly initialize our class. Also, Core Data will handle saving and loading the entities for us, and we are specifically forbidden from overriding `isEqual:` or `hash` and strongly discouraged from overriding `description`.

That's it. Our new `WeightEntry` is complete. Of course, we still have a ton of errors and warnings. Let's fix a few of those before we move on.

First, delete `WeightEntry_old.h` and `WeightEntry_old.m` and then clean and build the application. Then, at the top of `HistoryTableViewController.m`, `EntryDetailViewController.m`, `AddEntryViewController.m`, and `GraphView.m`, import `WeightEntry+addons.h`.

Now, if we build the application again, we should have only a single error. The call to `entryWithWeight…` in `HistoryTableViewController`'s `addEntrySaved:` method. Unfortunately, before we can fix that, we need to replace our `WeightHistoryDocument` class.

CREATING A NEW WEIGHTHISTORYDOCUMENT CLASS

Again, let's start by renaming our `WeightHistoryDocument` to `WeightHistoryDocument_old`. Be sure to change both the `.h` and `.m` files and then remove the `.m` file from the target, so it won't get compiled into our build.

Next, create a new Objective-C class in Model group. This class should be named **WeightHistoryDocument** (no surprise there). This time, make it a subclass of **UIManagedDocument**.

Since our `WeightHistoryDocument` is now a `UIManagedDocument`, it will create the complete Core Data stack for us. We can access the stack through `UIManageDocument`'s `managedObjectContext` and `managedObjectModel` properties.

There's still a lot of work to do, though. We have a lot of custom code to go through before we successfully switch our model over to Core Data. Fortunately, most of the code is simple, and a lot can be copied from our old document class. However, let's break it up into chunks, starting with the header file.

HEADER FILE

We need to copy most of the old `.h` file over to the new `.h` file. In fact, it's probably easiest to copy everything and then make the following changes:

- Delete the `CallbackHandler` typedef.
- Change `UIDocument` to `UIManagedDocument` in the `@interface` line.
- Delete the `migrateToCloud:` method declaration.
- Delete the `setupCloudContainer:` method declaration.
- Add a `WeightHistoryDocumentRefreshAllNotification` string constant.
- Replace the `addEntry:` method declaration with `addEntryWithWeightInLbs: units:date:`.

The finished header file should look like this:

```
#import <UIKit/UIKit.h>
#import "WeightUnits.h"

@class WeightEntry;
@protocol WeightHistoryDocumentSubscriber;
typedef void (^EntryEnumeratorBlock) (WeightEntry *entry);

// Use to register for update notifications
extern NSString * const WeightHistoryDocumentBeginChangesNotification;
extern NSString * const WeightHistoryDocumentInsertWeightEntryNotification;
extern NSString * const WeightHistoryDocumentDeleteWeightEntryNotification;
extern NSString * const WeightHistoryDocumentChangesCompleteNotification;
extern NSString * const WeightHistoryDocumentRefreshAllNotification;

// Use to access data in the notifications
extern NSString * const WeightHistoryDocumentNotificationIndexPathKey;

@interface WeightHistoryDocument : UIManagedDocument

@property (nonatomic, readonly) NSUInteger count;

- (WeightEntry *)entryAtIndexPath:(NSIndexPath *)indexPath;
- (NSIndexPath *)indexPathForEntry:(WeightEntry *)weightEntry;

- (void)addEntryWithWeightInLbs:(float)weightInLbs
                          units:(WeightUnit)units
                           date:(NSDate *)date;
```

```
- (void)deleteEntryAtIndexPath:(NSIndexPath *)indexPath;

- (void)enumerateEntriesAscending:(BOOL)ascending
                     withBlock:(EntryEnumeratorBlock)block;

- (NSArray*)weightEntriesAfter:(NSDate *)startDate
                     before:(NSDate *)endDate;

- (NSArray *)allEntries;

- (void)addSubscriber:(id <WeightHistoryDocumentSubscriber>)subscriber;
- (void)removeSubscriber:(id <WeightHistoryDocumentSubscriber>)subscriber;

+ (NSURL *)localFileURL;
+ (BOOL)localFileExists;

@end

@protocol WeightHistoryDocumentSubscriber <NSObject>

- (void)weightHistoryDocument:(WeightHistoryDocument *)document
            stateDidChange:(UIDocumentState)state;

@end
```

THE IMPLEMENTATION FILE

Now, let's switch to WeightHistoryDocument.m. We're going to copy over most of the imports and the constant declarations; however, we are making a few changes.

- We need to import WeightEntry+addons.h.
- We need to define our WeightHistoryDocumentRefreshAllNotification constant.
- We need to change our file name to WeightHistoryCoreDataDocument. This isn't strictly necessary, but it will help prevent odd bugs if our new code tries to open an old file.
- We need to define a new WeightHistoryDocumentCountKey constant.
- We need to create a new CompletionHandler typedef.
- Finally, we can delete our WeightHistoryDocumentBackgroundQueue static variable.
- The final code is shown here:

```
#import "WeightHistoryDocument.h"
#import "WeightEntry.h"
#import "WeightEntry+addons.h"
```

```objc
#import "CloudManager.h"
#import <CoreData/CoreData.h>

// Use to register for update notifications
NSString * const WeightHistoryDocumentBeginChangesNotification =
@"WeightHistoryDocumentBeginChangesNotification";

NSString * const WeightHistoryDocumentInsertWeightEntryNotification =
@"WeightHistoryDocumentInsertWeightEntryNotification";

NSString * const WeightHistoryDocumentDeleteWeightEntryNotification =
@"WeightHistoryDocumentDeleteWeightEntryNotification";

NSString * const WeightHistoryDocumentChangesCompleteNotification =
@"WeightHistoryDocumentChangesCompleteNotification";

// Use to access data in the notifications
NSString * const WeightHistoryDocumentNotificationIndexPathKey =
@"WeightHistoryDocumentNotificationIndexPathKey";

NSString * const WeightHistoryDocumentRefreshAllNotification =
@"WeightHistoryDocumentRefreshAllNotification";

// Used to create our file URLs
static NSString * const WeightHistoryDocumentFileName =
@"WeightHistoryCoreDataDocument";

static NSString * const WeightHistoryDocumentCountKey = @"count";

typedef void (^CompletionHandler) (void);
```

Next, we need to add a class extension to hold our private data. Most of this is new.

```objc
@interface WeightHistoryDocument () <NSFetchedResultsControllerDelegate>
@property (strong,nonatomic) NSFetchedResultsController *resultsController;
@property (strong, nonatomic)NSHashTable *subscribers;
@property (strong, nonatomic) id documentStateObserver;
@property (strong, nonatomic) id storeWillChangeObserver;
@property (strong, nonatomic) id storeDidChangeObserver;
@property (strong, nonatomic) id iCloudUpdateObserver;
@end
```

Here, we're adopting the NSFetchedResultsControllerDelegate. Then we declare a resultsController property to hold an NSFetchedResultsController. This will fetch, sort, and monitor all of our WeightEntries and notify us of any changes to the fetched objects.

We can copy the subscribers and documentStateObserver properties directly from our old class. However, we do need to add three new observers: storeWillChangeObserver, storeDidChangeObserver, and iCloudUpdateObserver.

INIT AND DEALLOC METHODS

With the preliminary work done, we can begin implementing methods. Let's start with our init and dealloc methods. As always, these go inside the @implementation block.

```
@implementation WeightHistoryDocument

- (id)initWithFileURL:(NSURL *)url
{
    self = [super initWithFileURL:url];
    if (self) {
        _subscribers = [NSHashTable hashTableWithOptions:
                    NSHashTableWeakMemory];

        [self setupNotifications];
    }
    return self;
}


- (void)dealloc
{
    [self removeNotifications];
}
```

In initWithFileURL:, we set up our subscribers' hash table and then call setup Notifications. In dealloc, we just call removeNotifications.

ACCESSOR METHODS

Now, let's add a couple of custom accessor methods, starting with our count virtual property.

```
#pragma mark - Accessor Methods
- (NSUInteger)count
{
    NSArray *sections = self.resultsController.sections;
    id<NSFetchedResultsSectionInfo> sectionInfo = sections[0];
    return [sectionInfo numberOfObjects];
}
```

We start by grabbing the sections array from our results controller. This array contains opaque objects that adopt the NSFetchedResultsSectionInfo protocol. We should have one section info object per section in our results controller, and since we are not partitioning our data into multiple sections, there should be only one in this array.

We grab that object out of the array and then call its numberOfObjects method. This gives us the total number of entities in that section.

Unlike before, our count property is not directly dependent upon any other properties. It's loosely dependent upon the results controller; however, instead of trying to specify a reasonable set of dependent key paths, let's just manually call the KVO update methods whenever our underlying data changes.

Next, let's create a custom getter for our resultsController property.

```
- (NSFetchedResultsController *)resultsController
{
    if (_resultsController == nil)
    {
        [self setupResultsController];
    }
    return _resultsController;
}
```

Here we use lazy initialization to create our results controller. When the getter is called, we check to see whether we have a valid resultsController. If we don't, then we call setupResultsController to create one. Then we return our results controller.

This is conceptually similar to the singleton class code we used in the previous chapter. However, this version is a little simpler, since we're not using dispatch_once(). This has two important implications for our code. First, we can reset our resultsController by calling self.resultsController = nil. This will clear out the old results controller, and the next time we try to access this property, our code will create a new controller for us. Second, our lazy initialization code is no longer thread safe. But, that's OK. We declared our results Controller property as nonatomic, so it doesn't have to be thread safe.

PUBLIC METHODS

Now let's start implementing our public methods. Let me tell you a little secret. When I designed WeightHistoryDocument's public interface, I based much of it on the NSFetched ResultsController. This means many of our public methods will be thin wrappers around our resultsController property.

NSFetchedResultsController was clearly designed to work hand-in-hand with a UITableViewController. In fact, people often make the NSFetchedResultsController a property of their UITableViewController subclass and let the table view communicate directly with the fetched results. This works well, especially since the fetched results controller supports shared caches, so we could have multiple view controllers, each with their own fetched results controller, all looking at the same data, without requiring separate fetch requests.

However, I like pulling the fetched results controller back inside my model. I feel that adding it directly to the view controller tightly binds that view controller to Core Data. Putting the fetched results controller inside the model encourages a more modular design. This will make it easier to replace the Core Data model, if something better comes along.

Like all software engineering, this comes at a cost. We have to build a slightly more complex communication channel between our model and our view controllers; however, since we've already built that in previous chapters, there's no reason not to reuse it now.

Let's start by implementing our entryAtIndexPath: and indexPathForEntry: methods.

```
#pragma mark - Public Methods


- (WeightEntry *)entryAtIndexPath:(NSIndexPath *)indexPath
{
    return [self.resultsController objectAtIndexPath:indexPath];
}


- (NSIndexPath *)indexPathForEntry:(WeightEntry *)weightEntry
{
    return [self.resultsController indexPathForObject:weightEntry];
}
```

As you can see, these are simply wrappers around the corresponding NSFetchedResultsController methods.

Our addEntryWithWeightInLbs:units:date: method, on the other hand, requires a little more effort.

```
- (void)addEntryWithWeightInLbs:(float)weightInLbs
                          units:(WeightUnit)units
                           date:(NSDate *)date
{
    [self willChangeValueForKey:WeightHistoryDocumentCountKey];
    WeightEntry *entry =
    [WeightEntry entryWithWeight:weightInLbs
                      usingUnits:units
                         forDate:date
                           inMOC:self.managedObjectContext];
    [self didChangeValueForKey:WeightHistoryDocumentCountKey];

    [self.undoManager setActionName:
     [NSString stringWithFormat:@"Do you want to remove the %@.",
      entry]];
}
```

Here, we call the entryWithWeight:usingUnits:forDate:inMOC: convenience method that we defined in our WeightHistory class. This returns an entry object—but we use that object only locally—we never save it or pass it on to the rest of our application. This is because entryWithWeight... also adds the entity to our managed object context. Our fetched results controller will notice this addition and will update our user interface.

The rest of the code is simply infrastructure. We bracket the creation of a new entry with the KVO notification methods. Core Data automatically adds the undo action, but we still need to set the undo action name for our previous shake-to-undo code to function properly.

In normal Core Data code, we would also have to save our managed object context here. However, since we are using a UIManagedDocument, it will detect the undo action and automatically save our data for us.

Next, let's look at deleteEntryAtIndexPath:. Deleting is similarly simple, and again, most of our code goes to supporting KVO and our shake-to-undo.

```
- (void)deleteEntryAtIndexPath:(NSIndexPath *)indexPath
{
    WeightEntry *entry = [self entryAtIndexPath:indexPath];
    NSManagedObjectContext *moc =self.managedObjectContext;
    __weak WeightHistoryDocument *_self = self;

    [moc performBlock:^{
        NSString *undoString =
        [NSString stringWithFormat:
         @"Do you want to restore the %@.", entry];

        [_self willChangeValueForKey:WeightHistoryDocumentCountKey];
        [_self.managedObjectContext deleteObject:entry];
        [_self didChangeValueForKey:WeightHistoryDocumentCountKey];

        [_self.undoManager setActionName:undoString];
    }];
}
```

We start by grabbing local copies of our entry, our managed object context, and a weak reference to self. Then we call performBlock: on our managed object context. This guarantees that the code inside the block will be called on the context's queue. The context is on the main thread, and this method should always be called from the main thread—so this isn't actually required. However, it's easy to have a notification method called from a background queue that accidentally triggers other methods unexpectedly. Better safe than sorry.

We create our undo action name. Next, we delete the entry, bracketing this call with the proper KVO notification methods. And, finally, we set the undo action name.

Now, let's look at enumerateEntriesAscending:withBlock:.

```objc
- (void)enumerateEntriesAscending:(BOOL)ascending
                        withBlock:(EntryEnumeratorBlock)block
{
    NSUInteger options = 0;
    if (ascending)
    {
        options = NSEnumerationReverse;
    }

    [[self allEntries]
     enumerateObjectsWithOptions:options
     usingBlock:^(id obj, NSUInteger idx, BOOL *stop) {
        block(obj);
     }];
}
```

This is almost the same as our old implementation. The only change is that we're calling [self allEntries], not self.weightHistory.

Next, let's look at weightEntriesAfter:before:. This method has some serious new code.

```objc
- (NSArray*)weightEntriesAfter:(NSDate *)startDate before:(NSDate *)endDate
{
    NSParameterAssert(startDate != nil);
    NSParameterAssert(endDate != nil);

    NSDictionary *variables =
    @{@"StartDate":startDate,
      @"EndDate":endDate};

    NSFetchRequest *fetchRequest =
    [self.managedObjectModel
     fetchRequestFromTemplateWithName:@"EntriesBetweenDates"
     substitutionVariables:variables];

    NSSortDescriptor *descendingByDate =
    [NSSortDescriptor sortDescriptorWithKey:@"date" ascending:NO];

    fetchRequest.sortDescriptors = @[descendingByDate];
```

```objc
    __block NSArray *results;
    NSManagedObjectContext *moc = self.managedObjectContext;
    [moc performBlockAndWait:^{
        NSError *fetchError;

        results = [moc executeFetchRequest:fetchRequest
                                     error:&fetchError];

        if (!results)
        {
            // We will want more-thorough error checking; however,
            // at this point, the main cause for errors tends to be
            // invalid keys in the sort descriptor. Let's fail fast
            // so we're sure to catch that during development.

            [NSException
             raise:NSGenericException
             format:@"An error occurred when performing our fetch %@",
             [fetchError localizedDescription]];
        }
    }];

    return results;
}
```

This method performs a fetch request, grabbing all the weight entries between the two dates. We start by getting the EntriesBetweenDates fetch request from our managed object model. Note that we pass in a dictionary containing the substitution data for our request. This dictionary's keys need to match the variables' names (without the dollar sign). The dictionary's values will be placed into the request, replacing the corresponding variables.

Next, we create a sort descriptor. Sort descriptors let us sort collections of objects. We can use them to compare two objects (compareObject:toObject), to generate sorted copies of an array or a set (sortedArrayUsingDescriptors:), or to sort a mutable array (sortUsingDescriptors:). We also use them to sort the results of a fetch request.

At their most basic, sort descriptors specify the property to use when comparing objects and the order (ascending or descending). We can optionally specify the selector to use when comparing as well. However, by default, the sort descriptor can compare C scalar data such as BOOL, NSInteger, or CGFloat. It will also use the compare: selector when comparing objects. This means it can compare many common objects, including NSDate, NSString, and NSIndexPath. Still, when we are comparing strings, we will often want to use a more-specific selector like caseInsensitiveCompare: or localizedCompare:. The localized compare methods are particularly important, since they take into account the current locale's sorting order for case and diacritics. Also note, if the objects being sorted do not have the specified property or do not respond to the specified comparison selector, the sort descriptor will throw an exception.

By themselves, sort descriptors are somewhat interesting but not life changing. However, they really start becoming powerful when we begin combining them. Most of the methods that take sort descriptors actually take arrays of descriptors. We can provide as many as we want. The system will apply the first descriptor from the array. If there are any ties, it will then apply the second descriptor to break those ties. If there are still ties, it moves on to the third, and so forth. This lets us define complex sort orders for our objects.

To get back to our fetch request, we want to sort the entries by date in descending order. The entities returned by a fetch request are unordered by default. If we want them in a particular order, we need to sort them.

Once our fetch request is ready, we call `performBlockAndWait:`. Like `performBlock:` this guarantees that our block's code is run on the context's queue. However, unlike `performBlock:` this method runs synchronously. That is important, since our calling method needs to return the result of this fetch.

Inside the block, we execute our fetch request and check for errors. If we find an error, we throw an exception—however, as the comment suggests, most errors during development are because of misspelled keys. We want our code to fail fast, so we can find and fix these mistakes. However, we'll probably want to replace this code with more-thorough error checking during beta testing.

Finally, if everything goes as expected, we return the array of `WeightEntry` objects.

NOTE: Since our context is on the main queue, all of our fetch requests will block the main thread. Most of the time, the request should be fast, so we shouldn't notice any lag or delays in our user interface. However, if we start noticing performance issues, we may want to fine-tune the fetch request—for example, setting a batch size. Of course, we should always profile the application before and after making any changes, just to make sure we're actually improving performance. Returning faults usually seems like a good idea, however, if we end up triggering a number of individual fetch requests, it could actually hurt performance.

Now let's get back to something a bit easier:

```
- (NSArray *)allEntries
{
    return self.resultsController.fetchedObjects;
}
```

Again, this is just a thin wrapper around our `NSFetchedResultsController`. Its `fetchedObjects` property returns a snapshot of all the objects currently returned by the controller's fetch request. Note, however, that this array is not updated as managed objects are inserted or deleted.

Finally, the addSubscriber:, removeSubscriber:, localFileURL, and localFileExists methods are copied exactly from WeightHistoryDocument_old.m. I am including them here as a reference.

```
- (void)addSubscriber:(id<WeightHistoryDocumentSubscriber>)subscriber
{
    [self.subscribers addObject:subscriber];
}


- (void)removeSubscriber:(id<WeightHistoryDocumentSubscriber>)subscriber
{
    [self.subscribers removeObject:subscriber];
}


#pragma mark - Public Class Methods

+ (NSURL *)localFileURL
{
    NSArray *urls = [[NSFileManager defaultManager]
                    URLsForDirectory:NSDocumentDirectory
                    inDomains:NSUserDomainMask];

    NSURL *documentURL = [urls lastObject];
    return [documentURL URLByAppendingPathComponent:
            WeightHistoryDocumentFileName];
}


+ (BOOL)localFileExists
{
    NSFileManager *manager = [NSFileManager defaultManager];
    return [manager fileExistsAtPath:[[self localFileURL] path]];
}
```

NSFETCHEDRESULTSCONTROLLERDELEGATE METHODS

Our `WeightHistoryDocument` will act as our fetched results controller's delegate. This means we will receive updates whenever a change occurs. However, to receive these updates, we must implement the corresponding delegate method.

Most of the time, we're just going to turn around and post our corresponding notification. Anyone listening to our notification will then be able to update their state as appropriate.

Let's start with `controllerWillChangeContent:` and `controllerDidChangeContent:`. These are called before and after our actual changes. If a large number of changes occur at once (for example, because of an incoming iCloud sync), Will Change is called, followed by each actual change, one at a time, and then Did Change is called.

```
#pragma mark - NSFetchedResultsControllerDelegate methods


- (void)controllerWillChangeContent:
(NSFetchedResultsController *)controller
{
    [[NSNotificationCenter defaultCenter]
     postNotificationName:WeightHistoryDocumentBeginChangesNotification
     object:self];
}


- (void)controllerDidChangeContent:
(NSFetchedResultsController *)controller
{
    [[NSNotificationCenter defaultCenter]
     postNotificationName:WeightHistoryDocumentChangesCompleteNotification
     object:self];
}
```

In both cases, we simply post our corresponding notification.

Next, let's implement `controller:didChangeObject:atIndexPath:forChangeType:new IndexPath:`. This method is called once for each object that changes. It also requires a little more work. We need to determine what type of change it is, before we can post the correct notification.

```
- (void)controller:(NSFetchedResultsController *)controller
    didChangeObject:(id)anObject
        atIndexPath:(NSIndexPath *)indexPath
      forChangeType:(NSFetchedResultsChangeType)type
       newIndexPath:(NSIndexPath *)newIndexPath
{
```

```objc
NSNotificationCenter *center = [NSNotificationCenter defaultCenter];

switch (type) {
    case NSFetchedResultsChangeDelete:

        [center
         postNotificationName:
         WeightHistoryDocumentDeleteWeightEntryNotification
         object:self
         userInfo:@{WeightHistoryDocumentNotificationIndexPathKey:
                        indexPath}];

        break;

    case NSFetchedResultsChangeInsert:

        [center
         postNotificationName:
         WeightHistoryDocumentInsertWeightEntryNotification
         object:self
         userInfo:@{WeightHistoryDocumentNotificationIndexPathKey:
                        newIndexPath}];

        break;

    default:

        [NSException
         raise:NSGenericException
         format:@"Invalid change type: %@",
         @(type)];

        break;
}
}
```

Here, we create a switch statement for the different types. There are actually four different types of changes: insert, delete, move, and update. However, since our entities are immutable, they cannot change. Also, since their order is defined by their date property, they cannot move. That means we need to respond to only two of the four.

In both cases, we post our corresponding notification. However, in these cases, we also need to pass the index of the object that was inserted or deleted in the `userInfo` dictionary.

Just to make things confusing, this method takes two index path arguments. This is necessary when an object is moving, since we need to know their original location and their destination. However, for the other changes, it's often hard to know which index path to use. I usually can't remember from project to project, so I ran a quick test to see. It turns out that *delete* uses the old index path while *insert* uses the new one.

PRIVATE METHODS

Now, we just need to implement the private methods that we've been calling in our earlier code. Let's start with `setupNotifications`. This is a long method, but it follows the same basic pattern that we've seen before. First, we gather together all the local variables that we'll need. Then we set up each of our notifications.

Most of the notifications are relatively simple. Many of them just call out to other private methods to do the real work.

```
#pragma mark - Private Methods

- (void)setupNotifications
{
    NSNotificationCenter *center = [NSNotificationCenter defaultCenter];
    NSOperationQueue *mainQueue = [NSOperationQueue mainQueue];
    NSManagedObjectContext *moc = self.managedObjectContext;
    NSManagedObjectContext *parent = moc.parentContext;

    NSPersistentStoreCoordinator *storeCoordinator =
    [moc persistentStoreCoordinator];

    [moc setMergePolicy:NSOverwriteMergePolicy];
    [parent setMergePolicy:NSOverwriteMergePolicy];

    __weak WeightHistoryDocument *_self = self;

    self.documentStateObserver =
    [center
     addObserverForName:UIDocumentStateChangedNotification
     object:self
```

```
 queue:mainQueue
 usingBlock:^(NSNotification *note) {
     for (id <WeightHistoryDocumentSubscriber> subscriber
          in _self.subscribers)
     {
         [subscriber weightHistoryDocument:_self
                        stateDidChange:_self.documentState];
     }
 }];


self.storeWillChangeObserver =
[center
 addObserverForName:
 NSPersistentStoreCoordinatorStoresWillChangeNotification
 object:storeCoordinator
 queue:nil
 usingBlock:^(NSNotification *note) {
     NSLog(@"*** Store Will Change ***");
     [_self resetMocs];
 }];


self.storeDidChangeObserver =
[center
 addObserverForName:
 NSPersistentStoreCoordinatorStoresDidChangeNotification
 object:storeCoordinator
 queue:mainQueue
 usingBlock:^(NSNotification *note) {
     NSLog(@"*** Store Did Change ***");
     [_self refreshAll];
 }];


self.iCloudUpdateObserver =
[center
 addObserverForName:
 NSPersistentStoreDidImportUbiquitousContentChangesNotification
 object:storeCoordinator
 queue:mainQueue
```

```
    usingBlock:^(NSNotification *note) {
        NSLog(@"*** Importing Data from iCloud ***");
        NSSet *deleted = note.userInfo[@"deleted"];
        NSUInteger initialCount = [[moc deletedObjects] count];
        [_self updateMOCFromNote:note completionHandler:^{
            if ([deleted count] !=
                [[moc deletedObjects] count] - initialCount)
            {
                [_self refreshAll];
            }
        }];
    }];
}
```

Before we begin looking at the notifications themselves, there are a couple of lines I want to draw attention to. After we create local variables for our managed object context and its parent context, we then set both context's merge policy to NSOverwriteMergePolicy.

This is important, because it solves one of the three iCloud bugs I identified earlier. In fact, these lines of code solve what I consider the most serious of the three bugs.

As I'm writing this, if we delete an entity on one device and then sync the change to a second device, the next time the second device saves, it will throw a merge conflict error. By using the NSOverwriteMergePolicy, we're saying that the entities in the context should overwrite the entities in the persistent store when there's a conflict. This lets Core Data automatically resolve these conflicts.

Alternatively, we could use NSMergeByPropertyObjectTrumpMergePolicy, which will overwrite the store on a property-by-property basis. However, since our objects are all immutable, there's no reason to use fine-grained conflict resolution. Merging object-by-object is sufficient.

Next, let's look at the notifications.

- UIDocumentStateChangedNotification: This notification was copied exactly from our old document. Just to remind you, when we receive the notification, we call the weightHi storyDocument:statedidChange: method on all our subscribers.

- NSPersistentStoreCoordinatorStoresWillChangeNotification: This notification is sent just before our Core Data stack switches from one persistent store to another. Our code appears deceptively simple. We just call a resetMocs private method. However, there's one subtle but interesting point. Notice that we're passing nil for the queue. That means our block will run on whatever thread the notification was posted from.

This is important, because we must perform a synchronous save and reset on our managed object contexts from that background thread. As long as our code is blocking that thread, we can safely make calls to our managed object context. However, once we stop blocking the thread, the system will begin tearing down and rebuilding our Core Data stack, and the contents of our context will become invalid.

- `NSPersistentStoreCoordinatorStoresDidChangeNotification`: This notification is sent once our Core Data stack has successfully moved to the new persistent store. This is our chance to update our user interface. We do this by calling `refreshAll`, which performs a new fetch, grabbing all the `WeightEntry` objects from our persistent store. Then it tells our view controllers to update their contents.

  This is actually a little heavy-handed. Most of the time the fetched request controller will automatically reload its data when the store changes. However, explicitly reloading the fetched request controller fixes one of the iCloud bugs I discussed earlier.

  If the user deletes and then reloads the application, the fetched request controller won't pick up any existing iCloud data during its first launch. By explicitly forcing the request controller to fetch new data, we make sure that the user always gets the correct data from the persistent store—even in these somewhat rare corner cases.

- `NSPersistentStoreDidImportUbiquitousContentChangesNotification`: Finally, this notification is sent whenever we receive an update from iCloud. At this point, the persistent store has been updated, but we still need to merge these changes with our managed object context.

  In theory, we should need to call only `mergeChangesFromContextDidSaveNotification:` on our context, and we'd be done. However, I've added some extra code to deal with an apparent delete bug.

  This is the last of the iCloud bugs that I mentioned earlier. Basically, if an update is deleting more than one entity, sometimes not all of the deletes are processed properly.

  To work around this, we grab the set of IDs for all the entities that will be deleted. We also count the number of deleted entities in the context. These represent objects that we've already deleted but whose changes have not been saved yet.

  Next, we call `updateMOCFromNote:completionHandler:`. This will update our contexts asynchronously and call our completion handler when it's done. In the completion handler, we check and see whether our update actually deleted the number of items we expected it to delete. If not, we call `refreshAll`. This will re-fetch all our `WeightEntry` objects from the persistent store.

  Again, this is a bit heavy-handed, but it also guarantees that the data we're displaying is correct and up to date.

Whenever we set up notification observers, we also need to tear them down again. Since we now have a number of observers to remove, let's create a `removeNotifications` method to handle it all.

```
- (void)removeNotifications
{
    NSNotificationCenter *center = [NSNotificationCenter defaultCenter];

    if (self.documentStateObserver)
    {
        [center removeObserver:self.documentStateObserver];
    }

    if (self.storeWillChangeObserver)
    {
        [center removeObserver:self.storeWillChangeObserver];
    }

    if (self.storeDidChangeObserver)
    {
        [center removeObserver:self.storeDidChangeObserver];
    }

    if (self.iCloudUpdateObserver)
    {
        [center removeObserver:self.iCloudUpdateObserver];
    }
}
```

We've seen this pattern before. There shouldn't be anything surprising here. Next, we need a method to set up our fetched request controller.

```
- (void)setupResultsController
{
    if (self.documentState != UIDocumentStateNormal) return;
    NSManagedObjectContext *moc = self.managedObjectContext;

    NSFetchRequest *fetchRequest =
    [NSFetchRequest fetchRequestWithEntityName:
     NSStringFromClass([WeightEntry class])];

    [fetchRequest setFetchBatchSize:15];

    NSSortDescriptor *descendingByDate =
    [NSSortDescriptor sortDescriptorWithKey:@"date" ascending:NO];
```

```
    fetchRequest.sortDescriptors = @[descendingByDate];

    self.resultsController =
    [[NSFetchedResultsController alloc]
     initWithFetchRequest:fetchRequest
     managedObjectContext:moc
     sectionNameKeyPath:nil
     cacheName:@"Document Data"];

    self.resultsController.delegate = self;
    [self fetchAllEntries];
}
```

We start by making sure our document is in a normal state. If it's not in a normal state (for example, if it hasn't finished loading yet), then there's no point in performing the fetch request.

Next, we need to create the fetch request that our controller will use. This time we're programmatically creating our fetch request. We want all of our WeightEntries, but we want to grab only the first 15. All the others should be returned as faults.

We call fetchRequestWithEntityName: to create the basic fetch request. By default, it will return all the entities of the given name (and their subentities). Again, we use the NSStringFromClass() trick to avoid hard-coding in the class name.

Then we set the batch size to 15. This will be more than enough to fill a screen full of information. It will then download the others in 15-entry chunks when they are needed.

We also provide a sort descriptor. Just like before, we want to sort our WeightEntry objects in descending order by their date property.

Once the fetch request is ready, we instantiate our NSFetchedResultsController and assign our WeightHistoryDocument as its delegate. Then we call fetchAllEntries to perform the fetch. We're breaking the actual fetch out to its own method, since we will also call fetchAllEntries when refreshing our user interface.

```
- (void)fetchAllEntries
{
    NSError *fetchError = nil;

    if (![self.resultsController performFetch:&fetchError])
    {
        [NSException
         raise:NSGenericException
         format:@"An error occurred when performing our fetch %@",
         [fetchError localizedDescription]];
    }
}
```

This method is fairly straightforward. We simply call our fetched results controller's performFetch: method, and then we check for errors. If an error occurred, we throw an exception. Again, this is geared toward catching misspelled keys during development. We will undoubtedly want to replace it as we get closer to releasing the application.

Next, let's implement the resetMocs method.

```objc
- (void)resetMocs
{
    NSManagedObjectContext *moc = self.managedObjectContext;
    NSManagedObjectContext *parent = moc.parentContext;
    __block NSError *saveError;

    [moc performBlockAndWait:^{
        if ([moc hasChanges])
        {
            if (![moc save:&saveError])
            {
                [NSException
                 raise:NSGenericException
                 format:@"Unable to save the chld moc: %@ (%@)",
                 [saveError localizedDescription],
                 saveError.userInfo];
            }
            else
            {
                [parent performBlockAndWait:^{
                    if (![parent save:&saveError])
                    {
                        [NSException
                         raise:NSGenericException
                         format:@"Unable to save the parent moc: %@ (%@)",
                         [saveError localizedDescription],
                         saveError.userInfo];
                    }
                }];
            }
        }
    }];

    [moc reset];
```

```
    }];

    [parent performBlockAndWait:^{
        [parent reset];
    }];
}
```

As mentioned earlier, this method needs to run synchronously. Therefore, we use performBlockAndWait: to do all our work on our managed object contexts. Additionally, we want to save and then refresh things in a particular order.

First we want to save our child context. This pushes all our changes up to the parent context. Then we want to save the parent context. Once both contexts are saved, we want to reset them both.

To get everything to work out right, we have a number of nested blocks. But, don't let the blocks confuse you. If you strip everything else away, we're just saving and resetting our contexts.

Now, let's implement updateMOCFromNote:CompletionHandler:. Our notification code calls this whenever we receive an update from iCloud.

```
- (void)updateMOCFromNote:(NSNotification *)note
        completionHandler:(CompletionHandler)completionHandler
{
    NSManagedObjectContext *moc = self.managedObjectContext;
    NSManagedObjectContext *parent = self.managedObjectContext.parentContext;

    [parent performBlock:^{
        [parent mergeChangesFromContextDidSaveNotification:note];

        [moc performBlock:^{
            [self willChangeValueForKey:WeightHistoryDocumentCountKey];
            [moc mergeChangesFromContextDidSaveNotification:note];
            [self didChangeValueForKey:WeightHistoryDocumentCountKey];

            if (completionHandler)
            {
                [[NSOperationQueue mainQueue]
                 addOperationWithBlock:completionHandler];
            }
        }];
    }];
}
```

Like resetMocs, we're trying to do something quite simple. We just want to merge the incoming changes with our managed object contexts. This time we start with the parent and then merge the child.

Also, this time we are using the asynchronous API. So, we will pass our block to the parent context's private queue, and it will update the parent context in the background. When this is done, we pass the next block back to the main queue so we can update our child context. We also call the KVO notification methods, just in case someone is observing our count property.

Finally, once both updates are complete, we check to see whether we have a completion handler. If we do, we execute it on the main queue.

NOTE: Our child context already performs its blocks on the main queue, so passing the completion handler to the main queue is a bit redundant. We could simply execute the block and be done. However, this is a little bit of defensive coding. If we change our child context so that it uses a private queue, this code will still run as expected.

One last method to go. Implement refreshAll as shown here:

```
- (void)refreshAll
{
    if (_resultsController)
    {
        [self fetchAllEntries];

        [[NSNotificationCenter defaultCenter]
         postNotificationName:WeightHistoryDocumentRefreshAllNotification
         object:self];
    }
}
```

This method is called whenever we switch to a new persistent store. It checks to see whether we have a valid results controller. Notice that we need to directly access the instance variable here. If we use the accessor, it will try to instantiate the controller, if one didn't already exist.

If we do have a controller, we simply re-fetch all its data. Then we post our Weight HistoryDocumentRefreshAllNotification, telling any listening view controllers to update their content.

That's it. Our document now uses Core Data, and it's ready to use iCloud. We just need to specify the correct options when loading and creating our document.

LOADING OR CREATING OUR DOCUMENT

We need to make a number of changes to our `RootTabBarController` to properly load and create our Core Data document. Open `RootTabBarController.m`. Let's start at the top of the file and work our way down. We need to make only six changes.

1. Replace `setupDocument` with the following implementation:

```objc
- (void)setupDocument
{
    NSURL *fileURL = [WeightHistoryDocument localFileURL];
    [self createWeightHistoryForURL:fileURL];

//    [self addMocData];
    if ([WeightHistoryDocument localFileExists])
    {
        [self loadFile];
    }
    else
    {
        [self createNewFileAtURL:fileURL];
    }
}
```

As you can see, we're moving back to a much simpler setup procedure. We start by creating our `WeightHistoryDocument` object. Then we check to see whether we have a copy of the document on disk. If we do, we load it. Otherwise, we create a new file.

2. Replace `createWeightHistoryForURL:`.

```objc
- (void)createWeightHistoryForURL:(NSURL *)fileURL
{
    self.weightHistoryDocument = [[WeightHistoryDocument alloc]
                                  initWithFileURL:fileURL];

    self.weightHistoryDocument.persistentStoreOptions =
    @{NSPersistentStoreUbiquitousContentNameKey:
          @"com~freelancemadscience~HealthBeat",
      NSMigratePersistentStoresAutomaticallyOption:@YES,
      NSInferMappingModelAutomaticallyOption:@YES};

    [self.weightHistoryDocument addSubscriber:self];
    [self passDocumentToViewControllers];
}
```

Here, we instantiate our WeightHistoryDocument property. Then we set its persistent store options. We're setting three options, as described here:

- NSPersistentStoreUbiquitousContentNameKey: This key tells Core Data to sync via iCloud. The value of this key is the unique identifier for this particular persistent store inside our Ubiquity Container. If an application uses multiple documents, each one must have their own, unique content name.

- NSMigratePersistentStoresAutomaticallyOption: If this option is set to YES, then when we try to load a persistent store that is from an older version of our model, Core Data will attempt to automatically migrate the store. Note that because we are using iCloud, we cannot use a mapping model to migrate from one version to the next.

- NSInferMappingModelAutomaticallyOption: If this option is set to YES, Core Data will attempt to infer the mapping between versions when automatically migrating from one version to the next. Inferred mapping supports only a limited range of changes. For example, we can add a new attribute to an entity. However, it's easy to use, and iCloud supports inferred mapping between versions.

Once the options are done, we set our RootTabBarController as a subscriber, and we pass the document on to all of our child view controllers.

3. Delete the following methods: searchForCloudDocument, processQuery:, and searchForLocalDocument.

4. Replace loadFile with the following implementation:

```
- (void)loadFile
{
    NSLog(@"Loading File");
    __weak RootTabBarController *_self = self;
    [self.weightHistoryDocument
     openWithCompletionHandler:^(BOOL success) {

        if (!success)
        {
            NSLog(@"*** Corrupt file at %@, "
                @"attempting to delete it and try again. ***",
                _self.weightHistoryDocument.fileURL);

            [self rebuildFromiCloud];
            return;
        }
        else
        {
```

```
            NSLog(@"File Loaded");
        }
    }];
}
```

Again, this is considerably simpler than our previous version. We just call openWithCompletionHandler: to load our persistent store. If that's not successful, we call rebuildFromiCloud to try to rebuild the persistent store.

5. Delete the following code from the end of createNewFileAtURL:.

```
if (isCloudAvailable())
{
    [self.weightHistoryDocument migrateToCloud];
}
```

6. Implement the following new method:

```
- (void)rebuildFromiCloud
{
    NSURL *fileURL = [WeightHistoryDocument localFileURL];
    self.weightHistoryDocument = [[WeightHistoryDocument alloc]
                                  initWithFileURL:fileURL];

    self.weightHistoryDocument.persistentStoreOptions =
    @{NSPersistentStoreUbiquitousContentNameKey:
          @"com~freelancemadscience~HealthBeat",
      NSPersistentStoreRebuildFromUbiquitousContentOption:@YES,
      NSMigratePersistentStoresAutomaticallyOption:@YES,
      NSInferMappingModelAutomaticallyOption:@YES};

    [self.weightHistoryDocument addSubscriber:self];
    [self passDocumentToViewControllers];

    NSLog(@"Rebuilding File");
    [self.weightHistoryDocument
     openWithCompletionHandler:^(BOOL success) {

        if (!success)
        {
            [NSException
             raise:NSGenericException
```

```
                format:@"Unable to rebuild the Core Data "
                @"database from iCloud"];
        }
        else
        {
            NSLog(@"File Rebuilt");
        }
    }];
}
```

We call this method whenever we run into errors while trying to load our persistent store. We're going to try to create the store again, but instead of loading the local data, we want to delete the local store and rebuild everything from iCloud.

We start by creating a new WeightHistoryDocument object. This time we set an additional option: NSPersistentStoreRebuildFromUbiquitousContentOption. This tells Core Data to delete the local persistent store and rebuild it using data from iCloud.

Next, we subscribe to the document and pass it on to the children view as normal. Then we try to open the document.

That's it, our document is ready to use both Core Data and iCloud—and with considerably less code than the previous version. We just need to update a couple of view controllers, and we're ready to run.

UPDATING OUR VIEW CONTROLLERS

Let's start with our HistoryTableViewController. Open HistoryTableViewController.m, and in the class extension, add the following property:

```
@property (strong, nonatomic) id documentRefreshAllObserver;
```

Next, we can finally get rid of our last compilation error. Modify addNewEntrySaved: as shown here:

```
- (IBAction)addNewEntrySaved:(UIStoryboardSegue *)segue
{
    AddEntryViewController *controller = segue.sourceViewController;

    [self.weightHistoryDocument addEntryWithWeightInLbs:controller.weight
                                          units:getDefaultUnits()
                                          date:controller.date];

    [self dismissViewControllerAnimated:YES completion:nil];
    [self becomeFirstResponder];
}
```

This just replaces the old code to create our `WeightEntry` object and adds it to the document with our new (and somewhat longer named) method.

Next, add the following code to the bottom of `setupNotifications`:

```
self.documentRefreshAllObserver =
[center
 addObserverForName:WeightHistoryDocumentRefreshAllNotification
 object:doc
 queue:mainQueue
 usingBlock:^(NSNotification *note) {
     [_self.tableView reloadData];
 }];
```

This reloads our entire table view whenever we receive a refresh notification.

Finally, we need to remove our new observer. Add the following code to the bottom of `removeNotifications`:

```
if (self.documentRefreshAllObserver)
{
    [center removeObserver:self.documentRefreshAllObserver];
    self.documentRefreshAllObserver = nil;
}
```

That's it. Delete `WeightHistoryDocument_old.h` and `WeightHistoryDocument_old.m`, and then clean the project. Run the application. Try adding and deleting weights. Navigate to the history view, and shake to undo. Everything should work as expected.

Launch it on a second device; all the weights should transfer. Put the first device on the graph view. Then enter a new weight on the second device, and put that app into the background. Within a minute or so, the first device's screen should change.

Try disabling iCloud Document Storage. All the weight entries that we saved to the cloud should disappear. Reenable document storage, and they will reappear again.

Next, put one device into airplane mode, and then create conflicting changes on both devices. Force-save the changes by putting the app temporarily in the background. Then take the device out of airplane mode. Everything should sync, and the conflicts should resolve properly.

And, one final test. Shut down the app, and then delete it from one device. Rerun the app. It will take a long time, sometimes five minutes or more, but eventually it will download and display all the old data from iCloud.

NOTE: There is one other odd bit about Core Data and iCloud. If we delete the data from iCloud (either in the Settings app or from System Preferences) and re-launch one of our applications, it will actually repopulate the cloud data from its local store. If we want to erase all the iCloud data, we need to delete the data from the cloud and remove the application from all our devices. Then we can reload and relaunch our devices with a clean slate.

Alternatively, we can call `removeUbiquitousContentAndPersistentStoreAtURL:options:error:` and wait for the changes to sync to all our devices. This method deletes the local store and then deletes the iCloud data, providing us with a fresh, clean slate.

WRAPPING UP

We just finished what amounts to open-heart surgery on our application, gutting and replacing its entire model. It was a long haul with a lot of code, but none of the individual parts was terribly complicated. Most importantly, we could rebuild it. We could make it better than it was before. Better. Stronger. Faster.

Core Data is a complex framework with a number of very powerful features, and we're only scratching the surface here. Unfortunately, Health Beat's data model is so simple, you get only a smallest taste of what Core Data has to offer. Still, this chapter should give you a strong understanding of the fundamentals and enough hands-on experience to build a solid foundation for your own explorations.

Next up, we're going to go back to the user interface. We're going to use a few of iOS 7's flashiest new features to spice things up a bit.

OTHER RESOURCES

- **Core Data Programming Guide**

  iOS Developer's Library

  Core Data is a deep, rich topic. Unfortunately, there is only so much that we can cover in one chapter. If you want to learn more, I highly recommend reading through the Core Data Programming Guide. It provides in-depth explanations on every aspect of Core Data.

- **Predicate Programming Guide**

  iOS Developer's Library

  This guide covers a number of advanced topics on both creating and using predicates. If you would like to learn how to programmatically create predicates, or how to dynamically set key paths, this is your guide. It also includes a full description of the predicate format string syntax.

- **What's New in Core Data and iCloud**

  WWDC 2013 Videos

  Unfortunately, it looks like Apple has not yet updated their documentation on iCloud and Core Data. The existing documentation continues to refer to techniques used in iOS 6, which are no longer recommended when building iOS 7 apps. For now, this WWDC session remains the best resource for learning about syncing Core Data with iCloud.

CHAPTER 8

Advanced User Interfaces

A lot of digital ink has been spent discussing Apple's move away from skeuomorphism in iOS 7. In this context, *skeuomorphism* refers to a style of user interface design where digital objects retain characteristics of their physical ancestors. Most famously, previous versions of Apple's Calendar was designed to look like a physical calendar, down to its stitched leather trim and the torn remains of previous pages along the top edge.

When the iPhone first came out, it was a new type of device. Those skeuomorphic queues often helped orient new users. The calendar felt familiar, which made it easier to understand and use.

Unfortunately, this also limited what we, as developers, could do with our user interfaces. As purely digital constructs, our applications are really limited only by our imaginations. There are any number of designs and features we could explore that have no analog in the real world. So, while pursuing skeuomorphic designs, we often sacrificed functionality for familiarity.

iOS 7 has abandoned this type of skeumorphic design. Partially this is a pragmatic response to the changes in its users. The iPhone is now a mature technology. Users understand how to manipulate the world under the glass screen. They no longer need the handholding that skeumorphic design provided. Partially this change reflects current trends and styles. We can argue about what had the biggest effect, but in iOS 7 the flatter, simpler interface dominates.

Or does it? If you take a snapshot of the user interface, it appears flatter. However, if you actually use the device, there's a lot going on. iOS 7 emphasizes motion and animation. Some of these are playful, like the parallax effect on the home screen or the slight bounce and wiggle in Messages' conversation bubbles. Some are informative, such as the zooming transitions in Calendar, as we drill down from year to month to day.

Ironically, these motion effects mean that we may have simply moved from one type of skeumorphic design to another. Instead of trying to build interfaces that look like real objects, we're now trying to build interfaces that move like real objects. Even Calendar's zoom has a natural feeling of acceleration and deceleration to the effect. In its own applications, Apple has worked hard to create a sense of motion that feels right. More importantly, it has given us the tools to do the same thing in our own apps.

In Chapter 4, "Custom Views and Custom Transitions" we learned how to make custom transitions using Core Animation. In this chapter, we will focus on techniques for making those animations and transitions feel more alive and real.

We will start with UIMotionEffect. This is the technology behind the parallax effect on the home screen. We will use it to add a similar effect to our Add Entry view. Then we will dig into UIKit Dynamics. UIKit Dynamics lets us design animation sequences using a 2D physics engine. This lets us easily design transitions that appear physically real.

CREATING MOTION EFFECTS

iOS devices contain a wide range of sensors that let them respond to user motion. On the small scale, they contain accelerometers, gyroscopes, and a magnetic compass. This lets the system detect changes in the device's orientation, shake gestures, and more.

On the large scale, it can both triangulate its location based on cell towers and known Wi-Fi hot-spots and use its GPS. In both cases, iOS integrates information from multiple sensors, letting it calculate its position and orientation with more precision than using a single sensor alone.

The iPhone 5s further expands these capabilities with its M7 motion coprocessor. This lets the iPhone monitor, process, and store data from the accelerometers, gyroscopes, and compass outside its main CPU. This greatly reduces the amount of power needed to handle these motions, enabling continual monitoring of the device's motion even when the device is asleep.

It's important to note that we could duplicate the parallax effect, even in previous versions of iOS, using the `CMMotionManager` class. We register for device motion updates and then adjust our user interface based on these updates. Of course, we'd have to handle a lot of the low-level details—and a lot of the math—on our own.

While this fine-grained approach is great if we want to create a tilt-based game control or a Fitbit-like fitness tracker, if we just want to have our views react to our device's motion, there's a much simpler way.

`UIMotionEffect` is an abstract class designed to automatically respond to changes in the device's motion and update our user interface. We cannot instantiate this class directly; instead, we must subclass it, overriding its `keyPathsAndRelativeValuesForViewerOffset:` method.

When this method is called, the system hands us a `UIOffset`. This structure contains the horizontal and vertical rotation information. Each of these is rated from -1.0 to 1.0. An offset value of {0.0, 0.0} means the device is facing directly toward the user. A value of {1.0, 0.0} means it's rotated 90° to the right, and {-1.0, 0.0} is 90° to the left. A value of {0.0, 1.0} is face down, while {0.0, -1.0} is face up.

Given these offsets, we calculate and return a dictionary containing a number of key-value pairs for properties that we want to change. The keys must be key paths to animatable properties in our view, its layer, or a subview that is accessible through our view's properties. The value is the new value for the property.

While this gives us a lot of flexibility, it still involves a lot of work. If we want something even simpler, we can use its concrete subclass `UIInterpolatingMotionEffect`.

Here, we just create an instance of `UIInterpolatingMotionEffect`. In the `initWithKeyPath:type:` method we specify both the key path we want to modify and the type—whether the effect is based on horizontal or vertical motion. Note that we can affect only one key path in one direction with a single `UIInterpolatingMotionEffect`. This means we usually need at least two motion effects to create the desired visual effect.

Once we have our motion effect, we still need to set its `minimumRelativeValue` and its `maximumRelativeValue`. These measure the amount the key path's value will change relative to its starting value. For example, when modifying the view's `center.x` property with a horizontal motion effect, the `minimumRelativeValue` would be the distance that the center would shift when the view was rotated completely to the left. The `maximumRelativeValue` would be the distance that the center would shift when the view was rotated completely to the right.

Once configured, we add the motion effect to our view by calling `-[UIView addMotionEffect:]`. The system will handle everything else.

> **NOTE:** Users can disable motion effects using the Settings app. Just go to General > Accessibility > Reduce Motion. Turning this setting on will automatically disable all `UIMotionEffect` subclasses.
>
> This is one of the major advantages of using `UIMotionEffect`s. While we could duplicate the basic behaviors using custom code, we couldn't tie ourselves into the accessibility settings like this.

ADDING MOTION EFFECTS TO ADD ENTRY VIEW

Many of the built-in pop-up views automatically respond to device motion. Alert views, for example, will wiggle around as you rotate the device. We want to duplicate this behavior with our Add Entry View.

Let's start by opening AddEntryViewController.m. At the top of the file, declare the following constant variable:

```
static const CGFloat MaximumMotion = 15.0;
```

This defines the maximum range of motion. Our view will shift up to 15 points to the right, left, up, or down. We can then modify this value to increase or decrease the amount of motion.

> **NOTE:** Fifteen may be a bit high for a production app. I picked a value large enough to make the effect easy to see, ideally without being overwhelming. Still, you might want to use a slightly subtler range of motion in your final app.

Next, at the bottom of the class extension, add the following two properties:

```
@property (strong, nonatomic) UIInterpolatingMotionEffect
*horizontalMotionEffect;

@property (strong, nonatomic) UIInterpolatingMotionEffect
*verticalMotionEffect;
```

When using the UIInterpolatingMotionEffect, we must create a separate effect for each axis. Therefore, we almost always create two effects (unless we're just animating changes along one axis, of course).

Now, scroll down to viewDidLoad. Modify it as shown here:

```
- (void)viewDidLoad
{
    [super viewDidLoad];
    self.date = [NSDate date];
    self.weight = 0.0;
    [self setupInputAccessories];
    [self setupNotifications];
    [self setupMotionEffects];
}
```

We're just adding a call to our yet-undefined `setupMotionEffects` method. So far so good; however, now things get complicated. Remember, our Add Entry View is displayed as part of a custom modal view transition. As you may remember from Chapter 4, the container view does not rotate for modal transitions. This means we need to programmatically adjust for any difference between our Add Entry View's orientation and the container view's orientation. For more information about this issue, refer to Chapter 4. We will handle this by rebuilding our motion effects after each rotation.

Navigate to `willAnimateRotationToInterfaceOrientation:toInterfaceOrientation:` and modify the method as shown here:

```
- (void)willAnimateRotationToInterfaceOrientation:
(UIInterfaceOrientation)toInterfaceOrientation
duration:(NSTimeInterval)duration
{
    [self centerViewInParent];

    if ([self.view.motionEffects count] > 0)
    {
        [self setupMotionEffects];
    }
}
```

Here, we just check to see whether we have any active motion effects. If we do, we rebuild them for the new orientation.

Also, much of the time the keyboard covers our Add Entry View. We don't really want the view to move around while the keyboard is displayed—that just looks odd. Therefore, we should disable the motion when the keyboard appears and reenable it when the keyboard disappears. We will do this by adding and removing the motion events in response to our keyboard notifications.

Scroll down to the `setupNotifications` method. Add the following code to the top of the `UIKeyboardWillShowNotification` block (right before `_self.keyboardIsShown = YES;`):

```
[self.view removeMotionEffect:self.horizontalMotionEffect];
[self.view removeMotionEffect:self.verticalMotionEffect];
```

This removes our motion effects, disabling them.

We also need to enable them when the keyboard appears. Again, we want to make sure they are set up correctly for the current orientation, so let's rebuild them again. Add the following line to the top of the `UIKeyboardWillHideNotification` block:

```
[self setupMotionEffects];
```

Now we just need to set up our motion effects. Add the following to the bottom of our private methods:

```objc
- (void)setupMotionEffects
{
    if ([self.view.motionEffects count] > 0)
    {
        [self.view removeMotionEffect:self.horizontalMotionEffect];
        [self.view removeMotionEffect:self.verticalMotionEffect];
    }

    NSString *horizontalKeyPath;
    NSString *verticalKeyPath;
    NSNumber *horizontalMax;
    NSNumber *horizontalMin;
    NSNumber *verticalMax;
    NSNumber *verticalMin;

    switch (self.interfaceOrientation) {
        case UIInterfaceOrientationPortrait:
            horizontalKeyPath = @"center.x";
            verticalKeyPath = @"center.y";
            horizontalMin = @(-MaximumMotion);
            horizontalMax = @(MaximumMotion);
            verticalMin = @(-MaximumMotion);
            verticalMax = @(MaximumMotion);
            break;

        case UIInterfaceOrientationLandscapeLeft:
            horizontalKeyPath = @"center.y";
            verticalKeyPath = @"center.x";
            horizontalMin = @(MaximumMotion);
            horizontalMax = @(-MaximumMotion);
            verticalMin = @(-MaximumMotion);
            verticalMax = @(MaximumMotion);
            break;

        case UIInterfaceOrientationLandscapeRight:
            horizontalKeyPath = @"center.y";
            verticalKeyPath = @"center.x";
```

```
            horizontalMin = @(-MaximumMotion);
            horizontalMax = @(MaximumMotion);
            verticalMin = @(MaximumMotion);
            verticalMax = @(-MaximumMotion);
            break;

        default:
            [NSException
             raise:NSGenericException
             format:@"Invalid orientation %@",
             @(self.interfaceOrientation)];
    }


    self.horizontalMotionEffect =
    [[UIInterpolatingMotionEffect alloc]
     initWithKeyPath:horizontalKeyPath
     type:UIInterpolatingMotionEffectTypeTiltAlongHorizontalAxis];

    self.horizontalMotionEffect.minimumRelativeValue = horizontalMin;
    self.horizontalMotionEffect.maximumRelativeValue = horizontalMax;

    self.verticalMotionEffect =
    [[UIInterpolatingMotionEffect alloc]
     initWithKeyPath:verticalKeyPath
     type:UIInterpolatingMotionEffectTypeTiltAlongVerticalAxis];

    self.verticalMotionEffect.minimumRelativeValue = verticalMin;
    self.verticalMotionEffect.maximumRelativeValue = verticalMax;

    [self.view addMotionEffect:self.horizontalMotionEffect];
    [self.view addMotionEffect:self.verticalMotionEffect];
}
```

That's a large chunk of code. Most of the time it's not nearly this hard. In an ideal world (basically anything other than a modal custom transition), we would just create a horizontal motion effect that modified our view's center.x and create a vertical motion effect that modified its center.y. For both effects, we set the minimum relative value to –MaximumMotion and the maximum to MaximumMotion. Notice that we must assign objects to these properties, not C scalar values. Then we would just add the motion effects to our views.

Unfortunately, we're not in that world. Instead, we create a bunch of local variables to hold all the values that could change based on the orientation. Basically, that's the key path and both the minimum and maximum relative values for each axis. Then, in a switch statement, we set those values based on our current orientation. Only then can we create our motion effects and assign them to our views.

That's it. Build and run the application. You will need to test it on an actual iOS device—the simulator does not simulate motion effects. When you bring up the Add Entry View, it should have the keyboard displayed above it. Notice that the view does not move as you tilt the device. Dismiss the keyboard. Notice how the view now moves. Try rotating the device into different orientations and verify that the motion effects still work by tilting it. You can also try changing the `MaximumMotion` value, and observe how that changes the application's look and feel.

CREATING PHYSICALLY REAL ANIMATIONS

UIKit Dynamics is a physics-based, declarative animation and interaction system. It is designed to be composable. We will create complex behaviors by combining multiple low-level behaviors. Furthermore, the behavior's tree-like structure lets us easily add or remove an entire subtree of behaviors at once. This makes it easy to design and reuse custom behaviors.

UIKit Dynamics is not a replacement for Core Animation. In fact, it is built upon Core Animation and is designed to work well within custom transitions. Instead, UIKit Dynamics lets us create animation effects that would be difficult, if not impossible, to build with Core Animation directly.

There are three main components to UIKit Dynamics: `UIDynamicItem`, `UIDynamic Behavior`, and `UIDynamicAnimator`.

`UIDynamicItem` defines a protocol for items that can be modified by UIKit Dynamics. The protocol simply declares a `bounds`, `center`, and `transform` property. Both `UIView` and `UICollectionViewLayoutAttributes` adopt this protocol, but we are free to create our own custom objects. This is particularly useful if we want to have "invisible" objects on the screen that respond to or affect other `UIDynamicItems`.

`UIDynamicBehaviors` define a single type of behavior inside our 2D physics world. The `UIDynamicBehavior` class is the parent class for a number of low-level behaviors: `UIAttachmentBehavior`, `UICollisionBehavior`, `UIDynamicItemBehavior`, `UIGravityBehavior`, `UIPushBehavior`, and `UISnapBehavior`. We will often create custom `UIDynamicBehavior` classes that combine multiple low-level behaviors into a single effect. For example, combining gravity and collisions to create a bounce effect. We will assign one or more `UIDynamicItems` to each behavior, and the behavior will animate those items.

Each behavior also has an `action` property that takes a simple block. The animator will call these blocks during each update step. This lets us inject our own code into the animation.

The UIDynamicAnimator runs our physics-based animations. We instantiate an animator and then provide it with one or more dynamic behaviors. These behaviors, in turn, hold the dynamic items that they affect. The dynamic animator also has a reference view, which provides the coordinate system for our animations.

As long as the animator exists, it will run its behaviors. We can cancel or disable a behavior either by removing the behavior from the animator or by deallocating the animator.

> **NOTE:** Make sure you have a strong reference to your UIDynamicAnimator instance somewhere in your code. If you ever set up UIKit Dynamics and nothing happens, it's probably because your animator was not retained and was therefore automatically deallocated, canceling the animations.

EXPLORING UIDYNAMICBEHAVIOR

The UIDynamicBehavior subclasses are where the digital tires meet the electronic super highway. As we have seen, iOS provides a number of pre-defined, low-level behaviors that we can combine into more complex effects. In fact, most of our UIKit Dynamics code focuses on creating, configuring, and combining behaviors. However, before we can do that, we need to understand the existing, primitive behaviors.

- UIAttachmentBehavior: This behavior defines a connection between two dynamic items or between an item and an anchor point. By default, the attachment connects to the center of each item, though we can modify that if we want. Attachments can act either as fixed rods or as springs. We can configure both its frequency and its damping, letting us control the amount of bounce. Attachments also provide a convenient way to add interactivity to our layout. We can use a gesture recognizer to move the anchor point, letting us drag items around the screen.

- UICollisionBehavior: This behavior lets its items collide with each other and with the collision's boundaries. Items that belong to the same collision behavior cannot overlap each other. Collisions are often the basis for letting one view bounce off, push, or stack on top of another view.

    We can define a collision delegate, allowing us to programmatically respond to collisions. We also have a number of methods to set the collision's boundaries—either by setting them relative to the dynamic animator's reference view's bounds or by explicitly defining them using a UIBezierPath.

    Many of the properties that define collision (especially density, elasticity, and allowsRotation) are actually defined using UIDynamicItemBehavior.

- UIDynamicItemBehavior: This behavior lets us customize the physical properties of our dynamic items, thus letting us modify other behaviors. The dynamic item behavior includes properties for our object's angularResistance, density, elasticity, friction, and resistance. Other properties may be calculated using these. For example, a dynamic item's bounds and density determine its mass. We can also use this item to directly get or set the angular and linear velocity of our object.

We have to be a little careful when using multiple dynamic item behaviors within a behavior hierarchy. If more than one behavior has a given property, the last behavior wins. Behavior order is determined using a pre-order depth-first walk of the tree. This is not necessarily the order in which behaviors were created and added to the tree.

- `UIGravityBehavior`: All items included in the gravity behavior will accelerate along the gravity's vector. By default, the vector is {0.0, 1.0}, indicating that all items will accelerate at 1000 pt/s2 down. We can adjust this by modifying the angle, magnitude, or the gravity vector.

- `UIPushBehavior`: This behavior lets us apply force to our items, moving them around the screen. We can either apply an instantaneous or continuous force. Just like gravity, we can set the `angle`, `magnitude`, or `pushDirection`. However, unlike gravity, the acceleration will vary depending on the item's mass. Applying a continuous force of magnitude 1.0 to a 100 pt x 100 pt item with a density of 1.0 will accelerate it by 100 pt/s2.

  By default, the force is applied to the center of the item; however, we can specify an offset—letting us spin or wrench our items around.

- `UISnapBehavior`: This behavior lets us move an item to a point with a spring-like behavior. We specify a single dynamic item and a point. We can also set the behavior's `damping`, which will affect the number of oscillations before the animation comes to rest.

  While this can be useful as part of a more complex behavior, if you just want to move something with a spring-like bounce, consider using +[UIView animateWithDuration: delay:usingSpringWithDamping:initialSpringVelocity:options:animations: completion] instead.

PERFORMANCE NOTES

While generally well behaved, there are a few points to consider when implementing a dynamic system.

- The `UIDynamicAnimator` will continue processing the behaviors for all the items in the behavior hierarchy until the system comes to rest. Once all items are resting, the animator will pause.

- Not all systems will come to rest. We may need to explicitly cancel some animations after a fixed duration, or after its items leave the screen.

- The animator will continue to process items that are not on the screen.

- Collision behaviors can be quite costly, especially if you define a large number of items that can all interact with each other. Try to limit the number of colliding items or possible combinations.

- Since UIKit Dynamics modifies a view's position by modifying its bounds or center, it may not play nicely with Auto Layout. If we're working with views that are part of a custom transition or views that we programmatically add to the view hierarchy, then we shouldn't have any problems. If we are trying to animate and move items that are part of our existing layout and that have explicit Auto Layout constraints, we may need to remove the constraints before we animate the object and then add new constraints after we're done.

MAKING OUR ADD ENTRY VIEW BOUNCE

Currently, our Add Entry View fades in and out. Let's have it drop from the top of the screen and bounce slightly, like it landed on a hard surface. Then, when the view's dismissed, we want it to accelerate upward, matching the acceleration of its fall. While we're at it, let's let the user dismiss the view by dragging it upward.

We will implement some, but not all, of this using UIKit Dynamics. That is probably the most important lesson here. Don't feel the need to use UIKit Dynamics for everything. We can freely mix and match it with other animation or gesture-based techniques.

BUILDING OUR BEHAVIORS

Let's start by building our behaviors. We need two separate, complex behaviors: a bounce behavior for when the view appears and a lift behavior for when it disappears. However, in both cases we will want to be able to set an initial velocity. Additionally, since these behaviors will run during a custom transition, we need to track the device's orientation. That's a lot of common behaviors between the two classes. Let's extract all of that out to an abstract superclass.

Create a new Objective-C class in the Animators group. Name it AbstractBehavior, and set its superclass to UIDynamicBehavior. Now open `AbstractBehavior.h` and modify it as shown here:

```objc
#import <UIKit/UIKit.h>

@interface AbstractBehavior : UIDynamicBehavior

@property (strong, nonatomic, readonly) id<UIDynamicItem> item;
@property (assign, nonatomic, readonly) UIInterfaceOrientation orientation;

- (id)initWithItem:(id<UIDynamicItem>)item
          velocity:(CGPoint)velocity
       orientation:(UIInterfaceOrientation)orientation;

- (void)setupBehaviors;
@end
```

We're simply declaring two read-only properties. The first will let us access the dynamic item that we're animating. The second lets us access the current user interface. Then we declare a custom `init` method that takes three arguments: our item, our item's current velocity, and our orientation. Finally, we declare a `setupBehaviors` method. Our subclasses will have to override this method to set up their behaviors.

Switch to `AbstractBehavior.m`. Let's start by declaring a class extension containing three properties.

```
@interface AbstractBehavior ()
@property (strong, nonatomic, readwrite) id<UIDynamicItem> item;
@property (assign, nonatomic, readwrite) UIInterfaceOrientation
orientation;
@property (assign, nonatomic) CGPoint velocity;
@end
```

We start by redeclare the `item` and `orientation` properties as read-write. Then we declare a private `velocity` property. With those in place, let's move on to the methods. Define our init methods as shown here:

```
// Designated Initializer
- (id)initWithItem:(id<UIDynamicItem>)item
          velocity:(CGPoint)velocity
       orientation:(UIInterfaceOrientation)orientation
{
    self = [super init];
    if (self) {
        _item = item;
        _velocity = velocity;
        _orientation = orientation;
        [self setupPrivateBehaviors];
        [self setupBehaviors];
    }
    return self;
}


- (id)init
{
    [self doesNotRecognizeSelector:_cmd];
    return nil;
}
```

`initWithItem:velocity:orientation:` is our new designated initializer. It sets our properties' initial values and then calls the `setupPrivateBehaviors` and `setupBehaviors` methods. `setupPrivateBehaviors` will set up the common behaviors shared by all subclasses, while `setupBehaviors` will be overridden by each individual subclass to set up their individual behaviors.

Since we're creating a custom `init` method, we also need to override our superclass's designated initializer. In this case, that's just `init`. Here, we simply call `doesNotRecognizeSelector:`. By default this will throw an exception if `init` is called. This forces us to always create our classes using the designated initializer.

Next, let's implement `setupBehaviors`. This ends up looking similar to our `init` method, though it has a very different meaning.

```
#pragma mark - Abstract Methods

- (void)setupBehaviors
{
    [self doesNotRecognizeSelector:_cmd];
}
```

Like `init`, this will throw an exception if called. However, with `init`, we were trying to prevent developers from calling `init`, forcing them to use `initWithItem:velocity:orientation:`. Here, we're forcing the developers to override `setupBehaviors` in their subclasses. This method will be automatically called when the behavior is instantiated. If we forget to override `setupBehaviors`, our application will crash.

Finally, let's implement `setupBehaviors`.

```
#pragma mark - Private Methods

- (void)setupPrivateBehaviors
{
    UIDynamicItemBehavior *itemBehavior =
    [[UIDynamicItemBehavior alloc] initWithItems:@[self.item]];

    [itemBehavior addLinearVelocity:self.velocity
                            forItem:self.item];

    [self addChildBehavior:itemBehavior];
}
```

In this method, we instantiate a dynamic item behavior. We typically use item behaviors to configure an item's physical characteristics for the 2D physics engine such as its density, the amount of bounce it has in collisions, and the amount of friction it has while sliding along another item or boundary. In our case, we're adding a linear velocity to our item. We will use this to match our pan gesture's velocity when implementing the interactive code.

After we create the item behavior, we add it as a child of the current behavior. And that's it. We're done with our abstract class.

Now we need to create our concrete subclasses. Let's start with the bounce behavior. We will use this to animate the Add Entry View's appearance. We will also use it when the pan gesture is canceled to return the view to its original position.

Add another Objective-C class to the Animators group. This time name it BounceBehavior and make it a subclass of AbstractBehavior.

Open BounceBehavior.m. Let's declare a class extension with a single property.

```
@interface BounceBehavior ()
@property (weak, nonatomic) UICollisionBehavior *collision;
@end
```

Here, we're just creating a property to store our collision behavior. We will be modifying this behavior programmatically, so we need to hold onto a reference.

Next, inside the @implementation block, override willMoveToAnimator: as shown. This method will be called whenever our behavior is added to a dynamic animator. This is important because we need access to the dynamic animator's reference view before we can properly set up our collision boundary.

```
- (void)willMoveToAnimator:(UIDynamicAnimator *)dynamicAnimator
{
    [super willMoveToAnimator:dynamicAnimator];
    CGRect containerBounds = dynamicAnimator.referenceView.bounds;

    CGFloat itemHeight = CGRectGetHeight(self.item.bounds);

    CGFloat top = 0.0;
    CGFloat bottom = 0.0;
    CGFloat left = 0.0;
    CGFloat right = 0.0;

    switch (self.orientation)
    {
        case UIInterfaceOrientationPortrait:
            top = -1000.0;
            bottom = CGRectGetMidY(containerBounds) -
            itemHeight / (CGFloat)2.0;
            break;

        case UIInterfaceOrientationLandscapeLeft:
            left = -1000.0;
            right = CGRectGetMidX(containerBounds) -
            itemHeight / (CGFloat)2.0;
```

```
        break;

    case UIInterfaceOrientationLandscapeRight:
        right = CGRectGetMaxX(containerBounds) +
        (CGFloat)1000.0;
        left = CGRectGetMidX(containerBounds) -
        itemHeight / (CGFloat)2.0;
        break;

    default:
        [NSException
         raise:NSGenericException
         format:@"Invalid orientation %@",
         @(self.orientation)];
    }

    UIEdgeInsets insets = UIEdgeInsetsMake(top, left, bottom, right);
    [self.collision
      setTranslatesReferenceBoundsIntoBoundaryWithInsets:insets];
}
```

While this looks complex, it's mostly just the extra code to support our different orientations between our Add Entry View and the transition's container view.

We want our collision boundary to roughly match our reference view's bounds—however, we don't really want a top. While I could create an open-topped UIBezierPath, it's easier to just offset the top by 1,000 points—that's high enough that it won't matter. We also want our bottom to be slightly below the center of the reference view—half our Add Entry View's height, to be precise. This way when our Add Entry View is resting on the boundary, it will be centered in the reference view.

The rest of the code is dedicated to calculating the correct insets given our current orientation. Remember, we pass the orientation as one of the arguments to our abstract superclass's designated initializer. The superclass saved it in a property and exposed the public property as read-only. That means we can access (but not modify) the orientation here in our subclass. Once we have the correct inset values, we create our insets and call setTranslatesReferenceBoundsIntoBoundaryWithInsets: to create our collision boundary.

Next, we need to implement the setupBehaviors method. Here, we're going to create three behaviors. A gravity behavior will cause our view to accelerate downward. A collision behavior will cause our view to bounce off and then settle into position atop the bottom boundary. Finally, an item behavior lets us set our view's elasticity, controlling how much it bounces. It also lets us disable rotations—guaranteeing that the view falls and bounces straight up and down.

The only tricky part is defining what *up* and *down* mean.

```
#pragma mark - AbstractBehavior Methods


- (void)setupBehaviors
{
    NSArray *items = @[self.item];
    UIGravityBehavior *gravity =
    [[UIGravityBehavior alloc] initWithItems:items];


    CGVector gravityDirection;
    switch (self.orientation)
    {
        case UIInterfaceOrientationPortrait:
            gravityDirection = CGVectorMake(0.0, 2.0);
            break;
        case UIInterfaceOrientationLandscapeLeft:
            gravityDirection = CGVectorMake(2.0, 0.0);
            break;
        case UIInterfaceOrientationLandscapeRight:
            gravityDirection = CGVectorMake(-2.0, 0.0);
            break;
        default:
            [NSException
             raise:NSGenericException
             format:@"Invalid orientation %@",
             @(self.orientation)];
    }


    gravity.gravityDirection = gravityDirection;


    UICollisionBehavior *collision =
    [[UICollisionBehavior alloc] initWithItems:items];


    UIDynamicItemBehavior *itemBehavior =
    [[UIDynamicItemBehavior alloc] initWithItems:@[self.item]];
    itemBehavior.elasticity = 0.4;
    itemBehavior.allowsRotation = NO;
```

```
[self addChildBehavior:gravity];
[self addChildBehavior:collision];
[self addChildBehavior:itemBehavior];

self.collision = collision;
}
```

We start by creating our gravity behavior. Then we set the gravity's direction based on our orientation. Note that we're using 2.0 for the vector's length. This means our gravity will be twice as strong as the default 1000 pt/s2. The default gravity felt a little too slow for my tastes, but feel free to fine-tune the value on your own.

Next, we create our collision behavior; however, we delay its configuration until willMoveToAnimator:.

After that we instantiate our item behavior. Here, we set the elasticity to 0.4. An elasticity of 0.0 means there will be no bounce at all. A 1.0 means the item will be perfectly elastic. After a collision it will leave the boundary going the same speed but in the opposite direction. Here, we are giving our view a fair bit of bounce, but it still settles down relatively quickly. Again, you can fine-tune this value to better suit your own tastes.

We also disable rotation by setting allowsRotation to NO.

With all our behaviors are ready, we add them as child behaviors. This lets us simply add our BounceBehavior to—or remove it from—the dynamic animator. Its entire subtree comes along for the ride.

Finally, we assign our collision behavior to the collision property. This lets us access and configure it during willMoveToAnimator:.

Our LiftBehavior class is similar, but even simpler, since we don't need to create the collision boundary. Start by creating a new class named LiftBehavior that subclasses Abstract-Behavior, placing it inside the Animators group. Then open LiftBehavior.m. We just need to implement one method, setupBehaviors.

```
- (void)setupBehaviors
{
    UIPushBehavior *push =
    [[UIPushBehavior alloc] initWithItems:@[self.item]
                                     mode:UIPushBehaviorModeContinuous];

    CGFloat area = CGRectGetHeight(self.item.bounds) *
    CGRectGetWidth(self.item.bounds);

    CGFloat magnitude =  area / (CGFloat)1000.0 * (CGFloat)2.0;
    CGFloat angle;
```

```
    switch (self.orientation)
    {
        case UIInterfaceOrientationPortrait:
            angle = (CGFloat)-M_PI_2;
            break;

        case UIInterfaceOrientationLandscapeLeft:
            angle = (CGFloat)M_PI;
            break;

        case UIInterfaceOrientationLandscapeRight:
            angle = 0.0;
            break;

        default:
            [NSException
             raise:NSGenericException
             format:@"Invalid orientation %@",
             @(self.orientation)];
    }

    [push setAngle:angle magnitude:magnitude];

    [self addChildBehavior:push];
}
```

This time we need to create only a single behavior, a continuous push behavior. However, we want to match the acceleration from our push behavior to the acceleration from gravity. We do that by finding the area of our view, dividing that by 1000.0, and multiplying it by the magnitude of our gravity. Unfortunately, that means if we modify the gravity in our Bounce Behavior, we will also need to modify this as well.

Next, we want to determine the correct angle for our push. It should be up—but up varies depending on our orientation. Once we have both the magnitude and the angle, we can call setAngle:magnitude: and then add our behavior as a child.

Our behaviors are ready to use. Now we just need to create new animation transition controllers to set up and kick off these animations.

ANIMATION TRANSITION CONTROLLERS

Currently, we're using a single animation controller for both the push and the dismiss animation. I cleverly named it AddEntryAnimator. Now, we're going to replace it with two separate controllers: a BouncePresentationController and a LiftDismissalController.

This eliminates some of the complications we saw when using a single class to perform both roles. However, this comes at a cost—it uses twice as many classes. In this case, I think splitting the animation into two separate classes works better, since the actual animation code is very different. However, there is a lot of setup and management code that can be shared between the two. Again, we can create an abstract superclass to handle all the common code.

Create a new class named AbstractTransitionController and make it a subclass of NSObject. Then open AbstractTransitionController.h and modify the header file as shown here:

```
#import <Foundation/Foundation.h>

@interface AbstractTransitionController : NSObject
<UIViewControllerAnimatedTransitioning>

@property (strong, nonatomic) UIDynamicAnimator *animator;

// Must Override and call super before the subclass's implementation
- (void)animateTransition:(id<UIViewControllerContextTransitioning>)
transitionContext;

// Must Override
- (NSTimeInterval)horizontalAnimationDuration;
- (NSTimeInterval)verticalAnimationDuration;

// Call to cancel the animation
- (void)cancelAnimation;

@end
```

We start by adopting the controller transitioning protocol, and then we declare a single property, our dynamic animator. Once that's done, we declare a few other methods. Abstract classes typically have a few methods that its subclasses need to override. Here, we're redeclaring animateTransition: just to document that it must be overridden and that our implementation must call super before it does any work. The horizontalAnimationDuration and verticalAnimationDuration methods must also be overridden; however, they should not call super.

Now, switch to AbstractTransitionController.m and create a class extension with a single property declaration.

```
@interface AbstractTransitionController ()<UIDynamicAnimatorDelegate>
@property (strong, nonatomic) id<UIViewControllerContextTransitioning>context;
@end
```

We start by adopting the UIDynamicAnimatorDelegate property. This will let us receive updates from the animator. We also need to save a copy of our context so we can call completeTransition: when our animation sequence has finished.

> **NOTE:** Animations created using UIKit Dynamics do not necessarily have a set end point. Instead, we declare the properties for our dynamic system, and then we let it run. Sometimes it will come to rest and the animator will pause. Other times it won't. We need to define what finished means for our particular system, so we can call completeTransition:. There are three common options: end the transition once our animation pauses, end the transition after a specified duration, or end the transition once our item leaves the screen.

Next, we need to implement our methods. Let's start with the UIViewControllerAnimatedTransitioning methods. Implement transitionDuration: as shown here:

```
#pragma mark - UIViewControllerAnimatedTransitioning Methods


- (NSTimeInterval)transitionDuration:
(id<UIViewControllerContextTransitioning>)transitionContext
{
    UIViewController *modalController =
    [transitionContext viewControllerForKey:
     UITransitionContextToViewControllerKey];

    UIInterfaceOrientation orientation =
    modalController.interfaceOrientation;

    if (UIInterfaceOrientationIsPortrait(orientation))
    {
        return [self verticalAnimationDuration];
    }

    return [self horizontalAnimationDuration];
}
```

Here, we get our pop-up view controller from our context. Then we ask the pop-up controller for its current orientation. We use that to return the correct duration value. Each concrete subclass will implement verticalAnimationDuration and horizontalAnimation-Duration to return the correct value based on their particular animation sequence.

Next, let's implement animateTransition:. We're not going to actually set up the animation in this implementation. Our concrete subclass will need to override this method to do that. Instead, we're going to set up some of the background infrastructure.

```objc
- (void)animateTransition:(id<UIViewControllerContextTransitioning>)
transitionContext
{
    self.context = transitionContext;

    UIDynamicAnimator *animator =
    [[UIDynamicAnimator alloc] initWithReferenceView:
     [transitionContext containerView]];

    animator.delegate = self;
    self.animator = animator;

    __weak AbstractTransitionController *_self = self;
    __weak NSNotificationCenter *notificationCenter =
    [NSNotificationCenter defaultCenter];

    __block id observer =
    [notificationCenter
     addObserverForName:UIDeviceOrientationDidChangeNotification
     object:[UIDevice currentDevice]
     queue:nil
     usingBlock:^(NSNotification *note) {

         if (_self.animator.running)
         {
             [_self cancelAnimation];
         }
         [notificationCenter removeObserver:observer];
     }];
}
```

We start by assigning the incoming transitionContext to our context property.

Next, we instantiate a UIDynamicAnimator object. We use the transition context's container view as our reference view, since all the animation will occur within that view. Then we assign ourselves as the animator's delegate and assign the animator to our animator property.

Finally, we set up a one-shot notification. Once we receive the notification, we're going to remove our observer, preventing us from receiving it a second time. Therefore, if the device is rotated during our animation, we will cancel the animation. Otherwise, we do nothing.

This is important since the user may rotate the device immediately after triggering our animation. We want to make sure our system responds reasonably. If we don't cancel the animation, the animation will run to completion, and then the user interface will rotate. This makes our application feel sluggish and nonresponsive—and we don't want that.

Now, let's implement our UIDynamicAnimator methods.

```
#pragma mark - UIDynamicAnimatorDelegate Methods


- (void)dynamicAnimatorDidPause:(UIDynamicAnimator *)animator
{
    NSLog(@"Animation took %0.2f seconds",
        [self.animator elapsedTime]);

    [self cancelAnimation];
}


- (void)dynamicAnimatorWillResume:(UIDynamicAnimator *)animator
{
    // doesn't do anything.
}
```

These methods will be called in response to changes in our dynamic animator. Both methods are required, but we're really interested only in dynamicAnimatorDidPause:. Here, we log the amount of time the animator took to complete, and then we call cancelAnimation to end the transition.

This means our animation will automatically end whenever the system comes to rest. This won't work for all our animations, but it provides a reasonable default *finished* state.

Next, let's implement our horizontal and vertical duration methods.

```
#pragma mark - Abstract Methods


- (NSTimeInterval)horizontalAnimationDuration
{
    [self doesNotRecognizeSelector:_cmd];
    return 0.0;
```

```
}

- (NSTimeInterval)verticalAnimationDuration
{
    [self doesNotRecognizeSelector:_cmd];
    return 0.0;
}
```

These methods need to be overridden by our concrete subclasses, so we simply call doesNotRecognizeSelector:. We've seen this design before. If we forget to override these methods (or if we call super in our subclass's implementation), this will throw an exception.

Finally, let's implement our cancelAnimation method.

```
#pragma mark - Public Methods

- (void)cancelAnimation
{
    self.animator = nil;
    [self.context completeTransition:YES];
}
```

Here, we set our animator to nil. This will deallocate the animator, canceling any animations that are currently running. Then we call completeTransition: to finish our transition.

> **NOTE:** While the animation may be canceled, the transition will not. This is not an interactive transition; we will always move from the from-controller to the to-controller. Therefore, we must always pass YES to the completeTransition: method.

With the backend infrastructure in place, we can implement our concrete subclasses. Let's start with the presentation controller. Create a new class named BouncePresentation Controller. It should be a subclass of AbstractTransitionController.

Now, open BouncePresentationController.m and import BounceBehavior.h. Let's start by overriding animateTransition:.

```
- (void)animateTransition:(id<UIViewControllerContextTransitioning>)
transitionContext
{
    [super animateTransition:transitionContext];

    UIViewController *modalController =
    [transitionContext viewControllerForKey:
```

```
                  UITransitionContextToViewControllerKey];

    UIView *modalView = modalController.view;
    UIView *containerView = [transitionContext containerView];

    UIInterfaceOrientation orientation =
    modalController.interfaceOrientation;

    [self calculateFrameForModalView:modalView
                  inContainerView:containerView
                     orientation:orientation];

    [containerView addSubview:modalView];



    BounceBehavior *bounceBehavior =
    [[BounceBehavior alloc] initWithItem:modalView
                          velocity:CGPointZero
                      orientation:orientation];

    [self.animator addBehavior:bounceBehavior];
}
```

We start by calling super. This performs the background setup from our abstract class, including setting up our dynamic animator. Then we proceed to set up our animation. We start by grabbing our to-controller, our to-controller's view, and our context's container view.

Next, we need to calculate the proper starting position for our incoming view. It should be positioned just above the screen. Unfortunately, as we have seen already, the definition of *above* varies depending on our device's orientation. Therefore, we grab the current orientation, call a helper method to set up our frame, and then add the to-view to our container view.

We also need to instantiate our bounce behavior. It's going to start from a complete rest, so we set the initial velocity to {0.0, 0.0}, and we pass along our current orientation. Finally, we add the bounce behavior to our animator. This will start the animation. The animation ends when the system comes to rest and the animator pauses.

Next, we need to implement our duration methods, as shown here:

```
#pragma mark - Public Methods

- (NSTimeInterval)horizontalAnimationDuration
{
```

```
    return 1.62;
}

- (NSTimeInterval)verticalAnimationDuration
{
    return 1.86;
}
```

Since we're animating a view dropping from the top of our screen, the duration will vary depending on the device's orientation and the screen size. The farther the object must move, the longer the animation takes.

Fortunately, this does not need to be super precise. The system just uses this value if it needs to sync other animations with ours. To determine these values, I simply ran the animation and looked at the duration values that it printed to the console. Also, I used the 4-inch phone for both of these. We might want to modify the vertical animation duration—having it check the screen size before determining the duration. However, that's probably more complicated than is absolutely necessary. Instead, let's simply use the longer value unless we discover that it causes problems.

One last method: Implement calculateFrameForModalView:inContainerView: as shown here:

```
#pragma mark - Private Methods

- (void)calculateFrameForModalView:(UIView *)modalView
                  inContainerView:(UIView *)containerView
                      orientation:(UIInterfaceOrientation)orientation
{
    CGFloat containerViewWidth = CGRectGetWidth(containerView.bounds);
    CGPoint center;

    switch (orientation)
    {
        case UIInterfaceOrientationPortrait:
            modalView.frame = CGRectMake(0.0, -170.0, 280.0, 170.0);
            center = modalView.center;
            center.x = CGRectGetMidX(containerView.bounds);
            break;
        case UIInterfaceOrientationLandscapeLeft:
            modalView.frame = CGRectMake(-170.0, 0.0, 170.0, 280.0);
            center = modalView.center;
            center.y = CGRectGetMidY(containerView.bounds);
```

```
            break;
        case UIInterfaceOrientationLandscapeRight:
            modalView.frame =
            CGRectMake(containerViewWidth, 0.0, 170.0, 280.0);
            center = modalView.center;
            center.y = CGRectGetMidY(containerView.bounds);
            break;
        default:
            [NSException raise:NSGenericException
                        format:@"Invalid orientation %@", @(orientation)];
    }

    modalView.center = center;
}
```

This code is similar to the code to set the to-view's frame in -[AddEntryAnimator presentAddEntryViewController:overParentViewController:usingContainerView: transitionContext:]. However, there are two important differences. First, we're centering the view only horizontally, not vertically. Next, we need to move the view above the top of its superview. Unfortunately, this means we need to calculate a different frame for each of the three different orientations.

When aligning views, I often find that it's easier to create an initial frame and then modify the center. That's what we're doing here. We create a frame that is left aligned and just above the superview. Then we grab our center value, modify its horizontal component (x for portrait and y for landscape orientations), and then reassign it to our view.

That's it for the presentation controller; however, we still need our dismissal controller. Create yet another new class. Name this one LiftDismissalController and make it a subclass of AbstractTransitionController. Then open LiftDismissalController.h and declare a custom init method as shown here:

```
@interface LiftDismissalController : AbstractTransitionController
- (id)initWithVelocity:(CGPoint)velocity;
@end
```

Next, open LiftDismissalController.m and import LiftBehavior.h. Then declare a class extension with a single velocity property.

```
@interface LiftDismissalController ()
@property (assign, nonatomic) CGPoint velocity;
@end
```

And then implement our init methods. We need both our custom `initWithVelocity:` method and our superclass's designated initializer.

```
- (id)initWithVelocity:(CGPoint)velocity
{
    self = [super init];
    if (self) {
        _velocity = velocity;
    }
    return self;
}


- (id)init
{
    return [self initWithVelocity:CGPointZero];
}
```

There's nothing surprising going on here. We simply assign the velocity argument to our property. For the `init` method, we default to a velocity of {0.0, 0.0}.

Now we just need to override our three methods. Let's start with `animateTransition:`.

```
#pragma mark - UIViewControllerAnimatedTransitioning Methods


- (void)animateTransition:(id<UIViewControllerContextTransitioning>)
transitionContext
{
    [super animateTransition:transitionContext];

    UIViewController *modalController =
    [transitionContext viewControllerForKey:
     UITransitionContextFromViewControllerKey];

    UIView *modalView = modalController.view;
    UIView *containerView = [transitionContext containerView];

    LiftBehavior *lift =
    [[LiftBehavior alloc]
      initWithItem:modalView
      velocity:self.velocity
      orientation:modalController.interfaceOrientation];
```

```
    __weak LiftDismissalController *_self = self;
    lift.action = ^{
        CGRect intersection =
        CGRectIntersection(modalView.frame, containerView.bounds);

        if (CGRectIsEmpty(intersection))
        {
            NSLog(@"Duration = %0.2f", [_self.animator elapsedTime]);
            [_self cancelAnimation];
        }
    };

    [self.animator addBehavior:lift];
}
```

Again, we grab a reference to our pop-up view controller, its view, and the container view. Remember, the to- and from-controllers are reversed. In the presentation controller our pop-up controller was the to-controller. In the dismiss, our pop-up is the from-controller.

Next, we create or lift behavior, setting its initial velocity and orientation. Unlike our bounce behavior, this will never come to rest. Our view will continue to accelerate upward. Therefore, we need some way to stop the animation once we're finished. In this case, *finished* means our pop-up view is no longer on the screen.

To do this, we need to add an action to our behavior. The system will call our action's block during each update step. Here, we simply take the intersection of our pop-up view's frame and our container view's bounds. If the intersection is empty, the two views no longer overlap. We log out the duration and cancel the animation, ending the transition.

With everything done, we add our behavior to the animator. This starts the animation.

Finally, let's add our duration methods as shown here:

```
#pragma mark - Public Methods


- (NSTimeInterval)horizontalAnimationDuration
{
    return 0.51;
}


- (NSTimeInterval)verticalAnimationDuration
{
    return 0.62;
}
```

Again, I calculated these values by running the code and looking at the duration messages printed to the console. If you change the animation parameters, you may need to change these as well.

And that's it. Now we just need to use these transition controllers during our modal segue and then add a bit of interactivity.

MODIFYING HISTORYTABLEVIEWCONTROLLER

Switching our animation controllers is easy. We just need to change the controllers returned by HistoryTableViewController's animationControllerForPresentedController:presentingController:sourceController and animationControllerForDismissedController:. However, before we get there, let's add some infrastructure to support a bit interactivity as well.

Let's start by opening HistoryTableViewController.m and importing both Bounce PresentationController and LiftDismissalController. Then add the following property to the class extension:

```
@property (assign, nonatomic) CGPoint addEntryDismissVelocity;
```

We will use this to hold our Add Entry View Controller's velocity when it is dismissed using a gesture.

We also need to modify viewDidLoad as shown here:

```
- (void)viewDidLoad
{
    [super viewDidLoad];
    self.addEntryDismissVelocity = CGPointZero;
    self.navigationItem.leftBarButtonItem = self.editButtonItem;
}
```

We're just setting our dismiss velocity to {0.0, 0.0}. We will also need to set our dismiss velocity whenever our view is saved or canceled. Navigate down to addNewEntrySaved: and modify these methods as shown here:

```
- (IBAction)addNewEntrySaved:(UIStoryboardSegue *)segue
{
    self.addEntryDismissVelocity = CGPointZero;
    AddEntryViewController *controller = segue.sourceViewController;

    [self.weightHistoryDocument addEntryWithWeightInLbs:controller.weight
                                                  units:getDefaultUnits()
                                                   date:controller.date];

    [self dismissViewControllerAnimated:YES completion:nil];
    [self becomeFirstResponder];
}
```

Again, we just set our dismiss velocity to {0.0, 0.0}. We don't save our entry as part of a dismiss gesture. We save only when the user explicitly presses the Save button. This means our corresponding dismiss animation will always start from a dead stop.

Next, modify addNewEntryCanceled:.

```
- (IBAction)addNewEntryCanceled:(UIStoryboardSegue *)segue
{
    AddEntryViewController *controller = segue.sourceViewController;
    self.addEntryDismissVelocity = controller.velocity;
    [self dismissViewControllerAnimated:YES completion:nil];
    [self becomeFirstResponder];
}
```

Unlike the save action, we will provide a gesture for canceling the Add Entry View. This means the dismiss action might actually have an initial velocity. If it does, we want to grab it so we can use it in our animation.

Now, we can finally modify the UIViewControllerTransitioningDelegate methods. Navigate to animationControllerForPresentedController:presentingController: sourceController: and replace the current implementation with the following:

```
#pragma mark - UIViewControllerTransitioningDelegate Methods


- (id<UIViewControllerAnimatedTransitioning>)
animationControllerForPresentedController:(UIViewController *)presented
presentingController:(UIViewController *)presenting
sourceController:(UIViewController *)source
{
    return [[BouncePresentationController alloc] init];
}
```

Here, we just instantiate and return our BouncePresentationController. The dismiss controller is similar. The only difference is that we pass our dismiss velocity to its init method. Also replace the current implementation of animationControllerForDismissed Controller with the following:

```
- (id<UIViewControllerAnimatedTransitioning>)
animationControllerForDismissedController:(UIViewController *)dismissed
{
    return [[LiftDismissalController alloc]
            initWithVelocity:self.addEntryDismissVelocity];
}
```

That's it. Our new animation is ready to go. Unfortunately, we still have an error in addNewEntryCanceled:. However, we need that only for the interactive dismissals. If you comment out the top two lines of that method, you can build and run the application. Tap the + button. The Add Entry View should drop and bounce into place. It will then zoom out of the way when you tap either Save or Cancel.

Now, we just need to add the interactive bit. Uncomment the two lines in addNewEntry Canceled: and let's add our dismiss gesture.

IMPLEMENTING THE DISMISS GESTURE

We could implement the dismiss gesture in a number of ways. We could create an interactive transition controller, like we did in Chapter 4. However, that would be overkill. We don't need the extra framework to sync our gesture and our animation. Our lift behavior will work from any starting position. We just need to know its initial velocity, and we're good to go.

Similarly, we could implement everything using UIKit Dynamics. In this case, we add an attachment behavior to our view, and then we could move the attachment's anchor point with our gesture. However, UIKit Dynamics is also overkill. Our view doesn't interact with any other dynamic elements, so we don't need to use an attachment point to move it. We can just move it directly. Then, when our gesture is done, we create a new bounce or lift behavior to move it to the correct final position.

Let's start by opening AddEntryViewController.h. Create a read-only velocity property. This will let outside code access our gesture's final velocity.

```
@property (assign, nonatomic, readonly) CGPoint velocity;
```

Now, switch to AddEntryViewController.m and import our BounceBehavior.h. Then, at the top of the file, declare the following constant:

```
static const CGFloat DismissTriggerVelocity = 100.0;
```

We will use this value to determine whether our gesture should dismiss our view. If, when the gesture ends, our view is moving upward at a velocity greater than 100 pt/s we will dismiss the view. Otherwise, we'll just return it to its starting position.

Next, in the class extension, adopt the UIDynamicAnimatorDelegate protocol as shown here:

```
@interface AddEntryViewController ()
<UITextFieldDelegate, UIDynamicAnimatorDelegate>
```

We also need to declare two additional properties inside the class extension.

```
@property (assign, nonatomic, readwrite)CGPoint velocity;
@property (strong, nonatomic) UIDynamicAnimator *animator;
```

The velocity property simply redeclares our velocity property as read-write. Then we create a property to hold a dynamic animator.

Next, navigate down to `viewDidLoad` and modify it as shown here:

```
- (void)viewDidLoad
{
    [super viewDidLoad];
    self.date = [NSDate date];
    self.weight = 0.0;
    self.velocity = CGPointZero;
    [self setupInputAccessories];
    [self setupNotifications];
    [self setupMotionEffects];
}
```

Here, we just set our default velocity to {0.0, 0.0}.

Now, let's implement the gesture itself. Let's start with an action. We will eventually connect a gesture recognizer to this action, but for now just implement the drag method at the bottom of our action methods.

```
- (IBAction)drag:(UIPanGestureRecognizer *)sender {

    // ignore drag events if the keyboard is showing
    if (self.keyboardIsShown) return;

    static CGPoint originalCenter;

    UIView *superview = self.view.superview;
    CGPoint translation = [sender translationInView:superview];
    CGPoint velocity = [sender velocityInView:superview];

    switch (sender.state) {
        case UIGestureRecognizerStateBegan:
            [self weightEditingDone];
            originalCenter = self.view.center;
            break;

        case UIGestureRecognizerStateChanged:
            [self updateCenterUsingTranslation:translation
                            originalCenter:originalCenter];

            break;
```

```
    case UIGestureRecognizerStateEnded:
    case UIGestureRecognizerStateCancelled:
        [self endDragWithVelocity:velocity];
        break;

    default:
        [NSException
         raise:NSGenericException
         format:@"Invalid Gesture State: %@",
         @(sender.state)];
    }
}
```

We will move our view using a pan gesture recognizer, so we type the sender appropriately. Next, we check to see whether our keyboard is being displayed. If it is, we shouldn't respond to gestures, so we simply return.

Next we declare a static variable to hold our original center position. We've used static variables before. They are created when the application is compiled, not at runtime. Local static variables can be accessed only inside the method in which they are declared. They will hold their value, even after the method returns.

In this case, we're using a static local variable instead of using an instance variable. As I have said before, I dislike using instance variables for values that really need to be shared only temporarily among a handful of methods. It feels like we're leaking implementation details about those methods to the entire class.

The static local variable solves that problem, but it has its own problems. Every version of our class will share the same static local variable. This means if we ever had more than one AddEntryViewController class, they might set conflicting values to the same variable.

A static local variable works here, because we will only ever have one instance of AddEntryViewController at a time. However, you really need to think through all the possible edge cases before you use them.

Next, we grab our current superview, which should be our transition context's container view. We also grab our gesture's current translation. That is the distance our finger has moved from the original point of contact. Finally, we grab our velocity—or how fast our finger is moving.

With the data in hand, we check the gesture's state. Again, we need to respond to four different states: UIGestureRecognizerStateBegan, UIGestureRecognizerStateChanged, UIGestureRecognizerStateEnded, and UIGestureRecognizerStateCancelled.

For UIGestureRecognizerStateBegan, we just record our view's current center in the originalCenter static variable. For UIGestureRecognizerStateChanged we call updateCenterUsingTransition:originalCenter:. For both UIGestureRecognizerStateEnded and UIGestureRecognizerStateCancelled, we call endDragWithVelocity:.

Next, just below this method, let's implement our UIDynamicAnimatorDelegate methods. When we're dismissing the view, we can simply use our dismissal controller. However, when we want to bounce the view back into place, we cannot use the presentation controller—our view is already being presented as part of a modal transition. Instead, we will create a dynamic animator and a bounce behavior directly. Unfortunately, this means we also need to monitor the dynamic animator's delegate methods to cancel the animation once everything comes to rest.

```
#pragma mark - UIDynamicAnimatorDelegate Methods


- (void)dynamicAnimatorDidPause:(UIDynamicAnimator *)animator
{
    [self.animator removeAllBehaviors];
    self.animator = nil;
}


- (void)dynamicAnimatorWillResume:(UIDynamicAnimator *)animator
{

}
```

Now, we just need to add our private methods. Let's start with updateCenterUsingTranslation:originalCenter:.

```
- (void)updateCenterUsingTranslation:(CGPoint)translation
                       originalCenter:(CGPoint)originalCenter
{
    CGPoint center = self.view.center;

    switch (self.interfaceOrientation)
    {
        case UIInterfaceOrientationPortrait:
            center.y = MIN(originalCenter.y + translation.y,
                        CGRectGetMidY(self.view.superview.bounds));
            break;

        case UIInterfaceOrientationLandscapeLeft:
            center.x = MIN(originalCenter.x + translation.x,
                        CGRectGetMidX(self.view.superview.bounds));
            break;

        case UIInterfaceOrientationLandscapeRight:
```

```
        center.x = MAX(originalCenter.x + translation.x,
                       CGRectGetMidX(self.view.superview.bounds));
        break;

    default:
        [NSException
         raise:NSGenericException
         format:@"Invalid orientation %@",
         @(self.interfaceOrientation)];
    }

    self.view.center = center;
}
```

Here, we want to offset our original center by the translation distance. However, things get a bit tricky. We only want to let the user move the view vertically, not horizontally. Also, we don't want the view to move down, below its starting position. The code here will accomplish both of those tasks.

Now, let's implement endDragWithVelocity:.

```
- (void)endDragWithVelocity:(CGPoint)velocity
{
    switch (self.interfaceOrientation)
    {
        case UIInterfaceOrientationPortrait:
            velocity.x = 0.0;
            if (velocity.y < -DismissTriggerVelocity)
            {
                self.velocity = velocity;
                [self performSegueWithIdentifier:
                 @"Dismiss Popup" sender:self];
            }
            else
            {
                [self bounceBackToCenter:velocity];
            }

            break;

        case UIInterfaceOrientationLandscapeLeft:
            velocity.y = 0.0;
```

```
        if (velocity.x < -DismissTriggerVelocity)
        {
            self.velocity = velocity;
            [self performSegueWithIdentifier:
             @"Dismiss Popup" sender:self];
        }
        else
        {
            [self bounceBackToCenter:velocity];
        }
        break;

    case UIInterfaceOrientationLandscapeRight:
        velocity.y = 0.0;
        if (velocity.x > DismissTriggerVelocity)
        {
            self.velocity = velocity;
            [self performSegueWithIdentifier:
             @"Dismiss Popup" sender:self];
        }
        else
        {
            [self bounceBackToCenter:velocity];
        }
        break;

    default:
        [NSException
         raise:NSGenericException
         format:@"Invalid orientation %@",
         @(self.interfaceOrientation)];
    }
}
```

Again, the fact that we need to treat each orientation differently obscures the actual intent of this code. Basically, we check to see whether the velocity is greater than our trigger in the correct direction (up, in whichever orientation the device happens to be in). If the velocity is greater, we clear out the velocity in the other coordinate, and we assign it to our velocity property. Then we call performSegueWithIndentifier: to dismiss our Add Entry View Controller.

We still need to go into Interface Builder and set the correct unwind segue's identifier. But, eventually, this will trigger the Cancel button's unwind segue, which will dismiss our view.

If our velocity is not greater than our trigger value, we call bounceBackToCenter: to bounce the view back into position. bounceBacktoCenter: is also the last method we need to implement.

```
- (void)bounceBackToCenter:(CGPoint)velocity
{
    UIDynamicAnimator *animator =
    [[UIDynamicAnimator alloc]
     initWithReferenceView:self.view.superview];

    animator.delegate = self;

    BounceBehavior *bounce =
    [[BounceBehavior alloc]
     initWithItem:self.view
     velocity:velocity
     orientation:self.interfaceOrientation];

    [animator addBehavior:bounce];
    self.animator = animator;
}
```

Here, we're just creating a new bounce behavior to return our view to its original position. We start by instantiating a dynamic animator, using our view's superview as its reference view. Again, this should still be our transition's container view. Then we set our AddEntryViewController object as the animator's delegate.

Once that's done, we instantiate our bounce behavior, passing in our view, the gesture's velocity, and our current orientation. Then we add the behavior to the animator. That starts the animation.

Finally, we need to make sure our animator remains in memory until the animation is finished. Therefore, we assign it to our animator property.

That's it for the code. A couple quick changes in Interface Builder, and our project will be ready to run.

Open Main.storyboard and zoom in on the Add Entry View Controller Scene. Then, in the Document Outline, expand the Add Entry View Controller Scene, and select "Unwind segue from Cancel to Exit." In the Attributes inspector, change the Identifier to Dismiss Popup. This must match the segue identifier we used in endDragWithVelocity:.

Next, drag a Pan Gesture Recognizer from the Object library and drop it on our Add Entry view. Select the gesture recognizer from the Document Outline, and in the Attributes inspector, change the Maximum touches to 1. Finally, Control-drag from the gesture recognizer to the Add Entry View Controller, and select Drag: from the pop-up HUD.

That's it. Run the application. Bring up the Add Entry View, and then dismiss the keyboard. You should now be able to drag the view upward. You have to be careful to avoid the text fields or buttons, but there's still plenty of space you can drag from.

Notice, if you bring your finger to a stop before letting go, the view drops back down into place. If your finger is still moving up when you let go, the view zooms away. It starts at the same speed as your finger and accelerates from there. In this case, we're triggering the same segue as the Cancel button, but our animation code properly takes the view's velocity into account.

Finally, you can lift the view and throw it down toward the bottom of the screen. Here, we're passing our view's velocity to our bounce behavior. Notice that our view bounces off the boundary considerably higher. You can actually get it to bounce completely off the screen, though it will eventually come back and settle into place.

WRAPPING UP

In this chapter, we looked at two, very different ways of animating objects on the screen. We began with UIMotionEffects. This provides an easy API for accessing the device motion (combined data from the accelerometers, gyroscopes, and compass). It is primarily used for building parallax effects, though we can use it to modify any animatable property of our view, its layers or its subview.

Next, we looked at UIKit Dynamics. This lets us simulate 2D physics-based animations with our views. It's worth repeating, UIKit Dynamics is really designed to create physically realistic-looking animations. It's not intended to be a full-featured game engine. Most of the time we will use it in limited ways—like the lift and bounce behaviors in this chapter.

If you're trying to build a game, Sprite Kit presents a much better option. It is interesting to note, however, that both Sprite Kit and UIKit Dynamics share the same underlying physics engine.

The end of the chapter also marks the end of development on our Health Beat application. All the features have been implemented. All the code is complete. We're not quite done, however. In the next chapter, we will look at all the little tasks remaining before we can submit our application to the App Store.

OTHER RESOURCES

Unfortunately, there are no programming guides that I can point you toward for this chapter. Most of the existing documentation is limited to the individual class references. However, there are a few other resources worth looking at.

- **Event Handling Guide for iOS: Motion Events**

  IOS Developer's Library

  I've recommended the Event Handling Guide before. This time, however, I wanted to highlight the section on motion events. This covers a number of different ways we can detect and respond to device's motion. This includes low-level motion detection using the Core Motion framework.

- **Getting Started with UIKit Dynamics**

  WWDC 2013 Session Videos

  This session provides an initial overview of UIKit Dynamics, covering the basics in how the behaviors and animators work.

- **Advanced Techniques with UIKit Dynamics**

  WWDC 2013 Session Videos

  This goes into more depth in UIKit Dynamics, covering a number of advanced topics and recommended best practices. I highly recommend watching both the Getting Started and the Advanced Techniques videos.

CHAPTER 9
The Last Mile

This chapter covers additional tasks needed to get our app ready for sale in the App Store. We'll look at the details that go into a finished app, from icons and start-up screens to localization and build settings. Finally, we'll examine the process of building the app for distribution—both for ad hoc distribution and for sale.

THE FINAL TOUCHES

This is a grab bag of additional features and settings. Some are required before we can submit our application, others are strongly recommended, and a few merely add a touch of convenience to our apps.

APPLICATION ARTWORK

Our application expects a number of icons and other images. These are not functional parts of the application itself. Rather, they are used by the system to represent our application in a variety of circumstances.

ICONS

We should provide at least four icons for our device: Application, Spotlight, Settings, and iTunesArtwork. Application is used on our devices home screen, Spotlight appears inside search results, Settings identifies our app inside the Settings application, and iTunesArtwork is displayed in the App Store and iTunes.

All the icons must be a PNG format image. They should fill the full rectangle without any transparent or translucent areas. The system will automatically apply the rounded corner effect.

Each icon is a different size. Additionally, these sizes may differ between the iPhone and the iPad. On the iPad we also need to provide both Retina and standard versions for each icon. Fortunately, all of the iPhones and iPod touches that support iOS 7 are Retina devices. This means we need only one version of each icon on the phone. **Table 9.1** gives details about the icon sizes.

TABLE 9.1 Icon Sizes

DEVICE	RESOLUTION	ICON TYPE	SIZE (IN PIXELS)
iPhone	Retina	Application	120 x 120
iPad	Standard	Application	76 x 76
iPad	Retina	Application	152 x 152
iPad	Standard	Spotlight	40 x 40
All	Retina	Spotlight	80 x 80
iPad	Standard	Settings	29 x 29
All	Retina	Settings	58 x 58

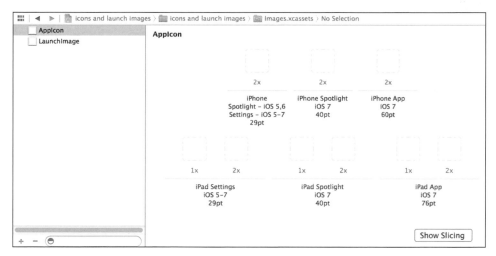

FIGURE 9.1 Placeholders for our icons in the assets catalog

iTunesArtwork is somewhat different from the rest. Its size does not depend on the device or the device's resolution. Apple recommends that we provide two versions of this icon, a 512 x 512 version and a 1024 x 1024 version. We will upload both of these icons to iTunes Connect when we submit our application; however, I recommend including them in the project as well. When included in the project, the 512 x 512 version should be named iTunesArtwork. Notice there's no file extension. The 1024 x 1024 version should be named iTunesArtwork@2x. This allows iTunes to properly display our application's icon when we create ad hoc builds (for example, during beta testing).

The Application icon and iTunesArtwork are required. All other icons can be derived from the Application icon. However, for best results, you should custom design an icon for each resolution.

We can easily add the icons to our application using the assets catalog. Our application's assets catalog should already have an AppIcon collection. If we select this, we will see the various icon sizes required by our application. **Figure 9.1** shows the AppIcon collection for a universal application; therefore, it requires both iPhone and iPad icons. Note that all sizes are shown in points, not pixels.

To add an icon, simply drag correctly sized PNG files from the Finder and drop them in the appropriate place. For the iTunesArtwork icon, Control-click an appropriate group (for example, the Supporting Files group), and select the Add Files To "<Project Name>"... menu item.

> **NOTE:** If you are supporting older versions of iOS, you will need to provide both the Retina and the standard resolution icons for the iPhone. Also, some of the icon sizes have changed with iOS 7. Most importantly, however, we cannot use the assets catalog for older versions of iOS. This means we need to add the icons directly to the project and identify them in our project's info.plist file.

FIGURE 9.2 Health
Beat's launch image

LAUNCH IMAGES

The system displays our application's launch image while the application loads. Many developers use this as an opportunity to display a splash screen or advertisement, but Apple's Human Interface Guidelines actively discourage this.

Instead, we should provide a streamlined version of the application's main interface as the launch image. We want to strip out anything that might change. Obviously, this includes date fields and table view contents, but it also includes button titles and other labels that need to be localized. In fact, it's often best to remove the buttons entirely. When in doubt, go for the simplest possible launch image. For example, **Figure 9.2** is an excellent launch image for our Health Beat application. I created this by taking a screen shot from the simulator and then editing it to remove the status bar, navigation bar contents, and tab bar contents.

Displaying only a partial user interface has a psychological advantage. The user won't accidentally try to use it until all the details are filled in. Furthermore, it creates the illusion that our application is launching faster. Our app seems snappier, and the users appreciate being able to get to work immediately.

For iPhone projects, we need two launch images: a 640 x 960 image for the 3.5-inch screens and a 640 x 1136 image for the 4-inch screens. iPhone always launches into the portrait orientation.

For iPad projects, we need both portrait and landscape images. We also need them in both standard and Retina resolution. That means we need four versions: 768 x 1024, 1024 x 768, 1536 x 2048, and 2048 x 1536.

We can add the launch images using the assets catalog. Simply select the LaunchImage collection and drag the images to the correct placeholders.

However, don't spend too much time on the launch image. It will be used only the first time the application launches. After that, our application will take a snapshot of its user interface when the app goes to the background. The next time the app launches, it will use that snapshot.

This snapshot is also displayed in the application switcher (the row of icons and views that appear when you double-tap the home button). This means we need to make sure we don't accidentally take a snapshot of any confidential or sensitive information. As a result, we may need to hide items like passwords in our app delegate's `applicationDidEnterBackground:` method. We can also call `ignoreSnapshotOnNextApplicationLaunch` to prevent our app from using the snapshot on its next lunch.

Our application will also update its snapshot whenever it downloads data using a background fetch. This keeps the image of our application up-to-date, both when it relaunches and when it's in the application switcher.

REQUIRED CAPABILITIES

We must declare any special capabilities that our application requires (or explicitly prohibits). Most of the defined capabilities are hardware-based, but some (like Game Center or Location Services) have a software component.

The iOS system will not launch the application if the device does not meet its required capabilities. Furthermore, the iTunes App Store will use this information to generate its device requirements—preventing users from downloading applications that they cannot run.

To set the required capabilities, add a `UIRequiredDeviceCapabilities` key to the application's `Info.plist` file. Set this key to either an array or a dictionary. If we use an array, then simply adding a feature's key to the array means that the feature is required. If it's not listed, the app can manage without it.

> **NOTE:** Your app may be rejected from the App Store if it needs a capability but does not properly declare that requirement in `Info.plist`.

If you use a dictionary, you should give each feature in the dictionary a `true` or `false` Boolean value. If it's `true`, the app requires the capability. If it's `false`, the app explicitly prohibits the capability. If the feature is not included in the dictionary, it's optional.

All the capability keys are listed here. For more information about these keys, refer to the "App-Related Resources" section of the iOS App Programming Guide. Some of these may be set automatically by our project's Capabilities settings; however, most will need to be set by hand.

- `accelerometer`
- `armv6`
- `armv7`
- `auto-focus-camera`
- `bluetooth-le`
- `camera-flash`
- `front-facing-camera`
- `gamekit`
- `gps`
- `gyroscope`
- `location-services`
- `magnetometer`
- `microphone`
- `opengles-1`
- `opengles-2`
- `peer-peer`
- `sms`
- `still-camera`
- `telephony`
- `video-camera`
- `wifi`

DEPLOYMENT TARGET

There are two build settings that determine which SDK our application uses to compile and which version of the OS it supports: the base SDK and the iOS deployment target.

The base SDK should always be set to the latest version of iOS. In fact, each version of Xcode includes only the latest SDK—so we typically cannot change it to anything lower.

The deployment target, on the other hand, lets us specify the earliest version of the OS that can still run our app. To see the deployment target, click the project icon and select the General tab. By default, new projects are set with the deployment target equal to the base SDK. We can change this to support any version of iOS 6.0 and above. Actually, we can support anything down to iOS 4.3, but to support anything lower than 6.0, we need to turn off 64-bit support.

Just to be clear, the application is compiled using the latest SDK, but it may still run on earlier devices. This works through the magic of weak linking.

The compiler will compare the symbols in the frameworks of the base SDK and the deployment target SDK. Anything that's available in the base SDK but not available in the deployment target will be weak linked. This means that when the process is running, the symbol does not need to be present. As long as a missing symbol isn't actually called, the application will continue to run normally. Of course, calling a missing symbol will crash the app.

This lets us include iOS 7-only features in an app targeting iOS 6.0. We just need to perform runtime checks before calling any iOS 7–only code and degrade gracefully when those features are not available.

To check whether a class is available, we simply call [<class name> class]. If this returns nil, the class is not available. To see whether a method is available, we call the object's respondsToSelector: method. To see whether a function is available, check to see whether the function's name evaluates to NULL.

```
if ([UIInterpolatingMotionEffect class]) {
    // We can use motion effects.
}


if ([self respondsToSelector:
    @selector(setTransitionCoordinator)]) {
    // We can set a custom transition
}


if (UIStatusBarStyleLightContent != NULL) {
    // we can use the new light content status bar setting
}
```

On the surface, this is amazing. It means we can have our cake and eat it too. We can support old iOS 4.3 phones while also enabling all the latest and greatest features on the most recent devices. However, there is one huge problem here. There is no way to check the code at compile time and verify that we aren't accidentally calling something above the deployment target in a generally reachable branch.

Things aren't so bad when you're just adding a new feature to an existing app. You know that the code you're adding is above the deployment target, and you can take care to isolate it properly. The real problem comes in when you're doing general coding or debugging. It's so easy to unknowingly use parts of the SDK that are above the deployment target—especially when using autocomplete.

Some third-party tools can help. AppCode from JetBrains will search for and identify code that's above the deployment target. However, the only real solution is testing.

OK, I like testing; I'm a huge fan of testing. Unfortunately, testing alone is not a sufficient solution for this problem. Here's the hard, cold truth: It's hard (I would say impractical if not impossible) to make sure we actually execute every possible branch of our code during our test cycles. And if we don't test every branch, we don't really know if we're safe. Above-deployment API calls may be scattered throughout any part of our code, laying around like little land mines, just waiting to kill our apps.

So, if you go down this route, test your code. Test it hard and test it often. If possible, find a bunch of beta testers who still run older versions of iOS. Otherwise, you're just asking for a bunch of bad reviews when your app starts crashing on older devices.

Finally, there are also some important limitations that weak linking just cannot work around. Storyboards are available only on iOS 5 and later. Auto Layout and unwinding segues are available only on iOS 6 and later. The assets catalog is available only for iOS 7.

LOCALIZATION

Localization involves adapting our application for two or more culturally distinct markets. People often think about localization in terms of translating written text, and it can involve a lot of translation. However, it also involves a wide range of other cultural aspects that have nothing to do with language. For example, we've already used `NSNumberFormatter` to create locally formatted numbers. In that case, it's not about language—we're not translating the number; we're simply choosing the best representation based on our user's locale. Similarly, a stop sign icon should look very different in Japan than it does in the United States. Both of these are prime examples of localization.

Localization affects a wide range of application features, including the following:

- Storyboards and nibs
- Static text
- Icons and graphics
- Sounds and spoken words

- Dynamically generated text
- Text editing
- Sorting orders

Xcode supports localization by creating localized bundles. These bundles are represented by directories ending in `.lproj`. The localized bundles can be used to distinguish between different languages or, in some cases, even different regional dialects. iOS will try to select the best match, based on the device's settings; however, it's generally best to use the most general location specifiers possible.

When we load a resource from our application bundle, the system starts searching in the general bundle. If it cannot find a match, it begins searching through the localized bundles. The actual search order is based on the user's preferences. By placing localized resources in the correct bundles, we ensure that our application loads the correct versions at runtime.

We have a number of tools to help ease the internationalization effort, especially when it comes to finding and translating string values.

- `ibtool`: This command-line utility can be used to extract strings from a nib file. The resulting string file can then be translated into another language. Once that is done, `ibtool` can merge the translated strings back with the original nib to create a translated nib.

- `NSLocalizedString()`: This method and its siblings will return a localized string value for a given key. `NSLocalizedString()` is the simplest. It takes two parameters: the key and a comment. It searches the bundle for the `Localizable.strings` file, and then it searches that file for the key. If a match is found, it returns the string associated with the key; otherwise, it returns the key itself. The other variants let us search different files, return different default values, or otherwise modify the search. Also note that the comment argument is not used at runtime. Instead, it is used by `genstrings` when creating our `.strings` files.

- `genstrings`: This command-line utility can parse C and Objective-C files and can find all the keys declared using one of the `NSLocalizedString()` methods. It will then build the `.strings` files containing all the unique values it found. This file can then be sent to translators, and the translated versions can be placed in the appropriate language bundles.

Additionally, we don't need to translate every single string in our application. We only need to localize the strings that the user actually sees. Strings used as internal keys or as the names of notifications should be left alone.

ACCESSIBILITY

Recently, iOS has received a lot of praise and press for its excellent accessibility features. Out of the box, iOS provides a wide range of alternate input and output settings to assist people with low vision or blindness, hearing disabilities, and motor or physical disabilities. For the most part, these features are available to our application for free. We may need to be a little careful when creating custom gestures, since assistive touch won't support them, but other than that, most of the work is done for us.

In fact, when developers talk about accessibility, we're really talking about supporting VoiceOver. VoiceOver helps visually impaired users navigate through our application. It tells them about the contents of the screen and assists with performing actions such as pressing buttons or selecting links.

Fortunately, VoiceOver is easy to use. For most standard controls, we just need to set the Accessibility settings in Interface Builder. These can be found in the Identity inspector. The Label is a string that succinctly identifies the control. For example, "Units" or "Enter Weight." The Hint is a brief string that describes the effect of performing an action on the control. This should avoid mentioning either the control or the action. For example, "enter a new weight" not "select this text field to enter a new weight."

This, however, is just the beginning. iOS accessibility support provides a number of methods to help truly customize and refine the interface for visually impaired users.

SHARING FILES WITH OTHER APPLICATIONS

We have already seen that the cloud lets us share our files across multiple devices—but what if we want to share one file among many applications? Unfortunately, the application sandbox really gets in our way here. If we want to open the file in another application, we must copy it into that application's sandbox. We do this using the "Open in" menu.

To transfer a document to other applications, create an instance of UIDocumentInteraction Controller. Then call either presentOpenInMenuFromBarButtonItem:animated: or present OpenInMenuFromRect:inView:animated:, depending on whether you want to anchor the menu to an arbitrary rectangle or to a bar button.

For example, the following code will display the "Open in" menu when the attached button is pressed. The system will then dynamically create a menu, listing all the applications that have registered support for the given document type.

```
- (IBAction) exportButtonPressed:(id)sender {
    // Open file in other apps.
    UIDocumentInteractionController *controller =
    [UIDocumentInteractionController interactionControllerWithURL:
```

```
        fileURL];
    [controller presentOpenInMenuFromBarButtonItem:sender
                                           animated:YES];
}
```

To receive documents from other applications, we must register all the documents that our application supports. This requires two steps. First, add an appropriate document type to the target's Document Types list. Click the project icon and select the Info tab. Next, expand the Document Types list. Click the + button to add a new document type.

In the Name field, give the document a name. Then, in the Types field enter its UTI. You can find a complete list of system-supported UTIs in the "System-Declared Uniform Type Identifiers" section of the Uniform Type Identifiers Reference. For example, to register text files, set the document Types field to **public.text**.

Next, in application:didFinishLaunchingWithOptions:, we need to check the options argument for the UIApplicationLaunchOptionsURLKey. If this key is present, we need to try to open the file at the corresponding URL.

```
NSURL *url =
[launchOptions objectForKey:UIApplicationLaunchOptionsURLKey];
if (url != nil) {
    // Open the file from the URL.
}
```

BUILDING FOR DISTRIBUTION

Once everything's ready, it's time to build our application for distribution. There are two ways to do this. First, we can build an ad hoc distribution. This allows us to distribute our application to up to 100 devices. We often do this as part of our application's testing, letting us send the application out to a select group of beta testers. Once that's done, we can build and submit to the iOS App Store.

NOTE: There's actually a third option. If you have an enterprise developer license, you can build and distribute applications internally. This lets large corporations create proprietary tools for use within the company.

CREATING AD HOC BUILDS

Before we can create an ad hoc build, we need to create a distribution provisioning profile containing the UDIDs of all our test devices. Log into your account at Apple's Developer site (http://developer.apple.com/iphone), and click the Certificates, Identifiers & Profiles link in the upper-right corner.

Before creating a new profile, be sure to add all of your test devices. In the left column, select Devices, and then click the "+" button to add a new device. You will need the unique device identifier (UDID) from each device. Your testers can get their UDID by viewing the device's summary in iTunes. Click the serial number to view the UDID. It's also best if they Control-click the UDID and copy/paste it. Trying to copy it by hand is a recipe for disaster.

We can have up to 100 test devices at any time. With all the test devices in place, select Provisioning Profiles from the left column and select the Distribution tab. Then click the + button, and then select the Ad Hoc distribution. Then click Continue.

In the next screen, select the appropriate App ID. If you haven't created a specific App ID for your application, you should just choose the Generic ID. Then select the developer certificate to use. Unless you have installed multiple developer certificates, there will be only one option here. In the next screen, select the devices that can run this application. In many cases, you can just check the Select All box.

Finally, give the profile a name and click the Generate button. Once it's done creating the profile, we can download the profile. Simply double-click the file to install it into Xcode.

Now we can create the ad hoc build. Make sure you have either iOS Device or an actual, tethered test device selected in the active schema and then select the Product > Archive menu item. This will build and save a release version of your app. When it's finished, it automatically opens the Archive tab in Xcode's Organizer.

Select the most recent archived file, and click the Distribute button. Then select Save for Enterprise or Ad Hoc Deployment and click Next. Finally select the deployment profile we created earlier and click Export. This creates an IPA file for your application. Email this file to your beta testers. They can load it into iTunes and sync it to their devices.

SUBMITTING TO THE APP STORE

Finally, we can submit our application to the App Store for distribution. The procedure is similar. We need to create a distribution profile for the App Store. We also need to sign up for an iTunes Connect account. Finally, we need to gather all the required information for our app.

- Description
- Categories
- Parental control rating
- Keywords
- SKU number
- Application URL
- Support URL

- Screen shots
- Support email address
- End user license agreement
- The iTunesArtwork icons
- Price
- Availability date
- Available territories

Once we have everything we need, we can log into iTunes Connect and set up our application. When iTunes Connect is ready, we archive and distribute our application for the App Store. Xcode will automatically upload it to iTunes Connect.

Remember that all applications submitted to the iTunes App Store must follow both the App Store Review Guidelines and the Human Interface Guidelines. Reviews are typically performed within seven days, and you can monitor the status from iTunes Connect. You will also receive email updates about the status as it moves through the review process.

While some applications have notoriously had trouble getting through Apple's review process, most applications pass without any issues. The best thing is to be prepared. Test your application. Make sure it doesn't crash. You'll also want to review Apple's policies and make sure you're not violating anything. If you've done your job correctly, you shouldn't have any problems. Good luck!

WRAPPING UP

This chapter covered a broad range of topics. If it didn't answer all your questions, I hope it at least pointed you in the right direction and helped you find the solutions you need.

This is also the end of the book. I hope the information has proven useful. However, the fun doesn't end here. Check out the book's website at `www.freelancemadscience.com/books/` for bonus chapters—additional material that we just couldn't squeeze in between this book's covers.

- "Objective-C" provides a detailed rundown on the Objective-C programming language. It covers the fundamental building blocks of Objective-C, objects and object-oriented programming, new Objective-C syntax like dot notation and the literal syntax, memory management, and common design patterns.

- "Overview of iOS Notification Techniques" reviews all the notification techniques available to an iOS application, discussing the advantages and disadvantages of each approach.

- "State Persistence and Restoration" discusses saving the user interfaces state so that we can relaunch the application exactly where they last left off.

- "From iPhone to iPad" covers the differences in developing for the iPad.

- "Other Tools of the Trade" discusses the tools, tips, and techniques behind source control, unit testing, performance testing, and debugging.
  Others material may be added as we go along.

The website also hosts the book's FAQs and errata, as well as a forum for discussion. Please stop by and leave your questions or comments. I look forward to continuing the conversation with you online.

OTHER RESOURCES

- **Asset Catalog Help**

  iOS Developer's Library

  This provides additional information on using the asset catalog, including information about migrating app icons and launch images from older projects, and using the asset catalog to specify the resizable area of an image.

- **iOS Human Interface Guidelines**

  iOS Developer's Library

  While this document contains a wealth of information about all aspects of app design, it is particularly helpful when creating app icons and launch images. It contains details about the requirements, along with helpful suggestions, hints, and tips. Unfortunately, the information is somewhat scattered through the document—so you should probably just read the whole thing.

- **Supporting Multiple iOS Versions and Devices**

  http://www.raywenderlich.com/42591/supporting-multiple-ios-versions-and-devices

  This tutorial walks you through the process of building an app with a deployment target lower than the base SDK. If you're thinking about going that route, this should give you an idea of what to expect. Just remember, it can be a long and difficult road.

- **Internationalization Programming Topics**

  iOS Developer's Library

  This is the go-to guide when internationalizing your application. I cannot stress internationalization enough. The iOS App Store provides easy access to a truly global marketplace. You should do everything you can to take full advantage of the global market.

- **Accessibility Programming Guide for iOS**

  iOS Developer's Library

  This is the complete guide for making accessible apps. In an ideal world, all apps would be accessible. It's just the right thing to do, and it's not terribly difficult. If nothing else, start with the basics, and then add new features as needed.

- **Accessibility for iPhone and iPad Apps**

  http://mattgemmell.com/2010/12/19/accessibility-for-iphone-and-ipad-apps/

  This is a quick overview of accessibility on iOS. It provides a strong motivation for adding accessibility to all applications, covers some of the common misconceptions about visually impaired users, and gives a brief run-through over the different types of accessibility. It's a few years out of date at this point, but still well worth reading.

- **App Distribution Guide**

  iOS Developer's Library

  This guide contains detailed information on all aspects of distributing applications using Xcode 5. I'm not sure that I'd recommend reading it cover-to-cover, but it's definitely worth keeping in your back pocket, in case you run into trouble.

- **iTunes Connect Developer Guide**

  iOS Developer's Library

  This also falls into the "most of the time you shouldn't need it" category. It has extensive information on submitting and managing applications in iTunes Connect. If you ever have any questions when working with iTunes Connect, this is the first place you should look.

- **App Store Review Guidelines**

  https://developer.apple.com/appstore/resources/approval/guidelines.html

  We are playing in Apple's sandbox, so we must abide by their rules. I would highly recommend reading this document before you begin each iOS project. Apple's policies change—and if you're going to run up against their policies, it's best to know before you invest months in an idea. Also remember, this isn't an exhaustive list—creative developers can always find new ways to get rejected. But, it will highlight the most common issues and pitfalls.

A

passing data across segues, 95–96

properties in class extensions, 93

recycling cells, 94

reloading data, 92–93

return entries to history, 93

returning cells, 94

I

iCloud. *See also* file versioning

checking for conflicting state, 352

delayed updates, 351

document storage strategies, 322–323

fallback store, 390–391

hash methods, 358–359

integration with Core Data, 389

Logging Profile, 360

merging conflicting versions, 351

merging history, 354–356

migrating documents to, 339–342

moving files back from, 323

removeConflictedVersions, 356–358

resolveConflicts method, 352–353

resolving conflicts, 350–359

resources, 360, 429

showing versions to users, 351

three-way merges, 389

usage details, 360

iCloud APIs

Document Storage, 316–323, 359–360

Key-Value Storage, 314–316

saving files, 318

iCloud best practices

device bit size, 316

device-specific data, 316

passwords, 316

SQLite databases, 316

"sync storms," 316

iCloud syncing, 314, 390

iCloud users, monitoring, 334–337

icons

iTunesArtwork, 473

placeholders, 473

providing, 472–473

sizes, 472–473

Identity inspector, 14

images, adding to Health Beat, 60–61

info button, 28–29, 31, 36

init method

creating for `WeightHistoryDocument`, 73

using with line graph, 204

`WeightHistoryDocument` for Core Data, 404

initialization methods, adding to `WeightEntry`, 68

`initWithCoder:`, 193, 306

`insertSubview:*`, 116

inspectors, 13–14

`interactive` property, 247

interactive transitions

animator object, 242–246

canceling, 256

explained, 241

gesture recognizers, 249–256

percent-driven, 242

`TabInteractiveTransition`, 246–247

testing custom animation, 248

interactivity, adding, 248–249

Interface Builder

Align tool, 130–131

custom table view cells, 137

Dock, 23

Document Outline, 23

editing constraints, 129–132

explained, 21

Pin tool, 130–131

Resizing Behavior, 130–131

Resolve Auto Layout Issues, 130–131

segue, 23

interfaces, custom drawn, 219

internationalization, 483. *See also* localization tools

iOS

concurrent programming, 290–291

human interface guidelines, 483

versions and devices, 483

iOS 7, handling of bars, 201

iOS App Programming Guide, 49

iOS apps, state preservation and restoration, 311

modal view, 29

model, 52

model layer tasks. *See* Core Data

modules

    explained, 18–19

    model, 52

    view controllers, 52

    view hierarchies, 52

motion effects

    adding to Add Entry View, 434–438

    adding to views, 433

    creating, 432–433

    disabling, 433

    minimum relative value, 437

    removing, 435

    setting up, 436–437

    setupMotionEffects, 435

    UIInterpolatingMotionEffect, 434

    UIMotionEffect, 433

motion events resource, 469

Music app, 52

N

navigation bar

    button, 82

    fixing, 43

navigation items, adding to storyboard, 85–88

Navigation preferences, 16

navigation techniques, 83

Navigator, 11

Navigator tabs

    Breakpoint, 12

    Debug, 12

    Find, 12

    Issue, 12

    Log, 12

    Project, 12

    Symbol, 12

    Test, 12

nesting

    containers, 54

    managed object contexts, 373

.nib extension, 21

nib file

    creating UINib object for, 168

    using, 30

nibs

    explained, 86

    function, 86–87

    loading, 86

    loading objects from, 193

notifications

    Dynamic Type, 180–181

    listening for, 96–100

    private methods, 414–422

NSCalendar object, using, 155

NSCoder, 282

NSCoding, 282, 305–307

NSFetchedResultsControllerDelegate, 412–414

NSFileManager():, 269

NSHipster, 188

NSKeyedArchiver, 282–283

NSKeyedUnarchiver, 282–283, 305

NSUserDefaults, 270–272

O

Object library, 14

Objective-C, 5, 75

objects, loading from nibs, 193. *See also* data objects

observer

    removing, 275–276

    removing observer, 297

opaque views, 194–195

opening apps, best practices for, 102

opening files, 12

OpenWithCompletionHandler:, 288

Option-clicking, 34

outlets

    Add Entry button, 299–300

    adding, 40–42

    connecting, 139–140

    creating for Entry Detail View, 149–150

    graph view, 203

overriding loadFromContents:ofType:error:, 292–294

P

PaintCode, 257

passing data for line graph. *See also* line graph
    adding guidelines, 214–217
    calculating x-coordinate, 211–212
    calculating y-values, 212–213
    checking for entries, 211, 217
    copying history array, 207
    drawing graph, 209
    Dynamic Type font, 215
    GraphView.m, 207
    method for drawing dots, 213
    overriding HBT_updateFonts, 218
    private drawGraph method, 210–211
    rectangle for text, 215
    textRect, 216
    weight history document, 206
    weight values, 217
    weightEntries property, 208–209

passing data to scenes, 36

paths, exploring in sandbox, 267–268

persistent stores
    custom incremental, 384
    encryption options, 385
    faults, 383
    in-memory, 383
    reducing memory overhead, 383–384
    speed, 382–383

PNG files, using, 220

predicates
    key paths, 380–381, 384
    resource, 429
    using in managed object contexts, 379–381

preference page, 280

preferences
    dealloc method, 275–276
    explicit, 270
    fixing warnings, 273
    Health Beat in Settings app, 280
    history view, 274
    implicit, 270
    implicit property, 272
    managing, 270–271

    NSUserDefaults, 270–272
    passing selector, 275
    removing observer, 275–276
    resource, 311
    saving, 270
    saving defaults, 271–272
    setDefaultUnits(), 272
    Settings application, 271
    settings bundle, 278
    system settings support, 278–282
    updateUI method, 277
    updating fonts, 277

prefixes
    using with class names, 8–9
    using with shared code, 9

private methods
    fetchAllEntries, 419
    refreshAll, 422
    removeNotifications, 417–418
    resetMocs, 420–421
    setupNotifications, 414
    setupResultsController, 418–419
    updateMOCFromNote:CompletionHandler:, 421

processQuery: method, 347–348

programming
    concurrency, 290–291, 311
    file system, 311
    keychain services, 311
    preferences and settings, 311
    state preservation and restoration, 311

programming guides
    Core Data, 429
    iOS app, 49
    key-value coding, 107, 188
    predicates, 429
    Quartz 2D, 257
    resources, 107
    view controllers, 107, 188

Project tab in Navigator, 12

projects. *See also* Health Beat project; iOS Utility Application
    adding to workspace, 9
    walking through, 37